Requirements Engineering

Social and Technical Issues

Computers and People Series

Edited by

B. R. GAINES and A. MONK

Monographs

Communicating with Microcomputers. An introduction to the technology of
man–computer communication, *Ian H. Witten* 1980
The Computer in Experimental Psychology, *R. Bird* 1981
Principles of Computer Speech, *I. H. Witten* 1982
Cognitive Psychology of Planning, *J-M. Hoc* 1988
Formal Methods for Interactive Systems, *A. Dix* 1991
Human Reliability Analysis: Context and Control, *E. Hollnagel* 1993

Edited Works

Computing Skills and the User Interface, *M. J. Coombs and J. L. Alty (eds)* 1981
Fuzzy Reasoning and Its Applications, *E. H. Mamdani and B. R. Gaines (eds)* 1981
Intelligent Tutoring Systems, *D. Sleeman and J. S. Brown (eds)* 1982 (1986 paperback)
Designing for Human–Computer Communication, *M. E. Sime and M. J. Coombs (eds)*
1983
The Psychology of Computer Use, *T. R. G. Green, S. J. Payne and G. C. van der Veer
(eds)* 1983
Fundamentals of Human–Computer Interaction, *A. Monk (ed)* 1984, 1985
Working with Computers: Theory versus Outcome, *G. C. van der Veer, T. R. G. Green,
J-M. Hoc and D. Murray (eds)* 1988
Cognitive Engineering in Complex Dynamic Worlds, *E. Hollnagel, G. Mancini and
D. D. Woods (eds)* 1988
Computers and Conversation, *P. Luff, N. Gilbert and D. Frohlich (eds)* 1990
Adaptive User Interfaces, *D. Browne, P. Totterdell and M. Norman (eds)* 1990
Human–Computer Interaction and Complex Systems, *G. R. S. Weir and J. L. Alty (eds)*
1991
Computer-supported Cooperative Work and Groupware, *Saul Greenberg (ed)* 1991
The Separable User Interface, *E. A. Edmonds (ed)* 1992
Requirements Engineering: Social and Techical Issues, *M. Jirotka and J. A. Goguen (eds)*
1994

Practical Texts

Effective Color Displays: Theory and Practice, *D. Travis* 1991
Understanding Interfaces: A Handbook of Human-Computer Dialogue, *M. W. Lansdale
and T. C. Ormerod* 1994

EACE Publications
(Consulting Editors: *Y. WAERN and J-M. HOC*)

Cognitive Ergonomics, *P. Falzon (ed)* 1990
Psychology of Programming, *J-M. Hoc, T. R. G. Green, R. Samurcay and D. Gilmore
(eds)* 1990

Requirements Engineering

Social and Technical Issues

Edited by

Marina Jirotka and Joseph A. Goguen
*Centre for Requirements and Foundations,
Oxford University Computing Laboratory, UK*

Academic Press
Harcourt Brace & Company, Publishers
London   San Diego   New York
Boston   Sydney   Tokyo   Toronto

ACADEMIC PRESS LIMITED
24–28 Oval Road
LONDON NW1 7DX

U.S. Edition Published by
ACADEMIC PRESS INC.
San Diego, CA 92101

This book is printed on acid free paper

A catalogue record for this book is available from the British Library

ISBN 0-1238-5335-4

Typeset by Phoenix Photosetting, Chatham, Kent
Printed in Great Britain by T. J. Press (Padstow) Ltd., Padstow, Cornwall

Contents

Contributors

A. J. C. Blyth, *Department of Computing Science, University of Newcastle, Newcastle upon Tyne, NE1 7RU.*

David Bolton, *Department of Computer Science, City University, Northampton Square, London, EC1U 0HB.*

Graham Button, *Rank Xerox EuroPARC, 61 Regent Street, Cambridge, CB2 1AB.*

J. Chudge, *Department of Computing Science, University of Newcastle, Newcastle upon Tyne, NE1 7RU.*

J. E. Dobson, *Department of Computing Science, University of Newcastle, Newcastle upon Tyne, NE1 7RU.*

Steve Easterbrook, *School of Cognitive and Computing Sciences, University of Sussex, Falmer, Brighton, BN1 9QH.*

David Furber, *Department of Computing, King's College London, London WC2R 2LJ.*

David Greatbatch, *Department of Social Sciences, University of Nottingham, NG7 2RD.*

Stewart Green, *Department of Computer Science, City University, Northampton Square, London, EC1U 0HB.*

Joseph A. Goguen, *Centre for Requirements and Foundations, Programming Research Group, Oxford University Computing Laboratory, Oxford, OX1 3QD.*

Christian Heath, *Department of Sociology, University of Surrey, Guildford, GU2 5XH.*

John Hughes, *Department of Sociology and the Centre for Research into CSCW, Lancaster University, Bailrigg, Lancaster, LA1 4YR.*

Sara Jones, *Department of Computer Science, City University, Northampton Square, London, EC1U 0HB.*

Paul Luff, *Department of Sociology, University of Surrey, Guildford, GU2 5XH.*

Linda Macaulay, *Department of Computation, UMIST, P.O. Box 88, Manchester, M60 1QD.*

John A. McDermid, *Professor of Software Engineering, Department of Computer Science, University of York, YO1 5DD. Technical Director Dependable Computing Systems Centre, Director, York Software Engineering Ltd.*

Dave Randall, *Department of Interdisciplinary Studies, Manchester Metropolitan University, Cavendish Street, Manchester, MI5 6BG.*

Dan Shapiro, *Department of Sociology and the Centre for Research into CSCW, Lancaster University, Bailrigg, Lancaster, LA1 4YT.*

Wes Sharrock, *Department of Sociology, University of Manchester, Oxford Road, Manchester, M13 9PL.*

Ronald Stamper, *Department of Information Management, University of Twente, PO Box 217, 7500 AE Enschede, The Netherlands.*

R. Strens, *Department of Computing Science, University of Newcastle, Newcastle upon Tyne, NE1 7RU.*

David Till, *Department of Computer Science, City University, Northampton Square, London, EC1U 0HB.*

Steve Woolgar, *Centre for Research into Innovation, Culture and Technology, Brunel University, Uxbridge, Middlesex, UB8 3PH.*

Introduction

Marina Jirotka and Joseph A. Goguen
*Centre for Requirements and Foundations, Oxford University
Computing Laboratory, UK*

The problem of Requirements Engineering is to determine the 'requirements' for computer-based systems. There is currently a lively debate about the definition and scope of requirements. Consequently, it is not possible to give a neutral description of what Requirements Engineering is. For example, Somerville (1992) states that requirements capture and analysis is "the process of establishing the services the system should provide and the constraints under which it must operate." Davis (1990) suggests that Requirements Engineering is the analysis, documentation and ongoing evolution of both user needs and the external behaviour of the system to be built. The editors' view is that requirements are properties that a system should have in order to succeed in the environment in which it will be used (Goguen 1992). Inevitably, this definition betrays a bias through its *explicit* reference to the system's context in the phrase 'the environment where it will be used', which acknowledges the involvement of both social and technical concerns in requirements. The former concern has remained largely implicit in most definitions and methods for requirements.

This book focusses on the relationship between social and technical issues in Requirements Engineering. It aims to present a number of representative positions on this issue, ranging from classical approaches to those that are more recent. The various authors view the relationship between the social and technical in widely different ways, ranging from the view that they are completely separated, to the view that they are inseparable. This diversity can be seen as a healthy reflection of lively ongoing debate about what requirements actually are, and how requirements engineers should go about their business. We now briefly outline some of the key issues in this debate.

Capturing requirements

The requirements engineer is said (among other things) to 'capture', 'specify', 'elicit' or 'construct' requirements. It is interesting to note the position on the nature of requirements implicit in each term. 'Capturing' requirements suggests that although they may be elusive, they are 'out there' somewhere, while 'specifying' requirements may suggest that a straightforward engineering job needs to be done, in which the issues involved are largely technical. Alternatively, 'eliciting' requirements suggests that requirements are to be found among people – the users, managers, etc. Finally, 'constructing' requirements suggests that requirements may not be 'out there', but instead are a somewhat arbitrary product of the requirements engineering process. There is no term as yet in current use which suggests the ongoing evolution of requirements from processes of interaction, both social and technical, continuing through the whole lifecycle of the system, although this is the view taken by several chapters in this book.

The software lifecycle

Requirements are often considered to be confined to a distinct 'phase' of the software lifecycle, preceding design, construction and use. However, several chapters in this volume suggest that this is not the case in practice. In particular, Goguen suggests a reconceptualisation of the notion of phase based on work by Suchman (1987) on plans, arguing that it is more accurate to see the division of the lifecycle into phases as a management technique or a *post hoc* reconstruction, rather than as a model of how system development actually proceeds. The study of an actual software development project in the chapter by Button and Sharrock supports this view, and McDermid argues that some aspects traditionally thought of as design are crucial to requirements.

Managing the development process

It is all too familiar that many large computer-based system development efforts run over budget, over time, and fail to deliver everything that was expected of them. This has produced a strong desire to manage and control the development process more closely, which recently has particularly focussed on requirements, because it has been shown that the cost of requirements errors is much higher than that of errors made in other phases, and also the cost of their repair rises dramatically as the lifecycle advances (Boehm, 1981). Anecdotal evidence suggests that errors in requirements may account for something like 50% of the total cost of debugging. This may help to explain the popularity of the many 'requirements methodologies' that are available, often as expensive commercial products, involving CASE tools, as well as extensive documentation and training programmes.

Unfortunately, there is very little reliable information about the relative effectiveness of these various methods[1]. One important reason for this is the lack of any theory that is adequate to the empirical phenomena of Requirements Engineering;

---

[1]   Strictly speaking, the word 'methodology' should refer to the comparative study of methods that is so sorely needed, rather than to the individual methods themselves. Unfortunately, this misleading terminology is firmly entrenched in the world of practice. Nevertheless we will use the word 'method' here.

in fact, at this stage we have only the beginnings of an understanding of how requirements are actually constructed and used in large software development projects. But again, the chapter by Button and Sharrock provides some important and useful information.

Method and process

It seems to be useful to distinguish between a method and the actual process[2] by which it is enacted. That is, while methods are generally proscriptive, the way in which practising engineers relate to their rules and guidelines may be very different from what the promoters of the method envisioned, as shown with particular vividness in the chapter by Button and Sharrock. This may be explained by the work of Suchman (1987), which points out that plans serve as 'resources for action' rather than as rigidly executed programs; human users of plans typically use them as a basis for improvisation, and feel free to modify and discard aspects in response to the actual conditions in which they find themselves. The link of Suchman's work to software methods, and particularly to those that are given procedural 'process' descriptions, is made by noting that these methods in fact are plans in Suchman's rather broad sense.

These issues suggest the desirability of reconceptualising Requirements Engineering, by examining both *how* requirements are done (that is, the process by which requirements are determined in practice) and *what* is done (the actual content of the requirements exercise). Investigations of both areas of research necessarily involve the social.

Past interest in what has been termed 'social factors' in computing has primarily addressed issues like the effect of the explosive growth of microelectronics on work and leisure time (Forester, 1980). The current interest differs significantly from this, and is more concerned with design and development, including computer interfaces and interaction (HCI), systems for groups of users (CSCW), and the development process as a whole. This book focusses on the latter, as applied to requirements. Underlying much of the research in this book is an interest in more directly exploring the social and its relationship to design. The remainder of this introduction attempts to outline these new directions, and in particular to describe some different approaches to the treatment of the social, including general approaches to relating the social aspect to the requirements process.

In some ways, the social is of obvious concern to system design and development. For example, the requirements process takes place in an organisation, computer systems are used in organisations, and the requirements process itself is social, in that it involves interactions among different groups of people. However,

---

[2] Unfortunately, the word 'process' is often used in the computing community to describe methods that have been described particularly precisely, e.g. in a kind of programming notation. Other possible words such as 'history' have other difficulties because of their associations with other disciplines.

our understanding of the multiplicity of ways in which the social is incorporated into the requirements process is still very limited. In particular, it is unclear what it means to take the social into account and then incorporate it into the design process. As Hughes *et al.* (1988) state, there is an awareness that social factors are important to system designers, but the ways in which these factors relate to work and work practices is problematic. Large grain characterisations of work, such as 'job satisfaction', 'efficiency fit', 'ethical fit' are used with little understanding of how such characterisations relate to particular instances of work. This is most problematic in relation to analysing human and organisational conduct, where it is difficult to know the grounds for particular classification schemes, or for quantifying those schemes. Comprehensive critiques of measurement in the human sciences are given by Lynch (1991) and Benson and Hughes (1991). These authors, and many of those in this volume, consider that 'the social' and all relevant concepts for understanding it are not given a priori, but are ongoing achievements of participants in actual particular situations, which may differ from one another in significant ways, including how relevant category systems are seen and used.

1   CLASSICAL METHODS

The approaches taken in this book differ significantly. Let us first consider what might be called 'classical methods', which are largely concerned with notation for describing requirements, rather than with the nature of what is being described. The complexity of analysing and incorporating the social may or may not be recognised by those who propose and use such methods. In general, these methods leave the social for others to deal with, as input to the use of the notation, or as determinants for parameter values left open. For example, the chapter by Bolton *et al.* makes no commitment about where and how to obtain the information they are modelling. Rather, the effort goes into developing and improving the notation for use in domain modelling.

Classical system development methods tend to focus on well-established issues within computing science, perhaps because of a recognition of the complexity of analysing and then incorporating the social. For example, concerning 'political problems', DeMarco (1978) states that they "aren't going to go away and they won't be solved." He then states that structured methods can help "limit the effects of disruption due to politics" by formalising the development process.

Nevertheless, requirements engineers still have to deal with the social before they can use any notation. Requirements engineers are conventionally advised to use techniques such as interviews and questionnaires to gather their data. Though there are many guidelines on designing questionnaires and conducting interviews, the analysis of the materials gathered is largely left to intuition. Thus, classical methods seem to assume that once an analyst has the information, it should be a straightforward task to identify such analytic elements as 'objects', 'processes' and 'tasks'. This may be explained in part by the common belief that because these elements are 'natural' in some sense, they should be straightforward to recognise. However, several chapters in this volume suggest that even identifying a task can be quite complex, because tasks are socially produced and interactionally achieved (Luff *et al.*, Randall *et al.*) rather than given *a priori*. This is not inconsistent with a hope that more than unaided intuition can be brought to bear on requirements analysis, yielding an engineering approach with a more scientific basis.

These considerations raise the fundamental question of how design choices can be warranted by analysis, and in particular, how a requirements analyst can justify a given requirement. Most of the chapters in this volume try to address this question in one way or another

2   MANAGING THE DEVELOPMENT PROCESS

Recent approaches to the social have had some influence on the management of software design processes. In classical methods, social aspects such as conflict and cooperation between participants in the design process are largely viewed as unproblematic. However, Checkland's (1988) Soft Systems Methodology (SSM) recognises that large scale projects include groups of people who must decide on requirements and negotiate contractual issues between customers and suppliers. SSM suggests managing this kind of process by guided intervention in meetings where people with different objectives and perceptions discuss and therefore increase their understanding of the problem at hand.

Following Checkland, Easterbrook uses notions from social and organisational psychology to suggest that it is essential to reveal and manage conflict in the requirements phase; this work is related to research carried out by Finkelstein on viewpoints (Finkelstein, 1992). Easterbrook proposes a system called Synoptic, which provides a set of tools to support the exploration of conflicts by displaying different viewpoints and allowing participants to compare and annotate them. These tools are designed to encourage discussion of the conflict situation.

By contrast, Macaulay's chapter is concerned with achieving cooperation between stakeholders through the mediation of a human facilitator with special training, rather than through explicitly managing conflict. These methods intervene directly in the social processes with which they are concerned. Their claims to effectiveness are based on experience with the use of methods, rather than on a systematic analysis of the organisational contexts within which the intervention occurs. It is interesting that these two papers take somewhat opposing views on the issue of whether to focus on conflict itself or on its resolution.

The methods proposed by Easterbrook, Macaulay and Checkland rely on eliciting participants' own accounts of their organisation and activities. The production of such accounts is addressed by Bittner (1965), who suggests that using common-sense concepts in the analysis of people who themselves use those concepts is problematic, because analysts take these concepts to exist 'out there in the world' and then use them to explain and measure human behaviour, whereas for members, these concepts should be seen as common-sense productions of individuals, and the focus of study should be on revealing what they consist of and what work goes into accomplishing them.

For example, Bittner describes a 'gambit of compliance' in which, through skill and craftsmanship, members of an organisation are able to comply with rules while 'finding in the rule the means for doing whatever needs to be done' (Bittner, 1965). Descriptions of organisational activities and formal organisational designs are, therefore, schemes of interpretation that "competent and entitled users can invoke in yet unknown ways whenever it suits their purposes." For example, a member of an organisation may account for a particular action as 'what I am supposed to do in my job' on one occasion, as 'what the organisation needs to survive' on another, and 'because someone in Personnel phoned and asked me to do it' on a third occasion. Bittner's research suggests problems with the concept of organisation. If we take this work seriously, then a whole range of concepts in requirements and system design that have been accepted unproblematically need to be reconceived of in terms of the ways in which they may be flexibly and innovatively applied in specific contexts. Although such concepts as task, user, role, social, technical, cooperation and conflict are used by requirements engineers, Bittner's work suggests that a programme of research is needed to explore how these concepts are actually used in specific contexts. This also applies to such seemingly more technical concepts as task, object, event, process and data.

3 SOCIO-TECHNICAL APPROACHES

The socio-technical approach, pioneered by Trist (Trist et al., 1963; Trist, 1971), is similar to SSM, but has some important differences. One fundamental idea of this approach is that organisations are composed of social as well as technical aspects, each of which has its own dynamics. This approach stresses, above all, that these aspects are interdependent.

The Socio-Technical approach has been widened to allow for worker participation in choosing among existing technical solutions. The well-known and well documented ETHICS approach to requirements developed by Mumford (1983, 1986) tries to unify concepts such as user needs, participation, organisational structure and job design into an extension of the Socio-Technical approach. Although there are many strengths to this approach, not least that it draws people together across organisational boundaries to discuss problems, it seems that the ways the social has been incorporated have led to a neglect of *how* people actually carry out the activities that they do in the workplace.

The chapters by Stamper on the MEASUR method and by Dobson on the ORDIT method each try to provide a complete overall picture of the design process. Both focus upon the needs of the organisation as opposed to individuals, and both agree on the importance of social context. Stamper's MEASUR method, drawing from a wide variety of sources including semiotics, suggests some ways to determine significant semantic features of the domain, and discusses some elements and structures that should be considered during requirements elicitation. Dobson's work is an outgrowth of the original Socio-Technical approach, and its main focus is on organisational change.

There are several ways that an approach termed 'Socio-Technical' might proceed. First, approaches that take account of the social could be integrated with existing requirements methods. In this case, an extra level of analysis could be added that incorporates the social. This would preserve the separateness and apparent strengths of each in addressing different issues, which are to be combined subsequently in some way. The main difficulty with such an approach lies in determining what such analyses might consist of, given the problems of conceptualising 'the social' discussed previously. For example, how should the analysis be performed? What are the analytic categories and how can they be justified? What forms of measurement are appropriate for human conduct?

A second approach, often called 'participative design', tries to avoid such difficulties by involving participants directly in the requirements process. Here analysts use materials drawn from meetings between participants and designers, or from user trials of prototypes. Nevertheless, the fundamental problem of how design choices can be warranted by analysis still remains unaddressed.

A third approach suggests that the social and the technical are thoroughly intertwined, and attempts to develop analytic categories from the participants themselves. Such an approach is discussed in the next section.

4   ENTWINING THE SOCIAL AND THE TECHNICAL

Woolgar's chapter in this volume outlines some ways in which the technical is thoroughly embedded within the social. In this empirically-based analysis, Woolgar shows how the notion of 'user' serves as a resource for producing requirements and technology. His analysis reveals the different ways in which the people responsible for building a new system in one setting contribute to the very definition of user, and thereby constrain the possible actions that users can take. For example, there are certain people who claim the right to speak on behalf of users. There is also the view that it is useless to ask users what they want because they don't know. This view can provide a rationalisation for not taking users' views very seriously.

This form of research, which tries to avoid using *a priori* concepts from the social sciences, has many implications for Requirements Engineering, and begins to demonstrate how key concepts in system design, user interface design, CSCW and conventional HCI can be reconceptualised (see also Grudin, 1990; Bowers and Rodden, 1993).

What form would an analysis take that attempted to examine the work of requirements engineers themselves? The chapter by Button and Sharrock outlines how requirements get done in one organisation, suggesting that the work of requirements engineers might be seen as a web of interactional practices through which particular methods are used. They further argue that although it is important to take people's work practices seriously in order to develop better technology, it is also necessary to understand the organisational accountability of the use of technology. This analysis reveals some difficulties faced by engineers in following a prescribed ordering of phases, and it also documents some ways in which engineers used the prescriptions of producing a requirements analysis and specification before building the system. These observations are echoed in McDermid's 'heretical' suggestion in this volume that methods should be more sensitive to the contingencies of requirements, and in particular, should consider architectural issues during the requirements phase.

An important question arising from such research is whether the practical reasoning of participants in a particular domain can be used to inform the requirements process, and hence to build better systems. The chapter by Randall *et al.* describes the experience of an interdisciplinary team of sociologists and computing scientists collaborating in the design of a computer-based tool for air traffic control. Here the sociologists' main concern was initially to provide a sociological description of the work of controlling, including its activities, contexts and culture, as constituted by participants in the work. They would then provide that information to the requirements engineers designing a user interface for a flight progress database, through a series of debriefing sessions in the form of questions posed to the field worker. This exercise was not unproblematic, in that the sociologists and computing scientists had different views of what was interesting and relevant. Nevertheless, the ethnographic information was useful for design. Primarily, it demonstrated the collaborative nature of controlling, because this activity required an "orientation to the active coordination of tasks on the part of the personnel around the suite in ways that fundamentally go beyond the formal specification of roles."

One strength of the ethnographic account is that it sees activities as part of a socially organised setting, and thus avoids treating tasks as discrete, isolated units of behaviour, and then taking these representations to be how the work is actually done. By contrast, current methods, both in systems analysis, and task analysis, rely on an individualistic conception of tasks, and on pre-established categories. Randall *et al.* have gone some way towards revealing the collaborative nature of activities. However, for requirements engineers to take such an approach seriously, some form of analysis must replace current individualistic methods. Hence several researchers have suggested that ethnographic material may be useful in Requirements Engineering. Randall *et al.* provide an informative discussion of the strengths and weaknesses of one such approach. Further useful discussion of ethnography is given by Button and King (1992), who tackle the misconception that ethnography is no more than 'hanging around' the workplace.

5   VIDEO-BASED ANALYSIS

The chapters in the last part of the book share a common goal of reconceptualising and extending the requirements process. There is a stress on gathering data in empirical, naturalistic settings to avoid the pitfalls of experimental situations. In addition, such an approach is needed if the researcher wants to obtain analytic categories directly from the people or organisation that the technology is intended to serve.

Goguen's chapter suggests that there has been a shift from approaches where computing scientists impose their own view of the requirements of an organisation, to approaches where analysts try to reveal the organisational culture as seen by the members themselves, and then uses the member's own analytic categories to inform requirements and design. This chapter serves as a bridge between more traditional views and the more recent video-based techniques. Perhaps its major contribution is a discussion of various ways that abstract data types can be socially situated.

Commonly used requirements terms like 'user' and 'task' are the focus for a programme of research that tries to reveal how members of some community use these concepts as a resource for producing technology. In addition, our understanding of such concepts can be broadened. For example, task analysis can now be seen to demonstrate how activities are achieved in concert with others in the local environment, and how that work is produced and made recognisable for others. To reveal such information, use can be made of video recordings of naturalistic settings (see the chapter by Luff *et al.* in this volume, and also work by Jirotka *et al.,* 1993) where fragments can be subjected to repeated analysis. Video fragments also assist in the 'transportability of experience' so that throughout the software lifecycle analysts can access not only the domain in which the systems are to be placed, but also can trace certain design decisions back to their analysis of that domain.

Luff *et al.* base their observations on detailed analyses of video recordings taken in several naturalistic settings, in order to show the interactional organisation of task-based activities. Their analysis shows some ways in which the accomplishment of specific tasks is thoroughly embedded in interaction with other participants. This applies not only to obviously 'interactive' domains, but also to settings where an activity appears to be localised and individual. Here, too, the activity is systematically produced with respect to the coparticipation of others. They argue that the tacit work practices and socio-interactional organisation of the domain have been ignored in more conventional task and systems analysis, thereby constraining the requirements that are identified, and hence also the range of technological solutions that may be considered.

However, these new techniques are not without their own difficulties. As Randall *et al.* state, ethnographic studies are labour-intensive, and it is not always apparent what information may be relevant to design. In addition, it is not clear how Luff *et al.*'s approach using interaction analysis to augment ethnography can be employed prescriptively. For example, it is not yet apparent how to structure the use of ethnography and interaction analysis to support requirements and design. More research is needed on this topic, including a framework for conducting the analysis of work processes and addressing the problems of constructing requirements from such analyses. However, as Button and Sharrock remind us, even if such an orientation can be successfully incorporated into a method, the determination of requirements is itself enmeshed in organisational processes, so that any method must be open and flexible enough for the practical purposes of working analysts in their own actual work setting.

The studies described above offer a radically different approach to incorporating the social into requirements that might be termed 'bottom-up', starting from the details of the moment-to-moment interactional practices of people at work, then developing analytic categories from these observations, and finally assembling a body of such observations in different domains. The results of such research could inform requirements practice by providing methods for analysing data and making design decisions based on the analysis. However, such methods could also be used to examine how requirements engineers use current methods, with a view to developing and improving the requirements and design processes.

6 THE STRUCTURE OF THIS BOOK

The book is divided into two parts. The chapters in Part 1 examine issues in current requirements engineering methods and practice, while Part 2 describes some ways in which a particular orientation on the social can also increase our understanding of the requirements process and also inform current requirements practice. Part 1 is introduced by John McDermid who outlines some key issues in Requirements Engineering. He begins with a discussion of the problems of conflict and overspecification in the 'orthodox' approach. Then a 'heretical' view is proposed as a base from which to improve the requirements engineering process.

The following two chapters develop the issue of conflict and collaboration in the management of the development process, drawing on organisational, psychological and social psychological research. Steve Easterbrook argues for the need to incorporate and support conflict in the requirements process, identifying a model of computer-supported negotiation.

In contrast, Linda Macaulay presents a technique which relies on a team approach to requirements capture, and which facilitates agreement between participants in a limited time period. A case study is described where this technique was used to help a group of people cooperate in capturing the requirements for the information needs of the next generation of Electricity Distribution Control Rooms.

In response to such organisational issues in requirements engineering, the next two chapters describe methods which attempt to provide a complete overall picture of the design process. John Dobson describes the ORDIT approach to requirements identification and expression within the context of organisational change. ORDIT focusses on the representation of organisational requirements in the design of socio-technical systems so as to emphasise the relationships between organisational structure and information systems.

Ronald Stamper describes an approach which attempts to observe the social norms that are said to govern the regularities that constitute an organisation. Most norms are informal, but where necessary they are supplemented using explicit rules. If the norms of an organisation can be specified in sufficient detail, then its information requirements may be deduced as a logical consequence. These concepts are the foundation of MEASUR (Methods for Eliciting, Analysing and Specifying User Requirements).

In the final chapter of Part 1, David Bolton, Sara Jones, David Till, Dave Furber and Stewart Green investigate the use of generic domain knowledge in the capture of requirements for computer systems. The process of requirements capture is seen as involving a number of activities including elicitation, analysis and validation. This chapter discusses the development of a framework within which generic domain knowledge can be used to support each of these activities.

Joseph Goguen introduces Part 2 by considering how informal, situated information and formal, context insensitive information arise and interact in Requirements Engineering. Informal, situated information arises in social interaction, for example, in the worlds of users and managers. Formal structures occur in the internal representations of computer-based systems, which are subject to the formal syntactic and semantic rules of computers and computer languages. He argues that the essence of Requirements Engineering is the need to reconcile these two aspects of system design, and that ethnomethodology may provide an appropriate approach to this reconciliation. He also shows how formal structures (namely abstract data types) can be seen to arise in social interaction.

Steve Woolgar in Chapter 8 and Graham Button and Wes Sharrock in Chapter 9 offer two distinctive approaches to looking at the process of system development. Steve Woolgar describes results from recent ethnographic studies of Information Technology development. The main aim of the study is to illuminate the ways in which aspects of local and organisational cultures, including belief systems, language and material resources, shape the design, production and implementation of new IT systems and products.

Graham Button and Wes Sharrock, in a sociologically grounded case study, describe how requirements get done in one organisation. They reveal the difficulties faced by the team's management in their efforts to make their engineers produce 'a proper' analysis of requirements, and then write to specifications with full documentation. Due to a number of organisational factors the engineers had to work around the tools and methods that they were given in order to get the job done.

The final two chapters of the book discuss ways in which ethnographic description can reveal the skills of people in the workplace and consequently might inform system design. Dave Randall, John Hughes and Dan Shapiro report on the experiences of an interdisciplinary team of computer scientists and sociologists, collaborating in the design of a computer-based system for air traffic control. Some of the features and problems of cooperation that have emerged are identified, along with the ways in which the ethnography of air traffic controllers informed the design of a system to support an area of their work.

In the final chapter, Paul Luff, Christian Heath and David Greatbatch examine three different workplaces. By drawing on detailed analyses of tasks and interaction, they outline consequences for the elicitation of requirements and suggest novel methods for Requirements Engineering.

7 TOWARDS THE FUTURE

Making predictions about such a volatile area as Requirements Engineering is surely dangerous. Therefore we limit ourselves here to an attempt to extrapolate from the kind of work described in this book, and in particular, we restrict ourselves to considering the role of the social factor in Requirements Engineering.

One clear trend, at least within the research community, is to base requirements more firmly on an empirical understanding of the social organisation of the environment where the system will be used. The degree and kind of involvement with the social aspect is currently subject to variation and debate, but it seems likely that the use of the more rigorous empirical methods will be valuable in increasing our understanding of the problems in this difficult area, and will pave the way for developing methods that are both efficient and effective. It may be that methods based on ethnomethodology with its orientation towards revealing participants' own practices and examining the details of work practices and interaction, will be valuable in this regard. It also seems likely that video-based methods will be important, because they allow viewing of the source data again and again throughout the system development lifecycle.

Another interesting possibility is to use more 'open' development processes, in which the lifecycle, including the requirements phase, is broken into a number of independent subprocesses, which can be contracted and evaluated separately. For example, the construction of prototypes could be separated from the evaluation of those prototypes. Such an approach would allow much greater flexibility in responding to the new opportunities and challenges that typically arise for large systems, as well as to changes in the ambient social and technical environment of the system being developed. It would also allow more realistic estimates of the cost of later work to be made closer to the time of performance, instead of everything having to be estimated at the very beginning when adequate information is not available. Such processes should be more fluid, dynamic and adaptive, as opposed to the static processes that are currently used, and which so often result in large overruns in time and cost, as well as failure to adequately meet user needs.

The chapters in this book draw on a wide range of disciplinary backgrounds including Psychology, Sociology and Computer Science, and reveal an interest in theoretical and methodological issues as well as practical implications for requirements engineering. Though none present an approach that fully meets the requirements for a fluid and flexible process, taken together they do suggest that present methods for requirements engineering need to be radically reconsidered, and they also suggest some directions that reconsideration might take.

REFERENCES

Benson, D. and Hughes, J.A. (1991). Method: evidence and inference – evidence and inference for ethnomethodology, in Button, G. (Ed). *Ethnomethodology and the Human Sciences*. Cambridge University Press.

Bittner, E. (1965). The concept of organisation, *Social Research*, **32**, 239–255.

Bohm, D. W. (1981). *Software Engineering Economics*, Prentice Hall, NJ.

Bowers, J. and Rodden, T. (1993). Exploding the interface: Experiences of a CSCW Network, *INTERCHI '93*, Amsterdam, April 24–29.

Button, G. and King, V. (1992). Hanging around is not the point: calling ethnography to account. Paper presented to the *Workshop on Ethnography and CSCW System Design. CSCW '92*, Toronto.

Checkland, P. (1988). Soft systems methodology: An overview, *Journal of Applied System Analysis*, **15**.

Davis, A. (1990). *Software Requirements: analysis and specification*. Prentice Hall.

DeMarco, T. (1978). *Structured Analysis and System Specification*. Yourdon Inc.

Finkelstein, A., Kramer, J., Nuseibeh, B., Finkelstein, L. and Goedicke, M. (1992). Viewpoints: a framework for integrating multiple perspectives in systems development, *International Journal of Software Engineering and Knowledge Engineering*, **2**(1).

Forester, T. (Ed.) (1980). *The Microelectronics Revolution*. Blackwell.

Goguen, J. A. (1992). The Dry and the Wet, in *Information Systems Concepts: Improving the Understanding*. Proceedings of IFIP Working Group 8.1 Conference (Alexandra, Egypt) Elsevier Holland, 1992, pp. 1–17.

Grudin, J. (1990). The computer reaches out: The historical continuity of interface design, *CHI '90*. Seattle.

Hughes, J., Shapiro, D., Sharrock, W., Anderson, R., Harper, R. R. and Gibbons, S. C. (1988). *The Automation of Air Traffic Control*. Technical Report University of Lancaster.

Jirotka, M., Luff, P. and Heath, C. C. (1993). Requirements for technology in complex environments: Tasks and interaction in a city dealing room. Sigois Bulletin 14, 2, Dec. 1993.

Lynch, M. (1991). Method: measurement – ordinary and scientific measurement as ethnomethodological phenomena, in Button, G. (Ed.) *Ethnomethodology and the Human Sciences*, Cambridge University Press.

Mumford, E. (1983). *Designing Human Systems for New Technology: The ETHICS Method*. Manchester Business School.

Mumford, E. (1986). *Designing Systems for Business Success. The ETHICS Method*. Manchester Business School.

Somerville, I. (1989). *Software Engineering*: 3rd edition. Addison-Wesley, Norwood, NJ.

Suchman, L. (1987). *Plans and Situated Action*. Cambridge University Press.

Trist, E. L. (1971). Critique of scientific management in terms of socio-technical theory, *Prakseologia*, **39**.

Trist, E. L. Higgin, G. W., Murray, H. and Pollack, A. B. (1963). *Organisational Choice*. Tavistock, London.

Part One

One

Requirements analysis: Orthodoxy, fundamentalism and heresy

John A. McDermid
Professor of Software Engineering, University of York, UK
Technical Director, Dependable Computing Systems Centre,
Director, York Software Engineering Ltd

1 INTRODUCTION

This chapter[1] presents a critical review of accepted industrial practices in requirements capture and analysis, and outlines a proposed approach to resolving problems encountered with these practices. It analyses the function-centred approach to requirements elicitation and specification typically used for embedded systems, and illustrates some of the problems of the approach, including over-specification. It then advances the idea of 'fundamental' specifications, which are based on causal models of the high level objectives for the system, and shows how these are expected to overcome the difficulties associated with the more conventional approach. It also indicates particular strengths in the approach, including the ability to identify conflicting goals. The chapter also outlines a 'heretical' approach to requirements analysis which incorporates analysis of the ramifications of requirements in terms of an architectural design, as part of the process of developing and agreeing a requirements specification. Whilst much of the emphasis is on representational issues, some attention is given to the process of requirements elicitation and validation.

The overall objective of the chapter is to identify some of the more fundamental problems in requirements analysis, and to indicate a strategy for solving – or at least addressing – these problems. It is intended that the strategy outlined be capable of dealing with industrial scale problems, although we are far from being able

---

[1] This chapter is derived from a presentation given by the author at a workshop on Requirements Capture and Analysis, sponsored by British Telecom, and held in Oxford in December 1991. An aim in producing the chapter has been to 'remain faithful' to the presentation and, in effect, to present an 'improved and rationalised transcript' of the talk given.

Requirements Engineering
ISBN 0–1238–5335–4

to present all the details of an industrially applicable method[2]. The observations and judgements made in this chapter are, to some extent, hypothetical. The problems of requirements analysis techniques are now quite well understood and documented. The somewhat radical view of requirements analysis proposed herein is intended to address these problems. Whilst we can see some evidence to support our views, there is, as yet, no complete method based on our views – so they have only partially been experimentally validated. However, we are engaged in a number of projects which aim to develop and apply requirements analysis techniques, and we expect, in due course, to be able to put these ideas to the test. Further, the approach we suggest seems to respect the realities of industrial-scale requirements analysis and system development, as we hope to show.

To set the discussion in context, we first need to sketch a typical view of the software development process, which assumes that the process can be divided into a number of sequential steps, or stages, starting from requirements as articulated by the system's would-be users, and ending with the implementation. The definition of the set of stages varies, but the following is typical. Requirements analysis is concerned with the users' perception of what the system should do, and constraints on how that functionality may be delivered, e.g. space or weight considerations. Requirements are usually represented in natural language, supported by diagrams and mathematics applicable to the problem domain. The next stage is system specification, which identifies the system boundary, what information crosses the boundary, and (aims to) give enough information to enable the designers to develop the system without further recourse to the users. High level, or architectural design, is then a top-level view of the way in which the requirements will be met (the specification satisfied). There is a major shift in emphasis here: we have moved from an external view of a system as a 'black box' to an internal, design view. However the requirements, specification and architecture have something in common: they represent the system as a whole. The next stage, detailed design, considers components of the system in isolation (part of the aim of defining the architecture is to make this decomposition possible). Finally, the implementation is concerned with the programs, both source and object.

In addition to these technical stages, it is valuable to identify phases, which are temporally contiguous sets of activities, and are primarily a managerial artefact. Phases are often (confusingly) given the same name as the stages, but they normally span more than one stage. For example, the architectural design phase will primarily be concerned with developing the architecture, but it will also involve feasibility studies to determine whether certain aspects of the architecture are realisable, and activities modifying or correcting the requirements. Identification of the distinction between stages and phases is one of the keys to good project management (see, for example, McDermid and Rook, 1991). Models based on phases typically include module testing, integration testing, and so on, representing the progressive construction and testing of the system from the individual software modules once they have been implemented.

---

[2] This is the goal of several related research projects in York: see the conclusions.

There are many different forms of software development process model. However, most of them recognise at least the stages identified above, and the ensuing discussion will assume a conventional way of thinking about the development process stages. As the title implies, we first consider the *orthodox* view of requirements analysis, then present a revised approach which considers the *fundamental* objectives for systems, and finally give a *heretical* view which downplays the role of conventional requirements, and especially system specifications, in the development process, and stresses the need to consider architectural solutions during the requirements analysis phase of a development project. In more detail the aim of this chapter is threefold.

First, we discuss the accepted wisdom about how to represent requirements for computer systems, and present some arguments as to why this style of requirements may be thought of as a *source* of problems in system development, rather than a contribution to their solution.

Second, we discuss the nature and representation of the fundamental objectives for computer systems, and the way in which these provide a 'stable core' for the more orthodox forms of requirement.

Third, we argue that to resolve (partially) conflicting objectives which arise in requirements, we need to express their solution in terms of a system architecture. The corollary of this is that we need to give the architecture a much more central role in *requirements analysis* than has hitherto been the case[3].

Before discussing each of these views of requirements analysis, we first consider the background to, and scope of, our study.

2   BACKGROUND AND SCOPE

Requirements analysis is a very broad problem. Our aim in this section is to delineate the set of issues that we intend to address in this chapter. This is not intended to imply that other issues are unimportant, rather to restrict our focus so that we can treat the issues that we do address in reasonable depth. We start by setting out some terminology specific to requirements analysis.

2.1   Terminology

We use the term *requirements analysis* in the generic sense, covering issues of requirements elicitation, representation, validation, and so on. In other words we use 'requirements analysis' to cover all the aspects of the requirements stage of the development process. We use the more specific terms where necessary, and qualify the term 'analysis' if we are using it with a different or more specific meaning.

---

[3] It is widely recognised that architecture plays a pivotal role in system development. The essence of the heretical view is that it is not possible to complete a requirements analysis until an architecture has been developed and validated. This view was also taken by Zachman (1987).

The term *requirements elicitation*, or just *elicitation*, refers to the process of extracting information about the required functionality and other properties of the system from a number of sources, including potential users. It is used here in a fairly pure 'information gathering' sense, and is not intended to imply organisation or formalisation of requirements.

The information gathered needs to be organised and represented, perhaps in a diagrammatic or formal (mathematical) notation. We use the term *representation* for this process, and for the product. The term *requirements specification* is also used for the (usually documentary) result of the elicitation and representation processes.

The processes of elicitation and representation are difficult and error-prone for many reasons, some of which will be discussed below. Consequently, it is necessary to go through a process of *validation*, that is gaining confidence that the requirements specification does represent what is actually wanted. Validation is normally carried out with the people who were involved in requirements elicitation. In the classical models of software development, requirements specifications can only be used for developing the system specifications, once the requirements specification is complete and validated.

2.2 Background

We are primarily concerned with requirements for socio-technical systems, that is computerised systems which interact with people and organisations, as well as other engineered artefacts. A paradigm example is a control system where operators (e.g. pilots) control complex engineered artefacts. There are many requirements methods that try to deal with one or the other aspect of such systems, i.e. the social (organisational) interaction, e.g. ETHICS (Mumford, 1984), and the technical, e.g. CORE[4] (Mullery, 1979). These are usually referred to as *soft* and *hard* methods, respectively, although the terminology has little to recommend it. However, a key problem in many systems is the need to deal with both organisational and technical (i.e. soft and hard) issues, and it seems that there are few, if any, methods which cope well with both sorts of issue.

Traditionally the methods which deal with 'hard' issues focus on the system functionality. Loosely, functionality is what the system is intended to do. More precisely, functionality is represented by input-output relations: when this input occurs this output arises. In contrast, the methods that deal with 'soft' issues deal more with the so-called non-functional requirements[5], such as ease of use, compatibility

---

[4] Arguably, the version of CORE defined by Mullery (1979) does address some of the organisational issues through the notion of viewpoints; however, much of the usage of CORE in industry takes a much narrower technical focus.

[5] The term is intended simply to imply that the requirements are not concerned with functions, i.e. input–output relations. However, it is not a very helpful term as it leads to considerable difficulties in classification, and we eschew it so far as possible in this chapter.

with power structures in an organisation, and so on. However, it is clear that there are many non-functional issues which are relevant to engineered artefacts, e.g. intensity of displays (this is crucial in aircraft cockpits, for example), response time, and the like.

Requirements for socio-technical systems span the issues normally addressed by the 'hard' and 'soft' methods, and also cover other non-functional issues, such as those illustrated above. Thus we are considering systems which current requirements analysis methods do not adequately address, and which are handled in most 'real-world' developments in a variety of *ad hoc* ways. In fact, there is much anecdotal evidence that the absence of adequate ways of dealing with the range of requirements outlined above is one of the major sources of difficulty in software development[6].

2.3   Scope

As indicated above, this chapter aims to set out general principles (and prejudices), but does not purport to describe a complete requirements analysis method. It is intended to set out many of the key issues to be addressed in requirements analysis, although there are a number of important issues which we do not have space to address (see below). In a literal sense, we are more concerned with methodology than method, that is, we discuss some of the properties that an effective requirements analysis method should have, and hint at some solutions. For brevity, however, we do not describe a particular method or methods, nor delve deeply into comparative methodology.

We are primarily concerned with the representation and validation of requirements, with a particular focus on Non-Functional Requirements (NFRs) and their sources. This is an important issue, as it is often the NFRs which give most difficulty both in requirements elicitation and in producing satisfactory systems, i.e. it is often difficult to engineer systems so that the required non-functional requirements are obtained.

We do not address process issues (e.g. elicitation) in detail. However, we note that, in practice, requirements are *negotiated*, not captured, and it is very misleading to think of there being some complete and well-defined set of requirements for a system waiting to be discovered[7]. Indeed, it is clear that requirements are normally unstable, and only emerge as a side-effect of the elicitation process. In essence, the issue is that people often do not appreciate the ramifications of what they state as requirements, so many, and often important, requirements only emerge as designs are being produced, or the system is being implemented and demonstrated. For example, the effect of some technical requirements on staffing might only be apparent once the system performance is known – and this can lead to major

---

[6]   See McDermid (1991b) for some examples.

[7]   This point was stressed in the presentation at the workshop to indicate a disagreement with the use of the term 'capture' in the workshop title.

changes in user requirements. See, for example, Harker and Eason (1990) and Truex and Klein (1991) for a discussion of these issues.

Although we are critical of existing requirements analysis methods, we acknowledge that they are effective in appropriate circumstances. Determining what are appropriate circumstances for the application of a particular method (for requirements analysis or other purposes) is a methodological question. In the conclusions we consider effective domains for the three classes of method which we describe.

We start by considering the aims and objectives of requirements analysis, then discuss orthodoxy, fundamentalism and heresy, in turn.

3   AIMS AND OBJECTIVES OF REQUIREMENTS ANALYSIS

The main product of requirements analysis is a requirements specification. This specification has a number of roles – it is used for communication between client (user) and system developer; it may be used for contractual purposes in a development project; it will typically form the basis for acceptance testing; it may be a critical item of evidence in litigation. In all these roles the specification is functioning as a means of (a carrier for) *communication*. In the following, we focus primarily on the developmental role, but it should be noted that the other roles may best be supported by requirements of rather different characteristics.

An effective requirements analysis process will produce a 'good' requirements specification, i.e. one which is effective in its communication role. Paraphrasing Parnas and his colleagues (Hester *et al.*, 1981) we can characterise a good requirements specification as one which:

"says everything which the designer needs to know in order to produce a system which satisfies the customer/users – and nothing more."

This definition has a number of strengths, and we highlight the two most important. First, it is common (especially among academics) to say that a requirement says *what* a system should do and a design says *how* the system should do it. The above definition avoids this artificial distinction and recognises that it is a requirement if someone (with appropriate authority) requires it, i.e. the notion of requirement is intentional and not to do with levels of abstraction or ways of representing system functionality, or even the notion that requirements should treat the system as a 'black box'.

Second, it says *and nothing more* – a common failing is to produce requirements with excessive and irrelevant detail. Over-specification is a technical problem as it over-constrains the design process and may lead to inefficient and expensive solutions. Over-specification can also be a contractual problem as a client may be legally and financially committed to something he doesn't want, especially where he does not appreciate the ramifications of some aspect of the specification[8]. These ideas will be treated as guiding principles, and we return to them later when criticising existing requirements analysis techniques. They are also useful properties to consider in validating requirements specifications – asking 'how unhappy would you be if this wasn't achieved?' can often lead to requirements being deleted, or at least priorities established. The latter point is important as, in practice, it is often not possible to satisfy all requirements to an equal degree within budget constraints, and informed trade-offs need to be made on the basis of user priorities.

The notion of what constitutes a good requirements specification is really much more complex, and it would be possible to devote several complete papers to this topic. A full analysis of the qualities of a good requirements specification are beyond the scope of this chapter, but other authors (see, for example, the STARTS Handbook (NCC, 1989)), give much more detail on what constitutes good requirements, in terms of detailed attributes such as traceability, etc. However, we view the above notions as setting out the fundamental requirements for requirements specifications – at least from the point of view of their role as the media of communication in a development project.

4   ORTHODOXY

Our aim in this section is to outline the 'conventional wisdom' in the production of requirements in industry, and to illustrate the limitations of this approach. This is an important topic of study, as we are concerned with developing an industrially applicable requirements analysis strategy, and it is therefore encumbent upon us to understand current practices and problems.

4.1   Contents of a requirements specification

In practice, most requirements specifications are written in natural language, supported by diagrams. It is possible to produce effective specifications in this form, although the impracticality of checking consistency and completeness of such specifications is an unavoidable limitation. Most handbooks, standards and guidelines for requirements give guidance on the contents of the specification, assuming that it will be of this textual form. One of the most widely used is the US DoD Standard 2167A (DoD, 1985), and another similar outline of requirements specification con-

---

[8] The requirements might implicitly require the client to increase staffing levels to run the system, and this may be in direct opposition to what he wants, as indicated above (see also Section 5). There is much anecdotal evidence that this form of problem has affected many office automation projects.

tents is given in the STARTS Handbook (NCC, 1989), although this latter does avoid the pitfalls of specifying section headings for the specification, and does deal with some process issues. Our representation of orthodoxy is redolent of these two documents and others of the same genre, but is most influenced by the STARTS Handbook[9].

Typical orthodox requirements specifications have the following structure:

- the core of the specification is a set of function definitions, setting out the functions to be performed by the system, and supported by a description of the structure of the data to be processed; some requirements specifications are data-centred, but the above is true of most requirements specification standards and guidelines for *embedded* computer systems of which the author is aware;
- typical functional specifications cover, at least:

  — normal functioning, including inputs, outputs, operation, and control, e.g. starting and stopping of functions;
  — abnormal functioning, exceptions, etc.;
  — dependability properties, e.g. safety and security;
  — performance, e.g. throughput;
  — quality, e.g. maintainability or modifiability;
  — expected changes, e.g. likely modifications to interface devices.

  Details vary but, typically, these properties are simply presented in a list (perhaps a pre-defined set of sub-sections of the specification document) first covering functionality, then dealing with NFRs;
- data specifications:

  — definition of data structure;
  — volumetrics, e.g. data flow rate;
  — sources and sinks of data.

There are often also 'global' considerations, e.g. for uniform treatment of user interfaces and, arguably, quality issues should be treated as a global issue. By global here we mean a property of the system as a whole, and not one that can be unequivocally linked to a particular component, module or sub-function. Often these global issues are problematic aspects of requirements, both to analyse and to achieve, because they are holistic or emergent properties, rather than being decomposable.

Functionality can be decomposed, and sub-functions assigned to modules for individual software engineers to implement. Similarly, some non-functional properties (e.g. numeric precision) can be allocated to modules, given a proper understanding

---

[9] The author was responsible for co-ordinating and editing the requirements section of the Handbook. Although this work is now being criticised, it should be remembered that the STARTS guide is intended to represent industrial good practice, rather than unvalidated research concepts, no matter how appealing.

of the relevant science, e.g. numerical analysis. Properties such as 'maintainability' cannot be decomposed in this way as the cost of making a change depends on the overall structure and inter-dependencies of the design. Thus it is very difficult to manage developments which contain these global properties. Few researchers have addressed these problems directly, although Gilb (1988) is one notable exception. There are many other interesting and problematic facets of requirements specifications, but the above serves to indicate their essential character.

Process issues are usually given fairly scant attention. It is often stated, or implied, however, that the elicitation process is complete once such specifications are produced at a uniform and consistent level of detail covering all of the system functions.

4.2   Problems of the orthodox approach

Although it is possible to produce good specifications in the form described above, and they are much better (in general) than those produced in an entirely *ad hoc* way, they have severe limitations in many situations. Problems found with such specifications include the following.

Several problems relate to the level of detail produced. First, they violate the 'and nothing more' principle as problem owners[10] are forced to say more than they want, e.g. to define data formats where they are only concerned with overall information content; thus they prompt over-specification by the users. Second, this form of specification encourages 'specmanship' – requirements analysts feel they must say something about each function attribute, even if this is not really relevant to the user's needs, i.e. they prompt over-specification by the analysts. Third, in practice, such specifications effectively incorporate design decisions[11], and problem owners may not appreciate, or want, the ramifications of what they've signed off, e.g. on organisation or staffing. There is a consequential problem that they lead to low flexibility in design and implementation as the inherent over-specification obstructs change.

There are also some (technically) more fundamental problems to do with the semantics of natural language. First, they have weak semantics thus there is poor consistency checking and, as a consequence, requirements conflicts may go unnoticed. Second, such specifications are hard to validate as they document what it is that the analyst thought it was the problem owner said he thought he might want, not what he'll get[12]!

Finally, and perhaps most significantly, such specifications may violate the 'high level objectives' of the organisation the system is intended to serve (we return to this point when we discuss fundamentalism).

---

[10] Here we are using Checkland's (1981) terminology.

[11] In general, we should expect to see design decisions in requirements. However, it is unsatisfactory if they cannot be distinguished from 'genuine' requirements.

[12] This seems to reflect a basic psychological principle; perhaps it is a difficulty most people have in dealing with abstract concepts.

In general, there can be little confidence, using such techniques, that the system implemented will satisfy the problem owner and the users – at least in circumstances where requirements include stringent NFRs. The above critique outlines some of the reasons why such specifications are of limited utility, and practical experience has shown that projects using such specification techniques often run into difficulties (see, for example, McDermid, 1991b).

Some of the problems identified above are inherent in the form of the specifications, but many result from the way in which the specifications are derived, not from the form, itself. In the author's view the underlying cause of the difficulties is that the process which leads to such specifications is effectively 'starting at wrong place', that is with derived requirements not fundamental ones. By this we mean looking at the desired properties at a *presupposed* system boundary, instead of starting with business needs, or the objectives of the embedding system.

This may seem to be a surprising observation, but in many cases it is not clear what functions should be computerised, and the first (tentative) design decision is deciding what to automate, i.e. where to place the system boundary. By starting with a presupposed system boundary one is effectively taking this crucial design decision before determining a single requirement. This seems to be the root cause of many of the problems encountered in using this orthodox approach.

It should be noted, however, that we are not in a position to establish unequivocally cause and effect between the (supposedly) poor specification techniques and the unsuccessful projects, so our attribution of blame must be treated with some care. Indeed, there are circumstances where the specification techniques are effective, e.g. for defining the requirements for a 'straightforward' replacement of an existing system. However, there is some evidence in support of our view (see, for example, Eason, 1989), and the author has heard much anecdotal evidence which supports the view. We believe that the 'orthodox' approach is, at best, limited in applicability, and we hope to lend further credence to our view by developing improved techniques and by showing their efficacy on practical projects. In addition, it would be desirable to have a true comparative methodology which enabled us to determine when a particular method would be effective. We return to this point in the conclusions.

5   FUNDAMENTALISM

There are many ways of addressing the above problems. In the rest of this chapter we focus on one approach. As indicated earlier, our main tenet is that it is necessary to take a more fundamental stance to requirements elicitation than is normally the case. Our aim in this section is to indicate the main issues which a fundamental approach to requirements analysis must address, and to outline some of the steps in a possible elicitation method. However, we first consider the 'orthodox response' to the above set of criticisms, that is the production of 'cardinal points' specifications.

5.1   Cardinal points specifications

The problems indicated above have been recognised for some time. As a consequence, within the 'orthodox' view of requirements it has been common to talk in terms of 'cardinal points' specifications, that is a small number of key requirements for a system. This approach certainly addresses the issues of over-specification, but it introduces a number of other problems.

The use of cardinal points specifications is a procurement practice operated in Europe and North America, by major agencies such as the MoD. The approach consists of writing succinct specifications covering 'the things that really matter', but there are no published guidelines (of which the author is aware) which suggest ways of determining what 'really matters'.

Practical cardinal points specifications are typically very *ad hoc*, representing rather disparate requirements. Even though they are typically high level requirements, there is no guarantee that they are consistent, and there are very often problems caused by under-specification. Often this means that the system produced does not satisfy the users, as there is missing functionality, or important issues which did not feature in the cardinal points are not handled adequately.

A major source of difficulty is that such specifications often need a substantial amount of (non-obvious) problem domain knowledge to interpret correctly – and system developers rarely have enough of this knowledge. Although over-specification is a problem with the orthodox approach, it does have the benefit of drawing out some of this problem domain knowledge and, in effect, encoding it in the requirements specifications. Thus, this approach appears to solve one problem at the expense of introducing another. However, we believe it is possible to do an effective job of requirements specification by devising a systematic approach to fundamental requirements.

5.2   The components of fundamental specifications

A central thesis in this work is that to represent the fundamental requirements for computerised systems we need to be able to define:

- causality – model of cause and effect in the environment(s) in which the system is intended to operate;
- objectives[13] – what the system is intended to bring about (cause).

In essence, these objectives define the role that the computerised system is intended to play in the causal chains (identified in the model) of the environment. This is a somewhat unusual notion, and it seems helpful to illustrate what we mean by

---

[13] In the presentation I used the term 'goal'. Objective seems more appropriate due to the connotations that it is a long-term 'requirement' not simply discharged by a single action (and it may not be attainable). I am grateful to John Dobson for pointing out this useful shift in terminology.

objectives both for embedded systems and for 'IT' systems, before discussing the details behind these ideas.

Objectives are typically expressible in terms of (un)desirable states to be reached or invariants, that is properties which need to be preserved over some protracted period of time. Such objectives might be concerned with the structure of the organisation using the system, the environment, or competitive advantage.

An environmental objective might be to ensure that the level of radiation emitted from the nuclear reactor is within permitted limits and that the reactor is available for useful power generation for 99.8% of the time over a ten year period.

An example relating to the organisation might be the desire to reduce the number of staff in the accounts department by 20% (by the introduction of the new system). Let us say that the general requirement is for an invoice management system. Here the issue will be the extra administrative load of entering data into the system, off-set by the reduction in clerical load in typing and checking the invoices by hand. This trade-off is governed in part by the performance of the system, its ease of use, and so on.

Also, in such circumstances it is important to know what other systems exist, or are planned, as the above objective may only be obtainable when information from timesheets or goods inwards is entered into another system, and can be extracted automatically from the files held by these systems, thus meaning that there is little data entry. Other issues in such a situation will relate to how the integrity of the input data is checked – if it is all entered twice and cross-checked then there may be no saving in effort, or even increased workload and staffing. These issues need to be addressed when establishing the feasibility of the high level objectives.

Finally, an example to do with competitive advantage might be to keep project X (which will be developed with support from the new computer system) secret until product launch. This objective will generate security requirements which might be satisfied by doors and locks, or by mechanisms on the computer system, e.g. passwords. Note that none of these requirements mention the computer system's functionality directly, and are articulated primarily in terms of the human and engineered system in which the computer system is (will be) embedded.

Ignoring for the moment the subclass of situations involving avoidance of undesirable states, the requirement for a computing system being used in any of the above environments can be specified directly in causal terms. The computer system is required to cause the desirable state to be achieved/maintained (or contribute to achievement/maintenance of that desirable state). In other words, the requirement for the computing system is that it play its part in the identified causal chain. Dealing with avoidance is slightly more complex, but here we require the computerised system not to cause, or contribute to causing (with more than some probability or frequency), the undesirable state, via any causal chain in which it can play a part.

For clarity we have hinted at the role of the computerised system in the second and third examples – in general, however, the role of the computer system will not be part of the objective, and the decision to use a computer system in support of (meeting) the objective is one which should be made explicitly. Indeed, this is often the first major design decision (and perhaps the most serious error).

A great advantage of the above approach is that it may enable us to see conflicts in objectives, hence potential inconsistencies in requirements, very early on in the process. Even stating such objectives informally may enable specifiers and problem owners to identify difficulties, but provision of a more 'formal' basis for articulating objectives opens up the opportunity for analysing the objectives. We believe that this is one of the values of causal models, as they should enable us to analyse specifications and identify inconsistencies in the sense that incompatible states are (required to be) caused. We have experimented with the use of causal models for this purpose (Dobson and McDermid, 1991; Morris and McDermid, 1991), although it is far from clear whether such an approach is practical for large scale systems.

Identifying the objectives in the above manner, and specifying the role of the computer system, is a way of expressing cardinal points specifications – but with a systematic and traceable basis. However, as indicated above, this is not enough to enable the system to be fully specified and built – we need to derive further requirements based on the physics of the situation or the structure of the organisation in which the system will play a part, e.g. rate of change of pressure in a tank, sustainable data entry rates and error rates. Clearly, knowledge of properties of the environment and cause and effect are needed to derive more detailed requirements. In many cases, these derived requirements will be equivalent in level of detail to the orthodox requirements mentioned previously.

In general, the choice of environment model to support derivation of more detailed requirements will depend on the particular circumstances, i.e. the nature of the objectives, and the important properties of the environment. However, we can indicate key aspects of the models which are relevant in the vast majority of, if not all, circumstances. There appear to be different bases for the models for different classes of system, and we draw a simple distinction here to illustrate our ideas. We refer to the embedding equipment for an embedded computer system, as an *engineered system*, and the embedding system for an 'IT' system as a *human activity system*[14]. Full models of an engineered or human activity system might be very complex, but there are some fundamental properties which always appear to be relevant for these classes of system.

It is our hypothesis that, for human activity systems, the following are the most important facets of the model:

- information and/or knowledge (information plus interpretation) are crucial as they are the basis for specifying many NFRs such as security;
- structural issues such as roles, and relations such as responsibility and authority, are also important in models of the human activity systems;
- cause and effect with respect to knowledge/information states, e.g. knowing X and Y is sufficient to enable someone trained for role P to infer Z.

---

[14] Again we have borrowed the term from Checkland (1981).

In general, producing such models explicitly and completely is very difficult (which is one of the reasons simplifying devices such as the military classification schemes are produced). However, it is clearly crucial to have some 'handle' on these issues to be able to analyse specifications. For example, the notions of classifications and information flow are used widely in military security as simplifying concepts. Note that, to deal with security issues, we may need to model the objectives of adversaries to the organisation which the system is meant to serve.

Similarly, for engineered systems, the key facets appear to be:

- energy, in its varying forms, as this is what the computerised system is intended to control (e.g. aspects of dynamics), and other energy-related properties (e.g. temperature, velocity, and pressure) are needed to specify NFRs such as safety;
- the structure of the engineered system is important as it affects causality, e.g. we will need to know which fluid flows are controlled by which valves;
- cause and effect, with respect to energy states, e.g. opening valve V will cause the level of fluid in the vessel to fall at 1 cm/s;

Both these characterisations of key issues are hypothetical, and subject to validation or refutation. The notion that information is crucial to modelling 'IT' systems is perhaps unsurprising. The stress on energy for engineered systems is perhaps less obvious to software engineers, but it seems to be a central concept used by systems and control engineers (Beam, 1991). It seems reasonable that these concepts are necessary – perhaps the key question is whether or not they are sufficient for articulating the bulk of objectives (pertaining to the use of computerised systems).

5.3   Derived requirements

As indicated above, it is necessary to describe objectives, but not sufficient, as achievement of these objectives is constrained by the properties of the environment in which the system is situated. Thus we need to *derive* requirements taking into account these constraints. To derive more detailed requirements, we need to understand the way in which the computer system takes part in the causal chains identified. Although they seem rather trite, the following observations, based on the understanding that a computer is an information processing system, are crucial.

First, in the context of a human activity system, a computer operates on information which will often simply be an encoding of the information of concern in the environment, e.g. historical models of business activities, such as are typically found in database applications. The computer system 'perceives' and contributes to information in the human activity system through terminals, workstations and the like, thus the derived requirements must relate to these processes of perception and contribution.

For example, a derived requirement might be that individuals on project X with access to product specifications shall not have access to marketing plans, and *vice versa*[15] – note that this does not achieve the objective outlined above, but it does reduce certain sorts of risk, based on knowledge (assumptions) about the ability of individuals to make inferences from information they receive.

Second, in the context of an engineered system, a computer system operates on information which is modelling the state of the environment. The difference between engineered systems and more classical information systems is the fact that engineered systems often need very up-to-date information about the state of the environment (within a few milliseconds), and are less concerned with history. Also, they try to control the environment, rather than simply modelling it and providing information to the system's users. These temporal constraints mean that many engineered systems are classified as being 'real-time'. However, the distinctions between these two classes of systems are becoming less clear as requirements evolve, e.g. many banking systems are now becoming 'real-time'. Typically, in such situations, the computer system monitors and influences the state of the environment through sensors and actuators.

For example, a derived requirement in the context of reactor control might be that an over-temperature indication on a majority of core temperature sensors shall cause all valves in the primary cooling circuits to be opened – and this should occur within time periods dictated by the rate of change of physical quantities, e.g. reactor temperature.

The above simply illustrates the issues we need to address in defining fundamental requirements and then establishing derived requirements. Space does not permit us to give a full description of the issues we need to model in establishing objectives and producing derived requirements, but we have previously analysed the modelling issues in more detail (Dobson and McDermid, 1990, 1991), and believe it is possible to produce adequate models for the above purposes.

It may seem that all we have done is to provide an indirect way of producing orthodox requirements – derived requirements do look like orthodox requirements, but there are some differences. First, we now know the source of the orthodox level requirements, so if there are conflicts in requirements identified at this level, we know that we need to rectify the problems in terms of adjusting (making trade-offs between) the initial objectives. Second, we will only produce orthodox level derived requirements where there is a corresponding objective. Thus maximum design freedom is left, yet the key facets of the system that are constrained by the environment in which the system will work are (in principle) defined in sufficient detail for the system to be designed and built. At a semi-philosophical level, what we are dealing with is really a *specif*ication, that is it deals with the specifics of the system requirements for a particular situation, and avoids detailing issues which can be left open as 'normal for a system of that sort'. This is much closer to the traditional meaning of specification[16]. There are, however some limitations of this approach, which we set out below, having outlined a possible process.

---

[15] This is a simple example of a form of Chinese Wall security policy (Brewer and Nash, 1989).
[16] For example, see the *Oxford English Dictionary*.

5.4   An outline analysis process

Although our main concern in this chapter is with the representation of requirements in the non-standard framework which we have proposed, it seems essential to be able to indicate the way in which such requirements might be elicited and validated to lend credence to our hypotheses. Any practical process involves iteration through stages, but a conceptual process, ignoring these practical issues, might be to go through a series of six stages, as we now illustrate.

1. Produce a model of the environment and its causal properties, including those of adversaries in human activity systems. For engineered systems the primary concern is with 'mechanistic' cause, that is cause and effect through engineered mechanisms. For human activity systems the primary concern is teleological cause, i.e. what individuals and agents wish to bring about, or their purposes.

2. Identify objectives as illustrated above. These are the system owner's teleological causes, perhaps including those derived from other organisations and individuals who have authority with regard to the system, e.g. airworthiness authorities for aircraft. It should be noted that objectives are teleological concepts, even in engineered systems, as they represent purpose; however, we would expect achievement of these objectives to be constrained by mechanistic cause.

3. It is then necessary to analyse for inconsistencies, i.e. clashes in objectives, which will be manifest by requirements for the environment to be in more than one state at once. If clashes are found then these need to be resolved by considering relative priorities of the objectives, and this can normally only be done in consultation with the problem owners.

4. Identify the scope of the computerised system – that is, determine what parts of the causal structures identified in the first stage are to be automated. This involves trade-offs based on the objectives, taking into account economic constraints, knowledge about the capabilities of other technologies, e.g. sensors and actuators, data entry rates, and the like. Economic or timescale problems might be identified here, and this might also lead to a revision of objectives.

5. Derive more detailed requirements based on physical constraints and those in the human activity system, e.g. objectives of adversaries. Examples of the derived requirements are: sampling rate derived from rate of change of energy value; security rules derived from adversaries' goals and estimates of their knowledge; definition of roles for system operators determined by organisational policy.

6. Analyse for conflicts in the derived requirements. There may be aspects of the objectives which are not fundamentally in conflict, but which do conflict once a technological solution strategy has been chosen.

Following this set of stages will lead to orthodox level requirements, but based on fundamental objectives. Clearly, a 'real' process would be much more complex, but the above illustrates the broad structure of the process that would be needed to apply the above ideas.

5.5   Observations

The approach outlined above must be viewed as hypothetical, or tentative, since we have not developed the full details of a method; however, there is some evidence that 'components' of the ideas are practical. In the conclusions we identify some existing methods and experience upon which we could build in developing a method, following the strategy we have outlined, and thus give some indication that our hypothesised benefits can be realised. However, it is still informative to consider the strengths and weaknesses which such a method is likely to display, even if these conclusions are rather tentative. Key strengths are as follows:

1. The approach addresses key issues, including the 'and nothing more' principle. In principle, by focussing on objectives and deriving requirements only against these objectives we should reduce the tendency to over-specify.
2. It leads to appropriate degrees of detail, giving information where there are important objectives, and leaving design freedom where there are no specific objectives or constraints.
3. The approach can help detection of inconsistencies, including clashes between objectives, at an early stage rather than in implementation.

These strengths have been illustrated, albeit briefly, above. There is one further issue which is worthy of brief explanation, as it indicates the importance of some of the relations needed in modelling human organisations.

In many cases there is an interaction between function and NFRs which, once appreciated, can lead to a change in operator roles and the function of a system. Imagine a point defence system such as the US PATRIOT, used for defensive purposes in the Gulf War. Consider an initial system (requirement) where incoming missiles travel sufficiently slowly that the operator can have responsibility and authority for both target acquisition and weapon firing, then evolving to a stage where having a 'man in the loop' is impractical. This might arise because increases in speed of the incoming missile, even if intercepted, would mean that it could still explode sufficiently close to its target that considerable damage would be done. Given this change in situation we would expect to see the requirements evolve so that the point defence system was given authority for missile firing – but this leads to a situation where the operator has responsibility for, but not authority over, the actions of the machine. Under these circumstances, it might be appropriate to add an auto-destruct function for the defensive missile so that the operator could still retain overall authority (there is time in flight for the operator to make such a decision, even when he can not be involved in the launch decision)[17]. Thus, evolving requirements, especially NFRs, have led to a change in system *function*.

---

[17] The author believes that a similar evolution did occur for the PATRIOT, but is not aware of any documentary evidence to support this belief.

The above example illustrates one of the reasons for wishing to model responsibility and authority – in many cases, automation causes change in responsibility and authority, and this may lead to derived requirements, both functional and nonfunctional. It also highlights another very crucial aspect of a requirements analysis method, that is the ability to deal with change, including change in the environment in which the system operates (this is one of the reasons why we need the models).

There are weaknesses of the proposed method, not least that it is still largely hypothetical. However, there is one other major weakness which needs to be considered. It is possible that some requirements derived in the manner described above may be unsatisfiable, that is, the objectives may be technically unachievable – at the stated cost, given policies adopted by the problem owners, and so on. The difficulty is that some of these policies, and certainly constraints on cost, can only really be seen in the context of a design, so infeasibility can only be detected at this level, and not in terms of either fundamental or derived requirements. This leads us on to the heresy.

6   HERESY

In essence, the heresy is that it is, in general, impractical to produce complete, consistent and implementable requirements specifications, and *know* that this has been achieved, without modelling the system to be produced at the *architectural* level. In other words, analysis of architectures is an essential part of requirements analysis, at least for certain classes of system. The primary technical reason for this was identified above – there are potential conflicts in objectives which can only be unambiguously identified once there is an understanding of the design. This is in conflict to the principles behind software processes such as the 'waterfall model' and the procurement practices of many major companies and government agencies. Such problems have been found by observation of actual development projects (see, for example, the chapter by Button in this volume). However, we illustrate here the reason for these general observations by means of a sketch example, which we take from the domain of satellite systems.

In space applications (e.g. communications satellites), functional requirements may be incompatible with power, weight and radiation tolerance requirements because the silicon on sapphire processors which have to be used to satisfy the radiation requirements may have insufficient processing power to provide the required functions. However, to determine these conflicts we need to have, at least, a detailed model of the hardware architecture, the mapping of software function to hardware unit, and knowledge of algorithm complexity. These are obviously design issues, albeit aspects of architectural design, that is the 'gross level' structure of the system.

Space does not permit a full discussion of the issues involved in modelling and analysing architectures. We have previously discussed the philosophy behind giving more prominence to architectural issues in the requirements analysis process (McDermid, 1991a), and have drawn out the strong analogies with the way in which architects work for their clients. Work has been carried out on architectural design and analysis, and some of the primary modelling issues, including the need to distinguish the logical architecture, that is the set of processes and communications needed to achieve the required functionality, from physical architecture, that is the hardware structures and the hardware-software mapping have been identified (Burns *et al.*, 1991). We limit our discussion to the broad process issues, and indicate how the treatment of architecture can be viewed as an extension of the requirements analysis process identified above.

Following the principles we have outlined above, the basic process for arriving at complete, consistent and achievable requirements is to proceed in two broad epochs. First, it is necessary to establish the overall system objectives and derived requirements as described in Section 5. Second, we should then proceed directly to the specification of architecture, both logical and physical, without producing an elaborate system specification. Having done this, we should analyse for conflicts in objectives which are only apparent at this level. There is an analogy here with architects in the building profession, who produce design sketches based on brief specifications from clients, and who then agree what should be built in terms of these sketches, not some notion of requirements. These design models are also used for the analysis of design feasibility, and we would advocate a similar set of analyses within our 'heretical' approach.

Particular strengths of this unusual process (potentially) are as follows. First, we can identify conflicts between NFRs and, as we have fundamental objectives not orthodox requirements, we have more freedom to change requirements (or early design decisions) to achieve an implementable compromise. Second, drawing on the analogy with architects, it is easier, in principle, to validate the architecture with the customer than it is to get meaningful agreement to requirements. This is because the customer agrees to what he is going to get not what it is some analyst tells him he said he required. In practice, this is done by reading specifications, observing animations, and so on, although, in practice, we need improved techniques for 'scaling' from prototypes to the properties of the final system for this approach to be entirely satisfactory.

There are a number of reasons why what we have described is a heretical view, or at least why it goes against accepted practices, although others have advocated the approach (Ehn, 1988). The most fundamental heresy is that there is no fully elaborated requirements specification, and that the requirements can only be finalised once an architecture has been produced. Further, it is the architectural definition which is 'signed off' by customer/problem owner/user as what he will get. Thus there are both technical and procedural, or contractual, ramifications of the heresy.

Although we have used the term 'heresy', some (industrial) readers may find little that is surprising from a technical perspective, and think that the views described simply rationalise the reality of most complex projects. Similarly, it may come as no surprise to those who have carried out ethnomethodological studies on real software developments. However, there does seem to be an important point. The traditional wisdom, and teaching in academia is that it is good to produce orthodox requirements and to complete them before embarking on design, and that one only carries out design prior to agreeing requirements when the ideal/normal process does not work. Our view is that this perceived wisdom has matters exactly the wrong way round. It seems that it is normal to need and to use this heretical approach, and that the orthodox one only works when one is lucky – there happen to be no major conflicts in objectives, the domain is well understood, and so on. In other words we believe that the above ideas represent the typical situation, and that the normal teachings about how to develop requirements contribute to the difficulties, rather than help ameliorate them. Again, this seems to be supported by Button's findings reported elsewhere in this volume.

7 CONCLUSIONS

In the true spirit of a workshop we have presented current ideas and prejudices, rather than trying to describe complete and polished work. We have proposed an approach to the development of requirements which stresses fundamental objectives and the need for agreeing an architectural solution, rather than 'signing off' abstract requirements which may be unimplementable (for technical reasons and cost and timescale limitations). Specifically we have proposed an alternative approach to deriving, resolving and validating requirements which introduces the notion of objectives specified in a causal framework, and the need to reach agreement on a design proposal, not an abstract specification of requirements. The approach we have outlined is still in the form of a working hypothesis for the development of a new method, not a tried and tested method, but it is based on observation of the difficulties which arise in practice with standard development practices.

As we have been at pains to point out, our proposed process is somewhat hypothetical, but there are a number of possible and partial bases on which we could build a prototype method for experimental application. This work addresses most of the issues which would have to be resolved to provide a complete method based on the principles outlined above.

One key issue is the ability to articulate objectives, and to analyse conflicts. Work by Dardenne et al. in the ESPRIT funded KAOS project, indicates how to model objectives (which they call goals) and to analyse for potential conflicts (Dardenne et al., 1991). This work addresses many of the issues associated with identifying objectives in their organisational context.

The issues of analysing non-functional requirements have received some attention. Two studies have been funded by the Admiralty Research Establishment[18] into the modelling of non-functional requirements. These deal with broad requirements

---

[18] Now the Maritime Division of the Defence Research Agency.

modelling issues, and illustrate the use of causal modelling for expressing requirements (Dobson and McDermid, 1990, 1991).

The notions of the use of causal models, and formalisation of the notion of causality, have been addressed by a number of researchers. Some foundational work on analysing and modelling safety and security in causal terms has been carried out (Burns *et al.*, 1992). Further, there have been various research projects on causal logics which show how such formalisms can be used to model requirements and derive consequences of requirements statements/specifications. Two examples of this work are given in Stokes (1992) and Morris and McDermid (1991).

A major issue with the above approach is the need to involve users in the review of design specifications. There is some evidence that this is tractable. Extensive studies and experiments by Christiane Floyd in Berlin with her STEPS method have shown that even non-technical users can contribute effectively to such work. Specifically, STEPS involves users extensively in the design process, including validation of high level (architectural) designs (Floyd *et al.*, 1989).

The final aspect of the method at the requirements level is the modelling of the system's environment. Work on the modelling of the operational environment of safety critical systems in such a form that they can be linked to formal descriptions of the system to be developed, and hence be analysed using the same formalisms has been carried out using a variety of formalisms (Anderson *et al.*, 1990).

Finally, there is the issue of modelling and analysis at the architectural level. In the area of real-time systems architectures, there is work on the development of TARDIS which provides a basis for analysing architectural properties prior to making commitments to the details of an implementation (Burns *et al.*, 1991).

The above publications do not give an exhaustive review of relevant work, but they do indicate that our hypotheses may be well-founded, although, of course, they do not provide a complete and comprehensive method. To validate these hypotheses we would need to develop and document a fully detailed method (and perhaps provide tool support). This entails defining three broad aspects of a method:

1. We need to identify representations (notations) for all the relevant facets of the requirements specifications. These include objectives, responsibility and cause, as well the more classical notions of data, functions and non-functional requirements such as numeric precision. Ideally, the representations need to be formal to make it possible to analyse the consistency of requirements, and to derive consequences of the specification.
2. We need guidelines for carrying out the elicitation process and rules and guidelines for verification and validation, where verification is concerned with the internal consistency of the requirements specification. These activities include conflict detection, i.e. determining when objectives are incompatible, and ways of resolving these conflicts.
3. The third issue is to define ways of handling change – this is a major problem, which is only partly addressed by the approach outlined above. Handling of change is a major research problem in its own right.

In addition, it would also be necessary to carry out major case studies, that is to undertake worked examples to show that the overall approach is tractable (and where there are pitfalls). It is only through this form of experimental work that the method could be validated and refined.

In practice, work towards the above three objectives needs to be carried out in parallel so that the method is informed by experimental feedback as it is developed. This, in part, is why we have already contributed to a number of apparently fragmentary studies – without these our ideas would be more fully worked out, and much less likely to be useful and usable! Much needs to be done if the approach is to prove useful. It is our hope that this philosophy can be developed and exploited in the research being undertaken for BAe as part of the work of Dependable Computing Systems Centre.

As we noted earlier, there is a need for some comparative methodology. Although we are proposing a new approach to requirements, motivated by limitations in current techniques, the orthodox approaches do work in appropriate circumstances – but at present, we do not know what methods are effective in which contexts, and this problem needs to be addressed[19]. Perhaps this is a more fundamental limitation than the absence of effective methods. An important basis for a comparative methodology for requirements analysis would be to identify the circumstances under which different requirements methods are effective, e.g.:

- replacement of existing systems due to technological obsolescence, with minor changes to requirements – orthodox requirements methods;
- experimental development to prove concepts for a future major development project – cardinal points;
- system embedded in a complex engineered system where design of the engineered system and the balance of authority between man and machine evolves as the design proceeds – the 'heretical' approach defined above.

We believe that the 'heretical' approach would work in the other cases, but it may be unnecessary in the simpler cases. The above is illustrative, and a true comparative methodology would give more complete and systematic guidance on method selection.

Finally, we can summarise our views in a different way to that in which they have been introduced – and perhaps therefore give a fuller picture of their meaning. It is common to distinguish requirements and design as being concerned with *what* a system should do and *how* it should do it, respectively. Taking our approach, we can say that the primary purpose of:

- the objectives is to say what the system is *for*;
- the derived requirements is to say *what* the system should do;
- the architecture is to say *how* the system will do it.

[19] This view is one to which the author subscribes, but was not mentioned in the talk at the workshop. I am grateful to Geoff Mullery for pointing out this omission from the presentation.

In practice, these differences are somewhat blurred, but there are distinctions of principle. Our heresy is that, at least in some circumstances, one does not produce these definitions in sequence, but works on them in concert until they are consonant. We believe that this reflects industrial reality, and that we have begun to set out a basis for analysing the consistency of these levels of specification in a systematic way; in other words, that we have begun to set out the basis of an effective industrial requirements analysis method. Time will tell how well-founded this belief is.

NOTE ADDED IN PROOF

In the two years since this chapter was written, considerable progress has been made. We still espouse the above concepts, and have proposed ways of representing causal structures and the relationships between objectives/goals, system models and requirements. For up to date information, contact the author at: Department of Computer Science, University of York, Heslington, York, YO1 5DD; telephone 0904 432726; fax 0904 432708; email jam@minster.York.ac.UK.

ACKNOWLEDGEMENTS

Many of the ideas presented herein have been developed in joint work with John Dobson of the University of Newcastle upon Tyne. John has also reviewed and made constructive comments on this chapter. Thanks are also due to many other friends and colleagues who have been instrumental in helping me to form the views given above.

REFERENCES

Anderson, T., de Lemos, R. and Saeed, A. (1990). A formal model for safety critical computer systems, *Proceedings of Safecomp '90*, (B. K. Daniels, Ed.), IFAC/Pergamon Press.
Beam, W. (1991). *Systems Engineering: Architecture and Design*. McGraw-Hill.
Brewer, D. F. C. and Nash, M. J. (1989). The Chinese Wall security policy, *IEEE Symposium on Security and Privacy*, IEEE Press.
Burns, A., Lister, A. M. and McDermid, J. A. (1991). TARDIS: An architectural framework for timely and reliable distributed information systems. *Proceedings of the Australian Software Engineering Conference* (P. A. Bailes, Ed.), Australian Computer Society.
Burns, A., Dobson, J. E. and McDermid, J. A. (1992). On the meaning of safety and security, *Computer Journal*, **35**(1).
Checkland, P. (1981). *Systems Thinking, Systems Practice*, Wiley.
Dardenne, A., Fickas, S. and Lamsweerde, A. van (1991). Goal-directed concept acquisition

in requirements elicitation, *Proceedings 6th International Workshop on Software Specification and Design*, IEEE Computer Society, pp 14–21.

Department of Defense (1985) *Military Standard 2167A: Defense Systems Software Development*.

Dobson, J. E. and McDermid, J. A. (1990). *An Investigation into Modelling and Categorisation of Non-functional Requirements (for the Specification of Naval Command Systems)*, YCS 141, University of York.

Dobson, J. E. and McDermid, J. A. (1991). *An Investigation into Modelling and Categorisation of Non-functional Requirements: Part II: Methodology and Models*, YCS 160, University of York.

Eason, K. (1989). *Information Technology and Organisational Change*, Taylor and Francis.

Ehn, P. (1988). *Work Oriented Design of Computer Artifacts*, Lawrence Erlbaum.

Floyd, C., Reisin, F.-M. and Schmidt, G. (1989). STEPS to software development with users, *Proceedings of ESEC '89* (C. Ghezzi and J. A. McDermid, Eds.), *Lecture Notes in Computer Science, Vol. 387*, Springer-Verlag.

Gilb, T. (1988). Principles of software engineering management, Addison-Wesley.

Harker, S. D. P. and Eason K. D. (1990). Human factors in system design, Alvey Report from Project MMI 080, HUSAT, University of Loughborough.

Hester, S. D., Parnas, D. L. and Utter, D. F. (1981). Using documentation as a software design medium, *Bell System Technical Journal*, **60**(8).

McDermid, J. A. (1991a). In praise of architects, *Information and Software Technology*, **33**(8), 566–574.

McDermid, J. A. (1991b). Introduction to Part II, *Software Engineer's Reference Book* (J. A. McDermid, Ed.), Butterworth-Heinemann.

McDermid, J. A. and Rook, P. (1991). Software development and process models, *Software Engineer's Reference Book* (J. A. McDermid, Ed.), Butterworth-Heinemann.

Morris, J. and McDermid J. A. (1991). The structure of permissions: A normative framework for access rights, *Proceedings of Database Security IV* (C. E. Landwehr and S. Jajodia, Eds), IFIP/North-Holland, 1992.

Mullery, G. P. (1979). CORE: A method for controlled requirements expression, *Proceedings of the Fourth International Conference on Software Engineering*, IEEE Press.

Mumford, E. (1984). *Designing Human Systems*, Manchester Business School Publications.

NCC (1989). *The STARTS Purchasers' Handbook*, NCC, UK.

Stokes, D. A. (1992). *Improving Requirements Analysis: Support for an Extended CORE Method*, DPhil Thesis, YCST 92/03, University of York.

Truex, D. P. and Klein, H. K. (1991). A rejection of structure as a basis for systems development, *Collaborative Work, Social Communications and Information Systems* (R. K. Stamper, P. Kerola, R. Lee and K. Lyytinen, Eds), Elsevier.

Zachman, J. A. (1987). A framework for information system architecture, *IBM Systems Journal*, **26**(3), 276–292.

Two

Resolving requirements conflicts with computer-supported negotiation

Steve Easterbrook
School of Cognitive and Computing Sciences,
University of Sussex, UK

1   INTRODUCTION

Conflict is an inevitable part of both requirements elicitation and system design. As McDermid pointed out in the previous chapter, requirements are negotiated, not captured. During this process, the participants will disagree over how to interpret features of the application domain, what the requirements for a new system are, and how to meet those requirements. Conventional analysis techniques tend to suppress conflict, making any resolution untraceable and adding to the communication problems. This chapter argues the need for explicit support for conflict management, and presents a model of computer-supported negotiation to address this need.

In the software engineering literature, mention of the need to handle conflict is rare. This is surprising given the importance attached to it in the social sciences. For many years it has been recognised in management science and sociology that conflict is an inevitable feature of group interaction, often to be harnessed for its positive aspects, rather than suppressed (Robbins, 1974; Deutsch, 1973; Strauss, 1978). Some recent software engineering research has identified conflict as an issue (Curtis, *et al.*, 1988; Anderson and Fickas, 1989; Feather, 1989; Robinson, 1990), although as yet little progress has been made towards understanding how conflict might be handled.

An apt example of organisational conflict is given by Robbins (1974): a newly elected city manager has promised an immediate improvement in rubbish collection. After several months the citizens complained that there was no improvement. On investigation it turned out that the citizens regarded 'improved service' to mean

Requirements Engineering
ISBN 0–1238–5335–4

more frequent collection, whereas the city manager had meant earlier, quieter and more economical collection. It is not difficult to see how similar conflicts might arise during the introduction of a new software system.

The term 'conflict' can be taken to mean any interference in one party's activities, needs or goals, caused by the activities of another party. Conflict can be characterised as disagreement among the originators of the requirements (or *problem owners*) and this disagreement may lead to inconsistencies in the specification. However, disagreements do not always lead to inconsistency, and inconsistencies do not always indicate the presence of conflict.

Typical requirements analysis methods are geared towards the development of a consistent specification. They do not allow conflicts to be expressed, let alone constructively resolved. Indeed, we could characterise existing methods as conflict avoidance, in that they prescribe particular approaches, which assist software practitioners to break problems down and resolve design decisions in particular ways. Uncertainty is reduced by the provision of the collective wisdom embodied in the methodology (Lehman, 1990).

While this approach helps reduce conflict within the requirements specification, it does not help with conflicting requirements. The demand for a single consistent specification means that requirements conflicts are suppressed when the specification is written. Formal methods do not necessarily help, even though formal languages are intended to prevent ambiguity and inconsistency (Finkelstein *et al.*, 1990). The ability to reason formally with specifications is a huge step towards detecting the presence of conflict, but carries the implication that inconsistencies are errors which must be eliminated. Methods developed to support formal specification reflect this philosophy, and miss the chance to explore conflict.

If much of software engineering is geared towards conflict avoidance, this in itself may not be a problem, for two reasons: first, requirements conflict may not be as common as has been suggested. Second, avoidance may be a valid way of tackling conflict, especially where it prevents energy being wasted on fruitless confrontation. We argue in this chapter that requirements conflicts are extensive in socio-technical systems, and that avoidance is not a satisfactory approach to handling these conflicts. Furthermore, handling conflict in more direct ways actually improves understanding of the requirements and assists with requirements validation.

1.1   Sources of conflict

Conflict is a part of the nature of an organisation (Robbins, 1989). In particular, it is both a source of and a response to organisational change. Software design necessarily involves organisational change, and even end-user involvement in the design process does not remove conflict (Wastell, 1993). Two obvious sources of conflict in requirements engineering are conflict between the participants' perceptions of the problem, and conflict between the many goals of a design. Other sources of conflict include conflicts between suggested solution components; conflicts between stated constraints; conflicts between perceived needs; conflicts in resource usage; and discrepancies between evaluations of priority.

Curtis *et al.* (1988) reveal the effect of conflict in software engineering. They identified three major problem areas: the thin spread of application domain knowledge; fluctuating and conflicting requirements; and breakdowns in communication and coordination. Each of these areas is a source of conflict, and each depends crucially on communication between participants as a basis for any solution. A good conflict resolution approach necessarily emphasises communication between parties.

Conflicting and fluctuating requirements have many causes, from change in the organisational setting and business milieu, to the fact that the software will be used by different people with different goals and different needs. Handling constant change in requirements (*requirements maintenance*) requires an evolutionary approach that must be based on accurate capture of rationales and process information.

In many cases, there will be disagreement over the nature of the application (Dobson, 1993). This could be dealt with by restricting the scope of the new system so that only a single goal (or view of the application) is addressed. For large scale, open systems this is not practical (Blum, 1991). Hence, requirements analysis must recognise and deal with the existence of multiple, conflicting perspectives. Furthermore, the occurrence of conflicting perspectives may not always be distinguishable from instances where people are describing essentially the same concepts, but using different terms. Even formal representation schemes allow enough variation in style so that there may be many different ways of saying the same thing.

1.2   Conflict resolution

If there is no means of expressing conflict within the method, where conflicts do occur, they are likely to get suppressed. If they remain suppressed, it will lead to dissatisfaction with the requirements process. The requirements may be based on a single perspective, at the cost of any alternative perspectives. If the conflicts are eventually resolved, the resolution must be carried out outside the framework of the method, probably at an inappropriate time, using an undesirable means. Resolution thus achieved is untraceable, making decisions irreproducible, and rationale information invalid.

Suppression of conflict will have a serious effect on the remainder of the software development process. Suppressed conflict may lead to the breakdown of the requirements process, or the withdrawal of participants. Failure to recognise conflict between the perspectives of the participants will cause confusion throughout the lifecycle. Participants' understanding of the specification will differ, leading to further misunderstandings during design and implementation.

These problems make a study of conflict resolution desirable. In the next section, we survey research on conflict in relevant disciplines. We will then synthesise a model of computer-supported negotiation, which can be used as a basis for the requirements process.

2 SURVEY OF RELEVANT FIELDS

2.1 Terminology

We will talk about conflict between *parties*, meaning individuals, groups, organisations, or even different roles played by one person. Similarly, we will refer to *participants* of the resolution process, to cover a similar diversity. Not all parties to a conflict need necessarily be participants in its resolution. A *resolution method* may be used to settle a conflict, although some conflicts will not need to be explicitly resolved. We distinguish three broad types of resolution method: *co-operative* (or *collaborative*) methods, which include negotiation and education; *competitive* methods, which include combat, coercion and competition; and *third party* methods, which include arbitration and appeals to authority.

Negotiation is characterised by participants exploring the range of possibilities, to find a settlement which satisfies all parties as much as possible. Such an approach has been variously termed *integrative* or *constructive* negotiation (to distinguish it from *distributive*, or *competitive* negotiation). This definition of negotiation is not universal. Authors such as De Bono (1985) restrict negotiation to its distributive variety, implying a process of bidding and concession-making, and so attack it as being inferior to an integrative approach. We prefer to give negotiation its broader definition, and call the concession-making process *bargaining*.

There are other collaborative methods than negotiation. Some conflicts might be resolved by education, where the participants gain a better understanding of the problem, or simply learn about each other's viewpoint. This may include reformulation of the problem, so that it disappears, or becomes unimportant.

Competition concentrates on achieving maximum satisfaction for a participant, without regard for the degree of satisfaction of other parties. However, a competitive approach is not necessarily hostile.

Third party resolution covers any situation where participants appeal to an outside authority. There are two types of third party resolution: those in which the cases presented by each participant are taken into account, which we term *judicial*; and those where a decision is determined arbitrarily (e.g. tossing a coin), or by factors other than the cases presented (e.g. by the relative status of the participants), which we term *extra-judicial*.

2.2 Mathematical and economic models

Decision theory is a prescriptive approach to the analysis of pre-specified alternatives. The interesting problems are concerned with resolving multiple conflicting objectives (Keeney and Raiffa, 1976). Decision theory assumes a single entity is making a choice, in contrast to conflict where there is more than one entity, each with a different perspective. Decision theory has a role in conflict resolution in helping participants to evaluate bids, to justify such evaluations, and to persuade the other participant(s) that a solution is satisfactory.

Bargaining theory is an attempt to produce descriptive models of bargaining processes, and is especially concerned with commerce and politics. Patchen (1970) notes that the more complete models include wider concerns than bids and outcomes, including how participants influence each other's behaviour, and factors such as the cost of various actions and the cost of delaying agreement. Bargaining theory frequently makes use of the *joint outcome space* (Thomas, 1976) as a tool for illustrating how a party perceives the options (Figure 1). Note that there may be unperceived possibilities that provide better resolutions. Bargaining theory does not indicate how these might be found.

Game theory is the theory of rational decision in conflict situations (Rapoport, 1974). Participants are regarded as players, and game theory examines the strategies used by the players in the process of trying to achieve particular outcomes. Game theory makes use of the payoff matrix (Figure 2), reflecting the assumption that the set of outcomes is known (though not necessarily finite), and that associated with each outcome is a calculable payoff for each player. Limitations of game theory include the assumption that the payoffs for any action are known with cer-

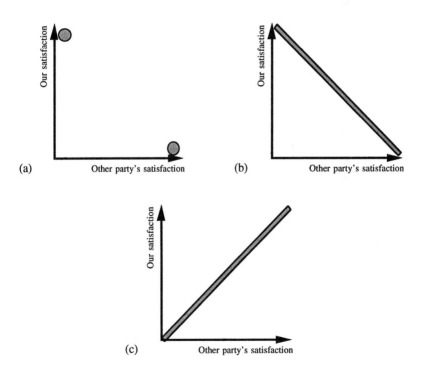

Figure 1 The Joint Outcome Space, illustrating how the options are perceived in (a) a win/lose conflict, (b) a zero-sum conflict, and (c) a common problem. In (a) only two outcomes are perceived, one party wins and the other loses. In (b) there are a range of possible outcomes, but any gain by one party is wholly at the expense of the other. In (c), any gain by one party is also a gain by the other.

Prisoner B

	Not Confess	Confess
Not Confess	1 year each	10 years for A and 3 months for B
Confess	3 months for A and 10 years for B	8 years each

Prisoner A (Not Confess / Confess rows)

Figure 2   The payoff matrix for the prisoner's dilemma. Each player must decide, in isolation from the other, whether to confess to a crime that the judge is sure they both committed. By confessing each will implicate the other, and their joint best strategy is for both to keep quiet.

tainty by all players. However, game theory does produce some useful information about the kinds of strategy that can be used to induce cooperation, and the relative success of various strategies (Axelrod, 1984).

Group decision making is the normative study of how individual preferences can be combined into a group decision. Luce and Raiffa (1957) define the problem as that of finding a method, or *welfare function* for combining individual preference rankings into a social preference, which satisfies properties such as fairness and representativeness. Work on group decision making extends decision theory to cope with more than one decision maker, but still suffers from the assumption that all the options are known.

2.3   Behavioural models

Conflict theory studies conflicting pressures in society, recognising that there are many different groups with different goals, and that conflict is a frequent occurrence. Deutsch (1973) gives a list of issues involved in conflicts:

- control over resources;
- preferences and nuisances, where the tastes or activities of one party impinge upon another;
- values ('what should be'), where there is a claim that a value or set of values should dominate;
- beliefs ('what is'), when there is a dispute over facts, information, reality, etc.;
- the nature of the relationship between the two parties.

Robbins (1989) adds that communication problems are a major cause of what he terms *pseudo-conflicts*.

A major concern of *organisational psychology* is how communication and coordination of teams can be effected. Early work tended to assume that all conflict was undesirable, and so should be eliminated, although empirical studies have demonstrated that conflict is endemic (Easterbrook *et al.*, 1993). Moreover, Robbins

(1974) advocates that conflict management includes not just resolution of conflict, but stimulation of conflict too. This is a result of observations that conflict has a useful role as a stimulus to innovation, by questioning and evaluating received wisdom. It is also a major weapon against stagnation and resistance to change.

A number of models have been proposed for conducting face-to-face negotiation in a commercial setting. Scott (1988) uses a four stage model to pace the negotiation: Exploration; Bidding; Bargaining; and Settling. The exploration stage allows participants to explore a range of possibilities before any confrontation takes place. Stefik *et al.* (1987) suggest that removing the personal attachment to positions prevents polarisation. If participants can dispense with the feeling of ownership of ideas, they can reduce the associated emotions when ideas are discarded or adopted. Similarly, Fisher and Ury (1981) recommend that rather than bargaining over positions, participants should focus on interests, and investigate options for mutual gain. This allows the participants to explain to each other their interests, and discover shared goals which were previously obscured from both.

2.4   Conflict in computing science

Various fields of computer science have addressed the problems of conflict. The ubiquity of conflict in the real world means that attempts to model the world, most notably in artificial intelligence, have to deal with it.

Knowledge-based systems rely on consistent knowledge for their inference mechanisms to work. In most cases, this is achieved by only consulting a single expert. Inconsistencies are attributed to mistakes, and are eliminated through debugging and refinement. This insistence that expertise must be consistent and rational means that knowledge acquisition becomes not so much the modelling of an expert's behaviour, but the synthesis of a rational domain model (Shaw and Woodward, 1989). This need not resemble any mental model used by the expert, and conflicts can be filtered out. Although this rationalisation process can be undertaken with a group, problems of conflict cannot be avoided so conveniently. A single expert will feel pressure to appear consistent and rational; for multiple experts, no such pressure can be applied.

Distributed Artificial Intelligence (DAI) divides up problem-solving activities among agents with specialist knowledge (Huhns, 1987). This handles conflicting knowledge by allowing different agents to develop and maintain alternative hypotheses. Most DAI systems assume agents share the same goal. Rosenschein (1985) notes that in real world situations, perfect cooperation never happens, as the goals of any two agents never coincide exactly. He uses payoff matrices from game theory to compare goals, and discusses various situations in which conflict of goals can occur, and how they can be resolved. However, DAI has not progressed much beyond work on models of belief and game theoretical studies of interaction.

Computer-Supported Co-operative Work (CSCW) provides a number of tools intended to improve group collaboration and hence manage conflict. *Argnoter*

(Stefik *et al.*, 1987) is intended for use in evolving designs. It attempts to overcome three major causes of dispute: personal attachment to positions; unstated assumptions; and unstated criteria. Proposals are presented using webs of interconnected windows. Reasons for and against are linked to each proposal. Finally, the assumptions made by the arguments and criteria for decision making are elicited. The assumptions can be grouped together into *belief sets*, to characterise points of view, and to explore the consequences of those views. Stefik compares the tool to a spreadsheet, in that it does not understand the proposals and arguments that it manipulates, but can compute logical relationships between them.

Hypertext offers the ability to support the collaborative elicitation and organisation of ideas over longer durations. As Schuler (1988) points out, hypertext provides an excellent vehicle for supporting (but not supplanting) negotiation. Differing opinions and viewpoints can be represented and linked in the same system, encouraging plurality rather than stifling it. For example, SYNVIEW uses a model of reasoning and debate to organise many viewpoints, with any group decision-making or voting based on access to a common body of material (Lowe, 1986). Similarly, IBIS explicitly represents and links together positions, issues and arguments (Conklin, 1989).

2.5   Conflict in requirements engineering

A number of studies have concluded that conflict has an important role to play in requirements engineering. For example, Curtis *et al.* (1988) identify *exceptional designers* who have a deep understanding of both the application domain and the design process which enables them "to integrate different, sometimes competing perspectives on the development process." Several recent models of the requirements process attempt to model such perspectives explicitly.

Nuseibeh and Finkelstein (1992) formalise the notion of a *ViewPoint* as having the following components:

- a style, which is the representation scheme used;
- a work plan, which describes development actions and strategy for the viewpoint, and any constraints on it;
- an area of concern, or domain;
- a specification, which is the set of statements in the viewpoint's style describing the area of concern;
- a work record, which describes how the specification developed, and its current status.

This model abstracts away from the people involved, allowing one person to have several viewpoints (as a person may have several areas of concern), and also for one viewpoint to represent several people (where people share an area of concern).

Feather (1989) uses a basic specification as a point of departure for development along separate lines of concern. At some later stage, these are merged to produce a single specification, which will then reflect all the concerns. This model delays the resolution of conflict between separate concerns until after the information gathering stage. While it is not yet entirely clear how best to merge the parallel elaborations, Feather has examined the different types of conflict that occur.

One approach to easing the integration of separate specification components is through tools which support negotiation. Robinson (1990) describes tools that allow a single arbitrator to evaluate the preferences expressed by various perspectives, and guide the search for new solutions which satisfy all perspectives. A single domain model is used, expressed as a hierarchy of goals in which perspectives associate different values with the goals. Integration involves searching for novel combinations of proposals, which increase the satisfaction of all perspectives' goals. This is done using a joint outcome space on which an ideal, but probably unachievable combination of perspectives is used to stimulate consideration of other combinations that come close to this ideal.

These approaches to requirements engineering all question conventional models that ignore conflict. Work is needed to clarify how conflicts based on differing requirements can be resolved. One major issue is the need to establish common ground between viewpoints. Participants need enough common ground to communicate; indeed, such common ground is needed before conflict can be expressed and recognised. In many of the above models, the common ground is assumed.

A second issue is how the resolution is devised. Anderson and Fickas (1989) suggest that in well charted domains, the experts will be aware of typical conflicts and how to deal with them. Hence, resolutions can be elicited from experts. However, standard solutions are not necessarily the best, nor will they always work in the environment introduced by computerisation. We would also add that the organisational environments of socio-technical systems are *not* well charted domains.

3   A MODEL FOR CONFLICT RESOLUTION

We now present a model for the management of conflict in requirements analysis. The model is based on the behavioural approaches used in organisational design, and addresses the need to separate the people from the problem, in order to avoid the polarising nature of arguing from entrenched positions. The twin goals of encouraging expression of conflict and providing productive resolution methods form the basis for this model.

A support tool, *Synoptic*, has been implemented to demonstrate the feasibility of the model. *Synoptic* displays viewpoints side-by-side, allowing the participants to compare and annotate them. Discrepancies noted by the participants are then used to prompt for underlying assumptions and issues. The support tools are designed to provoke discussion of the conflict situations as much as elicit a suitable resolution. Hence, the model is prescriptive, without being a rigid formal process.

3.1   Basis for the model

Research into group behaviour indicates that conflict can lead to higher quality solutions (Brown, 1988). In requirements analysis, exploration of the areas where participants' descriptions differ can lead to a much better understanding of the domain (Eden, 1989). This is a strong argument for conflict to be carefully managed, with participants encouraged to express divergent views. This will ensure that the requirements specification does not reflect just one point of view, and does not ignore concerns which interfere with the dominant concern.

In software design, effective collaboration is essential. Hence, encouragement of conflict must be matched with resolution methods which strive to satisfy all parties. An integrative approach should be adopted, to ensure that when divergent views arise they are incorporated into the process. The ultimate goal of requirements elicitation should be to identify and represent all concerns.

3.1.1   Specification context

We use the viewpoints model proposed by Nuseibeh and Finkelstein (1992) as a basis. Viewpoints allow the expression of conflict by providing alternative descriptions, while individually, each viewpoint remains consistent. Each viewpoint has an *originator* – the source associated with the viewpoint – and contains a self-consistent description of an area of knowledge. Easterbrook (1993) describes an architecture for eliciting viewpoints.

During elicitation, comparisons between viewpoints can shed new light on them. Such comparisons may involve conflict resolution, but are intended to be exploratory; they do not entail merging the viewpoints. Feedback from the comparisons can be used in the development of the viewpoints, for instance to modify terminology, or to elicit information that the originator neglected. The results of any exploratory integrations are treated as new viewpoints, representing coalitions (Figure 3). The process of parallel development of viewpoints – with exploratory integrations being initiated at any point – provides the context for our model of conflict resolution.

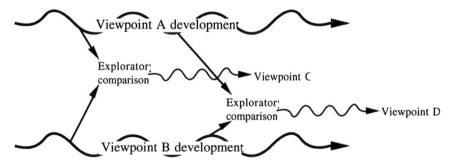

Figure 3   Our model of parallel viewpoints allows exploratory comparisons of viewpoints as they are elicited. These then may be discarded, or developed as new viewpoints.

3.1.2   Detection of conflict

The first problem for conflict resolution is to recognise that a conflict exists. This might be harder than it seems for a number of reasons. The terminology used by the participants is unlikely to match exactly (Shaw and Gaines, 1988), and the styles in which knowledge about an issue is expressed will differ. Also, participants will have different areas and different amounts of knowledge, making it difficult to make comparisons. These problems make it hard to tell where participants are agreeing, let alone where they are disagreeing.

Our definition of conflict was based on interference: two parties are in conflict if the activities of one adversely affect the interests of another. Hence, viewpoints are free to differ, and only conflict when that difference matters for some reason, leading to interference. There are a number of situations in which the differences matter:

- when viewpoints need to be compared;
- when there is a need to reason with knowledge from several viewpoints;
- when the originators insist their viewpoints are 'better' than others (and so perhaps should be adopted at the expense of them);
- when a coherent description is needed for further progress.

Under normal circumstances, differences between viewpoints are ignored, allowing them to develop independently. By only entering the conflict resolution process when differences between viewpoints matter, we avoid resolving conflicts unnecessarily.

Note that we deliberately ignore the distinction that Deutsch (1973) draws between real and apparent conflicts at this stage. Apparent conflicts would include: where one party has misunderstood another's position; where viewpoints use different terminology to describe the same thing; and where the interests do not interfere, and can be combined directly. All these are treated as conflicts, and part of the task of the negotiation process is to identify what type of conflict has occurred, and hence whether resolution is needed. The rationale for this approach is simple: it is impossible to tell without exploration whether a conflict is real or apparent.

3.1.3   Example

Take for example a library system. Two librarians offer different descriptions of the possible states of a book (Figure 4). One gives a description based roughly on a book's physical whereabouts, whereas the other gives a description based on how a book can be accessed. There is a conflict between their views of the library.

There appear to be a number of correspondences between the two descriptions. For example, the concepts ON SHELF and AVAILABLE are similar, except that the latter includes books waiting to be shelved: it assumes that unshelved books can still be lent. OUT and LENT are also similar, except that the former includes books being used within the library, while the latter only includes such books if they are

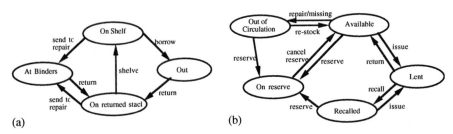

(a)   (b)

Figure 4   The possible states for a library book: (a) from the perspective of physical where-abouts; and (b): from the perspective of accessibility of a book.

from the reserve collection. To make things worse, both could have used the same terms.

3.2   Exploration phase

The aim of the exploration phase is to arrive at a better understanding of the conflict. Additional knowledge is elicited about the conflicting descriptions. This phase involves identifying why the conflict occurred, and hence the type of conflict, the extent of the conflict, and the issues involved. Such information is represented by annotating the descriptions and linking elements together. In particular, links showing correspondences and discrepancies are used.

The exploration phase begins once a conflict has been detected. It focuses on the conflicting parts of the viewpoint descriptions. For example, given the descriptions in Figure 4, imagine the analyst is trying to establish when a book is available for loan. The states ON SHELF in Figure 4(a), and AVAILABLE in Figure 4(b) correspond roughly, but there is conflict, as neither the names nor the transitions attached to these states match. In this case, we begin the exploration with these two diagrams and an indication that the conflict is between ON SHELF and AVAILABLE.

The result of the exploration phase is a map of the conflict. The original disparity between viewpoint descriptions is reduced to a list of items in the descriptions which correspond, and items which do not. Together, these comprise the *components* of the conflict. The exploration phase also elicits underlying issues.

3.2.1   Establishing correspondences

The first problem is to establish common ground between the descriptions to provide participants with a basis for communication. To determine the extent of the conflict, statements related to the conflicting ones are compared, as a *context* for the conflict. Initially, the context consists of those statements in the original viewpoints which are directly connected to those in question. In a graphical notation, these are the arcs and nodes connected to the items in question, and for a chain of inference, immediate antecedents and consequences are used.

The participants identify correspondences between items in the context.

Correspondences may be exact, where the items are identical, or approximate, where the items are similar, but differ in certain details. Many terminological differences will be discovered at this point. The tool support provided in *Synoptic* relies on the user to identify correspondences, although methodologies for recognising terminological mismatches, such as that of Shaw and Gaines (1988), and tools for detecting graph isomorphism could be added.

To illustrate this process, consider the library books example. The arcs attached to the bubbles ON SHELF and AVAILABLE, form the context. There is an approximate correspondence between SEND TO REPAIR and REPAIR/MISSING: the former appears to be included in the latter. This raises the issue of how books going missing are handled in the first diagram, and whether this needs to be represented. The actions BORROW and ISSUE appear to be identical, but note that the return action in one diagram is the inverse of issue, while in the other, it leads to a new state, ON RETURNED STACK. In this case, we can assume that the state AVAILABLE in the second diagram is the composition of ON RETURNED STACK and ON SHELF. Other correspondences can similarly be found, and items may be involved in more than one correspondence.

Figure 5 shows the different types of correspondence. For example, ISSUE and BORROW are equivalent (Figure 5(a)). In this case, one is the name of an action described by a librarian, and the other the same action described by a borrower. Both terms are useful, and could be recorded as synonyms. The comparison raises the issue of which term should be used where.

Figure 5(b) shows a correspondence between a single item in one description and a group in the other. In this case the representations are at different levels of abstraction. In such cases, the correspondences may not be exact, as decomposition will reveal details about a description not considered at a coarser grain. Again, such comparisons yield issues that one description does not address.

Figure 5(c) shows a correspondence between a group of items in one description and a different group of items in the other. In this case, different types of decomposition have taken place. In this example, both groups are decompositions of 'In the Library'. The two groups will not necessarily match exactly. For example, the RECALLED state seems to include recalled books both before and after they are returned, and so is not totally captured within the group ON SHELF/ON RETURNED STACK. Alternative decompositions reveal different concerns within the system modelling process.

Finally, an item or group of items in one description might have no correspondence in the other. It may have been omitted, or because the role played by such an item has been filled in other ways (Figure 5(d)).

The result of this stage is a list of correspondences between items in the viewpoints. Note that exact correspondences do not imply identical structure, but indicate where there is agreement, and so restrict the area of conflict. Where a correspondence is partial, there is still conflict to be resolved. In effect, the conflict has been broken down into its components: the initial rough description is replaced with a list of specific disparities between items in the descriptions.

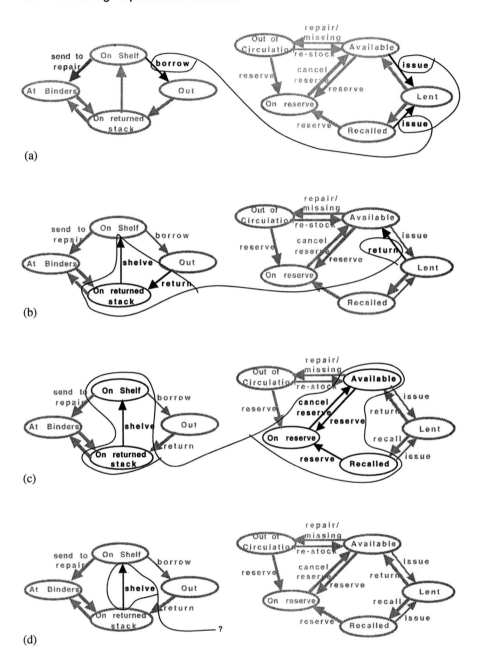

Figure 5 Correspondences between the descriptions of the library. (a) A correspondence between single items (although one of them recurs in the description); (b) a correspondence between a single item and a group; (c) a correspondence between two groups of items; and (d) an item for which there is no correspondence.

3.2.2   Identifying the conflict issues

For a conflict to be resolved constructively, the reasons the parties are in conflict must be ascertained. The apparent conflict might not reflect the underlying issues, as the descriptions being compared might not be based on the same initial assumptions and motivations. In fact, there will be many assumptions, goals and motivations involved in any description, some very trivial, and only a few will be relevant to the analyst. They are idiosyncratic in that what is obvious to one person may be an important decision to another (Kaplan, 1989). Discussion of *relevant* assumptions must be prompted in some way.

The systems gIBIS (Conklin, 1989) and Argnoter (Stefik *et al.*, 1987) use *issues*, which are simply points that the design needs to address. They may take the form of suggested requirements (e.g. 'The check-out process should ensure the borrower has not taken too many books'), or questions which need to be resolved (e.g. 'How many books is too many?'). However, in these systems, issues are elicited unprompted: in gIBIS as a prelude to identifying positions, and in Argnoter as supportive arguments for proposals. Our approach is to elicit issues only in response to specific conflicts. Conflict provokes discussion of the issues, as participants raise any issues they feel other parties' descriptions neglect. This avoids time wasted discussing issues on which there is already agreement, or which are irrelevant to the current context.

To assist with the elicitation of issues, four types of free-text annotation may be attached to the items in the descriptions, and to the correspondence links between items:

1. *Comments* – these are general purpose annotations, which can be attached to any item or group of items in the conflict. A typical use would be to attach to a correspondence between items to suggest a reason for the difference or similarity of items. Example: A comment might be attached to the state ON RETURNED STACK noting 'librarian B's description does not include a returned stack'.

2. *Assumptions* – these allow the user to note where a description appears to make some unstated assumption. They arise when comparisons reveal issues that have been neglected in either description. Example: An assumption may be attached to the comment above, to note that 'librarian B's model assumes that books waiting to be shelved can be located for loan'.

3. *Issues* – these are points that need to be addressed. There are many circumstances under which issues arise, but often comments and assumptions will result in an issue. Example: the assumption above might lead to the issue: 'How can books that have been returned but not shelved be traced?'.

4. *Justifications* – These are added to support a particular viewpoint or proposal. Often these will be added in response to assumptions and comments to provide a rationale for the original item. They will also be added in the next two phases of the process, to relate solution components to issues.

Several of the examples in the previous section showed how issues arise during the comparison of descriptions.

3.2.3   Agreeing resolution criteria

The final part of the exploration phase is the establishment of criteria by which to judge possible resolutions. These represent the participants' goals for the resolution process, and will allow potential resolutions to be judged and compared. Issues represent the key points in the conflict; criteria show how the participants feel about these key points.

In our model, every issue has a related criterion describing desirable outcomes for that issue. For example, the issue might pose a question, and the criteria attached specify what would constitute a satisfactory answer, with reference to the participants' concerns. Effectively, we treat issues as points that the original viewpoints left unclear, and the criteria as the clarification of these points. For some issues, participants will define opposing criteria. In this case, both are recorded, and the dispute added to the list of items in conflict.

Criteria can be used by participants to object to an issue. Issues are elicited in response to conflicts, and so will usually be agreed as being valid, if only because they are important enough to disagree over. However, occasionally a participant will object to an issue as irrelevant. In this case, they can attach a null criteria, effectively stating 'this issue can be ignored (in my opinion)'. A null criteria will have either an assumption or a justification attached, explaining why. For example, a participant may object to the issue 'There must be a way of locating unshelved books' because books can be assumed to be unavailable until shelved.

3.3   Generative phase

The result of the exploration phase is a 'map' of the conflict, which can be used to guide the search for possible resolutions. The second phase generates these resolutions, and is essentially a design process. The aim is to propose solutions which overcome the limitations of the original viewpoints, and respond to the issues identified in the exploration phase. At this stage, the proposals are not evaluated. This prevents the creative process being stifled by pragmatic considerations (Stefik *et al.*, 1987). The proposals might be generated in a variety of ways, from directly combining elements of existing viewpoints to techniques such as lateral thinking and brainstorming.

The result of the generative phase is a list of proposals for resolution. These are not intended to be complete resolutions, but might be combined in various ways to arrive at one. It is also possible that some proposals will be incompatible with one another: the evaluation phase will examine how they can be combined.

3.3.1   Types of conflict

It is useful at this stage to characterise the type of each component of the conflict revealed by the exploration process. This will help to decide what form the generative phase will take, and what a possible resolution might consist of. We can identify three broad categories of conflict that might arise in requirements analysis, as follows:

1. Conflicting interpretations – descriptions of the current situation or the current requirements do not match, usually because different perspectives interpret things differently. This category corresponds to the category *Beliefs* (or 'how things are'), as described by Deutsch (1973).
2. Conflicting designs – suggestions (or partial designs) for how the system should be do not match. This corresponds roughly to Deutsch's category *Values*, or 'How things should be'. While a requirements specification would not normally be expected to contain design information, participants are likely to express some of their requirements as partial designs, representing their preconceptions of the system.
3. Conflicting terminologies – the terms in which things are described do not match. This covers the communication problems suggested by Robbins (1989) as being a major cause of conflict.

In addition to these three categories, a scale of severity is used. This ranges from *non-interference* to *mutual exclusion*. The former implies that items can be combined directly without compromising either, whilst the latter indicates that each totally negates the other, and only one can be used (Figure 6).

Using this schema, conflicts identified as non-interfering can be eliminated from further resolution work, as the direct combination of the two viewpoints provides an instant resolution. Where the two viewpoints provide alternative views or alternative terms, the circumstances under which each should be used still need to be examined. For the remaining conflict types, there is plenty of scope for the design of novel resolutions which circumvent the conflict, by satisfying the underlying issues in other ways.

Table 1 describes examples of each of the categories and levels of severity. The examples are from the list of specific correspondences and differences discovered in the exploration phase. Some are phrased in a way that suggests possible resolutions; consideration of where these conflicts should appear in the table helped identify potential solutions. Note that these proposals are not exhaustive, and may obscure other possibilities. For example, exploration of this particular conflict revealed that one viewpoint was concerned with the physical whereabouts of a book, while the other is describing accessibility: it may make sense to retain both viewpoints entirely, and record for each book both its physical whereabouts and its loan status.

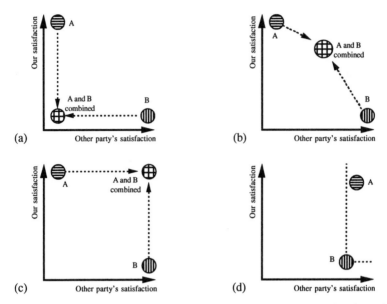

Figure 6   These diagrams show conflicts of different severity. In (a) the viewpoints are mutually exclusive, as their combination satisfies neither (the combination might not even be possible). In (b) the viewpoints can be combined, but with some loss of optimality for each party, and in (c) the viewpoints are non-interfering and can be directly combined. A variant of the non-interfering type is shown in (d), where one of the viewpoints already satisfies the other's concerns.

3.3.2   Generating resolution proposals

The model does not prescribe a method for generating resolutions. Consideration of the category and severity of the conflict components, as described in the previous section, provides an initial method. Beyond this, a range of design methods documented elsewhere (e.g. Finkelstein and Finkelstein, 1983) might be employed, depending on the components of the conflict, and the form of resolution required.

The categorisation of conflicts helps to determine what form a resolution should take. For example, conflicts in terminology, once detected, can be resolved by prompting for distinguishing terms. Each such suggestion is a possible resolution, to be evaluated in the same way as other resolutions. Proposals may include circumstances under which a particular term might be favoured. In many cases, negotiating terminological differences is a waste of time, and participants should agree to differ. It may be sufficient just for the participants to be aware of such conflicts.

Conflicting interpretations are slightly harder to resolve. Sometimes these will be based on incorrect information, which can be investigated. More often, they will arise from alternative ways of looking at things. Both interpretations might be useful, and proposals might attempt to combine them, or which suggest circumstances under which one or other might be used. Proposals might also recommend that one

Table 1   Different types and severity of conflict, and for each a description of the kind of situation covered, and an example from the library books conflict

	Conflicting interpretations	Conflicting designs	Conflicting terminology
Non-interfering	Either interpretation can be used without affecting the other (need to find out which to use when). *Example: The possibility of books going missing has been omitted from the first viewpoint, and could be added directly if necessary.*	The designs can be directly combined without compromising either. *Example: The recall facility, which is assumed to be a design suggestion, could be added directly to the first viewpoint.*	Different terms have been used for the same concept (need to find out which to use when). *Example: 'Borrow' and 'issue' apply to the same action. A borrower is more likely to use the former term, and a librarian the latter.*
Partially interfering	Interpretations are not wholly consistent: if both are to be used, some resolution is required. *Example: The 'shelve' action is not wholly consistent with the second viewpoint – 'available' does not quite correspond to 'on shelf'.*	Designs can be combined but interfere, and the direct combination may not be the ideal resolution. *Example: A reserve collection could be added to the first viewpoint by splitting the 'on shelf' state to indicate the type of shelf.*	The same labels have been used for similar concepts. The differences need to be resolved. *Example: 'Out of circulation' and 'At binders'. The latter is more specific, and implies that these books will eventually return.*
Mutually exclusive	Interpretations totally contradict one another, and cannot be used in conjunction. *Example: There is no 'return' action for recalled books in the second viewpoint, contradicting the notion of a returned book stack.*	Designs are completely incompatible, or tend to negate one another when combined.	The same labels have been used for different concepts, and some distinguishing terms are needed. *Example: The 'return' from 'at binders' is indistinguishable from the 'return' from 'lent'. These might be completely different actions.*

interpretation should be discarded, in which case the issues raised by the discarded description need to be satisfied in other ways.

Conflicting designs involve a higher level of uncertainty. Often the conflict will be the result of conflicts not tackled at earlier stages, and the issues arising out of conflicting designs will indicate the concerns that led to them. As the exploration stage has broken down the original conflict into its specific components, the designs can be examined more closely. Possible resolutions include combining the requirements underlying the designs, adapting one design to incorporate issues raised by another, or creating a new design which addresses the issues in new ways.

The result of this phase is a set of proposals for resolution. These will vary from the very specific (such as a particular change to a description), to entirely new viewpoints. Where a proposal is only applicable under certain conditions, these are described as part of the proposal. Note that the original viewpoints could be considered as possible resolutions: one or other could be accepted unaltered, if it turns out to be a satisfactory resolution. In addition, some proposals could be combined to produce a more complete resolution, while others might need to be dismantled. At this stage, the proposals have not been evaluated or compared in any way.

3.4   Evaluation phase

The final phase, evaluation, consists of taking the proposals for resolutions and relating them both to the map of the conflict generated in the exploration phase, and to each other. The aim is to find a proposal that best resolves the issues involved in the conflict. The approach is similar to that of the exploratory phase, and consists of linking items together and eliciting extra information to supplement the links.

The evaluation phase begins once a sufficient number of proposals has been generated. In fact, there is no distinct end to the generative phase. When participants feel that a good range of proposals has been generated, the evaluation phase can be initiated. The generative and evaluative phases are kept deliberately separate to prevent premature evaluation of the proposals from stifling generation of new suggestions. However, it is possible that the evaluation phase will also lead to new proposals, causing a cycling of these two phases.

3.4.1   Relating proposals to issues

The first task is to relate the suggested resolutions to the issues underlying the conflict. This may be done by taking a proposal, and selecting the issues that it satisfies, or by taking an issue, and deciding which proposals would satisfy it. Satisfaction of issues is measured using the criteria attached to them.

Links between proposals and issues vary in the extent to which the proposal satisfies the criteria. The relationship may be either positive or negative, depending on whether the proposal contributes to the satisfaction of the issue, or frustrates the issue. Unfortunately, the complex relationship between proposals and issues cannot be satisfactorily expressed using a simple numeric scale. Instead, a qualitative scale of five values is used: fully satisfies; partially satisfies; no effect; partially frustrates; and totally frustrates. The system attaches the value 'no effect' by default. The values will later be used to compare the proposals which contribute towards each issue. If the satisfaction or frustration is partial, an explanatory note is attached.

3.4.2   Relating proposals to one another

Individual proposals may interact in interesting ways. Some might be combined to produce a resolution which satisfies more issues than either individually: for example, the suggestion of adding a 'missing' state to the first viewpoint, and the suggestion of renaming the arrow from both this state and the 'at binders' state to 'restock' might be combined to give a more complete solution. For other proposals, combination will negate some of the benefits: for example the suggestion of adding a reserve collection to the first viewpoint is not compatible with the suggestion of maintaining two types of state information, whereabouts and loan status. The range of interactions between proposals is analogous to the possible interactions between conflicting items (see Figure 6), which were evaluated using a scale of severity.

Where two or more proposals can be combined, the combination is recorded as a new proposal. In creating the combination, the way in which the combination satisfies the issues may need to be reconsidered. In most cases the combination will satisfy all the issues that the individual proposals satisfied. However, this is not always the case, and in particular, it is not clear how proposals with differing strength links with an issue might be combined. This information needs to be elicited from the participants. Additionally, the combination might only be possible under certain circumstances, which need to be recorded as conditions for the new combined proposal.

3.4.3   Choosing a resolution

Once the proposals have been linked to the issues and to each other, the only remaining problem is to select the best proposal or combination of proposals as a final resolution. In many cases, an agreed resolution will have emerged during the process, making much of the evaluation phase redundant. In cases where there is no obvious resolution, the proposals need to be compared. If there is a proposal (or combination) which satisfies all the issues, then this is a likely candidate. If any participants are unhappy with such a resolution, their reasons need to be elicited: these are likely to indicate issues that were missed in the exploration phase.

To a certain extent, if there is still no clear resolution at this stage, this can be seen as a failure of the negotiation process. The aim of the entire process is to explore the conflict and educate participants about each other's viewpoint: if this is successful, a resolution should emerge from the process, or the conflict should disappear. In the last resort, the participants might either agree some decision making procedure, or agree to leave the conflict unresolved. This will depend on the perceived importance of the conflict.

The chosen resolution is represented as a new viewpoint which can be used instead of the original conflicting descriptions. The original descriptions are retained as a record of the resolution process. The conflict map is recorded as a rationale for the resolution viewpoint, so that it is available for later re-examination if necessary.

4 SUMMARY

This chapter has described a model for integrating conflicting domain descriptions. This forms part of a larger model of requirements engineering based on the representation of multiple viewpoints, as described in Easterbrook (1991). The model recognises that carefully managed conflict can improve the quality of the requirements specification, and encourages the expression of conflict by allowing participants to describe their viewpoints separately. Expression of conflict needs to be balanced with productive resolution methods, to ensure that conflicts do not become counter-productive. The model was designed with this aim in mind.

The model consists of three phases: exploration of the participants' viewpoints; generation of suggestions for resolving the conflict; and evaluation of these suggestions. During the exploration phase, the conflict is broken down into its components, represented as specific correspondences and differences between items in the viewpoint descriptions. These are annotated with comments describing any assumptions they make and issues they raise. These links and annotations act as a map of the conflict to guide the later stages. Resolution takes the form of designing novel ways of satisfying the issues. In the final phase, the ideas generated are then compared with one another and measured against the issues to determine the level of satisfaction. The proposal or combination of proposals which best satisfies the issues is chosen as a resolution.

The model combines the two most cooperative methods of conflict resolution: education and negotiation. Emphasis is placed on the exploratory phase in which participants learn about other viewpoints by comparing them to their own. Participants are encouraged to compare their viewpoint descriptions with others, and this comparison facilitates the elicitation of additional information, such as hidden assumptions. In fact, the resolution is not necessarily the most important product of the negotiation process – the extra information elicited during the process, and the participants new understanding of one another's viewpoints may be far more valuable.

The entire process is highly interactive, and acts to structure the elicitation of additional information concerning the conflict. Rather than imposing a strict methodology on the participants, the various activities can be freely interleaved, so as to support discussion and exploration. Where an agreement is not reached, the arguments and understanding that have been built up aid judicial arbitration.

The model does have limitations. One weakness is that there is no way of ensuring that all relevant viewpoints participate in the conflict resolution. When a difference between particular viewpoints becomes important enough to attempt to resolve, there may be other viewpoints which contain extra information relevant for the resolution. It is not clear how these relevant viewpoints can be detected, especially in the presence of the mismatches in terminology and style discussed in Section 1.1. If other viewpoints conflict with the generated resolution, then the resolution process may have to be repeated.

It is tempting to assume that the model provides a general framework for conflict resolution. However, the model was designed specifically for comparing and merging previously elicited viewpoint descriptions. The analyst would carry out most of the work, usually over a period of time, involving the viewpoint originators when necessary. The model is not intended to provide a form of meeting support, such as that provided in CoLab (Stefik *et al.*, 1987), nor is it intended to be a problem exploration tool, such as gIBIS (Conklin, 1989), although it shares some features of these systems. It is possible, however, that the model could be adapted for use in these situations.

The support system, *Synoptic*, is a prototype, built to demonstrate the working of the model. The support it provides is often minimal. Its main deficiency is that it requires the user to do much of the work. By incorporating more knowledge about the conflict resolution process, the system would provide much more guidance. For example, by comparing the issues which resolution proposals satisfy, the system might generate the most likely combinations of proposals, and use them to prompt the user for more information. Such a technique was used successfully in the knowledge acquisition system KSS0 (Shaw and Gaines, 1987). Another, major shortcoming of *Synoptic* is that it only allows two viewpoints to be compared at once.

We have described a solution to the problem of comparing viewpoints and resolving conflicts between them. We have demonstrated how an example conflict might be resolved using the model. Additional advantages include the ability to mix representations, and elicitation of additional information. The former is important as it is notoriously difficult to compare knowledge represented in different ways. *Synoptic* provides a means to explore correspondences between different representations. In using the comparison of existing descriptions as a basis for exploration, the system is able to elicit underlying assumptions which might otherwise have remained hidden. Furthermore, the comparison process draws out the issues that the descriptions address.

ACKNOWLEDGEMENTS

This work was carried out at Imperial College, London, funded by the SERC, studentship number 87311891. I am indebted to Anthony Finkelstein, Bill Robinson and Brian Gaines for discussion of the ideas presented.

REFERENCES

Anderson, J. S. and Fickas, S. (1989). A proposed perspective shift: Viewing specification design as a planning problem, *Proceedings Fifth IEEE International Workshop on Software Specification and Design*, Pittsburg, PN.

Axelrod, R. (1984). *The Evolution of Co-operation*, Basic Books.

Blum, B. I. (1991). Integration issues elucidated in large-scale information system development. *Journal of Systems Integration*, **1**, 35–53.

Brown, R. (1988). *Group Processes: Dynamics within and between Groups*, Basil Blackwell.

Conklin, J. (1989). Design rationale and maintainability, *Proceedings of the Twenty-Second Annual IEEE International Conference on System Sciences*, **2**, Hawaii.

Curtis, B., Krasner, H. and Iscoe, N. (1988). A field study of the software design process for large systems, *Communications of the ACM*, **31** (11).

De Bono, E. (1985). *Conflicts: A Better Way to Resolve Them*, Penguin Books.

Deutsch, M. (1973). *The Resolution of Conflict*, Yale University Press.

Dobson, J. (1993). The structure of the requirements engineering process and its implications for requirements analysis. *Proceedings of the DRA Colloquium on Analysis of Requirements for Software Intensive Systems*, Malvern, UK.

Easterbrook, S. M. (1989). Distributed knowledge acquisition as a model for requirements elicitation, *Proceedings Third European Workshop on Knowledge Acquisition for Knowledge Based Systems (EKAW-89)*, Paris.

Easterbrook, S. M. (1991). *Elicitation of Requirements from Multiple Perspectives*, PhD Thesis, Imperial College, University of London.

Easterbrook, S. M. (1993). Domain modelling with hierarchies of alternative viewpoints. *Proceedings First IEEE International Symposium on Requirements Engineering*, San Diego, CA.

Easterbrook, S.M., Beck, E.E., Goodlet, J.S., Plowman, L., Sharples, M. and Wood, C.C. (1993). A survey of empirical studies of conflict. In S. M. Easterbrook (Ed.), *CSCW: Co-operation or Conflict?* Springer-Verlag.

Eden, C. (1989). Using cognitive mapping for strategic options development and analysis (SODA). In J. Rosenhead (Ed.) *Rational Analysis for a Problematic World: Problem Structuring Methods for Complexity, Uncertainty and Conflict*. Wiley.

Feather, M. S. (1989). Constructing specifications by combining parallel elaborations, *IEEE Transactions on Software Engineering*, **15** (2), 198–208.

Finkelstein, A. C. W., Finkelstein, L. and Maibaum, T. S. E. (1990). Engineering-in-the-large: Software engineering and instrumentation, *Proceedings UK IT '90*, 1-8, Peter Peregrinus.

Finkelstein, L. and Finkelstein, A. C. W. (1983). Review of design methodology, *IEE Proceedings*, **130** (4).

Fisher, R. and Ury, W. (1981). *Getting to Yes: Negotiating Agreement Without Giving in*, Hutchinson.

Huhns, M. N. (Ed.) (1987). *Distributed Artificial Intelligence*, Morgan Kaufmann.

Kaplan, S. M. (1989). COED: Conversation-oriented software environments, *Draft Report*, University of Illinois at Urbana-Champaign.

Keeney, R. L. and Raiffa, H. (1976). *Decisions with Multiple Objectives: Preferences and Value Tradeoffs*, J. Wiley & Sons, NY.

Lehman, M. M. (1990). Uncertainty in computer application, technical correspondence, *Communications of the ACM*, **33** (5).

Lowe, D. G. (1986). SYNVIEW: The design of a system for co-operative structuring of information, *Proceedings, Conference on Computer-Supported Co-operative Work*, Austin, TX, 376–385.

Luce, D. L. and Raiffa, H. (1957). *Games and Decisions: Introduction and Critical Survey*, J. Wiley & Sons, NY.

Nuseibeh, B. and Finkelstein, A. C. W. (1992). ViewPoints: A vehicle for method and tool integration. *Proceedings of the IEEE International Workshop on Computer-Aided Software Engineering (CASE-92)*, Montreal, Canada.

Patchen, M. (1970). Models of co-operation and conflict: A critical review, *Journal of Conflict Resolution*, **14** (3).

Rapoport, A. (Ed.) (1974). *Game Theory as a Theory of Conflict Resolution*, Reidel.

Robbins, S. P. (1974). *Managing Organizational Conflict: A Non-traditional Approach*, Prentice-Hall.

Robbins, S. P. (1989). *Organizational Behaviour: Concepts, Controversies, and Applications*, (4th edn.) Prentice-Hall.

Robinson, W. N. (1990). Negotiation behaviour during multiple agent specification: A need for automated conflict resolution, *Proceedings ICSE-90* (to appear).

Rosenschein, J. S. (1985). *Rational Interaction: Co-operation Among Intelligent Agents*, Phd Thesis, Report No STAN-CS-85-1081, Department of Computer Science, Stanford University.

Schuler, D. (1988). AI and hypertext in support of negotiation, in Bernstein, M. (Ed.), *Proceedings AAAI-88 Workshop on AI and Hypertext: Issues and Directions*.

Scott, B. (1988). *Negotiating: Constructive and Competitive Negotiations*, Paradigm Publishing.

Shaw, M. L. G. and Gaines, B. R. (1988). A methodology for recognising consensus, correspondence, conflict, and contrast in a knowledge acquisition system, *Proceedings Third Knowledge Acquisition For Knowledge-Based Systems Workshop*, Banff.

Shaw, M. L. G. and Woodward, J. B. (1989). Mental models in the knowledge acquisition process, *Proceedings Fourth Knowledge Acquisition For Knowledge-Based Systems Workshop*, Banff.

Stefik, M., Foster, G., Bobrow, D. G., Kahn, K., Lanning, S. and Suchman, L. (1987). Beyond the chalkboard: Computer support for collaboration and problem solving in meetings, *Communications of the ACM* **30** (1).

Strauss, A. (1978). *Negotiations: Varieties, Contexts, Processes and Social Order*, Jossey-Bass.

Thomas, K. (1976). Conflict and conflict management, in M. D. Dunnette (Ed.), *Handbook of Industrial and Organizational Psychology*, Rand McNally College Publishing Co.

Wastell, D. G. (1993). The social dynamics of systems development: Conflict, change and organisational politics. In S. M. Easterbrook (Ed.), *CSCW: Cooperation or Conflict?* Springer-Verlag.

Three

Cooperative requirements capture: Control room 2000

Linda Macaulay
Department of Computation, UMIST, Manchester, UK

1 INTRODUCTION

This chapter is concerned with the very earliest stage of project development when the need for a new project is first perceived. This stage is sometimes referred to as the *project initiation stage* or the *feasibility stage* (Downs *et al.*, 1992). It can be considered as lying between a strategic study and the full systems analysis of the project. At this point the problem situation needs to be described to a sufficient level of detail to enable the scope of the new project to be identified. This involves investigation into a number of potential alternatives, and evaluation of alternatives according to the costs and benefits of change.

At this early stage there are particular difficulties with requirements capture since the scope of the new project has yet to be resolved. In Chapter 8, Woolgar points out that difficulties with requirements capture should not be considered as merely 'technical' problems:

> 'technical' in the sense that denotes the enduring assumption that actual requirements preexist our efforts to 'capture' them.

At this stage, requirements do not preexist as such; however, what does exist is a perceived need for change, and what has to be developed is an envisionment of that change.

The envisionment of change embodies a vision of the future which includes the proposed new system. The purpose of this chapter is to discuss who should participate in developing this vision of the future, and to consider what techniques can be used such that all those who have a stake in the proposed new system actually share the same vision.

The chapter falls broadly into five sections. The first is a discussion of different approaches to participation in this early stage of requirements capture. These are: (i) users are consulted; (ii) users participate; (iii) stakeholders participate; and

Requirements Engineering
ISBN 0–1238–5335–4

(iv) stakeholders cooperate. The second section describes a particular method of achieving cooperation between stakeholders called *Cooperative Requirements Capture* (CRC). The third section presents a case study in which shared envisionment of the future is achieved by stakeholders across three different organisational boundaries. The fourth and fifth sections consider the advantages and disadvantages of CRC, and discuss the need for computer support.

2 APPROACHES

In this section, we are concerned with approaches to gathering information about the problem situation, and using that information to identify the scope of the proposed new system.

2.1 Users are consulted

First, the most traditional approach is to think of the systems analyst as responsible for 'eliciting' requirements from users. This is usually achieved through the use of interviewing, questionnaires or by observation, where the user plays a relatively passive role. In structured analysis approaches, such as SSADM (Downs, 1992), user views are elicited at appropriate points in the method. The Requirements Analysis Module of SSADM has two stages: the first is an *Investigation of the Current Environment*, which is concerned with finding out about the business area and developing a logical picture of present activities and future needs. The second stage, *Business System Options*, derives a set of alternative courses of action for the project manager to select from. The scope of the investigation undertaken as part of the requirements analysis is relatively broad, in that it tries to be concerned with the whole situation which the information system is supposed to support, not solely the system itself. However, despite the various attempts by HUSAT (University of Loughborough) to change the approach to user involvement within SSADM (see Downs, 1992, pp 306–318), the techniques recommended within the Requirements Analysis Module are still largely process and data oriented. The method still relies heavily on the expertise of the analyst to model present activities, to elicit requirements, and to develop a vision of the future to present to the project manager and other stakeholders.

Other approaches explicitly seek to identify the viewpoints which must be incorporated; for example, CORE (Mullery, 1987) requires the analyst to identify the 'customer authority' and the 'viewpoint authority'. Each 'viewpoint authority' is the person responsible for providing the analyst with the information needed for some particular 'view' of the problem domain. That 'view' could be that of the end-user or of the user manager or, as is often the case, the 'view' of plant, machines or controllers or some already existing computer system. The 'viewpoint' must be responsible for processing information; it must receive input from some other viewpoint and send output to a viewpoint. Thus, although a user viewpoint might be a valid viewpoint, there is a tendency for users' needs to be considered only in as much as they have needs as information processors.

In contrast to the data- and process-oriented approaches, the object-oriented approach is now increasing in popularity. In particular, in Object Oriented Analysis (Coad and Yourdon, 1990) it is suggested that this approach improves analyst and problem domain expert interaction, because object-oriented is a natural way of thinking. The five stage method recommended by Coad and Yourdon still prescribes a passive role for the user, with the traditional view of users as sources of information and reviewers of models developed.

The methods discussed above assume that the analyst is responsible for understanding the problem domain and that users are a source of information and not normally active participants in deciding the scope of the proposed new system. Further, these methods tend to support the view that although there has been much discussion about participatory design since 1971 (Cross, 1972), the still prevalent view of the design process is that active involvement of the user is not only not required but it is to be avoided (Reich *et al.*, 1992).

The techniques employed within the above methods ensure that users are consulted, but do not encourage users to actively participate in the decision making process.

2.2   Users participate

According to Avison and Wood-Harper (1991), in participative approaches all users are expected to contribute to and gain from any information system, and that participation should increase the likelihood of success. Participation can take many forms, for example, in ETHICS (Mumford, 1986) the users assist in analysing their problems at work, complete job satisfaction questionnaires and set future objectives for efficiency, effectiveness and job satisfaction. Eason (1987), on the other hand, defines three categories of users whose needs should be taken into account. Primary users, who are those likely to be frequent hands-on users of the proposed system, secondary users, who are occasional users or those who use the system through an intermediary, and tertiary users, who are those affected by the introduction of the system or who will influence its purchase, but who are unlikely to be hands-on users.

In an attempt to smooth the transition from requirements to design, the formation of a 'design team' is recommended. More specifically, Eason (1987) offers a number of options for the construction of the design team (who also have responsibility for requirements capture) where the roles of the 'technical experts' and the 'customers' are clearly identified. The technical experts contribute their skills to the creation of a system, whilst the customers are concerned with the world they will have to inhabit after the change caused by the new system. The customers also have a wide range of specific knowledge about the way in which the organisation functions and the tasks it undertakes. The technical experts will want the system to help them advance their own design skills. Eason recommends, therefore, that the structure of the design team recognises the fact that both specialists and customers have expertise to contribute and vested interests in the solutions adopted.

Two of the team structures suggested by Eason are: (a) Technical Centred Design Team, where customers commission and accept the system and are informed and consulted throughout the design process, and (b) Joint Customer-Specialist Design Team, where user representatives are involved in all stages of the design process.

In his discussion on the alternative design team structures, Eason suggests eight criteria that could be used to evaluate the effectiveness of each structure. The first two criteria are concerned with the presence of technical skills needed, and with the human and organisation specific knowledge needed if the proposed system is concerned with organisational change. Criteria three and four refer to the expert contributions that can be made by potential users, particularly the extent to which users have the opportunity to contribute specific task knowledge or to assess the organisational effects of the proposed system. Criteria five and six are concerned with the vested interests of the different stakeholders; for example, are stakeholders able to negotiate their interests and are users able to develop a feeling of ownership? The last two criteria deal with the practicality and acceptability of the design team structure as far as the commissioning organisation is concerned.

Eason's own evaluation of the alternative team structures suggests that each approach has strengths and weaknesses. The Technical Centred Design Team scores favourably on having the technical skills where needed, is a practical use of resources and acceptable to the commissioning organisation, but fails on every other criterion. The Joint Customer Specialist Design Team on the other hand passes on all criteria except five and six suggesting that stakeholders cannot negotiate interests and users do not develop a feeling of ownership.

The Technical Centred Design Team finds favour with the commissioning organisation, but largely ignores the need for participation of users and other stakeholders. The Joint Customer-Specialist Design Team is widely accepted, but is likely to result in some stakeholder needs being ignored.

User participation is widely recommended by those concerned with socio-technical design, and as can be seen from the above discussion, the ability of users to participate effectively is determined as much by the structure and remit of the design team as by the provision of suitable techniques for allowing their views to be incorporated.

2.3   The stakeholders participate

A stakeholder is defined here, using Mitroff's (1980) terms, as all those who have a stake in the change being considered, those who stand to gain from it, and those who stand to lose.

The stakeholders in any computer system fall into four distinct categories (Macaulay, 1993) :

(a)   Those who are responsible for its design and development; for example, the project manager, software designers, communications experts, technical authors.

(b)   Those with a financial interest, responsible for its sale or for its purchase; for example, the business analyst, the marketing manager, the buyer.

(c)   Those responsible for its introduction and maintenance within an organisation; for example, training and user support staff, installation and maintenance engineers and user managers.

(d)   Those who have an interest in its use; for example, user managers and all classes of users, that is, primary, secondary or tertiary.

Some of the stakeholders identified above, particularly in categories (a) and (c), have a direct responsibility for the design and development of the various system components, and hence have a major interest in being involved in the requirements capture process. Those in category (b) have a financial responsibility for the success of the computer system, and therefore may also need to be involved. The stakeholders in category (d) will be the recipients of the resulting computer system, they also have a major contribution to make in terms of specific task knowledge and the ability to assess the likely effects of the new system.

A third design team structure suggested by Eason (1987) is the User-Centred Design Team where the technical experts provide a technical service to the users, and all users and stakeholders contribute to the design. In this case, stakeholders are able to negotiate their interests and users are able to develop a feeling of ownership. This option scores favourably on most counts; however, it most noticeably fails on the last two criteria. It is not perceived as a practical use of resources, and is generally not acceptable to the commissioning organisation.

Despite Eason's observations concerning the acceptability of stakeholder participation in requirements and design, there is an increasing recognition of the need to develop a shared meaning of the system being specified and designed. For example, Konda et al. (1992) argue that increasing design effectiveness is essentially increasing the breadth and depth of a shared meaning between the designers participating in the process of a specific design situation.

Reich et al. (1992) extend this notion to include not only different experts in creating this shared meaning, but also a range of non-expert designers such as users, resellers and maintainers. They also argue that extracting needs from users is a dynamic ongoing activity, where the central purpose is to continually evolve the design on the basis of multilateral participation of all relevant actors.

The problem of multilateral participation of a range of non-expert designers is one of potentially incompatible perspectives and conflicting objectives. Thus it is argued here that while stakeholder participation is desirable, it will not necessarily lead to agreement or consensus as to the way forward.

2.4   The stakeholders cooperate

The case being made here is not only for stakeholders to participate in requirements capture, but that they cooperate with each other and are actively involved in making decisions as to the scope of the proposed new system. Similar arguments for cooperative design have been put forward by Pasch (1991), in a paper on 'Dialogical Software Design', in which he states that "Software development is not merely a mathematical or technological challenge, but a complex social process, in which the kind of communication and cooperative, creative interaction of the participants determine the quality of the collaboratively developed product." He proceeds to argue that design requires experience, intuition, imagination and common sense, and that the design process is guided by insights from all participants. If this is true in software design, then surely the case for cooperative requirements capture can be argued even more strongly?

Whilst it can be argued that requirements capture would be enriched by cooperation between stakeholders representative of the four categories described above, it is by no means clear that interaction between people with such a diversity of expertise and vested interests would result in anything but chaos. For example, Westley and Waters (1988) identify five *Generic Meeting Problem Syndromes* which could arise were such a requirements capture 'team' to meet to discuss requirements for a new system. These are the 'multi-headed beast', the 'feuding factions', the 'dominant species', the 'recycling meeting' and the 'sleeping meeting'. The 'multi-headed beast syndrome', for example, can arise when there is no agreement on the agenda, or when group members attempt to mix problem solving strategies because there is no listening taking place and no integration of ideas. Another syndrome identified is that of 'feuding factions' where arguments are repeated, subgroups form within the meeting, and there are hidden agendas being pursued. The 'dominant species' syndrome is often witnessed at design meetings where one member of the group attempts to dominate the rest; other members can become withdrawn, afraid or frustrated.

Therefore, for stakeholders to cooperate, it is argued that meetings need to be facilitated in some way so that they might agree on the agenda, agree on which problem solving strategies to adopt at given points in the discussion, and that all stakeholders are given the opportunity to participate.

In addition to facilitated meetings, the stakeholders need techniques which will encourage multiparty interaction and provide a focus for discussion and decision making. Examples of such techniques can be found in the QFD (Quality Function Deployment) method, where a large matrix called the *House of Quality* is drawn up by the requirements capture team to map the customer requirements onto the proposed product characteristics and features (Sullivan, 1986). The strength of the relationship between what the customer wants and what the supplier is intending to provide is entered in each cell of the matrix. Further analyses can be undertaken using the matrix as the focus such as prioritising requirements and competitor analysis. Reports on the usage of QFD claim that it encourages interaction and helps build consensus and shared team understanding (Burrows, 1991). Further examples of similar techniques which encourage multiparty interaction can be found in the HUFIT toolset (Galer and Taylor, 1989); for example, the *Functionality Matrix* receives user and task related input and outputs interface design data (Catterall, 1990).

3 COOPERATIVE REQUIREMENTS CAPTURE

Cooperative Requirements Capture (CRC) is an approach to early requirements capture which has two components: first an approach to facilitation of cooperation between the stakeholders; and second, a method of requirements capture which includes techniques that encourage multiparty interaction.

3.1 Achieving cooperation through facilitation

In its present form, the CRC approach relies on a human facilitator to achieve cooperation at face-to-face meetings. This is only one approach to facilitation of cooperation; in the Utopia project, for example, Bødker and Grønbaek (1991) and Grønbaek (1991) explore the use of 'cooperative prototyping' using mock-ups with materials which are familiar to the user, and more recently using commercially available prototyping environments such as Apple's HyperCard. Such an approach enables designers to make a number of changes 'on-line' in such a way that the participating users can follow what is happening. The emphasis of the Utopia project is, however, on cooperation at the design stage of a project, where the key idea is to move the focus from discussions of system descriptions to cooperative action, using mock-ups and prototypes to simulate prospective work situations (Kyng, 1991). In contrast, the emphasis in CRC is on cooperation at the earliest stage of a project, when the system descriptions are being developed and agreed upon by stakeholders.

The CRC approach involves the use of a human facilitator who is normally an 'external' person, that is, not a stakeholder in the sense discussed in Section 2.3. He or she must have knowledge of the method being followed, and be able to give guidance as to its application in a given situation.

According to Viller (1991), facilitating the meeting can be broken down into the following five sub-tasks: *manage the agenda, observe group process, diagnose problems, design solutions* and *make interventions* (see Figure 1).

Managing the agenda for a meeting will involve its initial *creation*, followed by its subsequent *update*, whenever necessary. Depending upon the circumstances, agenda creation may be a task private to the facilitator, or a cooperative exercise involving the whole group. For example, if the group is to be following a set sequence of tasks, as is the case when following USTM (Macaulay *et al.*, 1990), then the agenda will be pre-specified by the method, and the facilitator need only be

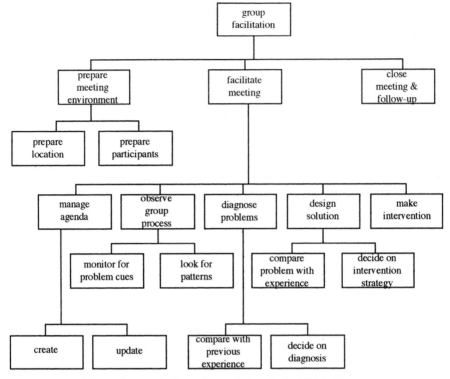

Figure 1   Facilitation tasks carried out by USTM facilitator.

concerned with the time to be allowed for the various tasks. Updating the agenda will always be a cooperative task, and may take place for a number of reasons. As already mentioned, the initial agenda may require amending at the very beginning of a meeting. At later stages of a meeting, however, the need for modifying the agenda may arise from the group attaining a greater understanding of their task, through items being made redundant by preceding items, and so on. Updates can take the form of adding new items, removing items, changing ordering, or changing the time allocated for an item.

The other four tasks mentioned above are all concerned with the facilitator monitoring the process of the group working together, and helping the other members balance their behaviour between task and socioemotional roles as they progress towards their goal. In a face-to-face meeting, the facilitator will observe the group process through both audio and visual channels, looking for cues that may indicate the existence of a problem. Having observed a set of problem cues, the facilitator must then make a diagnosis of what the problem is that has given rise to those cues. This will usually be achieved by referring to the facilitator's previous experiences in groups, as well as any training that they may have received. Having diagnosed the problem correctly, the facilitator must then design a solution (intervention).

Finally, armed with an appropriate solution, the facilitator intervenes to address, and hopefully put right, the problem initially identified.

At the end of a meeting, the facilitator will usually be responsible for ensuring that any relevant follow-up material is distributed to the group. If the meeting was a part of an ongoing series of meetings, then the facilitator should have made sure that the date, time, location, etc. for the following meeting have been agreed upon, and that any work in-between the meetings has been allocated to the relevant group members.

3.2   Achieving cooperation through a user centred method

In Cooperative Requirements Capture the user and the user environment provide the focus of attention for the stakeholders. They 'explore' the user environment together, they are encouraged to describe what users do now, and to envision how things might change in the future. They develop a shared understanding of the potential for change and a shared terminology for discussing the problem domain. Figure 2 gives an overview of the USTM method, which is the user-centred method used as a basis for cooperative requirements capture.

3.2.1   Formulate team

This will normally involve the project manager or project initiator and the facilitator in the identification of stakeholders, and hence of the requirements capture team. Ideally, between six and nine stakeholder representatives will participate in the CRC process.

3.2.2   Explore the user environment

Exploring the users' environment means that the requirements capture team must collectively investigate the organisational setting the target users are in, and identify and describe what the target users do. The term 'explore' is used because the team is encouraged to 'find out' afresh, to share knowledge about users, and to set aside preconceptions about what users need. They also assess the likely costs and benefits of change, and in the course of the workshop produce an initial document recording the shared view of the users' environment. This 'User Document' is structured into six levels: the business case; the workgroups; the users; the tasks; the objects; and an initial list of requirements. This involves a two day face-to-face meeting of the requirements capture team and the use of proformas and checklists.

The business case consists of a statement, by one of the stakeholders, of the rationale for the initiation of the project. This should include an initial description of the proposed system, and an initial view on who the target users are and on the perceived benefits of the proposed change to the customers, users and suppliers. In addition, the business case should identify the time perspective within which the proposed change will occur, for example, two years, five years or ten years from

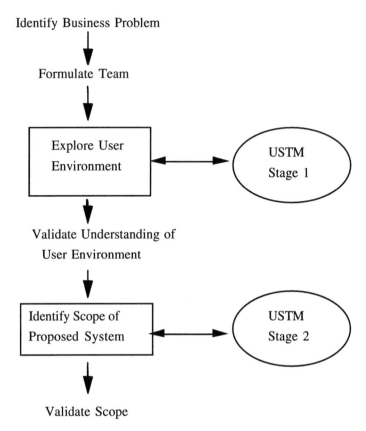

Figure 2   Overview of USTM, a method for cooperative requirements capture.

now. Thus in the remainder of the discussion, 'now' means at the time of the analysis and 'proposed' means 'n' years from now.

Each of the discussions concerning workgroups, users, tasks and objects includes a brainstorming session; an evaluation session; a prioritisation session; and an analysis of change session. For example, at the workgroup level the team: (i) identify the workgroups associated with the domain of interest through brainstorming a list onto the whiteboard, then evaluating that list until agreement is reached that it represents the collective view; (ii) classify the workgroups according to whether they are likely to be primary, secondary or tertiary users of the proposed system; then (iii) select one primary workgroup and describe the workgroup as it is 'now' in terms of social, organisational and job issues, and attempt to describe how it will change in the 'proposed' situation.

At the user level, a similar procedure as for workgroups is followed. A list of generic users is agreed upon; these are classified according to their relationship with the proposed system and selected users described according to three sets of issues. The first set is concerned with how the organisation views the generic user, both now and proposed. The second set concentrates on the personal attributes of the generic user now and proposed, and the third set deals with a typical 'day in the life of' the generic user, both now and proposed.

At the object level, the team is asked to brainstorm a list of objects which exist in the users' environment. These objects will normally be associated in some way with users and workgroups; they could be real world objects, knowledge about real world objects, procedures remembered by users, and so on. Once a list has been produced, it is then evaluated. This entails clarifying the meaning of object names, looking for similar objects with different names, or two different objects with similar names. In addition, it may be possible to aggregate some objects with others. Once an agreed list is produced, the objects are then classified according to whether they are likely to be of interest to the proposed system. Selected objects are then described in further detail in terms of their 'now' and 'proposed' characteristics.

A task is defined as an action carried out by a generic user on an object. A list of tasks is produced; a task hierarchy (i.e. a task and its subtasks) is produced, and the relationship between the tasks in the hierarchy and the proposed system is identified. Tasks are classified, and selected tasks are described using checklists of organisational issues, timing issues and human issues, both now and proposed.

The final level is concerned with consolidating the earlier analyses. In particular, combinations of user, object and task are examined to assess needs or requirements associated with the proposed system. The team is encouraged to make requirements statements of the form 'There is a need for . . .'; for example, 'There is a need for version control' as opposed to "The xyz system of version control will be implemented". The purpose of this is that the team should be trying to identify future needs rather than deciding on the solution. In addition, the consolidation session includes a review of each of the workgroups, users, objects and tasks in which the team is asked to make an honest assessment of the accuracy of their collective knowledge of the user environment. They are then encouraged to identify follow-up investigations that are needed to ensure the future stages of requirements capture and analysis are based on a sound understanding of the users. The User Document is initially a collection of the proformas completed at the workshop.

3.2.3   Validate understanding of user environment

This normally involves one or two members of the requirements capture team under the guidance of the facilitator. It involves validation of the information recorded in the User Document and expansion and updating where necessary. The techniques used for validation will depend on the specific problem; for a generic product further market research may be needed, for a bespoke product specific user interviews may be necessary. In any case, the extent of the information gathering task will depend on the extent of the knowledge and expertise of the stakeholders who took part in the workshop. A team who is highly conversant with their users may need to do very little validation.

3.2.4   Identify the scope of the proposed system

This also involves a two day face-to-face meeting of the requirements capture team and the use of proformas and checklists. At this stage, the scope of the system is discussed. The scope of the proposed system is determined at a number of levels: first, the stakeholders decide which work roles are to be affected, and then for each work role they decide what the role of the system should be in supporting that role. In particular, the role of the system is decided in terms of the extent of task sharing, and degree of control and monitoring of tasks. The likely acceptability of this proposed change is considered. In addition, for each work role identified an initial task model is produced. This helps to clarify and consolidate the understanding of the team with respect to specific roles. Second, the team is asked to consider which objects from the user environment that is, those contained in the User Document, are likely to be of interest to the system, that is, which objects will the system need to hold information about, which will it need to interact with, which will remain entirely in the user domain.

The scope of the proposed system is determined by the extent of support for the work roles, and by the list of objects the system will need to support. In addition, the scope of the system is reviewed from the point of view of each of the major stakeholders to identify whether their needs will be met. The list of requirements is also reviewed from the viewpoint of each stakeholder. Once the scope of the system is decided, and the list of requirements reviewed, the team is asked to identify and agree upon usability targets for the proposed system. The outcome from this stage is an *Initial Requirements Document* containing an agreed set of requirements for the first (or next) release of the system.

4   CASE STUDY: CONTROL ROOM 2000

To illustrate aspects of the CRC approach, the following case study is presented.

Identify Business Problem
One of the problems currently (1991) being addressed by the Electricity Research and Development Centre (ERDC) (a division of Electricity Association Technology Ltd.) is that of the increasing complexity of the control room wall-diagram. Several Regional Electricity Distribution Companies (DisCos) are currently examining the use of graphics to facilitate viewing images of the wall-diagram and associated data on a VDU screen. The concern of the ERDC is that the current approach is short-term, and too heavily conditioned by generations of experience with wall-diagrams.

The purpose of the 'Needs Analysis' project was to take a 'fresh look' at the information needs of the control room staff – in particular, to view the problem from a five to ten year perspective, and to use the knowledge and understanding gained by such an analysis to explore alternatives to the diagram that will be more suited to the next generation of computer-aided systems.

Formulate Team
Stakeholders of four types were identified, representing three different organisations:

1. Strategic thinkers who have a long-term financial interest in the success of the proposed system. Here staff from ERDC and from the DisCos were present.
2. Computer specialists who would ultimately be responsible for the design and development of the proposed system. Here staff from ERDC and the DisCos were present.
3. Control room engineers who would ultimately be users of the proposed system. Here staff from the DisCos were present.
4. Managers of the control rooms who would ultimately be responsible for the introduction of any proposed system. Here staff from the DisCos were present.

Explore the User Environment

The business case: One member of the team who has responsibility for the business case presents the initial justification for the proposed future system. In this case, the team was formed to establish the scope and nature of the proposed system, and hence only an initial tentative business case was presented.

After discussion it was agreed that the team should attempt to establish the basic requirements of the Control Room operation satisfied by the present (old) system, and to analyse what would be needed from a new (proposed) system. After debate, the consensus was to take a ten year perspective in view of the long implementation times for technology.

There was a need to avoid simply maintaining existing practice while not proposing unacceptable changes, recognising that the proposed system will cause changes to the human/organisational system.

The participants discussed the likely organisational benefits of cost savings, increased effectiveness, added value, improved network utilisation, etc., in qualitative terms. At this stage, it was agreed that a quantitative analysis was not feasible until an analysis of the technical specification of the proposed system had been undertaken.

Workgroups: An organisational structure chart showing the network control staff was not produced because of the wide variation between the two DisCos. However, the following workgroups were identified who interact with control room staff: Field/site staff; Control Room Engineers; Field Control Engineers; Technical Support Staff; Clerical Support Staff; Day Support/Outage Planning Staff; Planning

Staff; Third Parties; Management. A more detailed analysis of these workgroups was undertaken as described above. The team then decided to focus in upon the Control Room Engineers, and to describe this workgroup in some detail.

Users: The user level analysis was not considered to be relevant for this particular problem, because the team needed to consider Control Room Engineers as a workgroup and not as separate users.

Objects: The list of objects produced included: network model; network diagram; event log; outage program; plant records; forecasting tools; switching schedules; safety procedures; alarms; incidents.

Tasks: The team focussed upon the tasks of Control Room Engineers. One of the Control Engineers tasks which was analysed in detail was 'deal with incident'. The subtasks of 'deal with incident' were: identify incident; establish extent of incident; stabilise remaining network; formulate actions; coordinate response to actions; consider contingency action; report to management and press officer. The 'deal with incident' task was described using a checklist of organisational issues, timing issues and human issues, for the system both now and as proposed.

Consolidation: Some needs or requirements generated from specific object/task/ user combinations include:

- need for system to interrogate user
- needs to facilitate pattern recognition
- needs to initiate 'what if' analyses
- needs to display analysis results
- need for 24 hr/365 day access
- needs to support shift handover
- needs to store and correlate information for display at timed points or on demand
- need for display and analysis of incoming information
- needs to highlight weak links in the supply chain
- needs to 'police' the network.

At the consolidation stage, the need for further investigations was identified.

Validate Understanding of User Environment
Further investigations included interviews with Control Engineers from other DisCos not represented at the workshop to test whether they agreed with the requirements and with the 'future vision' for Control Rooms.

Identify Scope of Proposed System
The team felt that they had developed a sufficient 'vision' of what was needed at this stage. They used the outcome of the earlier stages as the basis for acquiring a budget to undertake a full scale investigation.

Shared Envisionment

It was clear from the results of this workshop that the information needs of the control room staff should not be centred around the discussion of the wall-diagram, but rather on the changing nature of the job of the Control Engineer.

This change is inextricably linked to the future changes within the electricity distribution industry itself, since in many ways the Control Engineer lies at the centre of the distribution network. This investigation has highlighted a number of potential and foreseeable changes which will affect the role of the Control Engineer, and which will, in turn, determine their information needs.

Although the two Regional Electricity Distribution Companies identified differences in their modes of operation and the allocation of duties to job titles, they were able to identify sufficient commonality in the tasks to be undertaken and in the operation of the Control Room to reach agreement on a number of fundamental issues.

The first major point of agreement was that significant changes will take place in the function and operation of the Control Room over the next five to ten years. A number of these changes could be predicted, and any new computer system development must be designed with these changes in view. In particular, recognition of the changing nature of the control room operations, the identification of changes in customer relationships, the recognition of the need to consolidate/reduce the number of control rooms, and identification of the need to provide a service to the Regulator *vis-à-vis* competitors.

The second major point of agreement was that the wall-diagram represented only one view of the network, and that the Control Engineer would typically need to view information from a number of different sources. Further, it was felt that there was a need for the Control Engineer to be able to view the diverse sources of information in a single, unified presentation.

These two points led to a recognition of the need for an Integrated Network Management System (see Figure 3), which provided support for the changing role of the Control Engineer, and which was capable of a unified, coordinated presentation of information from a variety of different sources. Some of the attributes of such a system were identified, and were summarised in the interim report under the headings: Presentation of Information, Security, Access, Timeliness and Provision of Support for the Control Engineer.

The results from the workshop provided an agreed baseline for the next phase of the investigation. The aim of the next phase was to identify the requirements of the proposed system to a sufficient level to enable an initial 'business case' to be developed.

5   DISCUSSION

CRC, and the earlier version USTM, have been used on a large number of projects over the last five years. Because the method is addressing the earliest stages of

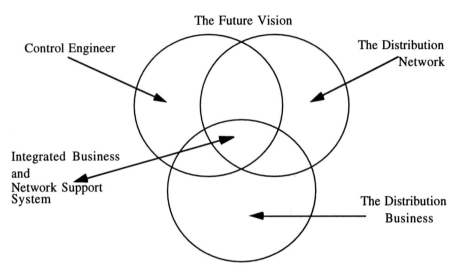

Figure 3   Shared vision of the future system.

requirements capture, it can be applied to virtually any project where the product being proposed has users of some type. Past projects include personnel systems, 'front-ends' to operating systems, decision aids for marketing managers, a student profiling system, a multi-media documentation support system, an inventory control system, application development tools, a theatre box office system, a travel agent system, and many others.

When the CRC approach is assessed against Eason's criteria, it is clear that the formulation of the requirements capture team is crucial to the success of the method; in particular, the first two criteria are concerned with the presence of technical skills needed and with the human and organisation specific knowledge needed. Criteria three and four, however, refer to the expert contributions that can be made by potential users, particularly the extent to which users have the opportunity to contribute specific task knowledge, or to assess the organisational effects of the proposed system.

The benefits of the approach are that it enables a number of stakeholders to come together and, for the period of the first workshop at least, to set aside their vested interests and develop a shared understanding of user needs with other stakeholders. Because of the techniques used and the discussion of change that occurs, the stakeholders are able to develop a shared envisionment of the future – a future which includes the proposed system, and embodies a projection of the changing needs of stakeholders, users and workgroups. Thus the approach scores favourably against Eason's fifth and sixth criteria, which are concerned with the vested interests of the different stakeholders, and with users being able to develop a feeling of ownership.

The CRC approach is intended to be used at the project initiation or feasibility stage of a project, and as such the amount of investment in investigating users *in situ* will be limited. This approach enables the stakeholders to share knowledge about users, to identify what they do not know, and to agree on what they need to know. Thus, any further investigation of users which is needed will be highly targetted and hence efficient in the use of resources.

The last two of Eason's criteria deal with the practicality and acceptability of the design team structure as far as the commissioning organisation is concerned. One of the drawbacks of the CRC approach is that it requires people to meet in a face-to-face setting; this is time consuming, and often difficult to arrange. Although it is important for the team to meet in order to develop a working relationship, the approach would be more cost effective if less time was spent in face-to-face meetings. A second drawback is that all the documentation produced, i.e. the User Document and the Initial Requirements Document, are paper-based. This tends to cause a lack of continuity between early requirements capture and later stages of analysis.

6   CONCLUSIONS

Cooperative Requirements Capture is an effective approach to early requirements capture. However, it would be greatly enhanced by the provision of computer support. The objectives of computer support would be (1) to reduce the amount of time spent in face-to-face meetings, (2) to enable the requirements capture team to work synchronously or asynchronously as appropriate for the particular stage of the method (e.g. brainstorming would be synchronous but prioritisation could be asynchronous), (3) to enable the requirements to evolve while systematically recording decisions taken and changes made, and (4) to provide support for facilitation of the interaction between members of the requirements capture team.

An initial prototype system has been developed at UMIST within the Cooperative Requirements Capture project (IED/1130), which seeks to achieve the above objectives, but with a limited subset of the method, namely the object level within the first stage. Thus the prototype supports brainstorming, evaluation, prioritisation and documentation of objects by a requirements capture team. Initial trials of the prototype by commercial requirements capture teams have been undertaken, and results are currently being analysed. The future for cooperative requirements capture lies in our ability to support flexible team working across organisational boundaries, and in enabling synchronous and asynchronous collaboration across time zones.

ACKNOWLEDGEMENTS

The author wishes to acknowledge the collaborators within the CRC (IED/1130) project. Cooperative Requirements Capture (CRC) is a collaborative project between UMIST, International Computers Ltd., Brameur Ltd. and Human Technology, with financial support from the Department of Trade and Industry and the Science and Engineering Research Council.

The author also wishes to acknowledge participants in the Control Room 2000 case study, particularly at the EA Technology and the Regional Electricity Distribution Companies.

REFERENCES

Avison, D. E. and Wood-Harper, A.T. (1991). Information systems development research: an exploration of ideas in practice, *The Computer Journal*, **34**(2), 98–112.

Bødker, S. and Grønbaek, K. (1991). Design in action: From prototyping by demonstration to cooperative prototyping, in J. Greenbaum and M. Kyng (Eds), *Design at Work: Cooperative Design of Computer Systems*, Lawrence Erlbaum Assoc.

Burrows, P. (1991). In search of the perfect product, in *Electronic Business Journal*, June.

Catterall, B. J. (1990). The HUFIT functionality matrix, in D. Diaper, D. Gilmore, G. Cockton and B. Shackel (Eds), *INTERACT'90*, Cambridge, IFIP, 377–381.

Coad, P. and Yourdon, E. (1990). Object-oriented analysis, in R. H. Thayer and M. Dorfman (Eds), *Systems and Software Requirements Engineering*, IEEE Press.

Cross, N. (Ed.) (1972). *Design Participation*, Academy Editions.

Downs, E., Clare, P. and Coe, I. (1992). *Structured Systems Analysis and Design Method: Application and Context*, Prentice-Hall.

Eason, K. (1987). *Information Technology and Organisational Change*, Taylor and Francis.

Galer, M. and Taylor, B. C. (1989) Internal report, ESPRIT Project, 385 HUSIT Human factors in Information Technology, HUSAT, Loughborough.

Grønbaek, K. (1991). *Prototyping and active user involvement in system development: Towards a cooperative prototyping approach*, PhD dissertation, Computer Science Department, Aarhus University, Denmark.

Kenny, A. (1988). A new paradigm for quality assurance, *Quality Progress*, **21**(6), 30–32.

Konda, S., Monarch, I., Sargent, P. and Subrahmanian, E. (1992). Shared memory in design: A unifying theme for research and practice, *Research in Engineering Design*, **4**(1) 23–42.

Kyng, M. (1991). Designing for cooperation: cooperating in design, *Communications of the ACM*, **34**(12), 65–73.

Macaulay, L. A., Fowler, C. J. H., Kirby, M. and Hutt A. T. F. (1990). USTM: a new approach to requirements specification, *Interacting With Computers*, **2**(1), 92–117.

Macaulay, L. A. (1993). Requirements as a cooperative activity, *Proceedings First IEEE Symposium on Requirements Engineering*, San Diego, CA.

Mitroff, I. I. (1980). Management myth information systems revisited: a strategic approach to asking nasty questions about system design, in Bjorn-Andersen, N. (Ed.), *The Human Side of Enterprise*, North-Holland.

Mullery, G. P. (1987). CORE – a method for controlled requirements expression, in R. H. Thayer and M. Dorfman (Eds), *System and Software Requirements Engineering*, IEEE Press, 304–313.

Mumford, E. (1986). *Designing Systems for Business Success, the ETHICS method,* Manchester Business School Publication.

Pasch, J. (1991). Dialogical software design, in H.-J. Bullinger (Ed.), *Human Aspects in Computing: Design and Use of Interactive Systems and Work with Terminals,* Elsevier, 556–560.

Reich, Y., Konda, S., Monarch, I. and Subrahmanian, E. (1992). Participation and design: An extended view, *Proceedings of the Participatory Design Conference PDC'92,* Boston, MA.

Sullivan, L. P. (1986). Quality function deployment, *Quality Progress,* **19**(6), 39–50.

Taylor, B. (1990). The HUFIT planning analysis and specification toolset, in D. Diaper, D. Gilmore, G. Cockton and B. Shackel (Eds), *INTERACT'90,* Cambridge, IFIP, 371–376.

Viller, S.A. (1991). The group facilitator: a CSCW perspective, in Bannon, L., Robinson, M. and Schmidt, K. (Eds), *ECSCW'91: The Second European Conference on Computer Support for Cooperative Work,* Amsterdam, Holland.

Westley, F. and Waters, J. A. (1988). Group facilitation skills for managers, *Management Education and Development,* **19**(2), 134–143.

Four

The ORDIT approach to organisational requirements

J. E. Dobson, A. J. C. Blyth, J. Chudge and R. Strens
Department of Computing Science, University of Newcastle, Newcastle upon Tyne, UK

1 INTRODUCTION

ORDIT, which is an Esprit II project, includes collaborators from industry and academia with expertise both in human factors and organisational issues and software design and engineering (Algotech srl, HUSAT Research Institute, the MARI Group Ltd., the Department of Computing Science of the University of Newcastle upon Tyne, and Work Research Centre). In this chapter, we describe the ORDIT (Organisational Requirements Definition for Information Technology) methodology for the design of socio-technical systems (Harker *et al.*, 1990), and discuss our experience in the four years of its development and application, which has used the case-study approach throughout.

1.1 Background to the ORDIT project

Conventional systems analysis has largely focussed on defining information processing requirements rather than looking at IT from a wider perspective, and so it is common for systems to be created which do not satisfy the needs of their human operators, although they are technically sound. Therefore, it is often the case that technical solutions to problems (the so-called 'hard' systems[1]) are created which do not adequately support the way in which the human components of the work system are organised. This problem is partly addressed by the soft systems approach (Checkland, 1981), but is taken a step further by the ORDIT project, which takes a socio-technical approach (Mumford, 1983) in which the system is viewed as a

---

[1] The standard terminology employed here is that a 'hard' system is one in which the definition of the system to be engineered or improved is taken to be unproblematic, whereas a 'soft' system is one in which this is not the case.

Requirements Engineering
ISBN 0–1238–5335–4

whole by placing it within the broad operational environment, with the user as an integral part of the system.

Organisational requirements are those which come out of a system being placed in a social context rather than those deriving from the functions to be performed or the tasks to be assisted. Examples of sources of such requirements are power structures, obligations and responsibilities, control and autonomy, values and ethics. The point about these sorts of requirements is that they are embedded in organisational structure and policies, and often in a way that cannot be directly observed or easily articulated[2]. Therefore (and this is a point to which we shall return), these policies are not so much captured or elicited as debated. In a sentence, then, ORDIT is an attempt to answer the question: what is the structure of this debating process?

Designers have generally ignored the importance of organisational issues in the design of IT products, and hence many of the difficulties encountered have been due not to limitations in technology, but to the disregard of organisational requirements. It is only fairly recently that organisational requirements, while acknowledged to be essential for successful implementation of socio-technical systems, have become an explicit focus of attention in systems design. The central tenet of the ORDIT philosophy is that design methods appropriate for technical systems cannot simply be applied to socio-technical ones, and that consideration must be given equally to both human and technical issues, with success being seen as the construction of a relevant socio-technical system that meets the 'real' requirements of the organisation.

Hence, the aim of the ORDIT project is to develop a methodology that will enable systems designers to reason about organisational goals, policies and structures, and the work roles of intended end users in a way which will facilitate the identification and expression of organisational requirements for information technology systems, and furthermore, one which will support these structures and roles. Our concern, therefore, is not solely with the creation of a framework in which such issues can be identified, but also with the development of a language with which to discuss human requirements of socio-technical systems, and to demonstrate how these are linked to the technical features of the system design.

We believe that our approach addresses the problems that arise when designing large and complex systems. The areas of complexity are both 'technical' and 'organisational'. Technical complexity is fairly well understood, the principal tool being that of abstraction, whereby the overall picture is constructed, with more detail being added as the design process proceeds. Organisational complexity, however, is another matter. The traditional notion of the software development lifecycle, with requirements capture being completed before the design stage, is no longer satisfactory. Requirements capture and design are now seen to be symbiotic. The initial set of requirements needed to start off the design process is gradually

---

[2] An interesting consequence is that the methods of the structural anthropologists seem more relevant to our work than the methods of the ethnological anthropologists (though it may be unfashionable to admit this).

refined into a systematic and coherent statement of requirements hand-in-hand with the refinement of the design.

1.2   Components of the ORDIT methodology

There are five main components of the ORDIT methodology:

1. *A Process Model*
    This is a model of the process of eliciting and modelling requirements. One of the main characteristics of the ORDIT process model is the way it has separated these two functions and shown the relation between them. Requirements are not considered as butterflies: they are not there to be captured and pinned down in a specification cabinet. Rather, the process of finding them is one involving at least three roles (requirements owner, requirements elicitor, requirements modeller), and a number of separate tasks involving some interesting feedback loops.

2. *An Enterprise Modelling Language*
    The ORDIT project has devised an enterprise modelling language to represent the structure of the organisation, in order to serve two related but distinct purposes: to determine the requirements owners and their positions and roles within the organisation; and to determine the user community (and others affected by the proposed IT system) and their roles and responsibilities within the organisation. The first purpose is to demonstrate completeness of the requirements elicitation process, and the second is required to demonstrate completeness of the requirements modelling process.

3. *An Information Modelling Language*
    The purpose of the information modelling language is not only to derive all the data models that are required, but also to determine all the so-called 'non-functional'[3] requirements (such as security and privacy) on the data, so that the data needs can be shown to be complete and fit for purpose in terms of the organisational responsibilities of the data owners and users.

4. *A Role Reference Model*
    The ORDIT concept of 'role' is perhaps the most sophisticated of all current role models, covering such things as functional and structural relationships, responsibilities, information access modes and rights, conversation structures and role evaluation criteria. The concept of the Role Reference Model has been developed by ORDIT to capture all these aspects of 'role' that are so important for a full definition of the organisational requirements placed on a system by the roles with which the system will interact. Although space does not allow us to describe the Role Reference Model in this chapter, we should mention that it differs from other models mainly in the number of related aspects that we have

---

[3]   Although we totally agree with McDermid, in Chapter 1 of this book, that this term, although in common use, is misleading and unhelpful.

identified (about one hundred) and in the way we have generalised it so that it can be used in examining all levels both of the power hierarchy (policy direction/management/execution) in an organisation and of granularity (for example, our coarsest model of a government department[4] describes it by reference to the interactions between just three roles: the funding, resourcing and operating agents).

5. *Supporting Tools*
   The ORDIT methodology is supported by a number of modelling tools which combine the power of hypertext-like structures with easy to use graphical interfaces and logical and analytic power. The development, prototyping and evaluation of these tools is a major feature of years 4 and 5 of the project.

In this chapter, we shall describe only the first two of these components. The third component has been described elsewhere with an example of its application (Dobson, 1992); the fourth and fifth components are still under active development.

2   ORGANISATIONAL REQUIREMENTS

2.1   Setting the context for organisational requirements

Within organisations, large tasks tend to be devolved to groups of people who work together in complex ways to achieve an overall objective. This has always been the case, and yet technical systems design often tends to assume a single user with a discrete task. The failure to recognise that users work in a collaborative or cooperative way, and to design systems to support this way of working, can account for the relatively low success rates of many complex technical systems[5]. One of the aims of the ORDIT methodology is therefore to enable design teams to address these organisational requirements, and thereby to produce IT systems that match not only the organisational and functional needs of the individual end user, but also those of groups of users and their associated usability and acceptability requirements.

The aims of a requirements methodology identified in order to achieve the aim of supporting different members of an organisational team are as follows:

- to identify the full range of relevant requirements in a specific organisational context;
- to derive appropriate functional specifications for any IT systems which take account of organisational as well as individual task requirements;

---

[4]   And one which was fully agreed by the department concerned as being the crucial one at this level of granularity.
[5]   We know that designers of Computer Supported Cooperative Work (CSCW) systems are aware of this problem, but there are many business applications other than CSCW.

- to compare the organisational requirements match of different design alternatives;
- to represent the range of organisational requirements to the problem owner and the systems designers in an iterative way;
- to identify organisational mechanisms or processes for fulfilling critical non-functional requirements.

The method used to determine requirements must allow the system designer to explore possible solutions (involving both the IT system and possible organisational change), and their consequences, at the same time as specifying the problem, thereby refining the understanding of the problem and developing the solution at the same time and by the same process. We have found it convenient to do this by representing the general requirements process within ORDIT as four broad interactive component subprocesses: scoping, modelling, requirements capture and solution options, as shown in Figure 1.

An important point to note is that there are no lines on the diagram. This absence signifies that the activities shown within the subprocesses and the subprocesses themselves are in no way sequential, and there is no set route through the diagram, the whole process being iterative with feedback to the client at every stage. For example, compared with other methods, modelling may be started at a very early stage to help in exploring the system boundaries and in identifying stakeholders. This process is in contrast to the traditional 'waterfall' approach to modelling, in which the output from one stage forms the input to the next stage, and so on, with all the stages following a predetermined order. The objective of the ORDIT model is to support the identification and transformation of organisational requirements into precise statements which can be operated upon by systems designers without being prescriptive as to the order in which the various operations involved in this process are carried out. We have found in practice, though, that the process described by Humphreys (1984) based on Checkland's Soft Systems Methodology works pretty well.

Another important point to note is that the subprocess called 'Solution Options' is not a requirements specification in the traditional sense. A 'solution' here is a solution to a socio-technical problem, and therefore identifies the feasible and desirable changes in the organisation which the IT system is intended to support or bring about. It thus acts as a base for a subsequent requirements specification process by providing the links between the designer's view of a requirement as a justification for a design decision, and the requirement owner's view of a requirement as a statement of a policy.

ORDIT is about navigation in this process space. In any requirements determination activity, all four places will be visited, often more than once, and from different directions and at different times in the overall process, and it is therefore important to have some kind of road map. For example, the use of modelling in determining the scope and boundaries of the system is quite different from the use of modelling in determining system requirements. It is therefore important to know for what purpose a model is being built.

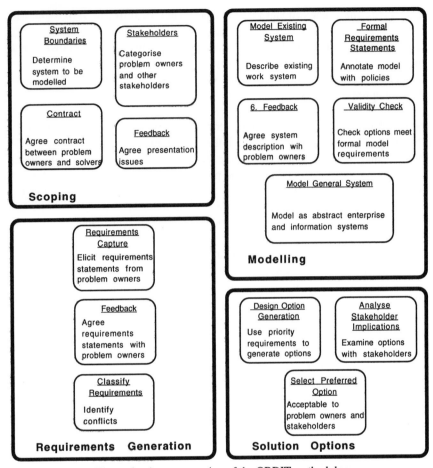

Figure 1   A representation of the ORDIT methodology.

Perhaps the most important requirement on the development of the methodology is that the navigation process be capable of being used in a number of ways, as dictated by the nature of the project in which it is being applied. This is an important aspect of the scoping process. There is a significant difference between a project which takes the form 'Here is the problem; what is the solution?' and one which takes the form 'We have the solution; what are its implications (and what problem does it solve)?' Different navigation strategies are required and different kinds of models will be needed. What is important about ORDIT is that it is a methodology for analysing organisational change, either to generate requirements on a system or as a consequence of a system being introduced.

To see ORDIT simply as a method for requirements determination, then, is to see it in only one of its aspects. Other aspects are in exploring implications, evaluating systems, analysing organisational policies and envisioning possible futures. ORDIT treats these as alternative ways of navigating through the same space, involving the same kinds of models and using the four subprocesses we have identified in various different ways.

2.2   Perspectives

A key concept of the ORDIT methodology is the notion of *perspective* – for example, efficiency, staff satisfaction, return on investment, client service orientation, etc. – as drivers of design decisions. A perspective is defined in terms of a model in the following way: if a person judges a model M to be sufficiently similar to a reality R for a particular purpose P, then P is the perspective of model M. These perspectives cannot always be expressed in terms of activities or resources; rather, they behave as policy generators and as evaluation criteria between options. Identification of perspectives is thus a vital part of the scoping and requirements phases of a project.

The way in which such perspectives are handled in ORDIT is through careful recording and exploration of the implications of the perspectives for a particular socio-technical system option. The Requirements Reference Model plays an important role here by linking design decisions to the conversations in which such decisions are made; for example, the distribution mechanisms used in the computer system may be specified in a conversation between the system architect and the system manager in the client organisation. The responsibilities of the parties to those conversations are examined to see whether the parties have agency over the related policies; for example, a highly distributed system will lead to lack of centralised control over information accessibility, and may therefore weaken a chain-of-command structure (which is largely enforced through control over information). If it is found that an agent has responsibility for merely executing a relevant policy and not for the making of that policy, then 'parent' conversations must be examined to see whether the implications of design decisions have been, or can be, explained upwards to the policy maker.

Where possible perspective and policy conflicts (e.g. efficiency *versus* staff satisfaction) are uncovered, the enterprise model is examined to determine the level in the organisation at which it is rational to resolve the conflict. This does not mean, of course, that it will necessarily be possible to have access to the relevant policy maker. If there is no rational decision role or mechanism, all that can sometimes be done is for the system designer to point this out. But this should be done in the domain of policy decision making, not in the domain of system design decision making. Hence the importance of the enterprise modelling, which must therefore include both the problem owner and the problem solver domains and the relations between them, so that such domains – which may span enterprises – can be properly identified.

This process of perspective identification often serves to uncover possible futures, in the sense that it may reveal alternative ways of grouping responsibilities and policy making loci and structures. Most policy changes do in fact turn out to be shifts of perspective; or, to put it another way, concentration on one chosen perspective can sometimes be shown to result in implications which are felt to be undesirable from the point of view of a particular policy holder. For example, in one of our case studies, a change proposed to increase communications efficiency was found to have the effect of centralising the scheduling of a certain resource, which went against the organisation's objective of localised autonomy of such decisions.

Thus when ORDIT talks abut exploring possible futures, the terms in which such futures are expressed and evaluated is the perspectives involved, their implications for responsibility and policy structures, and the aspects of organisational change which might be induced by those implications. The information technology system itself is seen as an agent of change, and the benefits and penalties of the change as seen from each perspective must be carefully worked out. Many of the concepts and techniques of ORDIT are *primarily* designed to achieve just this evaluation, which is seen as the main generator of organisational requirements.

2.3   The requirements process

The four major sections in Figure 1 are the outline of a process for arriving at a set of organisational requirements on an information technology system.

2.3.1   Scoping

The purpose of scoping is to establish territory and to determine the important players. It involves generating models of an area so as to be able to create scenarios about the future. The purpose of generating scenarios is to explore what the requirements might be, and whether such generated requirements fall within the scope of the system (as currently defined), or whether the scope has to be changed to encompass them.

Thus the major tasks of scoping are:

- to determine the nature of the contract with the client;
- to establish the boundaries for the system;
- to gain an understanding of the purpose and structure of the organisational unit/s which are to be involved;
- to identify the principal stakeholders involved.

All of these tasks are essential to the planning of the study, though they will all be revisited during the course of the study both to gain the detailed information required for the body of the study, and to adjust the terms and structure of the contract to meet new information or conditions.

2.3.2   Modelling

The purpose of this component subprocess is to represent the current understanding of the socio-technical system by producing a set of models. This provides not only information about the environment in which the IT system is to function, but also a context for understanding later policy and design decisions. One particularly important use of the description is to act as a focus for discussion on what sort of system the new system should be, and on how responsibilities and authorities in the organisation are going to change as a result of introducing the new system. Another important function is to assist in the scoping subprocess, by providing models for the determination of relevant stakeholders and system boundaries.

The existing system is described in terms of the system itself and its organisational environment, and then agreed with the problem owners. The next step is to model the existing system in terms of abstract agencies (see Section 3) and a general information and computational system. In addition, models are annotated with relevant requirements policies concerning issues such as combinations of agents into roles, access, authorisation, scope and objectives.

2.3.3   Requirements generation

There is much talk of requirements capture, as if requirements were butterflies to be caught and pinned down in a specification cabinet. In reality, of course, this is not so; requirements are often much better thought of as being elicited through such techniques as ethnomethodological study, structured interviews, dramaturgical exercises, and so on. This shift of emphasis from the requirements process as being formalising the explicit to making explicit what is merely implicit is clearly correct, but does not go far enough in many cases of organisational requirement, where the problem is one of envisioning the future rather than understanding the present.

One of the difficulties is that requirements often are emergent – that is, they are an artefact of the whole requirements process itself and their structure is often governed by the structure of the requirements process. In this sense, organisational requirements are not so much elicited as generated. In fact, a major focus of ORDIT is on exploring possible futures for the organisation, and the process of building a view of the future serves to generate new requirements as possible new ways of working are explored.

One of the consequences of considering requirements as being generated is that the process of interaction with the requirements owners has to be interactive and iterative. Further, the kind of requirements generated will be dependent on the kinds of models being used and the possible futures being explored, and both of these can be very speculative – but only in an exploratory (interactive and iterative) context. One of the main reasons why the requirements *capture* paradigm is so prevalent is that the standard systems analysis contract does not permit much scope for exploration – usually because the purseholder or contract authority does not wish it to, either out of ignorance or fear of possible risk. Competitive tendering policies also have the same effect.

It would, however, be a mistake to think that the ORDIT methodology cannot be operated in a context where exploration is discouraged or not permitted. ORDIT is not a prescriptive method, and just as it can accommodate the participative design and ethnomethodological elicitation methods (as used in the Utopia project (Ehn, 1988) for example, or those described in Chapter 11 of this volume by Luff *et al.*) it can also accommodate a more conventional approach (at least as practised in the UK) where users, if represented at all, are done so by 'user representatives' who may be completely the opposite. Both of these are alternative routes through our methodology. What is important is to know the strengths and weaknesses of each possible route, so that in those cases where client policy does permit a choice of route, an informed decision can be made; and in those cases where it does not, the risks and benefits of the dictated policy can be explained and debated with the client.

Thus our characterisation of requirements determination into three general modes – capture, elicitation, generation – is not to characterise ORDIT as espousing only the third, despite its manifest benefits (and undoubted associated costs), but is an indication of the three major routes through the requirements determination process. In practice, of course, some combination of routes is selected, probably on a basis of individual stakeholder prejudice or preference.

2.3.4   Solution options

Requirements and some priority ordering are used to generate possible design options for the socio-technical system, with conflicts and trade-offs being resolved with the client. One of the purposes of the earlier stakeholder analysis is to answer not only the question of how and by what criteria to prioritise stakeholders, but also whether different prioritisations are needed for different purposes (e.g. data collection, validation/feedback, policy decisions). The implications of the design options are analysed and discussed with relevant stakeholders in an iterative fashion. The acceptability of the preferred option is agreed with the problem owners and other stakeholders, ensuring that the option meets the formal model of requirements.

The 'space' in which solution options are discussed is a socio-technical space, that is, it encompasses possible changes in the organisation and new organisational constructs as well as changes in the technical system and new IT constructs. These must be considered together. For example, an organisation that wishes to improve its repair service carried out at customer premises might wish to consider making its repair service an integral part of its operations, or a separate organisation (wholly-owned or independent), or make its repairers a set of independent agents with a common coordinating service to which they all subscribe (the taxi-driver model). Each of these options will place its own distinctive set of requirements on an IT system to support the requesting, scheduling, use and monitoring of the repair service.

This is the final step in problem space of requirements analysis. Subsequent stages consist of a response by the system architects and designers to the requirements, and are therefore expressed in solution space terms.

3 ENTERPRISE MODELLING

The modelling concepts are perhaps the key aspect that makes ORDIT different from more conventional approaches to design. Enterprise modelling provides a framework for representing and reasoning about the IT system as a component of a wider environment which is the organisation whose needs it is designed to serve. We have found that this form of modelling ensures an adequate representation of the structural and organisational aspects of the problem, making explicit policy issues and assumptions which cannot so easily be stated. One of the main characteristics of the ORDIT approach is that we model responsibilities and relationships rather than activities, and base our understanding of the architectural framework on this and not on any current implementation of an activity model. In an analogous way to this we model information from the contractual view rather than the current structure of the information flow.

The ORDIT project has devised a diagrammatic enterprise modelling language to represent the structure of the organisation (Dobson and McDermid, 1989) in order to serve two related but distinct purposes: (1) to identify the requirements owners and their positions and roles within the organisation so as to demonstrate completeness of the requirements elicitation process, and (2) to identify the user community (and others affected by the proposed IT system) and their roles and responsibilities within the organisation in order to demonstrate completeness of the requirements modelling process.

3.1 Basic concepts of the Enterprise Model

The three essential elements of the Enterprise Model are *agency*, *activity* and *resources*. The relations between these entities are defined in Figure 2 (Dobson and McDermid, 1990). *Agency* is an intensional concept, in the sense that it is not an object but is a collection of responsibilities. The corresponding extensional concept is that of an agent who can be regarded as holding those responsibilities. An agent may be regarded as a primary manipulator of the state or structure of the system, and is the only object that through an activity can create, modify or destroy other objects, but may do so only by virtue of the responsibilities associated with the agency. An *activity* is an operation that changes the state of the system, and is performed by an agent. All activities must induce state changes in the system that are visible to one or more agents. A *resource* can be one of two types, consumable or non-consumable, where consumable resources are objects such as raw materials, time or money, and non-consumable resources include information, telecommunications services, etc. When modelling organisations from the enterprise projection viewpoint (ANSA, 1989), resources act either as tokens of responsibility, signifying that an agency has a binding responsibility upon some object, or as objects for which some agency is responsible. An important type of non-consumable resource is data. When data are passed from one activity to another, interactions occur, the data being the bearer of those interactions.

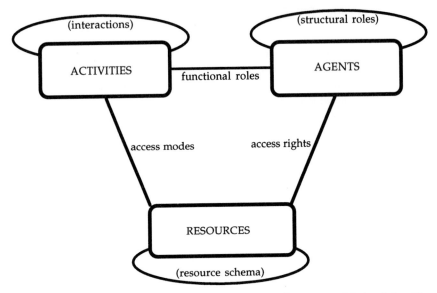

Figure 2   The basic elements of the enterprise modelling language and their relationships.

An enterprise model also provides us with a framework from within which it is possible to examine the kinds of relations between entities of the same and of different types. By examining these relationships a problem owner and solver can begin to understand how the basic objects influence and are related to each other. In our enterprise modelling we have chosen to concentrate on the concepts of 'role' and 'agency' as being central to our procedure.

3.2   The concept of role

We choose to describe an organisation as a set of related work roles for the following reasons:

1. A role is a descriptive concept that can be used to represent many different organisational realities, from the formal and structured to the fluid and unstructured.
2. Treating role as a basic building block makes it possible to move between organisational requirements and the requirements of individual users (e.g. from the organisation's role in a project to the way in which these responsibilities devolve to the roles of members of the project team).
3. A role defines task responsibilities and thereby functionality requirements.
4. A role defines the relationships between role holders and the behaviour they expect of one another, which in turn defines many non-functional requirements.

In fact, we distinguish between two major, and distinct, concepts of a role. A *functional role* is a relation between an agent and an activity, and so corresponds to the behavioural aspect of role. Examples of functional roles are executor (of an activity), owner, controller, and so on. This is in contrast to a *structural role*, which is a relation between agents, and so corresponds to the social aspect of role. Examples of structural roles are supervisor–subordinate, supplier–customer, provider–consumer, and so on. Hence our concept of role allows us to distinguish: (a) an agent with associated obligations such as accountabilities and responsibilities to other agents; and (b) activities that interact through information flows and are structured into tasks and operations. This enables us to represent and analyse the relations between these concepts, and to represent the way in which they operate in real organisations.

Figure 3 is an example of the basic building block of our enterprise modelling diagrams, which shows the roles involved in repairing a customer's appliance. We have used these diagrams in an actual case study to discuss options for reorganising an electricity supply company's policy on the future organisation of its customer premises repair service.

The main point to note about Figure 3 is that each box contains the names of what we have termed the functional role (in plain) and the structural role (in **bold**). The functional roles (*problem owner, problem repair*) are shorthand for the kind of behaviours that the parties may engage in (e.g. the problem owner can report the existence of a problem, the problem repairer can mend it). The structural roles (*consumer, supplier*) are shorthand for the framework of obligations that permit and give meaning to these behaviours.

The lines that join the functional and structural roles represent the fact that a relation between two agents may be one of interaction or one of commitment, these being derived from the corresponding agencies. Commitments and interactions are related to each other through activities such that commitments only arise and are fulfilled through interactions. So, properly speaking, the links between them are in fact functional and structural relationships.

This figure thus embodies the policy that the repair is effected by the supplier. An alternative scenario, in which the problem repair is effected by an approved independent agency, might be represented by Figure 4.

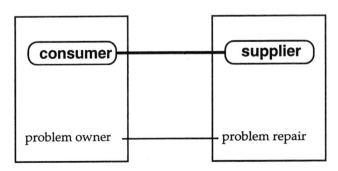

Figure 3   A very simple role-relation diagram.

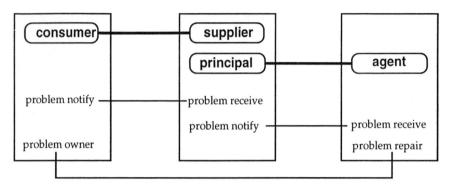

Figure 4   One possible decomposition of the repairing agency

Finally, Figure 5 represents the policy that the problem repair is effected by a separate agency within the supplying organisation. Note that we have used nesting to represent the organisational relationships involved.

3.3   The concept of agency

ORDIT aims to describe and reason about organisations that embody both a social and a technical system. These, however, comprise one single system, a socio-technical system, and as such cannot be described or modelled in terms of state and behaviour only as a purely technical system might be, since there is a fundamental difference between social and technical systems. It is in order to be able to differentiate between social and technical objects (i.e. between people and machines) that we introduce the idea of agency. A machine may perform the same tasks as a per-

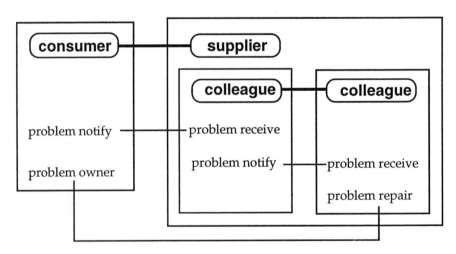

Figure 5   Another possible decomposition of the repairing agent.

son, but a person will hold responsibilities for those tasks in contrast to a machine which cannot hold responsibility. The person is said to be an agent and hold the agency.

It is important to realise that an agent is distinct from both an individual human and a role. An agent holds the particular set of responsibilities that comprise an agency. Thus, depending on how responsibilities in a social system are allocated and combined, agencies are composed and decomposed. An agent also differs from an individual in that an individual may hold more than one agency simultaneously. An agent differs from a role in that a role is not merely an agency or a collection of agencies, but also includes a set of relationships with other agents. These are structural or social in nature, arising from responsibilities that relate to the other agents.

This concept of agency is one of the strengths of the ORDIT approach to a possible *re*organisation of a socio-technical system, since it facilitates the reallocation of agency in a way that takes into account as fully as possible the structural and organisational implications of the change. Since agency is considered a coherent set of responsibilities, it permits the discussion of issues related to the change in and re-allocation of responsibilities when some functions or agents in the system are proposed to be automated.

3.4   Responsibility modelling

Although the abstractions we have chosen in our enterprise modelling language are rich enough to show many aspects of organisational structure, we have extended them to include responsibilities.

Dictionary definitions of responsibility seem to agree on distinguishing two different meaning groups: (i) being accountable for a state of affairs; and (ii) being the primary cause of a result. The first meaning group has connotations of blame for a mismatch between the actual and a desired or expected state of affairs, without any implication of a direct causal connection between the responsible agent and the mismatch, whereas the second meaning group does have explicit connotations of causality both for an event and the ensuing state of affairs. We shall therefore refer to these two distinct types of responsibility as *consequential* and *causal* responsibility, respectively. We must be clear about the sense in which we are using the term consequential here. It is being used to describe the type of responsibility where the agent is answerable to someone for a state of affairs: he is 'taking the consequences'. It must not be confused with causal responsibility for the consequences of an action, i.e. the ensuing state of affairs. For example, a child who throws a stone has causal responsibility for the action: he did it. He is also causally responsible for the immediate consequences of his action: he caused the window to get broken. Although the child can be blamed for breaking the window it is the parent who has consequential responsibility, since parents are held responsible by society in general for the actions of their children. We shall now examine these types of responsibility in more detail.

3.4.1   The responsibility relation

Our basic intuition is that one agent is responsible *to* another agent *for* something, and that this something can be described as a possible mismatch or non-conformance relation between an actual state of affairs and a desired, expected or feasible state of affairs. For example, an agent can be responsible for success (actual state of affairs better than expected) or failure (actual worse than expected) in some performance, or for the adequacy or inadequacy of a set of resources. The form of a consequential responsibility is therefore that it is a relation between a pair of agents and a mismatch relation, and it is important to note that all three elements are essential; in other words, the actual responsibilities held cannot be looked at on their own, but must always be considered within the responsibility relationship between the two agents.

We shall refer to the two agents as the *responsibility principal* and the *responsibility holder*, where the *responsibility holder* is responsible to the *responsibility principal* for a *responsibility target*.

Both in reality and in terms of the model, it is this relationship between the agencies that is important, and the question that we should be asking takes the form 'To whom are you responsible and in what respect?' Within an organisation these responsibility relationships determine the type of the structural relationships between pairs of co-workers. These relationships form an enduring framework for the basic 'socio' structure of the socio-technical system. In contrast, a responsibility relationship between an external agent and an organisation, where the relationship is essentially of the service type, is likely to be of a more transient nature, existing only for the duration of the specific contract. For example, a shipping company is responsible for safety to a particular passenger only while that person is a passenger.

3.4.2   Obligations and induced consequential responsibility

Although it is common to speak of responsibilities being transferred or delegated, and thus as having a dynamic aspect, the tripartite form of the responsibility relationship means that a responsibility holder cannot independently transfer his responsibilities to another agent. However what may be happening in the case of apparent transfer is that the responsibility is reallocated to a new holder by the responsibility principal by destroying the old relationship and establishing a new one. The case of apparent delegation is accounted for by the fact that a responsibility holder can set up new responsibility relationships between himself and other agents. He is then the principal of the new responsibility relationship, and the other agents are new responsibility holders.

Associated with any responsibility is a set of obligations which must be discharged in order to fulfil that responsibility. At this point, it is appropriate to make the distinction between responsibilities and obligations clear. Obligations, which are essentially constraints on the choice of action, are in effect the duties that must be performed to fulfil responsibilities. The distinction is apparent from the words we use: a responsibility is *for* something, whereas an obligation is *to do* (or not do) something. The binding between responsibilities and obligations is the state of affairs with which they are associated, the obligation being concerned with the maintenance or change of the state of affairs for which the responsibility is held.

Obligations or duties may be passed from one agent to another, provided that it is permitted by their relationship within the organisational structure, and one way in which an agent may discharge an obligation that he holds is to pass it on to another agent. However, inseparable from a specific obligation is a responsibility for the state of affairs resulting from the discharge of that obligation. This responsibility is held by the holder of the obligation. If an agent chooses to pass an obligation to another agent, the new obligation holder becomes responsible to the original obligation holder for discharging the obligation. Thus a new responsibility relationship is set up between them. In this way, a whole chain of responsibility relationships can be established.

3.5   Granularity and decomposition

A marked advantage of our modelling is the way in which we can compose and decompose our role-relation diagrams for the purposes of ascertaining requirements at the levels of agent (or individual), groups (or collections of distributed agencies), and organisations (policy holders). It is through using the features of role-relation diagrams in this way that we are able to specify the differences between relationships. To achieve this, it is essential that our diagrams (de)compose so that we can view the organisation at whatever level best fits the purpose. Furthermore, an advantage of this abstraction is the freedom it gives for the binding between the abstract and the concrete. Our use of the abstract term 'agency', for example, is deliberate so that we can discuss who or what corresponds to the agency. For instance, it allows us to investigate differing bindings and boundaries associated within agencies encapsulated within a role.

It is sometimes the case that binding turns out to be a fundamental policy issue – for example, it might be agreed that there should be a beneficiary from the existence of a market (e.g. the market landlord), but in the case of a public utility supply market, there might be debate as to whether this beneficiary is to be the public state or the private shareholder. Similarly for boundary drawing: it is useful to distinguish between, for example, the diagnosing agent and the prescribing agent in medical health care, but these may be combined into one role (as in the UK primary health care service) or separated (as in certain secondary health care services).

An important point that this serves to highlight is that differing requirements are expressed at differing levels within an organisation. At the organisation level, the most important requirements may be to do with policy issues, at a group level they may be concerned with being able to support collaborative work in an efficient manner, and at an individual level priority may be given to job satisfaction. We believe that enterprise modelling is capable not only of capturing what may be conflicting requirements within an organisation's structure, but that it can represent these qualitatively different requirements at their appropriate levels and then discuss issues of their conflict resolution, compatibility, desirability, and so on.

We have built many enterprise models using these concepts, and have found that in practice they are capable of being used successfully at all levels of granularity, from large scale systems where public policy is the main issue ('What is the structure of a National Health Service?') to small scale systems where individual roles and tasks are the main problem of concern ('What are the main organisational requirements on a pilot patient record system to be introduced into this accident and emergency ward in this small hospital?') What came out of this case study was the way in which we could directly track in terms of our models the way policy decisions set at the highest political level – doctors as resource managers, for example – influenced detailed requirements. The requirements reference model played a crucial role here in holding together the relations between the various levels of granularity, the agents involved in each, and the sources of responsibilities and requirements.

4   SUMMARY

ORDIT has its background in the socio-technical systems work such as ETHICS (Mumford, 1983), though it does not follow in detail all the stages of that approach. In general, ORDIT follows the recommendations of any structures systems analysis method, though it places far more emphasis on the initial stages than most. It is not unusual to find that determining the boundaries of the system is the single most time-consuming task of the whole of the requirements process. ORDIT is capable of adapting to a number of requirements engineering processes: capture, elicitation, generation or participation. ORDIT does not have an idiosyncratic method of its own, nor is it prescriptive about any particular method to be used, since this is often a matter of policy outwith the domain of the system analyst or consultant employed. ORDIT is, however, *normative* in the sense of understanding the relationships between organisational objectives and policy on the one hand, and system development methods on the other, and recommending the best choices for a particular culture (of both the owning and developing enterprises).

ORDIT is designed to enrich those poverty-stricken stages of systems analysis and design methodologies in which information requirements analysis is assumed to be straightforward, or organisations are naïvely documented as a set of unproblematical entities and functions. In this aim, of course, ORDIT resembles, and indeed has its roots in, the Soft Systems Methodology (Checkland, 1981; Checkland and Scholes, 1990). But where ORDIT has made an advance on SSM is, we claim, in its detailed linking to the detailed design of computerised information technology systems – an area identified by Checkland and Scholes (1990, p. 57) as being a weakness of SSM. Although this chapter, in presenting an overview, has not been able to show the details of this process, the richness of our enterprise and information models has turned out to be sufficient to make the crucial step from information categories and use to data structures which represent those information categories – for further details see Dobson (1992). Chapter 5 in this volume, by Stamper, rehearses very well many of these issues, which we have independently discovered, and we can but only loudly agree with his methods and conclusions. However, the reconciliation between common real-computer data structures with those which in principle would provide the information categories required by an enterprise analysis turns out to have a significant logical cost, in that current database concepts are insufficiently rich, and sufficiently confused, to preclude the use of commercial off-the-shelf databases without in many cases compromising the objective of fitness-for-purpose considered from the viewpoint of organisational policies and perspectives. Again, Chapter 5 by Stamper is a prime reference for the kinds of problems that arise.

We have found that our experience in ORDIT of constructing enterprise models and determining their bindings and boundaries has aided us in suggesting issues of job design and exploring organisational issues in a manner that pays heed to an organisation's requirements, goals and policies. For example, in the case presented, the choice between direct contact between the customer and the repair agency, or indirect contact, with the repair agency being either internal or external to the supplier, is an organisational choice that can easily be explained, and the implications on job design, responsibilities and information systems structure can be explored using the diagramming techniques we have outlined. The problem of determining system boundaries of complex IT systems has meant that mistakes have occurred where the boundaries turned out to have been drawn in the wrong place. We claim that our modelling techniques provide a sufficiently rich environment in which organisational structure and the roles of agents, information flow, resource management and the relationships between all of these are capable of being represented, and we are therefore able to capture the complexities of organisational structure.

The most common problem of requirements engineering in the design and implementation of complex IT systems is combining differing representations of the system and its environments; the operational, organisational and social environments of a system all possess different characteristics. Hence the driving thrust of the ORDIT philosophy is its advocation of involving policy makers and problem owners throughout the design of the system. It is a process of shifting the balance of responsibility between system owner and system designer away from the 'owner states, designer solves' model towards a relationship in which the problem solver helps the problem owner understand the problem, and the problem owner helps the problem solver understand the implications of possible solutions.

The ORDIT methodology has been developed over four years (1989–92) in a number of case studies used for testing and validating the approaches adopted, and more case studies are currently under way or being planned for the fifth year (1993) of the project. Explicit methods used to support each of the four major processes have been described in the ORDIT Manual of Tools and Techniques, which is currently in a draft version suitable for internal project use only. However, the final version of this manual, in four volumes, will be publicly available at the end of the project, together with a fifth process manual which describes the overall structure of the ORDIT methodology, gives guidance on selecting suitable techniques, and shows examples of navigation routes used in the case studies together with reasons for choosing those routes.

ACKNOWLEDGEMENTS

Acknowledgement is made to the contributions of all our colleagues in the ORDIT project to the ideas presented here. The project also gratefully acknowledges the financial assistance afforded by the ESPRIT programme of the CEC (Project 2301) and also by SERC (Bainbridge Project). Finally, Vic Maller as our project reviewer has unfailingly been a source of moral support and encouragement, and has done much to strengthen our faith in what we have been trying to do.

REFERENCES

ANSA (1989). *ANSA Reference Manual, Release 01.00*, Architecture Projects Management Ltd., Cambridge.

Checkland, P. (1981). *Systems Thinking, Systems Practice*, Wiley.

Checkland, P. and Scholes, J. (1990). *Soft Systems Methodology in Action*, Wiley.

Dobson, J. E. (1992). Information and denial of service, in C. E. Landwehr and S. Jajodia (Eds), *Database Security: Status and Prospects V*, pp. 21–46, Elsevier.

Dobson, J. E. and McDermid, J. A. (1989). Security models and enterprise models, in C. E. Landwehr (Ed.), *Database Security: Status and Prospects II*, pp. 1–39, Elsevier.

Dobson, J. E. and McDermid, J. A (1990). *An Investigation into Modelling and Categorisation of Non-Functional Requirements*, Report No. YCS 141, University of York, 1990.

Ehn, P. (1988). *Work-Oriented Design of Computer Artifacts*, Arbetslivscentrum, Stockholm.

Harker, S. D. P., Olphert, C. W. and Eason, K. D. (1990) The development of tools to assist in organisational requirements definition for information technology systems, *Proceedings Interact '90*, 295–300.

Humphreys, P. C. (1984). Levels of representation of decision problems, *Journal of Applied Systems Analysis*, **11**, 3–22.

Mumford, E. (1983). *Designing Human Systems*, Manchester Business School Publications.

Five

Social norms in requirements analysis – an outline of MEASUR

Ronald Stamper
Department of Information Management, University of Twente, The Netherlands

1 THE DISTINCT CHARACTER OF MEASUR

This chapter gives a brief outline of MEASUR, a radically new set of norm-oriented methods which generate requirements specifications for software development as a by-product of solving business problems. The concept underlying MEASUR is that organisations, themselves are information systems, and the social norm is the appropriate unit of specification. Business problems are solved in terms of actions, both particular actions and policies for action. MEASUR is concerned with both but, where policies are laid down for persistent patterns of action, formal and computer-based information systems can be used to support them. Policies can be defined in terms of norms from which the information requirements arise as a logical consequence. We can then use a system called a Normbase to transform the requirements into a default computer-implementation where the data are held in a semantic, temporal database together with formal versions of the norms. MEASUR and the Normbase together empower the users of computer-based systems by giving them tools for solving their problems which generate requirements specifications, succinct documentation that is rather easy to understand and prototype. Moreover, instead of the conventional database, the Normbase places all the business-oriented knowledge under their control rather than losing the functional part of it in the technical complexity of the application programs.

1.1 Business first, technology optional

MEASUR provides a link between the 'wet' and 'dry' cultures (Goguen, 1992) in the information systems field. 'MEASUR' is a rich acronym:

Requirements Engineering
ISBN 0–1238–5335–4

Methods, Means, Models ... for
Exploring, Eliciting, Evaluating ...
Articulating, Analysing, Assessing ... and
Structuring, Specifying, Simulating ...
Users'
Requirements

These methods enable one to start with a soaking wet problem and gradually dry it out until it is crisp and precise enough to generate supporting computer systems automatically.

MEASUR is focussed upon solving business problems in the broadest sense. Information system problems are appropriate for MEASUR, but so also are problems of designing systems for legislation, contractual rules, or other kinds of social norms. Such systems must be embedded within the social system as a means of solving the problem. In other cases, the emphasis may be upon understanding a situation or a complex problem domain, and MEASUR can also help in a more detached manner, as illustrated in Stamper (1992) where it is used to elucidate the concepts of semiotics.

Although it is not focussed on information technological problems, MEASUR can handle the 'up-stream' end of software engineering. In a conventional situation, it would primarily serve the managers and other system users, helping them to identify and solve their problems, and lead them to a precise statement of information requirements. In this role, it covers the domain of 'information strategy and planning', but it also provides detailed specifications of any problem domain where detailed requirements specifications are needed before designing a computer-based system. The default implementation, which can be generated directly from the specification, provides a benchmark for any software subsequently developed.

The underlying philosophy of MEASUR also distinguishes it from the mainstream of work in the information systems field. It is based on the assumption that the world is constructed socially and subjectively, whereas the majority of practitioners in this field tend to consider information systems as devices for representing and interacting with some objective reality. (The social construction, not only of social reality but of mathematics and programs, can be approached by reading such works as Berger and Luckmann, 1967, Bloor, 1976, 1983, DeMillo *et al.*, 1979, and Lakatos, 1976.) This philosophical difference may seem academic, but it has led to the creation of some very practical tools and techniques, and it can also have a profound effect on the attitude and approach adopted by the analyst using MEASUR.

The distinct character of MEASUR arises from its assumption that an information system is a social system and, indeed, mostly an informal system where formality and automation can play limited roles. The conventional view is that an information system is essentially a computer- and telecom-based system used within an organisation. The analyst using MEASUR must adopt the modest role of one who enables some limited amount of technology to be added to the real, infinitely rich and complex human information system, at points where its introduction is appropriate. The conventional analyst, as one of the members of a software engineering team, is responsible for introducing (even 'selling') information technology to the managers and other users in the organisation. These attitudes are institutionalised by placing the analyst in the computer-services department. MEASUR encourages and could be used to institutionalise the different view that information management should deal with business problems rather than the management of IT, because the organisation, not the computer, is the information system.

1.2   The organisation as IS

We can distinguish, perhaps, two main ways of thinking about organisational information systems: the plumbing paradigm and the field paradigm.

Look at the classical methods of requirements analysis for software engineering and you will find that they treat an organisational information system in much the same way as they treat the computer. This classical paradigm is the 'information plumbing' or 'chemical engineering' approach to information systems (Stamper, 1985a). Dataflow diagrams and data models of one kind or another appear in all of them. Dataflow analysis helps one to see how messages move from processor to processor in an organisation. The processors may be people or machines which act on the incoming flows to generate various flows of output messages. Some mechanical processors are storage devices where vast quantities of data are stored and there is a dual problem to solve. Instead of processors standing still and the data flowing, we now have the data standing still and the processor navigating through the storage space. Data models provide the maps for the navigating process. The tacit assumption behind both dataflow diagrams and data models is the same – data is a kind of abstract material being subjected to processes analogous to the mixing, distillation, packaging and so on, that take place in a factory. (The habit of saying 'data is …', instead of using 'data' as the plural of 'datum' also encourages this habit of treating 'data' as a mass term such as 'water', which underpins the flow metaphor.) The analytical and specification techniques in common use almost compel one to adopt this paradigm.

The concept of an information field encourages and enables us to adopt quite a different approach. If you want a physical analogy, think of a space vehicle under the interacting influences of many different internal and external fields, fields of gravitation, electro-magnetic forces as well as clouds of gas, and internal, elastic tensions. There is no point trying to explain the vehicle's behaviour in terms of energy, momentum and materials exchanged between its components – we need a macro-model – so we use the field concept. Information fields, similarly, help us to adopt a macro perspective before we work on details of flows, where that is possible.

Information fields can be thought of as a specialisation of the social group concept. (One may think of it as a special 'field' of discourse in the social semiotic sense, where the text concerns information. See Halliday 1978, p. 33, p. 143, for example.) The interesting work in the domain of ethnomethodology provides another view of information fields (See the chapters by Button and Sharrock, Luff *et al.* and Randall *et al.* in this volume). Ethnomethodological analysis does not aim to produce a conventional 'requirements specification' which stands apart from the context of the work which people do. The fact, overlooked by the conventional analyst, is that information and communication cannot be separated from the context of action. Except in relatively simple cases, it is dangerous to rely upon decontextualised specifications of requirements using flow charts, conceptual database schemas and functionality definitions. In the rich, subtle social context, where each syllable or gesture may have many possible, different effects, depending upon the whole situation in which the communicative action takes place, the consequences of implementing some formally specified software cannot be predicted. Ethnomethodology provides us with an approach to observing and understanding the complex situated reality. MEASUR acknowledges this complexity by placing the agents in their social setting at the centre of attention and in the core of its specification techniques.

An organisation behaves as it does under the interacting influences of many different social groups (= information fields, roughly speaking). The owners, managers, staff, clients, professional groups, local community, and so on, often subdivided into factions, will prefer rather different behaviour from or in relation to the organisation. They will have rather different norms relating to their habits of behaviour, beliefs, expectations, values, responsibilities and commitments, and these will affect their preferences concerning precisely how things should happen. A social group defines itself by its shared norms. Many of these norms will be cultural ones, but others will be standards and commitments that members have made explicitly (contracts are a good example). The organisation will operate according to some compromise between the forces exerted by these fields of social force, the compromise being influenced by the relative power of the groups. This is all rather obvious, so what is the connection with information systems?

1.3   Information and norms

The idea of a norm is the key concept. Every norm we assume has a structure which we can make explicit in many cases. For example, a behavioural norm has the form:

for a certain community and a certain purpose,
if x then A is obliged/permitted/forbidden to do y

where x is some perception of the situation, A is a responsible agent (a person or group of people, not a machine), and y may range across many alternatives including a specific concrete act (driving on the left), or a social act (acknowledging ownership), sending a message (paying a grant), invoking a rule (making use of trespass law), invoking a whole system of norms (applying the company rules for leave of absence), even making new rules. Given this structure, we know that *A* can only act in accordance with the norms of the community for the given purpose if he/she/it has the information necessary for perceiving the situation, and the power to communicate other information where the action calls for it. People obtain most of the information relating to the norms they have to obey through informal channels. Only in a minority of instances do we use formal or automated information systems to support the functioning of the norms. Hence, if we know the norms, we know what the information systems requirements are, as fully as it is possible to state them.

Let us take a range of examples, some that might be encountered when developing a routine administrative system, and some when developing a system for computer-supported cooperative work (CSCW). Using this information field paradigm we can be as vague or precise as the problem demands and permits. Very precise norms can be made explicit in rules. *In an administrative setting* where compensation is given to victims of minor crimes, rules might be made to calculate a maximum time to make a payment and to inform the person concerned. These are tasks that can be almost fully automated. Rather similar rules may be used *in a CSCW system* such as the collective articulation of a proposal for an innovation. All participants might be required to respond to a suggestion within a time that can be calculated, and that the members of the group must be polled for any missing replies five minutes before the deadline. Again, the computer can provide considerable help but, of course, only the people can complete the acts of conforming to typical social norms. When it is possible to find detailed and precise norms and we can say who exactly must obey them, then we can apply conventional methods to analyse the message flows from agent to agent and specify the exact functionality of the system.

But the problem may not admit that level of precision. We may only be able to say that any member of a certain group is subject to the norm and they must take into account certain information. For example, *in the administrative system* there may be a norm governing the level of compensation given to victims of minor crimes. The norm itself will be known to the responsible officials – they will discuss the 'tariffs' among themselves and with their superiors, and all of them will note what the general public, the politicians and the victims themselves say about the levels of compensation being provided. Every case will be unique, so the best we can do explicitly is to supply relevant facts and documents about it to the officer making the decision. The social norms involved are so complex that we cannot make them explicit for computer implementation, but we can have the computer supply data and document images to the right people, and also prompt them to scan the informal information field for relevant information outside the scope of the computer system. We could also add a rule requiring three officers to agree on any unusually high or low level of compensation, thereby making sure that the judgement was more firmly rooted in the information field. *In the CSCW application* supporting an innovation team, the participants may agree, in order to avoid the follow-my-leader effect, first to make individual judgements of cost expectations on the basis of factual information, and then to revise their judgements in the light of their colleagues' opinions. The computer would support the team by distributing the factual data, gathering initial judgements, sharing them and then collating final judgements. The participants can be expected to seek information and to discuss and negotiate outside the computer system, in other words, use the information field. Clearly, the design of a CSCW system should have as much regard for the creation of effective patterns of discourse outside as well as within the groupware system. Only the simplest norms can be made into explicit rules and separated from the people who know them; but we do have access to the complex rules through the people who know them while our computer provides data to the norm-subjects or decision-makers and applies rules to monitor their decisions or actions.

At the vaguest level we only specify the agents who are norm-subjects, and possibly the broad goals they are to achieve. We must rely upon these agents to apply the norms implicit in their experience, their skills and their social relationships. Most of these norms we cannot represent in any computer system. For example, in the compensation *administration system*, injury or illness may be caused by the crime – but how do we know? We have to rely on someone's judgement because the complexity of this decision defies analysis in formal rules. The administration of compensation must rely upon an appropriate medical practitioner to make this decision. The relevant norms are supplied by the medical profession, through its education, training and literature, modified in response to public opinion. The administration will have to monitor these norms in order periodically to revise its performance standards and budgets. All we can do with the computer system is to ensure that every episode is assessed by a properly qualified person. Compared with an administrative system, *CSCW applications* are likely to incorporate a far higher proportion of norms that cannot be modelled explicitly. A team of people working on a complex innovative proposal will have to make some collective judgements. They will include engineers of many kinds, marketing specialists, procurement experts, financial experts, business strategist, lawyers and so on, and they will have to contribute their specialist knowledge. The best we can do with the computer is to identify a responsible person or subgroups and give them goals – design something, procure something, estimate something. ... The groupware can do no more than identify relevant agents and goals. The CSCW system as a whole comprises the telematic groupware embedded in a social information field. This is not an abdication of responsibility by the analyst, it is an honest recognition that only a small fraction of the norms in any organisation can be expressed as computable rules, while the rest of our knowledge can only reside with the responsible agents.

Even with the precisely stated norms, imprecision cannot be avoided because the language of the rules has ultimately to be interpreted by responsible agents through their actual responses to a stream of particular cases. The absolute precision envisaged by the 'hard' school of analysis is unobtainable except as a mathematical exercise ignoring the underlying social reality. Using the 'norm-oriented' methods explained in this chapter, we are forced to relate the formal or automated information system to the agents who interpret the 'hard' components of the system, the explicit rules, by reference to the relevant information fields. In other words, the norm-oriented methods make clear that the hard system is only a mathematical fiction until it is *embedded* in a social structure.

Finding and understanding the information fields associated with the various stakeholders involved in the problem is one of the first tasks in dealing with the 'soft' part of requirements analysis. We also define the relevant goal structure and relate it to the mores of the community, in particular to the willingness of people to conform to norms and to exchange information. These stages belong in Phase I of MEASUR, to be explained in a little more detail below.

Norms are essential for interpreting data. No computer-based information system will perform a useful task unless there is a social system to supply data and interpret its outputs. Ultimately, responsibility for these functions must be allocated to agents – specific persons or groups or roles or members of a qualified community, such as a profession. In the final analysis, the meaning of the information in a system rests upon the conduct of these responsible agents. In MEASUR, the analysis of semantics is the task in Phase II of MEASUR, as explained below. Adding the precise allocation of responsibilities and, where appropriate defining norms at various levels of 'hardness' is the task of Phase III of MEASUR.

1.4   Overview of MEASUR

To understand MEASUR one needs to forget information technology and concentrate instead upon the organisation as an information system. This semiotic viewpoint (see for example, Nauta, 1972; Stamper, 1973, and forthcoming) treats the norms as the defining elements of organisations from which information requirements flow as a logical consequence. We evolve the norms needed to solve a problem in phases of increasing detail, as follows:

● *Phase I – Problem Articulation* to identify a significant issue and articulate the problems it raises in sufficient detail. This incorporates the methods of:

— semiotic analysis, which examines the organisation as a sign system;
— collateral analysis, which deals with an innovation in its infrastructure;
— functional morphology, which looks at the norms of communication and control and how they are allocated across the informal/formal and man/machine interfaces;
— valuation framing, which identifies the different stakeholder groups and analyses their valuations of the situation;
— contention management, which helps to resolve conflicts between the different world views revealed by the other analyses. (For more on Problem Articulation see Stamper and Kolkman, 1991, and Kolkman, 1993.)

- *Phase II – Semantic Analysis* to clarify the meanings of the language used to define the problem and its solution in operational terms, where all significant states of affairs are made explicit in readiness for
- *Phase III – Norm Specification* to assign authorities, responsibilities and design the norms governing all the relevant activities.

Phases II and III will be examined in more detail below. Phases IV and V are mentioned for completeness. These are only applications of the first three phases. The first round of analysis focusses on the substantive kernel of the system, disregarding all the problems of communication and control. Then we move to:

- *Phase IV – Communication and Control Definition* to apply the analysis methods of Phases I, II and III to problems of communication and control. This completes the work on the object system itself but leaves us with the meta-problem of instituting a solution within the organisation. This is handled in
- *Phase V – Project Definition and Management* to examine the scale, costs, potential benefits, task sequence, etc. for the implementation of a solution. Much of the input to Phase V can be taken directly from Phase I and, therefore, begun almost in parallel with it.

Phase I provides the minimum, rather fuzzy statement of the norms by identifying the stakeholder groups (information fields), their values and the tasks to be performed, all expressed in relatively informal language. Phase II produces a map of the relevant business concepts and terminology, which looks rather like a kind of data-structure. Phase III involves developing what looks rather like the 'legislation' that governs the organisation's functioning. Phase IV adds the norms governing procedures, message passing, rewards and punishments. In Phase V, we step outside the central problem and treat the meta-problem of how to solve the central problem.

Underlying the whole process is the concept of the organisation as a norm system. This ties all the methods and techniques together in a single conceptual framework, thus making MEASUR as a whole coherent and relatively easy to use.

Space does not permit us to survey the whole of MEASUR, so we concentrate on Phase II, which is concerned with the perceptual norms and the language associated with the concepts people use, with some mention of Phase III, which is concerned with assigning responsibilities and formalising social norms.

2 SEMANTIC ANALYSIS

Problem Articulation in Phase I belongs in the category of soft systems methods (Checkland, 1981). It produces a picture of the stakeholders involved, their value systems and the goals people have. It places a solution to the problem in the context of the socio-technical infrastructure: how the system which delivers the solution can be created, maintained, backed up, monitored, etc. It also reveals the internal structure of the system in terms of the communication and control norms which must be added to the substantive norms, and also the allocation of these norms to the three sub-systems: informal, formal and automated. Problem-solving groups using these techniques perform significantly better than unaided groups (Bruijn, 1993).

The key output of Phase I is sufficient terminology to represent the relevant actions and states of affairs about which the people involved need to communicate. Semantic Analysis will then lead one into a deeper exploration of these actions.

2.1   From articulated problem to semantic analysis

The result of articulating a problem is that we have the power to explain the situation and what we want to do about it in appropriate words and in an appropriate model. The question then arises: 'What precisely do we mean by those words?'

Why should we be bothered about meanings? Although the common expression 'mere semantics' suggests that practical people should not waste their time on philosophical disputes, policy makers and managers and those who negotiate with them, must be acutely alive to issues of semantics because doing business is getting things done through the use of language. The finer points of policy making, of negotiating, of making practical sense of our plans and intentions reduce to issues of meaning. To support this argument, one need look no further than the most important of our institutions for resolving conflicts – the judicial system – where disputes can nearly always be characterised as differences over semantics: one side favouring one interpretation of a law or a contract, say, and the other wanting the words to mean something different. Semantic Analysis supports the participants in the task of clarifying the meanings of the terms which have been developed during Problem Articulation.

In a business situation, it is crucial how the people involved in implementing a plan or conducting an activity translate into action the words through which they understand their tasks and duties. Thus we have identified as the right kind of semantic principle for solving business problems and interpreting language in the conduct of practical affairs, that *meaning must be treated as a relationship between signs and actions*.

The fundamental difference between the classical approach to requirements analysis and the Norm-Oriented approach of MEASUR is rooted in their underlying philosophical positions. They may be characterised crudely as the objectivist *versus* subjectivist positions, as in Figure 1.

The philosophical issues are discussed elsewhere (Hirschheim and Klein, 1989; Stamper, 1992), but we shall skirt them here. Anyone familiar with the classical methods will recognise some of the consequences as they appear in the techniques

Concept	Objectivist View	Subjectivist View
reality	objectively given, the same for everyone and composed of entities, their properties and relationships	created subjectively and socially with subtle differences between groups by knowing agents, through the repertoire of behaviour of which they are capable
data	a means of representing the truth about reality	a means of indicating intentions and coordinating actions
truth	the correct correspondence between data and reality	a consensus reached (temporarily) as a basis for coordinated action
meaning	a relationship between a sign and some real entity which it denotes, or points to	a relationship between a sign and some patterns of action established as norms within a group
information system	a kind of 'plumbing' system through which data flow	a semiological system, mainly informal but supplemented by formalised messages
role of the analyst	to specify the true data-structures and functions of the system needed by the users	to assist the users to articulate their problems, discover their information requirements and evolve a systemic solution

Figure 1   Typical objectivist and subjectivist positions compared

they use. The classical methods tacitly assume that there are simple answers to the deep questions about the nature of reality, meaning and truth:

- the world is divided up into entities (physical and abstract) which can be classified according to their properties and placed in relationship with one another, and this structure is independent of any observer;
- the words and numbers we use in our documents on our computer screens and in our databases point to entities, attributes and relationships in the real world, a view which leads to the E-A-R data models and to a commitment to a semantic function which maps from data onto reality;
- the truth is a correspondence between propositions (the facts in our databases and documents) and reality, a view that the database is a model of the enterprise and its environment.

MEASUR does not dismiss these assumptions, but it treats them as valid only for a limited class of rather simple problems of the kind on which the infant IT was weaned into the world of practical affairs. Where there is a high level of consensus about the problem area (for example, routine engineering and all the associated routine commercial transactions in a stable manufacturing business), the assumptions are valid for most practical purposes. But when things change rapidly, as increasingly we experience in all fields of business and social life today, these assumptions fail.

MEASUR is quite explicit with its philosophical assumptions. They provide the motivation for the specification language, NORMA, which it uses. For all practical purposes:

- there is no reality without involving agents who do things and, so doing, create their own, directly known reality;

- the agents draw boundaries round patterns of action when, in their judgement, doing so is biologically or socially desirable, and these boundaries establish invariants in the flux of activities and events.

(The common-sense objector may attempt to show that the world consists of individual objects by placing in one's hands a series of objects, what argument could be more convincing? But suppose one of these is an orange, I would say "So what! As far as I am concerned there is nothing here, for all practical purposes, unless I can do something with it: I can heft it, I can smell it, I can squash it on the carpet and make a mess, I can squash it in that machine and extract juice and leave pith and skin, with the juice I can ..., with the pith and skin I can ..." The Norm-Oriented analyst can demonstrate that all he can know about the orange is a repertoire of behaviour patterns which *he* can employ, and he will admit that, for *another person* who can do more or different things with an orange, the reality of the orange is different from his reality.) Continuing with the list:

- the words, numbers and propositions we agents use are names for the invariants in the flux of behaviour in which they are involved (meaning as a relationship between signs and actions).

(To represent the repertoire of behaviour associated with an orange you can do without language. Speakers of English label that repertoire 'orange', the Dutch speakers 'sinaassappel', the Chinese speakers 'ju zi', and so on. The behaviour can be represented in a semantic database by a numerical surrogate, in the linguistically neutral core to which different languages can be related.)

- truth is a provisional consensus among agents about how, for practical purposes, to relate propositions to the flux of their subjectively created reality – this expresses a commitment to the essential subjectivity of truth and knowledge.
- the data in an information system are instruments through which people act upon one another in a social system of which it forms a part.

These assumptions lead us to construct a specification language in which every proposition *must* contain a reference to an agent and to what the agent is doing. They also entail that anything we express in our specification language and use as a basis for action, must represent a commitment entered into by some responsible individual or group agent.

2.2   NORMA – The specification language of MEASUR

This analysis of what exists in terms of repertoires of behaviour has a profound practical consequence. The term 'affordance' was coined by James Gibson (1968,

1979; but also see Michaels and Carello, 1981) to describe the behavioural invariants which organisms perceive in the flux of their physical experience. Gibson developed a theory of perception based on this notion. Each invariant state is one in which the agent can act in a limited way defined by the repertoire of behaviour patterns which the world (physical and social) affords him/her/it. As an example, consider the very different repertoires of behaviour available to you when you are seated and when you are walking. In NORMA, everything, even objects such as an orange or a chair, are invariant repertoires of behaviour. Consider, for example, a copyright or a marriage, these are clearly repertoires of behaviour which society affords its members. Our social world is formed by the behavioural invariants we perceive in our social experience. The social world affords us patterns of behaviour which are established by our cultural and legal norms, the counterpart of the affordances of the physical world.

On this philosophical basis, we conclude that our description of the world must always refer to the agent who is doing the knowing and also refer to the action-repertoire known. No one knows what an orange is without him- or herself or someone else hefting it, smelling it, squeezing it ... So a sentence in this language, NORMA, has the following structure:

    agent behavioural-invariant
    e.g. John upright

The sentence structure introduced above can be applied recursively. An agent who adopts some invariant state for a period simply becomes a modified agent for that period, so

    (agent behavioural-invariant) behavioural-invariant
    e.g. John upright walk

represents a similar structure in which the existence of the second behavioural invariant depends upon the existence of the first. This is the notion of 'Ontological Dependency' used in a simple, practical analysis method described below. (The language is only sketched – for more detail see Stamper, 1992.)

Behavioural-invariants can be combined using operators that are NORMA's analogue of the logical operators 'and', 'or', 'not'. These are *while, whilenot* and *orwhile*. The difference is that these take account of time. An agent may be sitting *while* eating an orange, or eating an orange *while not* sitting – these provide ways of representing some simple composite invariants. The third represents an indifference between two invariants – *while* singing *or* speaking – so that either or both may be going on. In this way, we can construct expressions that represent complex situations and calculate their periods of existence from those of their components.

Norms tell us what should be done when various situations arise. Norms represent behavioural options that are socially determined. The simplest behavioural invariants are determined biologically and physically by the structure of the agent and his/her/their environment's structure. Norms and affordances, their physical counterpart, are, therefore, the mechanisms through which we perceive and act upon our world. The norms and affordances are universals (the analogue of data-types) and, as mechanisms (e.g. the ability to stand or walk), they have periods of existence, just as particular instances of things and behaviour have periods of existence (e.g. standing on one occasion). So nothing appears in a NORMA picture of the world without it being bounded in time. We write a norm in the form x *whenever* y where x may specify the putting out of a fire and y describes the circumstances of an uncontrolled fire in a building. The existence of the norm (unlike classical implication, its counterpart) cannot be computed from the existence of its components, but it is independently determined by a norm-making agency.

Notice that every sentence in NORMA has a number of others associated with it. A period of existence is associated with every statement in NORMA, the existence being bounded by a

start and a *finish.*

Start and finish are references to events, and we also have to consider the processes of

beginning and *ending*

which are further associated behavioural invariants. Other associated invariants are the

authorities

which are the agents or norms determining when things start and finish. There are also

signs

which are other behaviour patterns (such as the ink marks you are reading now), and

labels

which are the signs used in NORMA itself for making statements about the world. In this way every statement in NORMA has a rich associated structure, with the consequence that you can specify a lot very briefly in NORMA, so reducing the volume of documentation needed.

So much for a sketch of the theory, what about the practice?

2.3   Ontology charts

Given the words and expressions in which the issue or problem has been articulated, we have the names of the invariants, physical and social, that are relevant. We now need to make clear how these words relate to actions to be performed in the organisation.

In the previous section the concept of Ontological Dependency was introduced. Some things depend for their existence upon others. In Figure 2 an example is given.

Each element can only exist during the existence of the elements to the left of it, which are its various *ontological antecedents*. The marriage depends upon the existence of two persons as antecedents, hence the double line. The two people involved occupy the roles of husband and wife, which we can indicate as in Figure 3.

So 'husband' and 'wife' refer to persons in the context of marriage, and perform the dual role of selecting a marriage relationship and a person within it. Similarly, a runner is a person in the role of one who runs. The role name is a powerful semantic instrument because it picks up the whole of the ontological structure in which it is defined. However, we do not have natural language role names for every dependency.

Notice also that 'Society' appears as the ultimate antecedent. This is a way of acknowledging that the existence of the other elements depends upon the commonsense judgements about reality that are embedded in the perceptual norms of our culture. Different societies will give different interpretations to all the terms in this example.

We can also introduce the notation for processes of beginning and ending using this example. A marriage normally begins with a wedding, a process which if successfully performed results in the start of a marriage. A divorce is one way of ending a marriage. Birth and death are the beginning and ending processes for a person. We can use the forms:

marriage<　　marriage>　　person<　　and　　person>

to represent them. In many cases, there is no word for the beginning and ending processes, and then we have no option but to use these formulas.

We now have most of the basic concepts for performing some elementary Semantic Analysis, and we shall illustrate them with an example. As explained later, the method is not only useful for administrative systems, but is of quite general applicability, so do not read too much significance into the choice of example.

2.4　Example: Legislation for a national population register

In the particular case used below, the problem of developing the legislation for a Population Register in the Netherlands was reworked retrospectively to see how

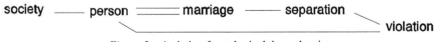

Figure 2　A chain of ontological dependencies.

$$\text{person} \quad \frac{\text{(husband)}}{\text{(wife)}} \quad \text{marriage} \qquad \text{person} \quad \frac{\text{(runner)}}{} \quad \text{runs}$$

Figure 3   Existence of roles within behaviour patterns.

this method could help in the preparation of legislation and, in parallel, the specification of the associated information systems.

The analysis could well have started from the first outline problem statement by the Minister for Home Affairs bringing forward the legislation (GBA-brief, 1984). In general, this is the best kind of starting point. However, it is interesting to present, instead, the list of data items which were produced by a conventional analysis, in order to illustrate some more of the differences between the Classical and this new Norm-Oriented approaches.

Population register – a list of data elements for a classical data model

The following categories of data may be collected about a person
a. identification
b. names
c. birth
d. civil status
e. address
f. parentage
g. cross-references
Identification
   local authority where personal index card is located
   date of entry into the register
   local authority where initially registered
Names
   family name, including prefixes
   forenames
   title
   indication of usage of name
Birth
   date of birth
   place of birth
   country and province of birth
   sex
   nationality
Civil status
   civil status
   date of marriage/dissolution

place of marriage/dissolution
reason for dissolution
country and province of marriage/dissolution
administrative number(s) of (ex-)spouse(s)
  OR List A

Address
date of registration and address at that time
actual date of settlement from abroad
date of earlier removal abroad
administrative date of settlement
actual date of removal abroad
date of death
current address
local authority area of previous residence
country of origin
local authority of new place of residence and address there
country to which removed
place of death
country and province of death
cause of death/post-mortem finding

Parentage
administrative number of father
  OR List A
administrative number of mother
  OR List A

Cross-references
for travel documents
  description and number of travel document issued
  expiry date
  issuing authority
for civil status
  birth certificate number
  death certificate number
  marriage certificate number
  divorce/annulment/separation certificate number
  certificate numbers relating to inherited status etc
  local authority relating to each certificate
for national authorities
  such items of data as mentioned in the present Schedule C of the
  population accounting manual, excluding medical topics
for driving licence administration
  licence number
for the administration of aliens
  residence entitlement and status

It is evident that the focus of attention is upon the data that have to be manipulated by the intended computer-based information system, rather than upon the substantive issues concerning the lives of people.

We may classify the items on the list as 'substantive' or 'semiological'. For the ultimate purposes of administration, we are interested in what happens to the substantive items such as *person, marriage, local authority*, etc. but in the case of the semiological items, such as *family name, administrative number, certificate*, etc., these are only the means by which we can interact with the substantive objects. The substantive objects are of primary juridical concern whilst the semiological objects, the means of representing the substantive objects, are the chief interest of the information systems designers.

In the classical methodology, all the elements on the data item list are treated as names for semiological items which, encoded in a suitable way, can be processed by computers, for example, a name or a birth certificate. Note that this is the ontological position implicit within object oriented methods. Most substantive items have nothing to do with computers or other information systems. These are the main focus of interest in a norm-oriented methodology, and the list can be thought of as denoting such 'real' objects. However, some real objects are signs which have to be handled physically outside the computer as well as in their encoded forms within.

Adopting this view, we can classify the items and simplify the process of analysis. We can subdivide the norms of a system into the substantive ones (the task we have to perform) and the others which allow a group to coordinate their actions: the norms about passing messages and about the use of rewards and sanctions (control norms). The message and control norms will not be missing from a system, but most of them will be handled by the informal system. So a Norm-Orientated analysis will begin with the substantive system on the assumption that we can hand over responsibility for all communications and control to the informal social system. Of course this is only an approximation, and we shall gradually add some norms about passing messages and about exerting social control to obtain conformity to the other norms. However, at some point we are forced to hand over to the informal system the rest of the norms.

A tentative version of an analysis into substantive and semiological items is given below. It has been constructed by going through the orthodox data-set and identifying the substantive and procedural items, and making a few slight changes, as follows:

Population register – list of items for a norm-oriented analysis

Substantive items	*Semiological items*
person	population register
local authority	personal index card
location	personal record
family	administrative number

Substantive items	Semiological items
place	title
country	usage of name
province	birth certificate
birth	death certificate
sex	marriage certificate
cause of death	divorce certificate
nationality	separation order
marriage	certification of title
cause of dissolution of marriage	driving licence
settlement ('brute fact')	residence permit
settlement ('institutional fact')	travel document
residence	
travel authorisation	
status	
mother	
father	
official body	

Whereas a classical data model is concerned with navigating through storage to find data items, an Ontology Chart in MEASUR is concerned with the business (governmental, in this case) activities and policies. The data are only instruments for reaching a substantive policy objective. On the other hand, semantic analysis is concerned with examining the policy problems, starting from the substantive ones and moving later to the procedural ones.

The MEASUR list is much shorter than the classical list of items. One reason for this is the fact that the NORMA structures always assume that every item has a name or label, a start, a finish and authorisations. These do not have to be specified explicitly in the Ontology Chart, thus reducing the complexity of the analysis needed by the users.

Figure 4 shows the first stage of semantic analysis. It is based on the list of substantive items in the classified list above, but with the addition of some of the items that are clearly missing. One may disagree with the analysis as it stands, what is important, however, is that one can find points of contention easily and then be able to say whether a change is definitely for the better or worse. The classical data models are not worth disputing because they tend to reflect arbitrary design choices and changes tend merely to reflect someone else's arbitrary choice. The notion of ontological dependency provides the criterion for finding in favour of one analysis rather than another.

The underlying principle is to picture the existence relationships among the items. The lines show that instances of items on the right (e.g. *divorce*) can only exist during the (co)existence of the items linked to them on the left (*divorce*

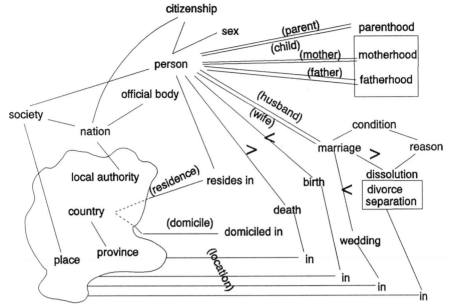

Figure 4   A partial ontology chart or semantic schema for a population register.

depends on *marriage* which depends on two *persons*). As mentioned above, every object has a start time and a finish time, so the semantic analysis is concerned with the constraints on these events and their related elements of data.

There are several features to notice. The first feature concerns another basic concept – the generic/specific relationship. This is illustrated by the *parenthood* as generic to the specific forms of *motherhood* and *fatherhood*, and by the other box labelled *dissolution* and containing *divorce* and *separation*. (Here there may be room for dispute.) Generic/specific relationships are not logically necessary ones – they are determined by norms of one kind or another.

The left-hand side of the chart is not complete. There is a fuzzy area around the concepts related to *place*. Some items do not have an antecedent. We could make all the loose items depend on a *Society* as the single source of common-sense meanings, or we could be more exact in our analysis. For example, the existence of a person will have a common-sense meaning, but we may want to distinguish *natural person* from a *legally recognised person* in a given legal order. We shall then need to redraw the chart, but first solve some tricky legal and political problems. The places we refer to are social constructions and, in most countries, for everyday purposes they are defined by a postal service which would, in a stricter analysis, be the antecedent. Notice that the *address* is the identifier of the *place*.

The process of semantic analysis forces us to think how *exactly* we intend our words to be interpreted operationally in the business by our own staff and by others. Semantic analysis has nothing to do with computers but it serves as a tool for solving business problems.

This example illustrates rather well how semantic analysis raises major policy issues. This law requires the concepts of *person, sex, mother, family, place,* and so on, to be clarified because the common-sense meanings are likely to cause problems in important marginal cases. (For a more detailed discussion, see Stamper, 1992.) Although this case is in the field of government administration, the same kinds of problems arise in business situations.

2.5   Choice of example

The choice of example should not mislead one into thinking that MEASUR is only for large administrative systems. The method has been applied to a very wide range of problems where meanings have to be clarified. All kinds of business and administrative issues have been examined this way to produce semantic analyses from which information systems could be developed, if required. In addition, scientific problems have been treated this way, for example, the terminology of the information systems field has been partially analysed in Stamper (1992). From this point of view semantic analysis may be considered a knowledge-elicitation technique. The method is well suited to dynamic CSCW applications, too, as indicated earlier. The importance of semantic analysis is not for producing an information system, but for solving a problem precisely enough for the operational meanings of terms to be assured.

Other chapters in this volume implicitly challenge any approach to requirements analysis to avoid the potentially catastrophic consequences of overlooking the delicate, seen but unnoticed socio-interactional practices of people in a real world, work setting (Luff *et al.,* in this volume). Perhaps, therefore, I should indicate how MEASUR might be employed in a case such as that of the work carried out in a control room in the London Underground. Recognising the complexity of problems of this kind and the sensitivity of the ethnomethodological approach to them, the few remarks that follow are tentative and intended only to indicate a possible line of enquiry.

A telescope will help you observe many parts of the heavens, but its design will not determine where you search or how you focus it. There is nothing in a method such as MEASUR to compel you to concern yourself with the socio-interactional practices of a team collaborating on a task. What I shall try to show is that one *can* usefully direct MEASUR towards this kind of problem and focus on it effectively.

Some requirements analysis techniques are actually incapable of registering many of the delicate interactions between team members. In particular, the flow-oriented techniques tend to treat the separate semiological acts performed by team members, such as changing a display, making an announcement to passengers,

handing a document to a colleague, and so on, as private to the one or two participants who handle the flow being represented. This is quite appropriate in the typical administrative situation, where tasks are separated by distance, hierarchy and
time, and communications have to be formalised as explicit information flows.
Social interactions where there is no regulated 'flow' of information tend to be
blotted out of the picture by the use of any technique based on the 'flow'
metaphor, virtually preventing the social aspects of the control room from being
described. On the other hand, by treating the members of the control team as an
information field governed by social norms, the social aspect would be brought to
the fore.

MEASUR is explicitly concerned with social behaviour. This encompasses the
social interactions where each person's behaviour is constantly monitored by other
members of the team who are up-dating their picture of events and of their colleagues' knowledge of and involvement in those events. The team in the control
room obtain some information from displays of many kinds, but in addition, much
of the communication is informal, and relevant information is obtained from the
ambient flux of signs of many kinds – speech, movements of hand or body, posture,
gesture, direction of gaze. The technique of Functional Morphology in Problem
Articulation would certainly draw attention to these processes (directing the telescope), but let us see how the semantic analysis technique examined in this chapter
might be used.

We can see the substantive problem very easily: the trains, their movements, the
crew and their work schedules, the delays, the bomb alerts, and so on. We should
soon incorporate these affordances into our semantic analysis. The concept of an
affordance treats each thing for which we have a name (even objects such as a
train) as a repertoire of behaviour. These repertoires are governed partially by the
nature of the physical world, but also by social norms. The same underlying
analytical concepts apply to the functioning of the team of controllers, but now we
are dealing with a totally different social system. Their behaviour is based upon a
constantly changing pattern of relationships within the group. The ethnomethodologist's sensitive observation can make these relationships perceptible. Semantic
analysis takes for its units of analysis invariants in the flux of human behaviour, so
if one person is explicitly monitoring the activities of another, we have a clear
example of an invariant which will be characterised by a certain repertoire of available behaviour, and its start and finish will be clearly signalled, unlike a period of
surreptitious monitoring which will be quite different. In the first case, that of
explicit monitoring, one could include within the permitted repertoire of behaviour
the direct registering of approval or disapproval, but such overt acts would be
excluded from surreptitious monitoring. These unnoticed affordances are what the
ethnomethodologist draws to our attention.

The ontological structuring principle will apply. One repertoire of behaviour will
depend upon another for its existence. For example *membership* of the team may be
basic, allowing current *engagement* in the team's work (leaving the control room or
being suddenly sick would terminate a period of engagement). *Engagement* would

include *monitoring* in its dependent affordances, with *approval* a further dependent, and so on. Each instance of each of these affordances will depend upon the exercise of norms which the participants must know. There is no implication in this analysis that these norms would be 'computerised' – they are strictly informal. Figure 5 shows a fragment of an ontology chart which might be used to report some findings of an ethnomethodological analysis.

A small point of interest is the appearance of the role 'subject' twice. This causes no confusion because the context disambiguates the meaning, so that, referring to a subject when using the Normbase, you would have to provide enough information to select the right meaning or make a choice when the system indicates the ambiguity.

This example has been concocted for purposes of illustrating the method; it is certainly not a report of ethnomethodological observations. Nevertheless, I hope it will suggest that the semantic analysis method in MEASUR is compatible with ethnomethodological enquiry.

3   NORM DEFINITION

The Ontology Chart provides a conceptual coat-hanger on which we can hang all the statements about the dynamics of the social system. Every instance of a universal (e.g. licence to drive) or a particular (e.g. Jan Jansen) has a start and a finish. The responsibilities and rule used to express a policy hang on the start and finish 'pegs' for the universal items, thus providing a check-list for our dynamic specifications.

3.1   From semantic analysis to norm definition

There is no need to complete semantic analysis before embarking on Norm Definition. In fact, it is desirable to make some preliminary Norm Definition

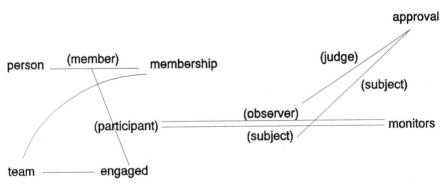

Figure 5   Some possible affordances in a communicating team.

throughout the process of semantic analysis. To be clear about the meaning of any term, we have to know the boundaries of the behavioural invariant it names. So we ask about each item: when does it come into existence? when does it go out of existence? who decides the precise times? and where do these rules apply? These are all essential aspects of meaning in our sense of meaning as a relationship of signs to actions. If we are not clear about the boundaries of things, then we are not clear about meanings.

The basis for Norm Definition is the Ontology Chart. Such a chart as in Figure 4 or the equivalent list of expressions which is a Semantic Schema, such as

    person
    nation
    citizenship (person, nation)
    parenthood (person #parent, person #child)
    resides (person, place)
    ...   and so on,

can be supplemented by adding the criteria for the start and finish of each item. These criteria would be discussed informally during semantic analysis and possibly defined in a piece of text which forms a part of the supplement to the Ontology Chart. The chart provides, in fact, a complete catalogue of the dynamic functions of the problem domain. Every relevant change must be the start or finish of one of the semantic elements. Norm Definition begins by providing a statement of the start and finish criteria at least in natural language text, and then translating these texts, into NORMA for the precise specification.

If we cannot be clear and precise about the criteria governing the start and finish of instances of some type of object, such as a marriage, we cannot be clear and precise about its meaning. For example: most often a marriage begins with a wedding but, for policy reasons we may want to include 'common-law marriages' which are established by the partners living together as man and wife. Political argument will involve this semantic problem when there are choices to make about when to use a broad or a narrow definition of marriage in making laws on taxation, social security, inheritance, and so on. Thus, at the start and the finish of each item in the semantic chart, we can attach hooks on which we then hang one or more norms determining when the object concerned comes into existence and when it ceases to exist.

Being forced to be explicit about the precise start and finish of every kind of thing in our problem domain imposes a semantic discipline that creates an agenda of policy issues, some simple but some quite difficult to resolve. By raising these issues, semantic analysis provides the starting point for Norm Definition.

In the formal specification we define the authorities governing starts and finishes. These can be either responsible agents or norms.

3.2 Responsible agents

In the simplest cases we allow starts and finishes to be determined at the discretion of some agent (individual or group) who may be named directly or indirectly through the role they occupy or the category they belong to. Thus to decide when a person's sickness starts and finishes, the person may decide himself, but, for the purposes of an insurance scheme, any qualified medical practitioner may be the authority, or perhaps only the medical officer in the person's employer's organisation can make this decision. The responsible agent can be specified more or less precisely. The least precise definition would be to say that society decides, which is to say a common-sense choice is to be made which can be delegated to any competent member of the society. A company will decide on the start and finish of its departments, and the start and finish of a machine may be determined at the discretion of the department with appropriate technical knowledge. The groups acting as responsible agents may delegate the decision to an individual selected by the circumstances (the member of the group who first encounters the problem) or it may use some voting procedure (parliament deciding to finish or repeal some Act), but we do not have to enquire into these details. Operationally, we need to know where to get a decision that will be regarded as good enough for practical purposes.

The subjectivist philosophy of MEASUR is carried through into practice using this idea of the responsible agent. No words simply have meanings that they carry around with them. We cannot legitimately ask: What is the meaning of X? We can only ask: How does A use the word X? Thus no meaning of a word can be known without knowing who is responsible for its use. Meanings in MEASUR cannot be specified by fiat of some analyst or data administrator. They have to be fully under the control of the users.

Earlier, the place of the informal information system as an essential component was emphasised. The classical methods have a tendency to lead to formal systems which stand on their own merits, using data that have their own meanings. This cannot happen using the methods of MEASUR, because the links between the formal and the informal systems must be made explicit. The problem that we face if we want to introduce the informal system into our specification is that we can say little about it without violating its intrinsic fluidity and pinning it down in some formalism. By specifying that the problem calls for the use of certain words and that certain agents are responsible for linking those words to actions, we get as close as we can to specifying the informal system. The natural words used in the organisation or society are effectively names for informal socio-linguistic norms governing their use in the context of action. What those norms are precisely we can never express formally. All we can do is provide an explicit link to the informal system by specifying the agent responsible for using the words according to his (usually tacit) knowledge of his culture. Thus we always treat the 'hard', formal system as no more than a neat little additional structure, depending for its foundations upon the strength of the informal system that interprets it.

3.3   Agents, communications and relevant information

Given the definition of the responsible agents in a given unit system, we have the foundation for a study of the communication system and, at the same time, we can begin to design the norms in detail. The agents who decide on starts and finishes are the sources of information. Who are the recipients?

Those who need information about changes in the state of the world are those who must act in response to the changes. Still leaving the system to be run under the control of human discretion, we can assist the decision-makers by stating what information should be taken into account when they make their choices. In the general case, the organisation will not make use of a computer-based system, how then can we get the right information to the decision-makers?

The first step towards a solution is simply to give them the schema and the allocation of responsibilities. The decision-makers can select the information that is relevant and then discover who is responsible for it. In some cases they can contact the relevant person, but often they will have to make use of their knowledge of the system (or acquire such knowledge) so that they can use secondary sources as best they can. Thus we give the decision-makers at least a rough map of the area and leave them to use the informal system to find what they want.

But if the organisation does provide a telematic environment then we can supply a default solution to this problem of helping the decision-makers with a supply of relevant information. If we build a Semantic Temporal Database using the semantic schema, then any available information can be held by this database and made accessible to all decision-makers. Parts of this database may contain no data on particulars, only the relevant part of the schema. In this case, the decision-maker will be thrown back on his skill in using the informal system. Where particular data are available, then we can write expressions in LEGOL defining the contents of reports which the decision-maker can request, using those expressions, whenever he faces a decision. This is a passive solution.

It is an obvious step to make the system active. This can be done by specifying norms which have a condition component that is satisfied in circumstances which require a decision to be made. The consequent side of the norm is not a mechanical result of the facts, but simply an obligation on the responsible agent to make a decision by whatever thought processes he chooses. This leaves open the option of requiring the decision-maker to account for his choice. The active system can monitor events for the decision-makers and monitor the decision-makers for the organisation or society.

3.4   Detailed norms

In some limited cases we can be precise about the norms to the extent that we can define exact conditions in which some definite actions must be taken. Usually, the action will require an agent to perform it. In these circumstances we can send a message to the right person directing what he should do. The results of his attempt may not be success, so the system will have to be informed what exactly happened. In the very narrow band of cases where the task can be performed by the computer itself, the task may be fully automated. Complete automation is relatively unusual in most real, organisational information systems. However, if you consider that an information system is essentially a computer-based system, then you will tend to overlook the majority of the norms governing the system because they cannot be performed without human discretion. Detailed norms define the small part of the organisation on which classical methods focus most attention.

4   SUPPORTING TOOLS

MEASUR is supported by a number of software tools. They first help to identify the areas where problems have to be solved, then they help to clarify exactly what is meant by the terminology introduced, and finally, they associate norms with the concepts introduced.

4.1   Problem articulation tool

The Problem Articulation Tool (PAT), supports the first phase. Basically, this is an hypertext system which leads the users, separately or in collaboration, through the analysis process and maintains a record of their ideas, judgements and expectations. Particularly valuable about PAT is the uniform structure which governs the hypertext linkages. Any innovation at the focus of attention gives rise to many others which form part of the supporting infrastructure (collateral systems) or are a part of the focal system (subsystems). Each of these secondary systems can be made the focus of attention and analysed in the same way. Thus, unlike many hypertext systems, this one is quite easy to navigate because the map is the same wherever you are in the structure.

The text generated by PAT provides input to semantic analysis.

4.2   LEGOL and the semantic, temporal database

The software tool that supports the use of semantic analysis is a Semantic Temporal Database (STB) which uses the Ontology Chart as a schema. It also has a data-manipulation language, LEGOL – a legally oriented language – in which norms can be written (see Jones *et al.*, 1979, for an account of an early version; and Liu, 1993).

LEGOL is a kind of ambiguous form of NORMA. When an expression in

LEGOL is interpreted by the STB, the system checks the terms against the schema in NORMA and either resolves any ambiguities from the context definition in operation, or it asks the user to select the interpretation from those it has found.

Anyone familiar with relational databases can think of the STB as a relational system containing only a single relational structure. Every element has a standard set of attributes which includes the start and finish times, the ontological antecedents and the authorities for start and finish.

This structure provides very tight semantic constraints on the data in the system and on the expressions in LEGOL or NORMA which make it virtually impossible to put meaningless symbols into the system. The normal relational system will tolerate all kinds of garbage as data, and will obediently perform all kinds of symbolic and arithmetic operations on them, subject to some data-typing and any explicit constraints that the analysts have remembered to include.

The presence of start and finish times which are handled by every LEGOL or NORMA operator makes it possible to write expressions involving time quite simply. In a few lines we can express what requires a page in SQL, the standard relational database language. For example, whereas in LEGOL 'a *while* b' needs one operator and two operands, in SQL the same basic function needs 39 operators and 86 operands – to an average person, a whole, incomprehensible page of code. Two examples of LEGOL appear in the next section. This brevity of expression also brings the more important virtue of clarity. LEGOL is a formal language, but not so far removed from ordinary language that a manager working on the requirements definition of a system cannot easily understand what is being said.

For achieving the goal of restoring the control of IT to management, the several features of MEASUR and its tools cited above play a vital role. We have found that documentation can be clarified and reduced in quantity by at least a factor of ten, as far as the business users are concerned. Thus:

- *Users' own words*: the words used in an Ontology Chart are the words and expressions of the users. The inventing of new terms (STK-AMT, DEL-DT, PRODN, and so on) which lend a spurious air of science to a majority of systems specification documents but which, in reality, only make the documentation even more impenetrable to the users than it need be if we use all the normal semantic units: *stock-amount, delivery-date, production*.
- *One word with many meanings but no ambiguity*: one of the motives for inventing special terms – the removal of ambiguity – is eliminated because the ontological structure disambiguates terms which can appear in many different places in the structure, their meanings being provided by the surrounding network of ontological dependencies and by the authorities governing starts and finishes.
- *Compactness*: every item in an Ontology Chart 'hides' a long, uniform list of items which the reader knows are implied. This 'hiding' accounts for most of the compression of the documentation. (A notable success in this area is reported in Liu *et al.*, 1991.)

- *Semantic constraints are implicit in the model*: the ontological dependencies contain most of the constraints that in classical methods must be specified in logical expressions accompanying the data model, and which are usually difficult for users to interpret.
- *Reusable modules*: the analysis of structures using semantic analysis does not allow them to incorporate features that are accidents of local practice, hence many features (such as 'contract' and 'transfer' in commercial problems) have standard solutions forming reusable modules of the system.

The reduction in quantity and improvement in quality of the requirements documentation should be sufficient reasons in themselves for adopting MEASUR.

Moreover, as a system is analysed using MEASUR, each increment to the semantic specification can be tested directly in a prototype. The Ontology Chart is both a specification for the users to understand and a schema for a supporting computer tool. As the specification grows, so does the Semantic Temporal Database. This can be used to hold a sample of data familiar to the users against which they can check their understanding of the problem.

4.3　The NORMBASE

The software tool to support Norm Definition is the NORMBASE (Stamper *et al.*, 1991). This builds on the foundation of the Semantic Temporal Database by adding facilities for storing and manipulating norms. Most of those facilities are afforded by the LEGOL interpreter.

Given the Semantic Schema or Ontology Chart and the associated norms which say how people should behave in the planned organisation, we have the means of generating a prototype computer system to support the organisation. This can be used as an analysis tool enabling the management and other users to see, at a fine level of detail, where their problem analysis has led them. They can easily modify both schema and norms.

To illustrate this, consider two examples where users want to write rules for extracting data from the Population Register database.

Example 1
One advantage of an automated system is that it can generate notifications of movements that are necessary for the work of administrative bodies of all kinds. For example, when a person returns from abroad, tax and social security, among others will have to resume official contact with that person. So we can have these movements notified automatically by writing a procedural norm such as:

if
finish of residence(person)

while not in(residence(person), Netherlands)
while today
then
notify (Tax, Social Security) "The following people have resumed residence"
#administration number(person)

which would send the relevant message, with a list of the administration numbers of the relevant persons to the named departments. This formula is correct logically but poorly written from a technical point of view because it would search for all finishes of residence before selecting today's cases. If the formula were to be used in practice, one would start it with

if today ...

This illustrates the difference between typical logical and the physical aspects of information system design.

Example 2

A policy group in a ministry has requested a study to be carried out on young persons between 16 and 18 years of age, from broken marriages. A database of relevant individuals is needed. There is no problem of selecting the age group – the formula

(15 years < age(person) < 19 years)

will do that. More difficult is to find 'broken' marriages because 'broken' has to be defined. One possibility would be to include children who have experienced any family life without both parents. This might include

divorce or separation at any time during the child's life
loss of one parent during the child's life
living with one parent when the other lives at a different address.

Evidently, the researchers would arrive at some definition of the population they wish to study. For the above categories, the formulae selecting them are

dissolution(marriage(parent(person))) *while* person *before* (age(person) = 19 years)
finish of parent(person) *while* person
residence(person) *while not* residence(parent(person))

which can be combined with the age criterion and an instruction to file the relevant data-set:

((15 years < age(person) < 19 years)
while

(dissolution(marriage(parent(person)))) *while* person *before* (age(person)=19 years))
or while
(*finish of* parent(person) *while* person)
or while
(residence(person) *while not* residence(parent(person))))
then
file#Young Person Survey(register-entry(person *or* parent))

This may not be exactly what is required but, at least, it is unequivocal and it can be subjected to careful critical scrutiny. We could use it in an experiment on a slightly more developed version of the prototype to investigate some of the practical consequences of having a distributed system or having constraints upon the supply of certain items of information. The Young Person Survey file is intended to contain data on the parents as well as on the relevant children but this might mean having to retrieve from several other local authorities, and this opens up the technical problem of generating a cascade of requests to chase up the necessary data.

5   PRACTICAL AIMS OF THIS NEW ORIENTATION

MEASUR was conceived with some important practical aims in mind when the research leading to it began in the early 1970s. The work has taken a long time to reach maturity because it has entailed making the radical shift to a subjectivist paradigm described above. This shift was dictated by the practical goals of the research.

Restoring control of IT to management and other users was always a primary aim. The poor organisational returns on investments in IT were visible even in the early 1970s when the scale of computer power was so limited that only organisationally simple problems could be addressed. The prospect of a 10-fold improvement in computer power per decade made it clear that sooner or later our need to understand very large and complex business problems and state their information requirements would outstrip our ability to do so with the conventional tools and techniques. Since then the conventional approaches have been given a superficial updating by packaging them in CASE tools, but more radical improvements are needed if the users are to be *empowered* rather than dazzled by smart colour-graphic interfaces. One advance has been a development of concern for the 'soft' systems problems and a wider use of relevant tools (see Rosenhead, 1989, for example), but these have not been integrated with the solving of 'hard' systems problems. MEASUR is based on radically new principles, generates computer tools for users (not biased to software engineering) and integrates the solving of 'soft' problems with fairly 'hard' specifications.

To achieve this goal the business side of systems analysis has been stripped of all

IT elements by the strategy described above of using the concept of social norms to define an organisational information system. If the requirements analysis process is intrinsically devoid of a technical content, then there is no special reason for placing it under the control of the computer-oriented information systems department. Changing the institutional position of the analysts can then reduce the dependence of users upon technological experts with different values and culture. Expertise is necessary for using MEASUR, but it is expertise in management and organisation rather than in IT.

A related aim is the removal of the technological/rational imperative. When analytical methods are used to solve business problems they usually imply the introduction of increased rationality and formality into the way the organisation is run. This tendency is absolutely necessary if the selected aspects of the organisation are to be automated. But increasing automation is not always effective. The alternative is to strengthen the informal system. So MEASUR provides ways of recognising how to push back the frontiers of formality (bureaucracy) in favour of a more effective organisational culture. Incidentally, formality does not necessarily lead to automation. Manual, paper-based formal systems will dominate organisations for the foreseeable future. They may substitute imaging and text for paper to some extent. These conventional forms of systems have not received the same methodological attention as structured, computer-based systems. MEASUR does not draw this distinction so that it can be used to design conventional organisational systems as well as automated ones.

One special ambition behind the development of MEASUR has been to reduce the costs of development and maintenance. In the trials so far, this appears to be a major success. Where the requirements are thoroughly understood by the users and are formulated in great detail, with precise semantics, the core structures in the requirements definition remain remarkably stable and the natural modularity of the system allows the specification to be modified without continual wholesale reconstruction of the system. Translated into the computer system, this appears to be capable of reducing maintenance costs perhaps by a factor of five. Equally, the thoroughness of analysis seems able to slash implementation costs.

Increasing the power of computers continually extends the horizon of our ambitions. It becomes feasible in principle to tackle organisational problems that are ever larger and more complex. Problems of size and complexity are accompanied by problems of vagueness of structure and rapid change that are difficult to deal with using the conventional requirements analysis tools. MEASUR is intended to make it easier to exploit increasing computer power in these more difficult areas. The strategy has been to build specification methods that reduce complexity, identify the natural modularity of the systems, and give the users intellectual command over their own problems. MEASUR tackles these problems.

Also, by representing, in a formal way, the social norms that define how we want to run the organisation, we can translate directly from business requirements into a functioning computer system. The central problem addressed by MEASUR is not how to give software engineers sufficient information about the organisation to enable them to develop a computer system, it concerns the more important issue of how the users can understand the business problems thoroughly before any software engineering is contemplated and how they can express them unequivocally to the software developers. By providing the intellectual tools for these tasks, MEASUR empowers the users.

REFERENCES

Berger, P. L. and Luckmann, T. (1967). *The Social Construction of Reality*, Penguin.

Bloor, D. (1976). *Knowledge and Social Imagery*, Routledge & Kegan Paul.

Bloor, D. (1983). *Wittgenstein: A Social Theory of Knowledge*, Macmillan.

Bruijn, J. (1993). *Groups Empowered with Problem Articulation*, Graduation Report, TBK, University of Twente, Enschede.

Checkland, P. (1981). *Systems Thinking, Systems Practice*, Wiley.

De Millo, R. A., Lipton, R. J. and Perlis, A. J. (1979). Social processes and proofs of theorems and programs, *Communications of the ACM*, **22**(5) 271–280.

Gibson, J. J. (1968). *The Senses Considered as Perceptual Systems*, Allen & Unwin.

Gibson, J. J. (1979). *The Ecological Approach to Visual Perception*, Houghton Mifflin.

Goguen, J. A. (1992). The dry and the wet, in E. D. Falkenberg, C. Rolland and E. N. El-Sayed (Eds), *Information Concepts: Improving the understanding*, North-Holland.

Halliday, M. A. K. (1978). *Language as Social Semiotic*, Edward Arnold.

Hirschheim, R. and Klein, H. K. (1989). Four paradigms of information systems development, *Communications of the ACM*, **32**(10) 1199–1216.

Jones, S., Mason, P. and Stamper, R. K. (1979). LEGOL 2.0: A relational specification language for complex rules. *Information Systems*, **4** 28–48.

Kolkman, M. (1993). *Problem Articulation Methodology*, Proefschrift, University of Twente, Enschede.

Lakatos, I. (1976). *Proofs and Refutations,* Cambridge University Press.

Liu, K. Boekkooi-Timminga, E. and Liu, S. (1991). *Systems Analysis of a Computerised Test Construction System (CONTEST)*, EMIR Programme, University of Twente.

Liu, K. (1993). *The Application of Semiotics to Information System Development*, Proefschrift, University of Twente.

Michaels, C. F. and Carello, C. (1981). *Direct Perception*, Prentice-Hall.

Nauta, D. (1972). *The Meaning of Information*, Mouton.

Rosenhead, J. (Ed.) (1989). *Rational Analysis for a Problematic World: problem structuring methods for complexity, uncertainty and conflict*, Wiley.

Stamper, R. K. (1973). *Information in Business and Administrative Systems*. John Wiley & Sons, New York. (2nd edition in preparation, to be published by Blackwell).

Stamper, R. K. (1985a). Information: mystical fluid or a subject for scientific enquiry, *The Computer Journal*, **28**(2).

Stamper, R. K. (1985b). Knowledge as action: a logic of social norms and individual affordances, in G. N. Gilbert and C. Heath (Eds), *Social Action and Artificial Intelligence*, Gower Press.

Stamper, R. K. (1992). Signs, organisations, norms and information systems. *Proceedings of*

Third Australian National Information Systems Conference. (To appear 1994, in a modi-fied form in Andersen, B. *et al., The Semiotics of the Workplace.*)

Stamper, R.K., Liu, K., Kolkman, M., Klarenberg, P., Slooten, F. van, Ades, Y. and Slooten, C. van (1991). From Normbase to database, *International Journal of Information Management,* **11** 62–79.

Stamper, R. K. and Kolkman, M. (1991). Problem articulation: A sharper-edged soft systems approach, *Journal of Applied Systems Analysis,* **18** 69–76.

Six

Using domain knowledge in requirements capture and formal specification construction

David Bolton, Sara Jones and David Till
City University, London, UK
David Furber and Stewart Green
King's College, London, UK

1 INTRODUCTION

This chapter introduces an approach to requirements engineering which uses structured domain knowledge as a starting point for the development of formal requirements models.

A number of recent research projects have investigated the use of information or knowledge about a domain in creating specifications for new systems in that domain. Some of these projects are briefly reviewed in Section 2.

The approach described in this chapter is intended to be used by requirements analysts and clients working together to create precise formal specifications of the requirements for particular applications. Domain knowledge is structured around a network of interrelated application goals. Goals are encapsulated with fragments of theory which describe behaviour needed to realise those goals. Requirements models are developed by navigating the network to select, modify and compose appropriate theory fragments. A more detailed introduction to this approach is given in Section 3, and Section 4 presents a small example of its use in the hypothetical domain of rail ticket reservation systems.

Using an approach such as that proposed in this chapter should, it is argued, facilitate the process of formal requirements specification and yield benefits in terms of the completeness and consistency of specifications generated. These and other advantages are discussed in Section 5.

Requirements Engineering
ISBN 0–1238–5335–4

2   DOMAIN-BASED APPROACHES TO REQUIREMENTS ENGINEERING

In recent years, considerable attention has been focussed on the use of domain models in the requirements engineering process.

The utility of domain-based approaches to requirements engineering depends on a number of factors (Prieto-Diaz and Arango, 1991). Firstly, there must be a community of users who have a stake in finding software-intensive solutions to problems in a particular domain. At least some knowledge of the problems of the domain must already exist in an accessible form, and it must be possible to use that knowledge in developing software applications specific to the domain in which they will have to operate. It must also be assumed that information about the domain is worth collecting because it will be possible to reuse that information in constructing a number of applications. Empirical evidence supporting each of these assumptions is reviewed by Prieto-Diaz and Arango (1991).

A number of projects have investigated the use of models of, or knowledge about the domain in the process of specifying the requirements for new applications. These include Draco (Neighbors, 1984), the Taxis project (Greenspan et al., 1982), the Requirements Apprentice (Rich et al., 1987), IDeA (Lubars, 1988), KBRA (Czuchry and Harris, 1988), Analyst-Assist (Loucopoulos and Champion, 1988), KATE (Fickas and Nagarajan, 1988; Anderson et al., 1990), and KAOS (Dardenne et al., 1991a). A review of this work can be found in Bolton et al. (1992c).

The process by which domain models are produced is generally referred to as 'domain analysis' and entails an attempt to identify the objects, relationships and operations which experts perceive to be important in the domain. Different projects have defined the notion of a 'domain' in different ways, and have therefore adopted different approaches to constructing domain models. Our approach has most in common with those of KATE and KAOS, as we describe in the following section.

Most of the tools developed by the projects listed above assume that domain knowledge will, in the first instance, be manually encoded into a particular form by knowledge engineers. Each project assumes the use of a different notation for encoding domain knowledge. In IDeA, for example, domain knowledge is represented in terms of abstract design schemata describing functional specifications in domain-specific terms. In KATE, the domain model takes the form of a set of domain-specific policies or potential specification goals described using KATE's augmented version of the Petri net formalism. These constraints on the form of domain knowledge often restrict the nature of requirements specifications that can be produced. The domain models used on the Taxis project are, for example, aimed solely at the production of requirements specifications written in RML, a specialised Requirements Modelling Language. Our approach also assumes that domain knowledge will be manually encoded into an appropriate form, and we provide, at present, little support for this process. However, the structure for domain knowledge we propose is intended to be independent of any particular formalism or notation for requirements specification. We believe the relationships between components of domain knowledge we use will be useful in developing specifications in a range of notations (such as Z (Spivey, 1989), or Modal Action Logic (Maibaum, 1986)) of the kind already available for use by software engineers in formal system specification.

Many potential uses for domain knowledge in the process of requirements capture and analysis have been proposed. The most commonly cited of these are: provision of support for effective, domain-specific communication including the provision of user guidance and explanations (Barr *et al.*, 1991); provision of support for the reuse of specification components (Neighbors, 1984; Arango and Freeman, 1985); provision of support for specification by users unfamiliar with the domain (Barr *et al.*, 1991); provision of support for automated reasoning including consistency checking (Rubenstein, 1990; van Lamsweerde *et al.*, 1990; Arango and Freeman, 1985; Fickas and Nagarajan, 1988), completeness checking and automatic completion (Fickas and Nagarajan, 1988; Loucopoulos and Champion, 1988; Reubenstein, 1990; van Lamsweerde *et al.*, 1990; Czuchry and Harris, 1988), automatic refinement (Neighbors, 1988), analogy detection for reuse (van Lamsweerde *et al.*, 1990; Mirayala and Harandi, 1989), and formalisation of informal initial specifications (Loucopoulos and Champion, 1988; Reubenstein, 1990). In the following sections, we aim to demonstrate how our approach uses domain knowledge in a number of these ways.

3 USING DOMAIN KNOWLEDGE TO CREATE REQUIREMENTS MODELS

In our approach, a *domain* is defined to be a set of existing and potential *situated systems* associated with a common area of endeavour. Examples of domains include: resource reservation, flight ticket reservation, air traffic control, flight planning, stock control, temperature control, banking and cash dispensing. As can be seen from this list of examples, the notion of a domain may be applied at varying levels of generality: both resource reservation and flight ticket reservation are counted as domains, as are air traffic control and flight planning, and banking and cash dispensing.

The idea of a *situated system* includes that of a *system* and its *environment*. A *system* is defined as an existing or potential collection of related entities which interact in such a way as to achieve aims associated with a particular area of endeavour. The *environment* of a system consists of those further elements which directly provide inputs to the system and respond to outputs from the system but are otherwise free agents. Examples of situated systems in the domains listed above include: the Barbican Centre ticket office (resource reservation), London air traffic control (air traffic control), City University library (stock control), the Nat West bank on Upper Street, and the Nat West cashpoint on Upper Street.

Like other domain-based approaches, we assume that knowledge about domains can be captured, encoded and used in specifying the requirements for particular situated systems. As in projects described above, attention has so far been focussed on the way in which domain knowledge of the form proposed can be used in the process of requirements capture. No work has yet been done on providing support for the capture and representation of domain knowledge.

Our approach builds particularly on work by Anderson *et al.* (1990) and Dardenne *et al.* (1991b). Anderson *et al.* have proposed a model of the specification construction process which is based on the notion of an evolving 'development state'. A 'development state' is said to comprise two main components: a set of goals to be achieved, and an operational model which has been proposed for achieving them. Specifications are constructed by iteratively modifying and validating an evolving development state, until the client is satisfied both with the goals and with the operational model it entails.

The specification of system goals is also a feature of the approach proposed by Dardenne *et al.* (1991b). Here, however, high level system goals are progressively decomposed through various intermediate levels down to 'leaf goals' which may be 'operationalised' or characterised in terms of constraints specified with respect to well defined system actions and objects. It is understood that if a goal is decomposed into one or more lower level goals, it means that the achievement of one of the lower level goals is deemed to support or contribute towards the achievement of the higher level goal. Dardenne *et al.* also recognised that conflict might exist between goals.

As in the work of Dardenne *et al.*, our approach assumes that common high and low level goals of a domain may be discovered and incorporated into a network of domain knowledge together with the important relationships between them. For certain goals, it is also assumed that behaviour which would directly realise those goals may be determined and encapsulated with the goal, formally expressed as a theory (or theory fragment) in a specification formalism such as Z or MAL. Formal requirements specifications are intended to be developed incrementally, in a manner similar to that described by Anderson *et al.*, by traversing the domain knowledge network. These proposals will now be described in more detail.

3.1 Domain knowledge structure and content

We define *domain knowledge* to include a model of that domain, as well as domain-specific knowledge about how that model may be developed and specialised to the point at which it becomes a requirements model for a particular situated system in the domain.

Knowledge about a domain is structured around a network of nodes and links. Nodes contain natural language names and statements of common domain goals. Many nodes also contain fragments of formal specification defining behaviour which would realise the relevant goals. These nodes also contain natural language explanations of the meaning and significance of components of the specification.

Goal names consist of phrases or short sentences which characterise the relevant goals. In the context of a hypothetical library domain, examples of goal names might include 'maintain adequate shelf stock for population' and 'remind borrowers of overdue books'. Such meaningful goal names are intended to be presented to the analyst and client in order to permit the client to compare them with their own goals for an application. More lengthy *goal descriptions* may also be included to provide more information about particular goals.

Some goals are also associated with fragments of *theory specification.* These fragments comprise expressions, formulated in a well defined specification language, representing behaviour intended to realise the related goals. Not all goals are associated with such fragments of specification. In general, it is thought that higher level goals will tend not to be embodied by supporting theory. For example a hypothetical library domain goal 'promote book use in the community', would probably not be directly associated with enabling theory, while it seems more likely that a hypothetical lower level goal such as 'enable persons to borrow books' would be. Theory is accompanied by appropriate natural language explanations, which are intended to allow clients and analysts to understand and validate the theory and to see how the theory realises the goal. It is envisaged that further appropriate 'views' of the theory should also be provided, perhaps using data flow diagrams or statecharts (Harel, 1987). These should further facilitate validation of the formal theory components by the client.

Four types of relationship are used to link the nodes in the domain knowledge network: is_supported_by, is_undermined_by, may_be_specialised_by, and must_be_considered_before.

A relationship of type *is_supported_by* may be used to link nodes corresponding to pairs of goals when the achievement of one goal is deemed to be either completely or partially realised by the achievement of the second. The idea of using this relationship was suggested by the notion of partial goal satisfaction introduced by Robinson (1990) and the notion of goal reduction as used by Dardenne *et al.* (1991). Nodes linked by a relationship of this type may or may not contain fragments of specification theory. For example, in the context of a hypothetical 'resource reservation' domain, neither of the nodes involved in the relationship 'maximise resource utilization is_supported_by maximise access to resource for clients' is likely to contain specification theory. However, in the relationship 'maintain adequate shelf stock for population is_supported_by limit book loan period' in the context of a hypothetical library domain, it seems likely that the supporting goal will be associated with some theory, although the supported goal may not be.

A relationship of type *is_undermined_by* may be used to link nodes in a domain knowledge network when the achievement of the goal held in one is deemed to be completely or partially inhibited by the achievement of the goal held in the other. The idea of using this relationship was suggested by the existence of the kinds of conflicting goals recognised by Dardenne *et al.* (1991). Again, nodes linked by a relationship of this type may or may not contain fragments of specification theory.

The *may_be_specialised_by* relationship type may be used to link two nodes in a domain knowledge network when both nodes contain some specification theory, and the theory in one node specialises the theory in the other. The object-oriented sense of the term specialisation is intended here (Birtwistle *et al.*, 1973; Booch, 1991), and specialisation may be either of object types or of behaviour. An example of object type specialisation would be the specialisation of theory introducing the notion of borrowable resource to include theory introducing the notions of book, tape and compact disc, respectively. An example of behaviour specialisation in the context of a 'rail ticket reservation' domain would be the specialisation of theory intended to model the notion of paying for a ticket to describe different payment mechanisms relating to cash, cheque or credit card payments.

Finally, our experience to date has suggested that nodes in the domain knowledge network will sometimes need to be considered in a particular order. The domain knowledge network is, in general, intended to be constructed in such a way that depth-first, left-to-right traversal via the specialisation relationships will yield a sensible ordering on nodes, in that higher level goals will be considered before lower level specialisations, and closely related goals will tend to be considered together. It is intended that the client and analyst should, at some points, be free to disregard this ordering and to browse freely through the network. At other times, it will, however, be important that certain orderings on the nodes in the network be enforced. Theory in certain nodes will frequently use or refer to theory in other nodes, and in these cases decisions about whether one fragment of theory should be included in a client's specification will need to be made before decisions about other dependent theory can be considered. Relationships of type *must_be_considered_before* are intended to be used in such cases.

3.2   Creating requirements specifications

As described earlier, the approach to requirements specification proposed in this chapter is intended to be used by requirements analysts and client representatives working together to create formal requirements specifications. Domain knowledge of the form described above should support the process of specification in various ways.

Initially, both analysts and clients may consult a paper document containing textual representations of the nodes and links in the domain knowledge network. In this way, they may familiarise themselves with (or remind themselves of) the terminology used and overall form of the knowledge.

Later, when both parties are ready to begin constructing a specification of the client's requirements, they may turn to a computer-based tool embodying an electronic representation of the domain knowledge, and the capability to compose a formal specification based on the fragments of theory specification held in various nodes. Requirements specifications are created by browsing through the domain knowledge choosing just those components of theory which are appropriate for inclusion into a specification of the particular client's requirements. Clients are able to view the natural language names and descriptions of domain goals to determine whether those goals correspond to their own requirements. If they do, the corresponding fragments of theory may be selected for inclusion into an evolving specification. Decisions regarding the selection of particular fragments of theory are facilitated by consideration of the 'supporting' and 'undermining' relationships between goals in the network. These relationships may also be useful to the client in tracing the rationale for inclusion of particular goals or theory fragments.

It is recognised that theory held in the domain knowledge network will not always match perfectly with a client's requirements. It must therefore be possible for the analyst to modify theory to meet particular client needs before incorporating it into the specification. Several different kinds of modification may be needed. It might prove necessary, for instance, to strengthen or weaken constraints specified in some theory. It also seems likely that clients will often have their own way of naming data types and values; so another kind of modification might involve the replacement of given values for a datatype with new, client-specific ones. Clients may also wish to define mechanisms for achieving goals which are different to those specified in the domain knowledge network. For example, in the context of a hypothetical library domain, a goal related to sending reminders to borrowers about overdue books might be associated with theory specifying that a first reminder is followed at regular intervals by others, and then by a letter threatening court action. It is easy to imagine a client who requires an application to embody functionality corresponding to this goal, but wants the goal to be achieved by different behaviour.

Finally, it seems likely that clients will sometimes want to build applications for which some goals have not been anticipated in the domain knowledge network. It must therefore be possible to add theory to the evolving specification independent of any goals in the domain knowledge network. We believe that the framework provided by the domain knowledge will, in many cases, facilitate even the creation of new theory, by providing the analyst and client with templates which can be modified with relative ease.

4   AN EXAMPLE

This section describes part of a worked example which illustrates the ideas set out above. The domain of interest is that of rail ticket reservation systems, and we consider the case of a client who requires a system in that domain. Although this is really no more than a toy example, it demonstrates most of the properties which are currently of interest.

We first illustrate the structure of domain knowledge by setting out a representation of the overall structure and content of knowledge about the hypothetical domain of rail ticket reservation systems. Names and descriptions of some of the goals in the network are presented, together with corresponding fragments of theory specification where appropriate. (Because of limitations on space, it is not possible to present a complete description of the contents of all nodes in this chapter. A fuller description of the content of the domain knowledge network as well as an example of the kind of specification it can be used to create may be found in Furber *et al.*, 1992.) The way in which the network can be used to create a specification of a particular system is demonstrated in Section 4.2.

The formal notation used in this example is Z (Spivey, 1989; Potter *et al.*, 1991), and the aim is to show how a basic specification of requirements, written in Z, could be developed incrementally by adding fragments of specification selected by a client from the domain knowledge network. It is anticipated that the basic ideas embodied in our approach will be applicable in the construction of specifications written using various notations. Z-specific mechanisms for theory composition are therefore not used in this example. The intention is to illustrate what mechanisms are involved in evolutionary specification development of the kind proposed, independent of any particular notation.

4.1   Knowledge about the domain of rail ticket reservation systems

Part of the rail ticket reservation domain knowledge network is shown in Figure 1. The structure of the network as a whole is as described in Section 3. It contains examples of is_supported_by, is_undermined_by, and may_be_specialised_by relationships between nodes.

Orderings on nodes of the kinds described in Section 3 are also illustrated by this example. As stated above, the user will, in general, be expected to traverse a network in a depth-first, left-to-right order. The specialisation of basic types is intended to be done at an early stage, here during the traversal of the subtrees beneath nodes 1 and 2. Specialisation of functionality would take place later during traversal of subtrees 3 and 4.

Some of the orderings implied by the structure of this network are essentially arbitrary. It does not really matter whether specialisations of the passenger type (relating to node 2) are performed before or after those of the seat type (currently described under node 1). Similarly, it does not matter which of the specialisations of the cancellation facility (represented in nodes 4.1 and 4.2) is considered first. Other orderings are, however, more significant. Detailed specifications of a fare structure (of the kind represented in nodes 3.1.1 and 3.1.2) cannot be chosen until specialisations of the passenger and seat types (nodes 1 and 2) have been at least partially specified. Nor can the details of a cancellation policy, which may involve payment of refunds (see node 4.1), be properly decided upon until payment facilities have been considered (see node 3). These necessary orderings are represented using the must_be_considered_before relationship.

The following paragraphs describe the content of certain nodes in the network. The numbers and names of goals are printed in sans serif together with appropriate goal descriptions. Fragments of theory specification are shown indented. They are

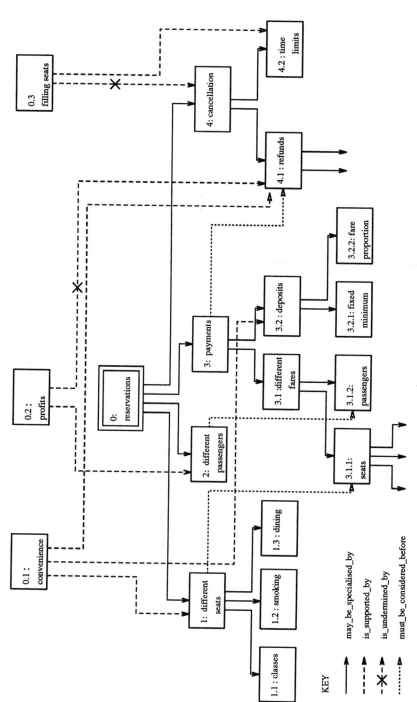

Figure 1 Part of the rail ticket reservation systems domain knowledge network.

surrounded by natural language explanations (also shown indented) of the meaning and significance of particular specification components. These explanations may be used by the client and analyst in validating fragments of specification. They are also intended to be included in the evolving specification whenever corresponding fragments of theory specification are selected, so that they can be used in the process of software development.

It may be noted that the core of the specification associated with the 'basic system node' (node 0) uses part of the 'Exclusive Resource' module of the general resource-user system specified in Flinn and Sorensen's (1993) paper on CAVIAR. The general sets T (Time slots), R (Resources) and U (Users) in that model are instantiated with sets of journeys, seats and passengers; it has been specialised by the addition of concepts such as those of scheduled trains and bookable seats, and some of the constraints in the original model have been expressed in different ways.

Ultimately, it would be useful to have a range of generic specifications such as CAVIAR available for use in domain knowledge construction. As in the present example, these generic specifications would be specialised to use domain-specific terms, and to define any further properties common to all systems in the domain. The development of more comprehensive support for the process described here would entail the construction of a range of such generic specifications.

4.1.1   High level goals

The example network contains three high level goals linked to other goals in the network by supporting or undermining relationships. For example, the goal of maximising utilisation of seats on trains (node 0.3) is shown to be undermined by the goal of permitting passengers to cancel reservations (node 4), but supported by the imposition of a time limit beyond which refunds were no longer given in the event of cancellation (node 4.2).

These high level goals are included in the network to assist clients in relating detailed and low level goals to their higher level organisational goals or policies. They are, however, not associated with any theory. Names and descriptions of the high level goals in the example network are given below (in sans serif).

0.1: convenience

The system should support maximum passenger convenience.

This is a high level goal which we might imagine to be appropriate to many client organisations in the hypothetical domain of rail ticket reservation systems. As can be seen from Figure 1, it is envisaged that such a goal will tend to be supported by the inclusion of distinctions between different kinds of seats (such as smoking and non-smoking – see node 1.2), and functionality which allows passengers to reserve seats on payment of a deposit rather than the full fare (node 3.2) and to receive refunds in the event of cancellation (node 4.1).

0.2: profits

The system should support the organisation in maximising its profits.

Again, this is a high level goal which we can imagine being appropriate to most client organisations. Such a goal might well be undermined by the provision of refunds on cancellation (node 4.1) but might be supported by the inclusion of a distinction between different kinds of passengers (node 2). It should, however, be noted that the degree of support in the latter case would depend on the nature of the client's policy regarding differential fares.

0.3: filling seats

The system should support the organisation in filling as many seats on its trains as possible.

This goal might tend to be undermined by the provision of facilities which allowed passengers to cancel reservations previously made (node 4). The degree to which it is undermined might, however, be lessened by the imposition of a time limit beyond which cancellation was not permitted (node 4.2).

4.1.2 The basic system node

It is, in general, intended that theory describing the basic functionality of any system in the domain should be held in a single node referred to as the 'basic system node' (shown as node 0 in Figure 1). The theory shown is all that is needed to specify the most basic of rail ticket reservation systems. If a client is satisfied that this simple specification forms a suitable basis on which to proceed, it may be selected to form the basis for the evolving specification. This basic specification may then be specialised by the addition of further fragments of theory selected from elsewhere in the domain knowledge network.

The basic system goal is set out below, with the relevant theory and explanation shown indented.

0: reservations

The system should support the organisation in permitting customers to reserve seats on trains making particular journeys.

Each seat on a train is assumed to have a unique identifier. The term $SEATID$ refers to the set of all such identifiers. The term $NAME$ refers to the set of all passenger names. $PLACE$ refers to the set of all stations at which trains either depart or leave. $TIME$ and $DATE$ refer to sets of times on a 24 hour clock and calendar dates respectively:

$$[SEATID, NAME, PLACE, TIME, DATE]$$

A point in time is defined to be identifiable by a time and date:

$$
\begin{array}{|l}
\_PointInTime _____ \\
Hour : TIME \\
Day : DATE \\
\hline
\end{array}
$$

There is a transitive relation *afterday* on the set of calendar dates, and a transitive relation *aftertime* on the set of times. A *PointInTime A isafter PointInTime B* if and only if the date of A is after the date of B, or the dates of A and B are the same but the time of A is after the time of B:

> $\_afterday\_ : DATE \leftrightarrow DATE$
> $\_aftertime\_ : TIME \leftrightarrow TIME$
> $\_isafter\_ : PointInTime \leftrightarrow PointInTime$
> ───────────────
> $\forall\, p1, p2 : PointInTime \bullet$
> $\quad p2\ isafter\ p1 \Leftrightarrow$
> $\quad\quad p2.Day\ afterday\ p1.Day$
> $\quad\quad \vee\ (p2.Day = p1.Day \wedge p2.Hour\ aftertime\ p1.Hour)$
> $.....plus\ other\ constraints\ to\ the\ effect\ that\ all\ three\ relations\ are\ total\ orderings$

The types *Seat* and *Passenger* are defined using easily extensible structures (since we are working with Z, we use schemas) so that they may later be specialised by the addition of further components and constraints (see, for example, node 2 in Section 4.1.3):

A seat on a train is defined in terms of its *Number*:

> ┌─ *Seat* ──────────────────────────
> │ $Number : SEATID$
> └──────────────────────────────────

A passenger is defined in terms of his or her *Name*:

> ┌─ *Passenger* ──────────────────────
> │ $Name : NAME$
> └──────────────────────────────────

A journey is defined to start and end at particular stations *From* and *To* and to depart and arrive at particular points in time, *DepTime* and *ArrTime*. The time of arrival must always be after the time of departure:

> ┌─ *Journey* ────────────────────────
> │ $From, To : PLACE$
> │ $DepTime, ArrTime : PointInTime$
> ├──────────────────────────────────
> │ $ArrTime\ isafter\ DepTime$
> └──────────────────────────────────

The term *scheduled* is used to refer to the set of trains scheduled to make journeys. For every train scheduled to make a journey, the function *bookable* identifies the set of bookable seats on that train:

> │ $scheduled : \mathbf{P}\ Journey$
> │ $bookable : Journey \nrightarrow \mathbf{P}\ Seat$
> ├──────────────────────────────────
> │ $scheduled = \mathrm{dom}\ bookable$

The seat reservation system *SeatResSys* is defined in terms of the function *reservations* which specifies that for each train scheduled to make a journey, some of the bookable seats will have been reserved by passengers. The function *reserved* identifies the set of seats which have been reserved on any scheduled train, and the function *passengers* identifies the passengers who have made those reservations:

$$
\begin{array}{|l}
\_SeatResSystem_____ \\
reservations : scheduled \rightarrow (Seat \nrightarrow Passenger) \\
reserved : scheduled \rightarrow \mathbf{P}\, Seat \\
passengers : scheduled \rightarrow \mathbf{P}\, Passenger \\
\hline
\forall j : scheduled \bullet \\
\quad reserved\, j = \mathrm{dom}(reservations\, j) \subseteq bookable\, j \wedge \\
\quad passengers\, j = \mathrm{ran}(reservations\, j)
\end{array}
$$

The initial state of the system is defined as a state in which no reservations have been made:

$$InitSeatRes \;\hat{=}\; [SeatResSystem' \mid \forall j : scheduled \bullet reservations'\, j = \varnothing]$$

The general notion of a change in the record of reservations resulting from an operation which takes place at a particular time (*now?*) and involves a particular *journey?* scheduled for some time after that is defined as:

$$
\begin{array}{|l}
\_Bookings_____ \\
\Delta SeatResSystem \\
journey? : Journey \\
now? : PointInTime \\
\hline
journey? \in scheduled \\
journey? \vartriangleleft reservations' = journey? \vartriangleleft reservations \\
journey?.DepTime\ isafter\ now?
\end{array}
$$

The booking operation is an operation of kind *Bookings* through which a *passenger?* reserves a *seat?*. In order for the operation to take place, the seat must be bookable but not already reserved. As a result of the operation, the relationship between the passenger and the seat is added to the set of reservations of which the seat reservation system has a record:

$$
\begin{array}{|l}
\_BookSeat_____ \\
Bookings \\
passenger? : Passenger \\
seat? : Seat \\
\hline
seat? \in (bookable\, journey?) \setminus (reserved\, journey?) \\
(seat? \mapsto passenger?) \in reservations'\, journey?
\end{array}
$$

It may be noted at this point that the operation *BookSeat* is the only instance of an operation of kind *Bookings* held in the basic system node. The general notion of making a change in bookings is kept separate from the notion of booking a seat so that the specification of a general change may be reused in defining other operations lower down in the network. For example, the notion of a general change in bookings also forms the basis for the definition of cancellation held in node 4.

4.1.3   Ordinary nodes

Further functionality which may commonly be required by particular clients is described in lower level components of the network which specialise descriptions of various aspects of the domain. The content of two of the lower level nodes in the example network is described below. The first of these nodes specialises a basic system type, and the second specialises the basic functionality defined above.

2: different passengers
The system should allow the organisation to distinguish between different kinds of passengers.

From Figure 1, we can see that this goal may support the high level goal of maximising profits, and that it must be considered before goal 3.1.2, which is concerned with charging different fares for different kinds of passengers. It may be selected by clients interested in either of these goals.

Two fragments of formal specification are held in node 2. The first provides a default definition of a new type which would be needed if the goal were selected:

A passenger may be either a senior citizen, a student, a railcardholder or none of these.

PassDescr ::= *seniorcitizen* | *student* | *railcardholder* | *standard*

Both the specification text and the accompanying natural language explanation can be edited if a different definition (for example, one which makes no distinction between students and other railcardholders) is required. It is then possible to include the edited version into the evolving specification in place of the default.

The second fragment of specification is concerned with augmenting the definition of the *Passenger* schema first introduced in the basic system node. If node 2 is selected, the line

Kind : *PassDescr*

must be added to the definition of type *Passenger*. The natural language explanation of the significance of the definition must also be amended, so we might have:

A passenger is defined in terms of his or her *Name* and *Kind* (see type *PassDescr*):

┌─ *Passenger* ────────────────────────────────
│ *Name* : *NAME*
│ *Kind* : *PassDescr*
└──

3: payments
The system should support the organisation in handling payments made for seat reservations.

Clients who wish their computer-based seat reservation system to handle information about payments for reservations may select this node. Associated fragments of specification are as follows.

Firstly, the domain knowledge provides a definition for a function *farecalc* which will be used to calculate the fare for any journey. By default, the fare is defined in a general way as being a function of the journey, seat and passenger in question. As with types *Seat* and *Passenger*, *farecalc* is defined using an easily extensible structure (here, an axiomatic description) so that it may later be specialised by the addition of further constraints:

Fares depend on the *Journey*, *Seat* and *Passenger* in question:

$$| \quad farecalc : Journey \times Seat \times Passenger \rightarrow \mathsf{N}$$

Secondly, if the goal in node 3 is selected, the definition of the basic system must be augmented to include notions of the organisation's current balance and of the fare paid for a seat on a scheduled train. This may mean adding the lines:

balance : **Z**
farespaid : *scheduled* → (*Seat* ↦ **N**)

above the line in schema *SeatResSystem*, and augmenting one of the constraints below the line. Assuming, for the purposes of illustration, that we started with the definition of *SeatResSystem* shown above (i.e. assuming that no other goals associated with specialisations of the basic system description had yet been selected), this would yield:

```
┌─ SeatResSystem ──────────────────────────────────────────────
│ reservations : scheduled → (Seat ↦ Passenger)
│ reserved : scheduled· → P Seat
│ passengers : scheduled → P Passenger
│ balance : Z
│ farespaid : scheduled → (Seat ↦ N)
├──────────────────────────────────────────────────────────────
│ ∀ j : scheduled •
│     reserved j = dom(reservations j) = dom(farespaid j) ⊆ bookable j ∧
│     passengers j = ran(reservations j)
└──────────────────────────────────────────────────────────────
```

Note again that the accompanying natural language explanation would also need to be amended.

A further associated fragment of specification concerns a specialisation of the initial state of the system. Assuming, once again, that no other specialisations had been requested since selection of the basic system node, the new version of the definition would be:

The initial state of the system is defined as a state in which no reservations or payments have been made:

$$InitSeatRes \; \widehat{=} \; [SeatResSystem' \mid \forall\, j : scheduled \bullet reservations'\, j = \varnothing \wedge farespaid'\, j = \varnothing]$$

Finally, some new theory to be added to the specification on selection of node 3 is as follows:

The general notion of a change in the record of reservations as a result of an operation which takes place at a particular time (*now?*), involves a particular *journey?* scheduled for some time after that and leaves the record of fares paid unchanged except for the particular journey in question, is defined as:

$$
\begin{array}{|l}
\underline{\;BookingsByPayment\;} \\
\;Bookings \\
\hline
\;\{journey?\} \lhd farespaid = \{journey?\} \lhd farespaid' \\
\end{array}
$$

The operation of booking by payment is an operation of kind *BookingsByPayment* through which a *passenger* reserves a *seat* by paying the *fare* for that seat on the relevant *journey*. In order for the operation to take place, the seat must be bookable but not already reserved. As a result of the operation, the relationship between the passenger and the seat is added to the set of reservations of which the seat reservation system has a record, the fare paid is recorded and the organisation's balance is increased by the relevant amount:

$$
\begin{array}{|l}
\underline{\;BookSeatByPayment\;} \\
\;BookingsByPayment \\
\;BookSeat \\
\;fare! : \mathbb{N} \\
\hline
\;balance' = balance + fare! \\
\;fare! = farecalc(journey?, seat?, passenger?) \\
\;farespaid'\,journey? = farespaid\,journey? \cup \{seat? \mapsto fare!\} \\
\end{array}
$$

Once again, *BookSeatByPayment* is the only instance of a *BookingsByPayment* operation shown here. The general notion of making a change in bookings and related payments is, however, kept separate from the notion of booking a seat by payment so that the specification of a general change may be reused, for example in specifying an operation involving cancellation and refund.

4.2   Selecting theories for the requirements specification

As suggested in Section 3.2, the analyst and client might typically begin the process of specifying requirements for a rail ticket reservation system by reviewing the domain knowledge network as a whole to gain an overall impression of the extent to which the client's goals match those represented. Both paper-based and electronic representations of the knowledge may be used. This process of joint review facilitates the development of an understanding of the domain which is shared by both the client and the analyst, and opens what should be an effective channel of communication between the two parties. The client may, through this process of review, also be prompted to consider goals which might previously have been overlooked. Early consideration of these goals increases the chances that the requirements model developed will be complete.

After spending some time on an overall review, the client and analyst may move on to consider individual nodes in more detail, selecting some nodes whose theory is to be included into the specification of the client's requirements and 'deselecting' others.

The first step of this stage will normally be to consider the basic system node. This is done in order to validate the theory it contains, or in other words, to ensure that it meets the basic requirements for the application of interest. In considering the node, clients are free to refer to descriptions of both the goal and the accompanying theory, and to examine either the theory specification itself or any available view on that specification. The client may also wish to modify the theory presented, though if the specification held in the basic node differs greatly from the client's basic needs, it may not be appropriate to proceed any further with that model of the domain.

Let us suppose, for the purposes of this example, that no modifications to the basic theory are required, and that the validated version of the basic theory is taken to form a basis for the evolving requirements specification. The next step is then to specialise the basic theory by selecting further fragments of specification from those held elsewhere in the network. In our example, the support tool may first lead the client and analyst to consider goals 1 and 2, which relate to the client's policy on distinguishing between seats and passengers of different kinds. Starting with node 1, let us suppose that the client wishes to distinguish between different classes of seat in the way described in node 1.1, and between dining and non-dining seats (as in node 1.3), but operates a no smoking policy on all journeys, and therefore has no need to be able to distinguish between smoking and non-smoking seats (node 1.2). The theory in nodes 1, 1.1 and 1.3 is in this case selected for inclusion in the evolving specification and that in node 1.2 is deselected.

Considering node 2, it may be noted that part of the theory does not match exactly with the client's requirements. If the client's organisation does not distinguish between students and other railcardholders, the definition of *PassDescr* must be changed from:

$PassDescr ::= seniorcitizen \mid student \mid railcardholder \mid standard$

to:

$PassDescr ::= seniorcitizen \mid railcardholder \mid standard$

before being selected for inclusion into the developing specification.

Let us suppose now that the client wishes to charge passengers for reserving seats and that the fare charged is to depend on the kind of seat booked and on the kind of passenger. The theory attached to node 3 relating to the provision of basic facilities for payment is added to the evolving specification. Node 3.1 (relating to the need to charge different fares under different circumstances) is also selected. This node contains no theory of its own, but its selection causes the nodes below it (3.1.1, 3.1.1.1, 3.1.1.2 and 3.1.1.3) to become available for selection. The client wishes to charge different rates for seats of different classes, but the same rates for dining and non-dining seats, and so selects nodes 3.1.1 and 3.1.1.1 but deselects node 3.1.1.3. (Note that node 3.1.1.2, which concerns charging different fares for smoking and non-smoking seats, is not presented to the client as an option at this stage since the goal of distinguishing between smoking and non-smoking seats – goal 1.2 – has already been deselected.) Finally, node 3.1.2 is selected to signify the fact that the the client wishes to charge different amounts for passengers of different kinds. The selection of this particular combination of the nodes below 3.1 results in an appropriate constraint being added below the line in the definition of *farecalc* held in node 3.

Further considering ideas related to the provision of payment facilities, the analyst and client move on to specify the fact that passengers are permitted to reserve any seat on payment of a fixed deposit, with the remainder of the fare being paid later. These ideas are modelled by the theory in nodes 3.2 and 3.2.1 which may therefore be incorporated into the evolving specification. Note here that as a result of selecting theory in node 3.2.1, theory in node 3.2.2 is automatically deselected as it is known to represent a policy which is incompatible with that described in 3.2.1.

Finally, the client considers the provision of facilities (described under node 4) which would permit passengers to cancel reservations made. The client is interested in providing such facilities, as the domain knowledge network shows that this would support the goal of maximising passenger convenience (node 0.1). The goal of maximising seat utilisation (node 0.3) is, however, undermined by permitting cancellation. To counteract this, the client decides to impose a limit on the time for which cancellation is permitted. Theory attached to nodes 4 and 4.2 specifies these requirements, and is therefore integrated into the specification. The client also decides to give a full refund on cancellation (as this further supports the goal of maximising passenger convenience), and selects node 4.1. Nodes below 4.1 in the network relating to the nature of the refund (not shown in Figure 1) may then be considered as well.

After fully traversing the network, it may become apparent that one of the client's goals has not been anticipated in the domain knowledge. If, for example, the client wishes passengers to be able to reserve sleeper seats, new theory must be added to the specification constructed in the manner described above. It is envisaged that theory held in the domain knowledge network may often act as a template for developing the new fragments of specification needed in such cases. Here, for example, theory held in nodes 1.1–1.3 might be used.

Owing to limitations on space, it has only been possible to give a small taste of our approach in this section. Readers are reminded that a fuller exposition can be found in Furber *et al.* (1992).

5   CONCLUSIONS

The approach to requirements specification described in this chapter has recently been embodied in a prototype support tool. The emphasis in the prototype is on simulating the user interface to a support tool of the kind described in Section 3.2. It has been built using NoteCards (Venue User Documentation, 1991), a hypertext tool, and the domain knowledge network is represented as a hypertext network which supports interactive browsing. Support for the selection and deselection of components of formal specification and for the generation of complete specifications has also been added. Initial trials with the prototype have used the domain knowledge network described above. Further information can be found in Bolton *et al.* (1992b).

Initial investigations into the use of the proposed approach in the domain of air traffic control have also been carried out (Bolton *et al.*, 1992a).

Experience with the prototype and with developing domain knowledge networks in both hypothetical and real domains suggests that the approach to requirements specification proposed may have the following advantages.

Firstly, the structured presentation of informally expressed domain goals is useful in permitting client representatives to understand and reason about the goals for their own applications in the broader context of the domain. Clients may find it easier to express their requirements by using informal domain goals as a starting point, and may also be prompted to state requirements they had forgotten, or had not previously considered. Specifications developed on the basis of such knowledge are therefore likely to be relatively complete. Requirements analysts, too, are likely to benefit from the existence of explicit and structured representations of domain goals: in particular, the existence of such domain knowledge might enable analysts to move more quickly between domains than would otherwise be possible.

Secondly, it is anticipated that it will be possible to reuse the components of formal theory in specifying any application with the relevant informal goals. Where theory components cannot be directly reused, they may still be used as templates to facilitate the creation of new theory to meet a client's requirements. Specifications constructed using fragments of theory which are known to be well-formed are more likely to be internally correct than those developed from scratch. Because of the formal nature of requirements specifications developed in the manner proposed, it will, in any case, be possible to check their syntax and logical consistency, and even to discharge formal proof obligations (Atkinson and Cunningham, 1991).

A number of concerns remain. Firstly, it is clear that the 'matching' of client requirements to components of formal theory is not trivial, and the goal-based approach described here does not entirely escape this problem. It is also not yet clear whether it will be possible to collect sufficient knowledge about large and complex domains to make the approach worthwhile. More than one formalism may be required to adequately express all behaviour in complex domains. In such cases, the method presented here would share problems of other approaches relating to the integration of pieces of theory expressed in different formalisms, in that mechanisms for integration are not yet well understood.

It is not yet clear whether the kind of incremental specification development which is a feature of our approach will always work safely; it seems at least possible that in some contexts adding new theory to an evolving specification – theory which references theory already in the specification – might produce undesirable or unintended effects. It is envisaged that the domain analyst or domain knowledge engineer should, in general, attempt to construct the domain knowledge in such a way that inconsistent specifications simply cannot be constructed out of the building blocks provided. The example presented in Section 4 is a very simple one, and it was therefore possible to construct the domain knowledge in such a way that most of the choices a user could make resulted in monotonic growth of the evolving specification. Even for such a simple domain, it was quite hard to construct the knowledge in this way. For larger and more complex domains, the task may be practically or theoretically impossible. Further research is needed to examine the way in which this problem might best be tackled.

While the selection of Z for use in our example is not intended to imply that Z is the only formalism with which our approach may be used, it does perhaps justify recording a few observations. First, it was noted that the schema inclusion mechanism, which allows the content of a schema to be assumed wherever the schema's name is written, is particularly useful for supporting incremental specification development. A further point concerns the methodology advocated by the Z community. In our example, we have only described normal (non-error case) behaviour of seat reservation systems. We have not dealt with the issues of invalid input to operations, or cases when those operations cannot be carried out; for example, we have not dealt with the case when a passenger wishes to reserve a seat on a journey but there are no seats available. A standard way to proceed when constructing a Z specification is first to describe the normal cases, then to compute the preconditions for each of the operations, so that the range of error cases is made manifest, and then to describe appropriate actions for those error cases. This idea could well be useful here, too; a first phase of domain knowledge traversal might be used to decide on the theory needed to describe normal operation, a second phase might be used to calculate preconditions for the operations selected, and a third might lead to descriptions of the kinds of action needed when error cases occur. One can well imagine that it might be possible to construct domain knowledge so that mutually consistent selections of desired theory could be added in to developing specifications. But since client requests can entail modification to theory fragments, it is unlikely that the domain knowledge could predict all possible error cases, and their corresponding actions, for all consistent selections. Even so, it seems that the domain knowledge network might have a useful role to play in providing a framework within which actions in error cases can easily be defined.

In summary, we claim that the structure for domain knowledge proposed provides a strong and useful bridge across the divide between informally and formally expressed requirements. We have shown how such a structure could be used to develop requirements specifications written in the Z notation and highlighted some advantages of the approach we propose. Some directions for further work have been identified.

ACKNOWLEDGEMENTS

Thanks are due to Professor Bernie Cohen and to Wing Lam for comments on earlier drafts of this chapter.

This research was carried out as part of the GMARC project which was jointly funded under the IED initiative by the Department for Trade and Industry and the Science and Engineering Research Council.

REFERENCES

Anderson, J., Fickas, S. and Robinson, W. (1990). *The Kate project: Supporting specification construction.* Technical Report CIS-TR-90-24, Department of Computer and Information Science, University of Oregon, Eugene, Oregon 97403.

Arango, G. and Freeman, P. (1985). Modeling knowledge for software development, *Proceedings of the Third International Workshop on Software Specification and Design*, IEEE Press.

Atkinson, W. and Cunningham, J. (1991). Proving properties of a safety-critical system, *Software Engineering Journal*, **6**(2): 41–50.

Barr, A., Cohen, P. and Feigenbaum, E. (1981). *The Handbook of Artificial Intelligence volume 4*, Pitman.

Birtwistle, G. M., Dahl, O.-J., Myrhang, B. and Nygard, K. (1973). *SIMULA Begin*, Student litteratur, Lund, Sweden.

Bolton, D., Jones, S., Till, D., Furber, D. and Green, S. (1992a). A generic modelling approach to requirements capture in the domain of air traffic control, in *Software in Air Traffic Control Systems – the Future*. IEE Digest number 1992/153. *Proceedings of a one day colloquium held by IEE Professional Groups C1 and E15.*

Bolton, D., Jones, S., Till, D., Furber, D. and Green, S. (1992b). *Prototype knowledge-based support for requirements elicitation*, Technical Report TCU/CS/1992/19, City University. GMARC Project Report R43.

Bolton, D., Jones, S. V., Till, D., Furber, D. and Green, S. (1992c). Knowledge based support for requirements engineering, *International Journal of Software Engineering and Knowledge Engineering*, **2**(2).

Booch, G. (1991). *Object Oriented Design with Applications*, Benjamin/Cummings.

Czuchry, A. J. and Harris, D. R. (1988). KBRA: A new paradigm for requirements engineering, *IEEE Expert*, Winter.

Dardenne, A., Fickas, S. and van Lamsweerde, A. (1991a). Goal-directed concept acquisition in requirements elicitation, *Proceedings of the Sixth International Workshop on Software Specification and Design*, IEEE Press.

Dardenne, A., Fickas, S. and van Lamsweerde, A. (1991b). *Goal-directed concept acquisition in requirements elicitation*, Technical Report CIS-TR-91-08, Department of Computer and Information Science, University of Oregon, Eugene, Oregon 97403.

Fickas, S. and Nagarajan, P. (1988). *Critiquing software specifications*. IEEE Software, November.

Flinn, B. and Sorensen, I. (1993). CAVIAR: A case study in specification, in I. Hayes (ed.), *Specification Case Studies* (2nd edn.), Prentice-Hall International.

Furber, D., Green, S., Bolton, D., Jones, S. and Till, D. (1992). *Using domain knowledge in requirements capture and formal specification construction*, City University technical Report number TCU/CS/1992/12 or King's College London, Department of Computing Technical Report number 92/04.

Greenspan, S., Mylopoulos, J. and Borgida, A. (1982). Principles for requirements and design languages: The Taxis project, in Y. Ohno (ed.), *Requirements Engineering Environments*, North-Holland.

Harel, D. (1987). Statecharts: a visual formalism for complex systems, *Science of Computer Programming*, **8** 231–274.

Loucopoulos, P. and Champion, R. (1988). Knowledge-based approach to requirements engineering using method and domain knowledge, *Knowledge-based Systems*, **1**(3).

Lubars, M. D. (1988). *Domain analysis and domain engineering in IDeA*, Technical report, Microelectronics and Computer Technology Corporation.

Maibaum, T. S. E. (1986). *A logic for the formal requirements specification of real-time embedded systems*, Technical report, FOREST Project, Department of Computing, Imperial College of Science, Technology and Medicine, London.

Mirayala, K. and Harandi, M. (1989). Analogical approach to specification derivation, *Proceedings of the Fifth International Workshop on Software Specification and Design*.

Neighbors, J. M. (1984). The Draco approach to constructing software from reusable components, *IEEE Transactions on Software Engineering*, **10**(5).

NoteCards Venue User Documentation (1991). *NoteCards User's Guide, Version 1.1*.

Potter, B., Sinclair, J. and Till, D. (1991). *An Introduction to Formal Specification and Z*, Prentice-Hall International.

Prieto-Diaz, R. and Arango, G. (1991). *Domain Analysis and Software Systems Modelling*. IEEE Press.

Reubenstein, H. B. (1990). *Automated Acquisition of Evolving Informal Descriptions*, PhD thesis, MIT AI Laboratory, Cambridge, MA 02139.

Rich, C., Waters, R. and Reubenstein, H. (1987). Toward a Requirements Apprentice, *Proceedings of the Fourth International Workshop on Software Specification and Design*, IEEE Press.

Robinson, W. (1990). Negotiation behavior during requirement specification. *Proceedings of the 12th International Conference on Software Engineering*, Nice.

Spivey, J. M. (1989). *The Z Notation: A Reference Manual*, Prentice-Hall International.

van Lamsweerde, A., Dardenne, A. and Dubisy, F. (1990). *KAOS knowledge representations as initial support for formal specification processes*, Technical Report 15, KAOS Project, Facultes Universitaires de Namur, Belgium.

Part Two

Seven

Requirements engineering as the reconciliation of social and technical issues*

Joseph A. Goguen†
Centre for Requirements and Foundations, Programming Research Group, Oxford University Computing Lab, Oxford, UK

1 INTRODUCTION

Much of the information that requirements engineers[1] need is embedded in the social worlds of users and managers, and is extracted through interactions with these people, e.g. through interviews and questionnaires. At its source, this information tends to be informal and highly dependent on its social context for interpretation. On the other hand, many representations that appear in constructing and using computer-based systems are formal, in that they are defined by the formal syntactic and semantic rules of computers and computer languages, so that their interpretation is relatively independent of social context. We suggest that both the formal, context insensitive, and the informal, socially situated aspects of information are crucial to the success of requirements engineering projects. Elsewhere, we have called these two aspects 'the dry' and 'the wet', respectively (Goguen, 1992b). Here, we suggest that requirements engineering has a strong practical need to reconcile them, and that this kind of reconciliation may be the very essence of requirements engineering. To this end, we suggest a new notion, the 'situated abstract data type', which joins the formal and informal aspects of information.

The need for progress in requirements engineering is acute: large projects have

* The research reported in this chapter has been supported in part by a contract from British Telecommunications plc, and grants from the Science and Engineering Research Council, and Fujitsu Laboratories.
† Written in part while on sabbatical at the Technical University of Nova Scotia, Halifax, Nova Scotia, Canada, with partial support from the Nova Scotia provincial government.

[1] A more traditional name for this rôle is 'systems analyst,' but we intend the name 'requirements engineer' to suggest an increasing importance, responsibility, and training for this profession.

an embarrassingly high failure rate[2]. Moreover, the requirements phase of a large system development project is the most error-prone, and these errors are the most expensive to correct (Boehm, 1981; Davis, 1990). Consequently, this phase has the greatest economic leverage. Unfortunately, it is also the least explored, and has the least satisfactory intellectual foundations. Therefore, it seems a promising area in which to invest research effort. The fact that the social issues at the root of many difficulties cannot be modelled by the usual technical methods suggests that novel approaches will be needed. Moreover, the immaturity of the field suggests that a willingness to be eclectic rather than dogmatic could be valuable. Consequently, we are exploring techniques from a variety of fields, especially ethnomethodology and discourse analysis, for analysing written texts, spoken language, and natural interactions in their social context. Section 2 reviews some of these techniques. Also, we use ideas from computing science and the sociology of science to help understand the formal aspect of requirements engineering. One outcome is some initial steps towards a social theory of information, as described in Section 2; another outcome is the situated abstract data type notion.

Sections 3, 4, 5 and 6 give examples to illustrate our approach. These are: the classification of system construction activities into so-called lifecycle 'phases'; a taxonomy for requirements engineering methods, using some ideas of Jean-François Lyotard on postmodernism; a value system for an organisation using some research on the structure of stories due to William Labov; and a conventional structure for a regatta, building on some work of Stephen Toulmin. Section 6 explains what abstract data types are, how they are specified, and what we mean by their being socially situated. A formal specification of the regatta abstract data type is given in the appendix. Some similarities and differences between these four examples are discussed in Section 7, explicating how some of their formal and informal aspects are related. We then draw some implications for requirements engineering.

2   TECHNIQUES FOR REQUIREMENTS ELICITATION

It can be difficult to find good data on which to base requirements. Experience shows that simply asking managers what they want often works poorly. They do not (usually) know what is technologically feasible, and they cannot accurately describe what their workers really do, what their clients really do, or even what they really do. This is not because managers are incompetent; on the contrary, they

---

[2] A 1979 study by the U.S. Government Accounting Office (1979) reported that 95% of funds spent in a sample of nine projects totalling nearly 7 million dollars did not result in a system that was actually used. Because the large organisations that commission large systems are understandably reluctant to release embarrassing information, it is difficult to obtain current data on this problem. However, there are indications that things may be somewhat better now, though still very far from ideal.

are (usually) genuine experts at their own job. Rather, it is due to what philosophers (Polanyi, 1967) call the problem of *tacit knowledge*, i.e. the phenomenon that people may know how to do something, without being able to articulate how they do it. Examples include riding bicycles, speaking languages, negotiating contracts, reconciling personal differences, and evaluating employees. One important reason for this difficulty is the social situatedness of the information involved.

However, to build a system that effectively meets a real business need, it may be necessary to find out what workers, clients and managers really do. But just asking workers what they do is subject to the same problems as asking their managers. Instead, if we really need this information, it would be best to go where the work is actually done, and carefully observe what actually happens. Various techniques from sociology and sociolinguistics seem promising for this purpose, and some of these are discussed later in this section; a more detailed exposition of these techniques with further comparison is given in Goguen and Linde (1993).

2.1 Ethnomethodology

Traditional sociology has been much influenced by what it considers to be orthodox science, where a scientist first formulates a theory, on the basis of which he makes predictions, which he then tests empirically. The aim is to achieve *objectivity*, in the sense that the desires and biases of the scientist cannot affect the conclusions. Hence, there is a rigid separation between subject and object, between observer and observed. Physics has already moved rather far from this kind of objectivity[3], and so it should not be surprising if sociology, and the social aspects of computing, had to go even further. In particular, if objective information is replaced by situated information, then the orthodox approach of formulating and then testing hypotheses objectively, for example through statistical sampling, will not be valid, because the random events observed can no longer be assumed to be statistically independent. However, statistical methods are the foundation for much of traditional sociology, for example, the design and evaluation of questionnaires. I do not suggest that statistics and questionnaires are never useful, only that they are *not always valid*, and in particular, that they should not be used in situations where context plays a significant rôle. (See Goguen and Linde, 1993, for a more detailed discussion of questionnaires and interviews.)

Ethnomethodology (Garfinkel, 1967) can be seen as a reaction against the 'scientific' methodology of traditional sociology. (More detailed discussion of ethnomethodology and science may be found in Sharrock and Anderson (1991) and Sharrock and Button (1991). Ethnomethodology tries to reconcile a radical empiricism with the situatedness of social data, by looking closely at how competent

---

[3] Penrose (1990) gives an elegant and readable exposition that illustrates just how strange the theories of contemporary physics can be.

members of a group actually organise their behaviour, and in particular, at the *categories* and *methods* that they use to render their actions intelligible to one another; this contrasts with presupposing that the categories and methods of the analyst are necessarily superior to those of members. The methods and categories of members are identifiable through the procedures by which members are held socially accountable by other members of their group. I like to describe this by saying that the analyst is used as a measuring instrument. Through experience, such an analyst gradually learns to pay attention to doubts and to hints of associations, and then follow them up with further questions. Through immersion in data from some particular social group (such as stockbrokers), the particular competencies are gradually acquired that enable the analyst to be a sensitive and effective instrument in that domain. In this way, subjectivity is harnessed rather than rejected.

One basic principle underlying ethnomethodology is that members are held *accountable* for certain actions by their social groups; moreover, exactly those actions are considered socially significant by those groups. A member performing such an action is always liable to be asked for an account, that is, a justification[4]. Let us call this the *principle of accountability*. From this follows the *principle of orderliness*, that social interaction is *orderly*, in the sense that it can be understood. This follows from the fact that the participants themselves understand it, because of accountability; therefore analysts should also be able to understand it, if they can discover the methods and categories that members themselves use to make sense of their interactions.

It is time to be more precise about what we mean by saying that social interaction is *situated*: we mean that the events that occur in some interaction can only be fully understood in relation to the particular, concrete situation in which they actually occur. The following list of *qualities of situatedness* (inspired in part by work of Lucy Suchman (1987) on plans) may help to further clarify this point:

1. *Emergent.* This refers to the claim that social events cannot be understood at the level of the individual, that is, in terms of individual psychology, because they are jointly constructed as social events by the members of some group through their on-going interaction.
2. *Local.* This refers to the claim that actions and their interpretations are constructed in some particular context, including a particular time and place.
3. *Contingent.* This refers to the claim that the construction and interpretation of events depends upon the current situation (potentially including the current interpretation of prior events). In particular, interpretations are subject to negotiation, and relevant rules are interpreted locally, and can even be modified locally.
4. *Embodied.* This refers to the claim that actions are linked to bodies that have particular physical contexts, and that the particular way that bodies are embedded in a context may be essential to the social interpretation of some events.

---

[4] Of course, this does not imply that such accounts are always, or even usually, requested by members of the group, or that they are necessarily given when requested.

5. *Open.* This refers to the claim that theories of social events (both those constructed by participants and by analysts) cannot in general be given a final and complete form, but must remain open to revision in the light of further analyses and further events.

6. *Vague.* This refers to the claim that practical information is only elaborated to the degree that it is useful to do so; the rest is left grounded in tacit knowledge. (This can be seen as a corollary of openness.)

I make no claims for the completeness of this list, let alone its superiority. On the contrary, it derives its plausibility from its general similarity to many other such lists. For example, qualities like these are familiar to anthropologists (e.g. see various comments in Lévi-Strauss (1964)); however, anthropologists have not (to my knowledge) been very precise in distinguishing among different qualities. Also, Suchman (1987) gives a rather similar list of qualities for plans.

Unfortunately, ethnomethodology can be difficult to understand; however, relatively comprehensible expositions of certain points have been given by Jirotka (1991), Levinson (1983), Suchman (1987) and Goguen and Linde (1993). Conversation analysis grew out of ethnomethodology through the work of Sacks on how speakers organise such details as timing, overlap, response, interruption, and repair in ordinary conversation (see Sacks *et al.*, 1974; Sacks, 1992). Interaction analysis extends conversation analysis to include video data, particularly in institutional settings. (See Goodwin and Heritage, 1990, for a recent overview of conversation analysis, and Kendon, 1990, for a collection of essays on and applications of interaction analysis.) All these fields are strongly empirically based. Typical projects can involve hundreds of hours of work in recording, transcribing and analysing data. In these approaches, it is important to use 'naturally occurring' data, collected in a situation where members are engaged in activities that they regularly and ordinarily do; otherwise, the basic principle of accountability will not apply, and we cannot be sure that events in the data have any natural social significance. For example, data collected from interviews cannot be used (unless one wants to study what happens in interviews!).

Although it is not usual in the literature of ethnomethodology, a distinction between the methods and categories used by members and those used by analysts can help to clarify the social status of requirements objects. Analysts often use categories and methods that members of the group they are studying do not use. For example, analysts of a telecommunications system may want to accumulate statistics on calls, even though these statistics would be incomprehensible to most of those making the calls. In fact, analysts form groups that have their own distinct cultures, with their own categories and methods, and it is necessary to evaluate their actions from this perspective. Nevertheless, analysts can often benefit from knowing the methods and categories of members, particularly when they want to understand something that members regularly and ordinarily do themselves, as is often the case with requirements engineering.

I believe that ethnomethodology provides useful general guidelines for how to collect high quality data about social interaction, and that conversation and interaction analyses embody these guidelines in ways that are directly applicable to many problems in requirements engineering. However, it is far from the only way to elicit requirements, and it is not the best method for all circumstances. (Further discussion of these issues, with examples, may be found in Goguen and Linde, 1993.)

2.2   Discourse analysis

Although natural language is often criticised, e.g. by advocates of formal methods, for its informality, ambiguity and lack of explicit structure, these features can actually be advantages for requirements. For example, these features of natural language can facilitate the gradual evolution of requirements, without forcing too early a resolution of the conflicts and ambiguities that may arise from the initial situation; it is important not to prejudge the many tradeoffs that will have to be explored later on, such as cost *versus* almost everything else, including speed and functionality. Also, natural language, possibly supplemented by graphics, is often the medium preferred by the individuals who represent the client. And finally, natural language can permit the 'diplomatic' resolution of conflicts through the careful construction of deliberate ambiguities; for example, this is rather common in large government financed projects.

There is a growing body of evidence that natural language is far more structured than most people realise, and that discourse structure carries much important information about what is being described. For example, work by Abbott (1983), and by Enomoto, Horai and others (Saeki *et al.*, 1987) shows that the nouns and verbs used in stating requirements can provide important clues to an object oriented design for the system. In particular, the nouns give clues about classes and their attributes, and the verbs give clues about methods. Syntactic structure can also indicate relationships of inheritance and clustering. However, one cannot expect to find mechanical algorithms that will always do such analyses reliably, in part because of the importance of context.

According to the principle of accountability, a member of some group who tells an informal story must establish to the audience the relevance of the actions reported. The classic case, studied by William Labov (1972), is the narrative of personal experience, where the narrator is an agent in the story. The most typical way to accomplish accountability is to include specific *evaluative material* within the body of the story that relates the *narrative material* to shared social values. It may be surprising that values are an integral part of the internal structure of stories, rather than being confined to an optional summary 'moral' at the end. But in fact, naturally occurring stories embody evaluative material in many complex and subtle ways, and its syntactic placement can be a significant clue to its importance.

To further explain and illustrate these ideas, let us analyse a simple story. The nursery rhyme that we use is not, strictly speaking, a naturally occurring spontaneous story, let alone a narrative of personal experience, as studied by Labov (1972). However, it is often read, or repeated from memory, to children in natural social settings, and thus an analysis of the values in it should tell us something about what our society teaches its children. Our analysis will be somewhat sketchy, omitting many details of argument; otherwise, it could be rather tedious to read. Here is the text:

> Jack and Jill went up the hill
>   to fetch a pail of water;
> Jack fell down and broke his crown,
>   and Jill came tumbling after.

> Up Jack got, and home did trot,
>   as fast as he could caper,
> Jill put him to bed and plastered his head
>   with vinegar and brown paper.

(The second verse is one among several variations; see Opie and Opie, 1951, for this and other background information.) The first line is a straightforward narrative clause, recounting an action in the narrative past tense, while the second line is an evaluative clause, giving a reason for the action of the first clause. The third and fourth lines give further narrative clauses (there are two in the third line).

A very basic feature of narrative is that the order of narrative clauses is taken as the order of the events that they report, unless some trouble is taken to indicate otherwise. Thus, in the first verse, they first went up, then Jack fell down, then he broke his crown, and then Jill came tumbling after. This basic principle is called the *narrative presupposition*. Note that it is a convention, and *not* a necessary feature of narratives; for example, Becker (1979) shows that in Balinese narratives, if no special care is taken then the events reported in a sequence of narrative clauses are taken as occurring *simultaneously* rather than sequentially[5].

Now that we know ordering is significant in English narratives, it is interesting to notice that Jack always comes before Jill. As far as the semantics is concerned, this ordering would not matter in the first line, but because it is part of a general pattern, we can consider it to be an evaluative feature of the narrative. (Note the delicacy, and not quite water-tight quality of this argument; rigorous proofs are impossible in this area.)

What can we now conclude? I think we may conclude that water is important to this (somewhat mythical) culture, and that males are more important than females in it.

This need not be the end of the analysis (although further elaboration might push the limits of tedium): one could get some further results by using the so called *causal presupposition*, which says that, other things being equal, given clauses in the order A, B, we may assume that A causes B. (For example, ''You touch that, you gonna die.'') The reader may wish to follow up this remark as an exercise. As

---

[5] A computing scientist might say that the default connective for a narrative sequence in English is sequential composition (';'), whereas in Balinese it is parallel composition ('||').

before, it is not so much a matter of *proving* something, or of *extracting the truth*, as it is of uncovering a resonance of the text with a possible interpretation. Any such analysis is contingent, local and open; moreover, it is best done in a group, so that the analyst is accountable to other analysts, in which case the analysis itself becomes emergent and embodied at that level. Nonetheless, any such interpretation can be considered to be some part of the meaning of the text; of course, each interpretation will seem more cogent to some analysts and groups than others, and some may seem dubious to most.

Work by Goguen and Linde (1978, 1981) shows that information extracted from naturally occurring instructional discourse can often be translated without much difficulty into dataflow diagrams of the kind used in structured design methodologies, such as those of De Marco (1978) and Yourdon (1989); nevertheless, there are questions about how such translations can be justified. Other research by Goguen, Linde and colleagues (1978, 1983, 1983a, 1984) shows that plans, explanations, directions, and other everyday types of discourse have a high level structure that relates directly to their social and semantic domains. What is called 'command and control' discourse (Goguen and Linde, 1983) seems especially relevant to requirements engineering, because its analysis can be used to reveal the structure of tasks unfolding in real time. Unfortunately, the data on which these structural theories of large grain discourse were based was not collected with the rigour of ethnomethodology (see Jirotka, 1991); nevertheless, we hope that a more careful ethnomethodological study might support at least some aspects of such theories.

2.3   Towards a social theory of information

If we knew more about what information is, and how it is used, then we might be in a better position to improve the practice of requirements engineering. This subsection presents what may be some initial steps towards a social theory of information. Objective and quantitative theories of information, such as the statistical theory of Shannon and Weaver (1964), as well as objective but qualitative theories, such as the situation semantics of Barwise and Perry (1983), are not adequate for our purpose. Although each may illuminate certain aspects of information, neither considers the social processes that create and sustain information through interpretation and negotiation. Shannon's theory is unable to take account of the meaning of information, even in the narrowest technical sense, and neither theory can explain how information can vary in its degree of context dependence, while remaining thoroughly situated. Discourse analysis provides one approach to such questions; this section discusses some other approaches that go even further in reconceptualising context.

2.3.1   Sociology of science

The study of the sociology of science is an important new development. One exciting voice in this field is Bruno Latour, who has identified certain properties that distinguish the work of scientists from other kinds of work (Latour, 1987). Latour introduced the phrase *immutable mobile* for a representation that can be interpreted in (what counts as) the same way in a variety of contexts; thus, immutable mobiles are information structures that have been (at least partially) dried out. These structures are frequently what Latour calls *re-representations*, which are representations that have undergone some form of concentration; for example, a large set of observations of planetary motion might be summarised by a single equation. Latour claims that the qualities of immutability, mobility and concentration are characteristic of the information that occurs in the discourse of science.

It would be interesting to take a similar approach to the study of information more generally, viewing Latour's work as exploring the special case of scientific information; this is because computing science must deal with information from a wide variety of fields other than science, such as commerce, government, law and literature, e.g. in designing information systems. It also seems promising to apply techniques from ethnomethodology to the information in computer-based systems. Work that may help point the way has been done by Eric Livingston (1987), showing the lived work involved in mathematical proofs. There are also ethnomethodological studies of several other aspects of science, and such an approach might help provide a richer empirical foundation for research in the sociology of science.

2.3.2   Dry and wet information

I suggest that *information* is distinguished from *mere signs* by the existence of a social group that can be held accountable for its appropriateness[6]. Signs, in the sense of semiotics, are configurations that do not necessarily have significance, so that 'mere signs' have no significance. But this is only a theoretical possibility, because the very notion of sign as configuration presupposes that a classification system for configurations has already been pre-selected (e.g. a certain character set), and because this classification system must be known to someone, it will impart to its signs at least the significance of its being known to be part of this system.

We can further distinguish information that can be understood in a wide variety of contexts from information that is so thoroughly situated that it cannot be understood except in relation to very particular contexts. We call these types of information *dry* and *wet*, respectively, following Goguen (1992b). Of course, there is really a continuum of intermediate cases, e.g. 'damp' information, such as cookery recipes. In general, information cannot be fully context sensitive (for then it could only be understood when and where it is produced) nor fully context insensitive (for then it could be understood by anyone at any time). A fairly extreme case is the 'raw data' collected in a scientific experiment; although it may be just a collection of numbers, it is very highly situated, because those numbers only make sense to a very small group who share a very particular context. On the other hand, an

---

[6] This is intended as a distinction that may be useful in practice, rather than as a metaphysical assertion about the nature of information.

equation that summarises the numbers is relatively more dry, and a physical law is even drier. It is important to notice that information, however dry, must still be interpreted in some local context. Therefore, the qualities of situatedness in Section 2.1 apply to information; that is, information is always emergent, contingent, local, embodied, open and vague. This has important implications for requirements engineering, in suggesting what we can reasonably expect from requirements documents, as opposed to the unattainable ideals of positivist philosophers.

These considerations suggest that formalisation may be a key technique for making information drier. Let us call this the *formalisation hypothesis*; several illustrations of it are given in the following sections. We can also relate this point to the immutable mobiles described by Bruno Latour (1987), which are distinguished by the possibility of their being interpreted in what counts as the same way for practical purposes in a variety of contexts. Latour discusses the example of cartographic maps: given the proper instruments and good weather, such maps can be used anywhere in the world; but each use is still a local interpretation. As Latour notes, immutable mobiles are often constructed by concentrating previously available information; this is a form of abstraction. But I wish to point out that there are other forms of abstraction; for example, a database can provide easy access to a large body of information through various search techniques, without actually compressing it in any way.

Latour also notes that the construction of immutable mobiles can be a way to mobilise support, by compressing large amounts of information into simple graphical representations; then anyone who wishes to disagree must mobilise the resources to represent and compress comparable amounts of information. The use of dataflow diagrams in requirements meetings seems to provide good examples of this phenonmenon. In general, the use of dataflow diagrams is beyond the capabilities of users and managers, in part due to the huge volume of information involved in large projects. Moreover, requirements engineering has recently developed special tools to help collect and organise large volumes of requirements information. One class of tools organises information about designs on selected requirements issues. For example, the gIBIS tool (Conklin and Bergman, 1988) is organised around issues, positions and arguments. These tools are based on normatively given presuppositions about the way that projects should be organised. Moreover, it is difficult for ordinary users and managers to use such tools themselves.

Information systems seem a particularly interesting site for research. Such systems are repositories for immutable mobiles, and increasingly they provide the means for producing new immutable mobiles, for transporting them into new contexts, and for further concentrating and summarising information. This means that they can be sources of power. Consequently, the design of an information system is a natural occasion for power struggles, and it is important that the human interests of all stakeholders should be recognised and protected; Boland (1991) describes an interesting case study that illustrates the importance of power struggles in understanding organisations. The failure to take account of such factors explains why many large information systems have not worked well in practice.

Leigh Star (1988) has introduced the term 'boundary object' to describe objects that are used in different ways by different social groups. For an information system to be successful, it must often serve different social groups in different ways, and so I suggest that research on boundary objects might be usefully applied to information systems. For example, the notion of a *view* in that field already reflects the idea that it may be useful to present information in different ways to different users. Similarly, a requirements document must serve a number of different stakeholders, and thus may need to incorporate multiple views (Finkelstein *et al.*, 1990). The work of Latour is also very relevant to these issues.

2.3.3   Interpretation versus representation

It is perhaps worth digressing briefly to contrast the view of information and meaning that has been suggested above with the *representational theory of meaning* that is considered more or less standard in computing science and more generally in the Anglo-American analytic tradition of philosophy.

According to our social theory of information, meaning is the on-going achievement of some social group; it takes *work* to interpret some signs so that they can be seen as information, and interpretation necessarily occurs in some particular time and place. By contrast, a representational theory of meaning claims that a meaningful configuration of signs *represents* something in the real world. In sophisticated representational theories, such as situation semantics (Barwise and Perry, 1983), what is represented by (say) a given phrase of English can vary with context, and need not be a simple object, but can be a complex relationship, such as a situation. This may be quite adequate for some purposes. However, even the most sophisticated representational theory leaves out the work of interpretation and the social accountability that goes with it.

2.4   Case studies

The Centre for Requirements and Foundations at Oxford is now involved in some case studies to test the practical application of techniques of ethnomethodology and interaction analysis to requirements engineering. One project, led by Marina Jirotka, involves the analysis of video tapes of stockbrokers at work, supplemented by ethnographic interviews, including feedback from the brokers on our interpretations of selected video clips. Another project will involve videotaping interviews conducted by requirements engineers, as well as their internal working sessions, in order to explicate their work practices, and suggest ways to improve requirements elicitation and analysis; the target domain here is software for multimedia communication.

Sections 3, 4, 5 and 6 give examples that illustrate some of the issues that arise in trying to reconcile the formal context insensitive with the situated social aspects of information. Although each example organises some data into what computing scientists call a tree structure, each structure is situated in its social context in a different way, as discussed in Section 7.

3   THE SITUATED LIFECYCLE

The *lifecycle* of a system is often considered to have a number of *phases*. There is no universal agreement on what these are, and in fact, their number, names and boundaries are somewhat vague and arbitrary. However, it seems that activities of the following kinds may be roughly distinguished with some consistency:

1. *need*, in which the desirability of a certain kind of system is identified at an executive level;
2. *requirement*, in which properties that the system must satisfy in order to succeed in its context are determined;
3. *design*, in which a rough architecture of the system is determined, e.g. as a block diagram of its major components;
4. *specification*, in which the behaviour of the components is described;
5. *construction*, in which the components are actually built, and then assembled to form the system;
6. *validation*, in which the resulting system is tested against its specifications;
7. *deployment*, in which the system is installed in its target environment; and
8. *maintenance*, in which the system is continually modified, upgraded and debugged.

In the so-called *waterfall model*, these (or similar) phases must be enacted in exactly the indicated order, as shown in Figure 1. However, experience with real projects shows that there is no such orderly progression from one phase to the next; instead, there is a continual projection forward and backward. For example, the client may perceive a new need (or reassess an old one), or an implementer may perceive a new opportunity (or impossibility); also, prototypes can suggest changes in requirements, specifications, etc. In fact, at least in successful large projects, the phases are constantly overlapping, and many actions and events are difficult to assign to phases. However, this is precisely what Suchman's (1987) work on plans should lead us to expect, because lifecycle models are actually plans. As Suchman points out, plans serve as resources for action, rather than as rigid programs for future action. Hence, actual lifecycles are contingent, emergent, local and open, and so their relationship to models of the software process will necessarily be problematic. But we might also note that because they abstract relevant prior experience, lifecycle models are also (partially) immutable mobiles.

The waterfall model has been widely criticised, and many so-called *process models* have been proposed as alternatives. Even so, the nature and limitations of

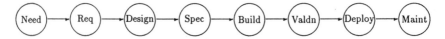

Figure 1   Information flow in the waterfall model.

such models do not seem to have been widely appreciated. For example, they still assume a division into phases. However, as the chapter by Button and Sharrock in this volume shows, a real project in a commercial environment may well have to deliver code before completing requirements. Also, McDermid's chapter argues that some high level design is often needed in defining requirements. It follows that rigidly following a fixed process model can severely limit adaptation. One very pernicious factor is procurement procedures that try to rigidly separate phases with contractual barriers in the name of competition; this approach fails to provide system developers with the on-going access to users that is often necessary for success.

The belief that lifecycle phases should be enacted sequentially follows from the myths that there is a more or less unique best system to be built, and that its construction can be controlled in a top-down hierarchical manner (Goguen, 1992a, discusses these and some related myths of system development).

Similarly in the requirements phase, it seems to be widely believed that there is some unique best model of the organisation and its needs. However, requirements are *emergent*, in the sense that they do not already exist in the minds of clients or requirements engineers (or anywhere else); instead, they gradually emerge from interactions between requirements engineers and the client organisation. Moreover, requirements are *open*: they are always subject to change, because organisations and their contexts continually change. Requirements are also *local*, in that requirements documents must be interpreted in the context of a particular organisation at a particular time. (For example, I conjecture that if you have not yet read the background material in Section 6 and the Appendix, then you will have difficulty in understanding Figure 6 on page 182.) Moreover, they are *contingent*, because they are an evolving outcome of an on-going process that builds on prior interactions and documents.

It is interesting to note that most of the effort for typical large systems goes into the maintenance phase. Some advocates of formal methods have argued that this is because not enough effort has been put into being precise in earlier phases, particularly specification. However, I believe a deeper reason is that much more is going on during so-called maintenance than is generally realised. In particular, reassessment and re-doing of requirements, specification, and code, as well as documentation and validation, are very much a part of maintenance; thus, the maintenance phase may contain smaller versions of the complete lifecycle. It therefore seems likely that problems with requirements will be a significant part of the maintenance cost, so that methods that help with requirements will also help with maintenance. Similar considerations apply to other phases, but perhaps less dramatically.

3.1   The principles of volume and inertia

Large systems seem to raise special problems because of the huge volume of information that they can produce, sometimes literally roomfuls. Consequently, special attention must be paid to the management of this information. Let us call this the *principle of volume.* Actually, it can be argued that no genuinely new problems arise for large systems, but rather it is merely necessary to devote considerable attention to issues that are trivial for small systems. These issues include version and configuration management for requirements, specifications, code, documentation, process requirements, standards, test data, financial data, as well as appropriate links among these.

A closely related principle may be called the *principle of inertia.* It says that the larger the volume of information involved in a system development effort, the more difficult it will be to make changes. For example, this principle can explain why large systems are often already out of date when they are delivered, why large organisations usually evolve slowly, and also why languages evolve slowly.

Perhaps it is misleading to dignify these observations with the title 'principle' because they are really only heuristics that may, in some circumstances, help in formulating an initial understanding of certain situations. Actually, this applies, to a greater or lesser degree, to all of the principles that we have formulated: they are intended as guidelines for practical action, rather than as metaphysical pronouncements about the nature of reality, or the nature of research. Notice that the proponents of particular methods may take a very different attitude to the principles that they claim underlie their methods.

3.2   The retrospective character of requirements

I wish to claim that the classification of events and objects into lifecycle phases makes the most sense retrospectively: from the viewpoint of some relatively stable state of a given system, one can determine the needs that it serves, the requirements that it meets, the design that it realises, etc. In general, such a retrospective reconstruction will have to delete or revise some of the original requirements, and add some new ones, in order to achieve the *traceability* of decisions back to some coherent basis in requirements objects. That is, a lifecycle only makes sense retrospectively, because only when one knows how the system works in its context can one tell whether particular events are important or trivial, successful or disastrous. In many projects, the work required to achieve a retrospective reconstruction is never done, and by the time the system is deployed (if it is), all that remains of the requirements process may be some colourful stories. (This is explained by the principle of volume.)

Another basic principle of a social theory of information may be an extension of Suchman's (1987) work on plans to the broader claim that only our *post hoc* explanations for situated events appear to attain relative stability and independence from context; let us call this the *retrospective hypothesis.* Support for this principle can be found in the empirical work on plans and explanations reported in Linde and Goguen (1978) and Goguen *et al.* (1983), as well as in the work of Suchman.

In particular, the interpretation of requirements, indicating whether or not they have been successfully met, is the outcome of a complex social process that typically involves negotiation and retrospective reconstruction; it may even involve legal action. Therefore, in many situations it can be quite misleading to think of requirements as pre-given; but of course, this does not hold for all situations. More radically, it may sometimes be useful to think that causal sequences, and in this sense, even time itself, are determined retrospectively, by the interpretations that we put upon events.

Software engineering has developed process models that are more flexible than the waterfall model, such as the 'spiral' models of Boehm (1986). However, we can predict that following any process model too rigidly will lead to difficulties, because one cannot really be certain where one is in the lifecycle except retrospectively. In particular, it will be impossible to say with certainty what the requirements are, let alone whether or not they are met, until the system is actually in place and running.

4   A CLASSIFICATION OF REQUIREMENTS METHODS

One project at the Centre for Requirements and Foundations at Oxford had as its goal to classify and evaluate existing requirements methods[7] and tools in an unbiased way; this is important because of the often exaggerated claims by vendors of the many competing methods and tools that can be found in the marketplace. This project is exploring the hypothesis that each requirements method has its own, usually unarticulated, theory of organisations, which is therefore an implicit sociological theory. From this it follows that a good classification of sociological theories would provide a good basis for classifying requirements methods.

We found a useful starting point in the work of French philosopher Jean-François Lyotard (1984). His scheme first distinguishes between (what he calls) *modern* and *postmodern* theories of society; a modern theory relies upon a so-called *metanarrative*, or 'grand unifying story', to legitimate its claim to universality. Modern theories are further divided into (what we call) *unitary* and *dual* theories. Unitary, or *systems* theoretic, approaches assume that there is some unique pre-existing 'real system' to be 'captured'. *Dualistic,* also called *critical* or neo-Marxist, approaches assume that the most important feature of an organisation is a split along class lines, for example, between workers and managers.

Lyotard's (1984) definition of postmodernism says that societies are composed of many 'local language games' that cannot necessarily be unified, or neatly divided into parts. Many other notions of postmodernism appear in the literature, some of which seem very superficial. Lyotard's definition appeared relatively early, and has some substantial content, being inspired by ideas from Wittgenstein's late period. In general, the word 'postmodern' seems to have been overworked.

---

[7] What we call 'methods' are often called 'methodologies' by practitioners. But in an academic context, the word 'methodology' should properly be used for the study and comparison of methods, and that is how it is used in this chapter.

We[8] have modified Lyotard's taxonomy, first by subdividing the *unitary* class into *hard* and *soft* subclasses, and second by extending the *dual* class to be *pluralistic*, with major subclasses *divisive* and *cooperative*, which are further subdivided into *dual* and *critical*, and *democratic* and *network*, respectively. ('Network' here refers to theories which claim that society is organised into a number of loosely coupled nodes; Bruno Latour is a leading advocate of this viewpoint.) Figure 2 gives a diagrammatic representation of this taxonomy.

Most existing work in requirements engineering falls within the unitary systems classification; in particular, the most familiar structured design methods are all hard unitary. Work in the so-called Scandinavian School falls under the cooperative democratic classification. There is very little work in requirements engineering that could be called postmodern; perhaps some recent directions in computer supported cooperative work come close, and there are also the studies described in the next two sections.

A major goal of this project was to compile a *Methods and Tools Handbook* that would be useful to managers in deciding how to organise actual projects. This document includes a taxonomy of relevant methods and related disciplines, with an annotated selection of relevant books, papers, individuals, groups and tools. It tries to identify the best of these, and to indicate the kind of application for which they may be particularly suitable. The first criterion used for classification is the social theory that underlies the method, based on our hypothesis that the most important determinant of success is that this social theory should match the actual social organisation where the system will be deployed. (See Bickerton and Siddiqi, 1992, for more details on this project.)

It is interesting to consider the methodological aspect of this classification scheme. It was not possible to base the scheme on the current practice of requirements engineers, because (we believe that) current practice does not take sufficient account of the social dimension of requirements. In particular, nearly all current

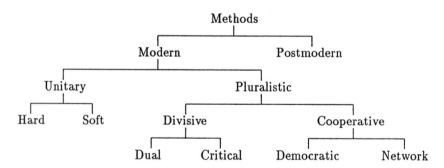

Figure 2   A taxonomy for requirements methods.

[8]   This version of the taxonomy is the result of much discussion within the Centre, including some very significant help from Dr Susan Leigh Star; Matthew Bickerton was the project leader.

industrial projects use hard unitary modern methods. Hence, this classification scheme was constructed by the researchers, using their judgement based on literature, their own experience, and discussions with others; it is not directly situated in the work of practising requirements engineers. Of course, the requirements methods that we classified are in the world of working requirements engineers, even though no single engineer can be expected to have had experience with all of them.

5 VALUE SYSTEMS

Goguen and Linde (1978, 1981) have developed a method that yields a value system for an organisation (or part thereof) from a collection of naturally occurring stories (and possibly jokes[9]) told by members of an organisation among themselves on informal occasions, such as their coffee and lunch breaks. Note that, unlike the nursery example given in Section 2.2, here we are primarily concerned with what Labov (1972) called narratives of personal experience, in which an individual relates events that were personally experienced. The method classifies the evaluative material (in the sense discussed in Section 2.2) of the stories collected, using a formal structure called a *value system tree*, in which higher level nodes correspond to higher level values, and lower level nodes correspond to refinements, applications, or corrections of superordinate nodes. Because members of an organisation who tell a story are socially accountable for doing so, the evaluative material that they use to justify their telling that story reveals their shared values.

Figure 3 shows part of a value system tree[10] obtained by Goguen and Linde in 1978. It represents the values of a small corporate recruitment (i.e. 'head hunting') firm. The tip nodes in this tree are situated in the sense that they are taken directly from actual narratives by members, and they require more background information in order to be understood. Many interior nodes, which express superordinate values, are also situated in this sense, but others were created by the analysts, by clustering nodes into larger and larger related groups, in the general style of the KJ method[11] (Kawakita, 1975).

The edges in Figure 3 express relationships of subordination; these are situated to the extent that there is evidence for them in the structure of the discourse; moreover, members could have been asked about them. The nodes at the three topmost levels are analysts' constructions, with support from the data. The phrases in the fourth level are taken from the evaluative clauses of stories and jokes collected at this firm. (Some nodes at the fourth level of Figure 3 have two more levels below them.)

Note the contradiction between the first two nodes on the fourth level. This illus-

---

[9] See the classical work on jokes by Harvey Sacks (1974).
[10] Note that this representation differs from trees on earth, which have their roots at the bottom.
[11] This method was introduced by the Japanese anthropologist Jiro Kawakita for classifying artefacts, and it is now rather widely used by Japanese businessmen and computing scientists. It provides useful guidelines for combining clusters, separating clusters, etc.

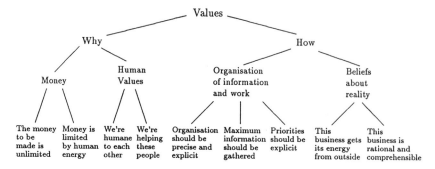

Figure 3   A value system tree.

trates the fact that real value systems are not necessarily consistent. This seems to be one reason why it is difficult (or even impossible) to elicit values from members just by asking for them. Indeed, value systems, like many other aspects of social life, are tacit knowledge.

The tree in Figure 3 is an analysts' construction: the members of the company analysed do not talk about the properties of their value system tree, such as its number of nodes or edges; they would not have names for these categories, and they would not regard questions about them as meaningful. Instead, this tree serves as a formal summary of the data that was collected, and of the analysts' understanding of that data; its structure is *open*, in the sense that it remains subject to revision in the light of further data and further analysis, and *contingent* in the sense that it is the result of many discussions, during which it gradually evolved to the form shown; quite possibly, further discussion would have led to further evolution. Nonetheless, we would expect that any changes produced by new data or analyses would be relatively small, based on the effort that had already gone into constructing this structure.

A value system tree can help requirements engineers to make appropriate trade-offs between conflicting requirements of the client and/or end user. The hierarchical structure of the tree suggests which requirements should be given precedence over others. Also, the nature of any conflicts that appear may be clarified, because the higher level values are more significant. For an even more detailed analysis, weights could be assigned to values based on their frequency in the data that support them.

6   THE STRUCTURE OF SPORTING EVENTS

An interestingly different example comes from Stephen Toulmin's (1958) suggestive book *The Uses of Argument*. Here the nodes and the tree itself are familiar categories to members; in particular, members have technical terms for these and many similar categories. This example is the annual regatta at Henley. Figures 4 and 5 show part of an initial 'draw' for this regatta. Toulmin (1958) presented his data in the form shown in Figure 4, saying that it came from 'the sports page of a

Visitors' Cup. Heat 1: Jesus, Cambridge *v.* Christ Church; Heat 2: Oriel *v.* New College; ... Heat 8: Lady Margaret *v.* winner of Heat 1; ... Heat 26: Winner of Heat 23 *v.* winner of Heat 24; Final: Winner of Heat 25 *v.* winner of Heat 26.

Figure 4   A draw for the Henley Regatta.

Sunday paper', presumably the (London) *Times* in the mid-1950s. Figure 5 presents the same information in the form of a traditional computing science tree.

The tip nodes in Figure 5 represent boats (i.e. crews), and the non-tip nodes represent individual 'heats' with their (not yet determined) winners. Such a structure represents a *regatta*, and the special case where no winners are filled in is called a *draw*. Each edge points to a participant in a heat, which in general is the winner of a 'subregatta', represented by a subtree. The number of non-tip nodes is the total number of heats, and the number of edges is the number of instances of boats racing. Note that each non-tip node is the root (i.e. topmost node) of a subregatta, and that the query marks represent winners that are not yet determined.

This formal structure is situated in the events of a particular actual regatta, and it is used in an emergent, local, contingent, open way. The query marks on the non-tip nodes of the draw in Figure 5 become instantiated with the actual winners as the concrete events of the regatta unfold in actual time, until the whole regatta is summarised by a single structure that tells what happened, including which boats raced in each heat, and who won. Another manifestation of openness and contingency is that a boat could be disqualified or withdrawn, resulting in fewer heats than scheduled in the original draw. Moreover, the structure is also open at the *meta* level, in that new methods could be added or old ones modified. For example, if we initially only have methods for constructing a draw and for setting the winners in that structure, then we would have to add a new method for restructuring regattas in order to allow stewards to drop and rearrange boats or heats, as would be needed for handling disqualifications and withdrawals. Thus, the regatta structure only attains immutability in retrospect, after the event is over. However, it is always mobile and compressible. As an example of compression, a radio announcer might tell the number of heats that have been held so far. In fact, sports fans are fascinated by statistics, which compress the structure of some event (or series of events) into a single number.

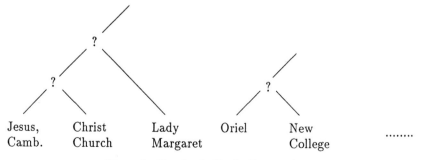

Figure 5   Tree for the Henley Regatta draw.

After a discussion of what formalisation is, we will formalise (some aspects of) the structure of the Henley Regatta as an abstract data type, and we will also formalise the meta language used to describe it.

6.1   What is formalisation?

Formalisation is not itself a formal activity, and in fact there are many interpretations for what formalisation may be. This subsection will give a rather precise explication of a fairly standard interpretation from computing science, but we will then relate it to social issues in a way that is far from standard.

The principles of accountability and orderliness suggest the possibility of formalising social interaction, but I hope our previous discussions have convinced the reader that there are limits to how successful any such formalisation could be. In particular, it will not be easy to formalise domains where there are many *ad hoc* special cases, or where much of the knowledge is tacit. Formalisation will be more successful on narrow and orderly domains, such as sporting events, that have long traditions, rule books, referees, regulating bodies, etc. For example, it would be more difficult to formalise a children's game than the Henley Regatta, and more difficult still to formalise queuing behaviour in Japan, where queues tend to be rather informal. In fact, there are degrees of formalisation, from dry to wet, and it can be important not to formalise beyond a certain appropriate degree. Cookery recipes are an interesting example, showing how an intermediate degree of formalisation is possible and helpful, whereas a very formal treatment would be unhelpful, even if it were possible.

Every formalisation requires a distinction between an *object* level, for describing that which is to be formalised, and a *meta* level, which provides a language for expressing the formalisation. The object level models the world of members, while the meta level is the language of the analysts who do the formalisation. The object level may have technical terms and rules not used by members themselves, but it is necessary to provide an interpretation for these terms into the members' world; in general, this cannot itself be formalised, and instead is a tacit part of the analysts' culture. Of course, any formalism is emergent, contingent, local, open and vague. These qualities of situatedness can therefore be considered to describe some basic limitations of formalisation. Note that the distinction between the object and meta levels of description is parallel to the distinction between the member and analyst cultures discussed in Section 2.1.

In the driest formalisations, the meta language is also formalised, so that the object level model is a formal theory in the meta language. In less fully formalised models, the meta language may simply be a natural language, such as English, or a somewhat stylised dialect. Note that there may be rules at both the object and meta levels. Rules at the object level are part of the model, while rules at the meta level define the language that is used for formalisation.

It is important to notice that a formal description of some real world domain cannot in itself capture the meanings assigned by members concerned with that domain; the analyst's interpretations of the formalism are necessary for making this bridge.

The next subsection will formalise the structure of the Henley Regatta, using the formal meta language of abstract algebra, and will also explain the the social situatedness of the formalisation.

6.2   Situated abstract data types

Members are aware that the same structure can be represented in a variety of ways; for example, it can be represented by a table in a newspaper as in Figure 4, by a verbally presented list, by a list displayed on a scoreboard, or by the tree shown in Figure 5. This means that there is a precise structure that is independent of how it happens to be represented, i.e. we have what computing scientists call an *abstract data type*. This subsection explains this concept in more detail, while applying it to the Henley Regatta. Unfortunately, the formalism is rather technical; further mathematical details may be found, for example, in Goguen *et al.* (1978) and Goguen (to appear).

Several different kinds of entity are involved in a regatta. Some of these can be arranged in a hierarchical classification scheme according to what we will call their *sorts*. Sorts correspond to an important class of members' categories, but not every members' category is formalised by a sort; for example, heats are not formalised this way. We will say that boats are of sort Boat, completed regattas are of sort Reg, possibly not yet specified boats are of sort Boat? (a supersort of Boat), and possibly not yet completed regattas have the supersort Reg?; the latter includes all draws. It is convenient to assume that Boat is a subsort of Reg and that Boat? is a subsort of Reg?; these assumptions imply that there are trivial regattas consisting of just one boat, which could even be the unknown boat, denoted '?'. Some sorts are *built in*, in the sense that they are already defined. Two examples are integers and identifiers. The latter have the sort Id (from the module QID that provides identifiers), here used for naming boats; it is convenient to accomplish this by considering Id to be a subsort of Boat. A diagram showing the subsort relations involved in this example is given in Figure 6 (the sorts 12 and Index are discussed in the appendix).

How can we avoid being tied to one particular representation, as Toulmin was? The key is to focus attention on the *methods* that members use to describe (or construct) representations. It is useful to distinguish two kinds of methods: *constructors*, for building representations from more primitive parts, and *selectors*, for extracting particular information[12]. For regattas, the most important method is a constructor that adds a new heat; it must specify the two contestants, and also provide a slot for the winner. In Figure 5, each non-tip node represents a heat, where the two contestants are the winners of subregattas, or else are given boats; the query

---

[12] In object oriented programming, the word 'method' refers to operations that can modify, and the word 'attribute' refers to operations that only extract information, that is, to what we have called selectors.

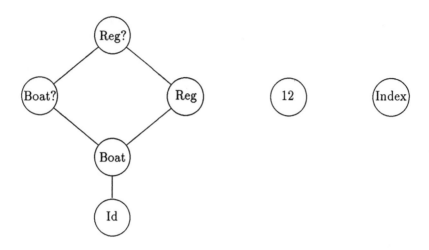

Figure 6   Classification scheme for some members' categories.

mark represents a not yet determined winner. In general, if R and R' are regattas and B is a boat, then heat(R,R',B) constructs a new regatta, by adding a heat in which the winners of the subregattas R and R' race against each other, with B the winner of that heat.

Selectors correspond to certain members' categories. For example, there is a selector that extracts the winner of a given regatta by taking the winner of its final heat. But we do not formalise 'winner' with a sort.

Methods respect the sorts of representations, in that it is only meaningful to apply a given method to representations of certain sorts, and not to others; moreover, each method has a *target sort*, for the kind of representation (information) that it yields. For example, the heat method takes three inputs, two of which are regattas, and one of which is a boat; it is not meaningful to give a regatta, or an integer, for its third input. We call the list of input sorts the *source* of the method. In addition, there can be 'constants' that do not have any inputs, but do have a target sort; for example, the unknown boat '?' has target sort Boat?. It is convenient to think of these as methods having no input, i.e. as having an empty source.

Given a particular representation, say by trees, we can collect all of the possible structures in that representation into a system called an *algebra*, in which each sort corresponds to the set of representations of that sort, and the methods (and selectors) correspond to functions that map representations to other representations (or else to built in values, such as numbers). If A denotes a given algebra, then A_s denotes its set of representations of sort s. If s' is a subsort of s, then we require that $A_{s'}$ is a subset of A_s.

For example, the method that adds a new heat to a regatta can be seen as a function

```
heat : Reg? Reg? Boat? -> Reg?
```

which takes two regatta representations and a boat, and constructs the new regatta where the winners of the subregattas race against each other. Similarly, the selector that gives the winner of a regatta is a function

```
winner : Reg? -> Boat?
```

from regattas to boats. Also, constant methods (such as '?') designate particular representations in an algebra.

It is often convenient to have two different versions of a method, one for not yet completed structures, and the other for completed structures; then we have an *overloaded* method. For example, in addition to heat as defined above, we may also have a method

```
heat : Reg Reg Boat -> Reg
```

for constructing completed regattas.

A collection of sorts (with their subsort relations) and a collection of operations (including methods and selectors) over it are together called a *signature*[13]. Given a signature, we can construct its 'well formed expressions', called *terms*: first, all constants are terms; and second, if o is an operation with source sorts $s_1,...,s_n$ and if $t_1,...,t_n$ are terms such that t_i has target sort s_i, then $o(t_1,...,t_n)$ is also a term, and it has the same sort as the target sort of o. For example,

```
heat(heat('JesusCam, 'ChristCh, ?), 'LadyM, ?)
```

is a well formed term, in which OBJ3-style identifiers are used as constants for the names of boats; these identifiers begin with a quote and contain no spaces (Goguen *et al.*, 1993b) (we have also further abbreviated the boat names).

Given any term t and algebra A over the same signature, that term denotes a unique representation in A. This *value*, or *denotation*, of t is determined just by first finding the values in A of any constants in t, and then applying the functions in A that correspond to the operations in t to those values, and then applying further functions to further values, and so on, until a final value is reached. For example, the above term denotes the left subtree in the representation shown in Figure 5.

We are now in a position to formalise what it means for two representation systems to be 'essentially the same', in the sense that they can represent exactly the same thing. The idea is that there must be a translation between the two representation systems that preserves the meaning of all operations. We have already for-

---

[13] We may also have to include some functions on built in values.

malised the notion of a representation system as an algebra. So it makes sense that the formalisation of translation should be a system of mappings between the sets of the algebras that preserve the operations. Let's say that the two algebras are A and A', and that the set of sorts in the signature is S. Then we want a collection of functions $f_s: A_s \rightarrow A'_s$ for each s in S, such that if o is an operation with target sort s, with source sorts $s_1,...,s_n$, and if A_o and A'_o are the functions that interpret o in A and A' respectively, then preserving the meaning of o amounts to requiring that

$$f_s(A_o(r_1, ..., r_n)) = A'_o(f_{s_1}(r_1), ..., f_{s_n}(r_n))$$

where $r_1, ..., r_n$ are representations in A of sorts $s_1, ..., s_n$, respectively. Also, if c is a constant of sort s, then we require that

$$f_s(A_c) = A'_c$$

where A_c and A'_c are the representations of c in A and A', respectively.

However, this isn't quite enough: we need the representations in A and A' to be in exact correspondence with each other. For this, we need to require that each of the functions f_s is bijective (i.e. is one-to-one and onto). A collection of functions f_s that has all these properties (of preserving all the operations and being bijective) is called an *isomorphism*.

The development and use of algebras in the sense explained above was a major advance in mathematics. Alfred North Whitehead (1898) prefigured this revolution in the late nineteenth century, but it was Emmy Nöther who is largely responsible for systematising and widely applying these concepts, thus creating what is now called 'modern algebra' or 'abstract algebra', and widely taught in undergraduate mathematics curricula.

But we are still dealing with representations. How can we abstract away from these, to obtain structures that are truly independent of how they are represented? The answer has two parts, of which the second is unfortunately a bit technical.

The first is just to describe the *relationships* that necessarily hold among the given operations; it turns out that it suffices to use equations for this purpose. For example, the fact that the winner of any regatta of the form heat(R,R',B) is B is expressed by the equation

```
winner(heat(R,R',B)) = B .
```

This is a relationship between the category 'winner' and the constructor method 'heat'.

So far, our approach for specifying an abstract data type consists of giving a collection of sorts with subsort relations, a collection of operations, and a collection of equations; let us call these three collections together a *specification*. Then a *model* for such a specification is an algebra that provides sets for the sorts (with subsets for the subsorts) and functions for the operations, such that all of the equations are satisfied. The elements of such a model provide a system of representations for the categories and operations in the signature. We now have a way of specifying representations that is truly abstract, in that it says nothing whatsoever about the representations themselves. But unfortunately, there are too many models, and they are not isomorphic to each other. We need one more principle to get what we want; this principle is called *initiality*, and it amounts to assuming the following two principles:

1. *No junk*: every representation in the algebra can be constructed using methods in the given signature.
2. *No confusion*: two terms denote the same representation if and only if they can be proved equal using the given equations.

So now we take as models only those algebras that satisfy not only the equations, but also the two principles above. Such models are called *initial models*, and it can be shown that any two initial algebras are necessarily isomorphic. Thus, we finally have the representation independent way of specifying structures that we have been seeking.

In this example, it is important to distinguish between the object and meta levels of description; a different language is used at each level, for a different purpose. The object level language involves boats, heats, and so on, and events here may construct draws, announce winners, etc. The meta language is also formal, and involves sorts, methods, equations, etc.; events at this level may add new methods, revise equations, etc. For example, in the OBJ3 code in the appendix, a method for restructuring regattas is given as an enrichment of the previously given specification that only involved methods for heats and winners.

The above has sketched a precise mathematical theory of abstract data types, in which an abstract type is an isomorphism class of many-sorted algebras; see Goguen *et al.* (1978) for some further details. One particular result in this theory is that any computable many-sorted algebra, and thus any abstract data type, has a representation by trees. Thus, it is not surprising that each of the examples discussed here has a tree representation[14]. (There is also a somewhat more sophisticated approach, based on behavioural satisfaction, that does not require initiality; see Goguen, 1991.) A complete formal specification of our Henley Regatta abstract data type is given in the appendix, using the specification language OBJ3 (Goguen *et al.*, 1993b). This specification is executable, and has actually been executed. (Experience shows that it is necessary to test all but the most trivial specifications in order to eliminate bugs.)

It may seem surprising how complex the complete specification is, with its various sorts, subsorts, methods, and especially equations. But the Henley Regatta really does have boats, heats, regattas, winners, not yet determined boats, etc., and the

---

[14] The linear ordering in Figure 1 is a particularly simple kind of tree having no branches, and just one tip node; it looks more like a tree if it is stood on its side.

relationships among them really are rather complex. Also, we know from experience that it can take quite some effort to learn how some new sport is structured. It is clear that the methods for constructing and restructuring a regatta really are rather complex. Moreover, this kind of complexity is not unique to this example, but is typical of sporting events, games, and many other social phenomena.

It may seem even more surprising how sophisticated is the meta level language that we used for formalising the structure of the Henley Regatta, with its categories of sort, subsort, signature, algebra, term, isomorphism, equation, etc. Perhaps this language could be simplified, but the approach presented here was developed in the context of computing science, where there is a strong preference for a rigorous mathematical development (Goguen *et al.*, 1978). In fact, the abstract data type concept is rather sophisticated, and I have simplified many details, and omitted others. However, the emphasis on the social situatedness of abstract data types seems to be entirely new.

Of course, the above discussion does not imply that members of a social group some of whose behaviour can be formalised by an abstract data type are familiar with the concept of an abstract data type; even Toulmin (1958) only uses concrete representations, without realising that they are algebras, that different representations give isomorphic algebras, or that there is no unique best representation. Similarly, there is no implication that members are familiar with the social aspects of formalisation. For example, much the same kind of process as described in this subsection occurs when a computing scientist formalises some aspect of computing practice by designing a new abstract data type, but this does not imply familiarity with (for example) the qualities of situatedness or the retrospective hypothesis, or even with the algebraic formalisation of abstract data types. On the other hand, perhaps such a familiarity would help to prevent some rather ill-advised formalisations.

7   DISCUSSION AND SUMMARY

Although each of our four examples (in Sections 3, 4, 5 and 6) has a tree structure, these structures are used for different purposes, and are embedded in their social contexts in different ways, because of their different relationships of accountability. Let's compare them.

The regatta example of Section 6 shows that abstract data types occur 'in nature', e.g. in ordinary social interaction, in the sense that the members of ordinary groups (such as sports fans) organise their talk in ways that correspond to instances of this concept. Different representations of the same abstract structure are displayed on scoreboards, printed in newspapers, shown on television in compact graphical forms, and are also presented in natural language. Of course, one expects to see abstract data types in the dry areas of computing science, such as programming languages and databases, and they are also familiar in the structured analysis notations of requirements engineering, but I was surprised to find abstract data types in live social interaction. However, we should not forget that these structures are still situated, and thus contingent, emergent, local and open; in particular, the categories and methods of our example need to be interpreted in the concrete events of an actual regatta. Moreover, new methods can be added, or old ones revised, to cope with new circumstances.

Note that even though we formalised both the object (member) and meta (analyst) levels of description in this example, contingence, emergence and openness occur at both levels in relation to any concrete instance: an analyst (the author) has constructed an abstraction which is now separated from the concrete instances that motivated its construction. This abstraction cannot be expected to precisely match any particular concrete instance. Of course, this is no different from the situation with maps, and such abstractions can still be a useful starting point for doing the practical work of understanding how some particular situation is produced by members.

In the case of the value system tree of Figure 3, the analysts are accountable for the structure, while the members of the organisation analysed are accountable for the bits of language attached to all but the highest level nodes. Thus, the tree structure itself is only meaningful to members of the analyst culture. All of the tip node labels were extracted from the data, and in fact so were most of the non-tip labels, although they get shorter and more abstract as they go further up; the analysts are accountable for the extraction and abstraction. Thus, this structure is open, contingent, emergent, and local with respect to two different communities, in two different ways.

The edges in the value system tree express relationships of subordination; these are situated in the members' culture to the extent that there is evidence for them in the structure of the data collected. Although the tree structure belongs to an abstract data type, the *meanings* of the labels on nodes are not captured by this formalism, nor is the restriction that the meaning of a higher level node is more general than that of its subordinates. In general, the lower a node is, the more background information about the organisation is needed to understand its meaning; this is because the tip nodes (and some of the interior nodes) are more situated, while the higher level nodes are more abstract immutable mobiles; these tend to be shorter, with fewer context bound terms.

The classification of requirements methods discussed in Section 4 is similar to the value system tree discussed in Section 5, in that the non-tip nodes were constructed by analysts. However, it differs in that the classification scheme was largely determined in advance, and the detailed assignment of methods to classes was done later. Nevertheless, there were some readjustments. For example, we originally had a category for methods based on psychology, but later realised that these were hard unitary modern methods; therefore we dropped that category. Assigning methods to classes could be considered a test of the hypothesis that implicit social theories are a significant property of requirements methods. It would appear that this hypothesis has been confirmed. Note that the requirements engineering community produced the tip nodes, the sociology community produced the internal nodes, and the analysts put the whole together. The *Handbook* is now in the hands of its user community, and we expect to receive further feedback, which will help us to assess the adequacy of our construction. Thus, the situatedness and accountability of this example involve three different communities, which are interrelated in a complex way.

In the waterfall lifecycle model of Section 3, each so-called phase is a members' concept, and so is each temporal ordering relationship; software engineers use these phase names frequently, to help them classify their activities. They also recognise the *logical* priority of 'earlier' phases over 'later' ones. However (based on informal ethnography), it seems to be mainly managers who insist upon the *temporal* priority of 'earlier' phases; practising software engineers, especially those with some years of experience, generally recognise that 'reality' often turns out differently (see also the chapter of Button and Sharrock in this volume). The preferred number of phases, their names, and their definitions all vary somewhat with the organisation, textbook, method, or individual practitioner examined. Thus, the structure shown in Figure 1 does not represent a consensus, but rather an analyst's idealisation, necessarily involving some arbitrary choice. Nevertheless, any trained software engineer will recognise that Figure 1 does represent (a version of) the waterfall model.

In the regatta example, all the structure in the abstract data type can be referred back to the community of members; in particular, members have categories for both the nodes and the edges in Figure 5. However, the tree representation is only one among several that are used by members; others include tables (as in Figure 4) and verbal listings. But all of these are isomorphic when viewed as algebras. This is the precise sense in which we have an *abstract* data type. But we should not forget that any concrete instance, i.e. any particular Henley Regatta, is still very much socially situated.

The other three examples use a simple tree structure to support a hierarchical classification, in a way that resembles classes with inheritance in object oriented programming. This kind of tree can easily be described as an abstract data type. But it would be problematic to try to formalise the meanings of the labels, the relationships of subordination among them, or the meta language used for these. The classification scheme for methods is somewhat more of an analysts' construction than the value system tree. The analysts' rôle in the waterfall phases example was a fairly minimal tidying up. Figure 6 is also a hierarchical classification scheme.

It is important to recognise that in all four examples, the operations of abstraction have, to a varying extent, diminished the connection of resulting formal structure with its original social context. I wish to argue that this is not the result of an inadequate method, but rather that it is *always and necessarily* the case that operations of systematising, abstracting, theorising and concluding will have such an effect, even if carried out according to the most rigorous canons of ethnomethodology. The construction of immutable mobiles necessarily reduces the situatedness of data and makes it drier, and any assertions made by analysts necessarily fall into this area.

Note also that dryness comes not merely in different degrees, but also in a wide variety of kinds, resulting from the complex relationships of accountability between different communities, including that of analysts.

Thus, the relationship between the formal and the social aspects of information is not one of antagonism, where one must be rejected and the other accepted; rather, these two aspects of information are *complementary*, and they are both essential for successful requirements engineering. Moreover, the relationship between the formal context insensitive and the social context sensitive aspects of information is very *complex*, in that there may be several different facets, which arise in different social contexts, have different levels of abstraction, and are interconnected in complex ways.

7.1   Summary

We have used some ideas from ethnomethodology, such as the principles of accountability and orderliness, to better understand information. We have argued that the situatedness of information has consequences that are important for analysts to understand, including the emergent, local, contingent and open qualities. In general, traditional sociology has tried to avoid such consequences, in the misguided pursuit of objectivity. Ethnomethodology can be seen as a reaction against this, in its efforts to reconcile a radical empiricism with a deep appreciation of the situatedness of social data.

We have also used ideas from the sociology of science (especially work of Latour) and from computing science to explicate the nature of dry information (especially abstract data types). Dry information often loses the property of embodiedness, and is also less emergent, contingent and local. However, even the most formal information is still situated, and in particular, is open, emergent, contingent and even embodied at the meta level, where analysts are accountable for its formalisation. Similarly, even the wettest information about social interaction is necessarily partially abstracted from its social context, in order to be presented to an audience of analysts. In particular, the analyst must always speak in a meta language.

We have suggested the *formalisation hypothesis*, which says that formalisation is a key way to make information drier, i.e. more immutable and mobile. We have also suggested the *retrospective hypothesis*, which says that plans and explanations (and much other socially situated information) can only become dry after the events to which they refer have reached some stage of completion.

We have argued that abstract data types can be found in the discourse of ordinary social groups, such as sports fans. It seems likely that many other instances of abstract data types can be found in social interaction. The 'language games' proposed by Wittgenstein seem a suggestive hint, because we have seen that abstract data types provide a natural way of formalising games. However, it does not seem likely that all socially situated information can be represented by abstract data types. In particular, the use of the terms 'category' and 'method' in ethnomethodology seems to cover a much larger ground than that formalised by abstract data types.

We have also suggested the importance of not adhering dogmatically to any one research method, whether it is ethnomethodology, discourse analysis, questionnaires, object oriented analysis, or formal domain modelling. Instead, we have argued for the flexibility to use whatever method seems best to fit the given circumstances.

7.2 Implications for requirements engineering

The retrospective hypothesis explains why it can be so difficult to manage the requirements of a large system: it only becomes clear what the requirements really are when the system is successfully operating in its social and organisational context. Thus, a reasonably complete and consistent set of requirements for a large, complex system can only emerge from a retrospective reconstruction. The retrospective hypothesis also explains why it can be so difficult to enforce process models on actual system development projects: it is difficult even to know what phase a given action fits into until some coherence has emerged retrospectively. Note that it takes work by members to achieve a retrospective reconstruction, and that this work is often not done for many projects, because of the principle of volume.

We can now understand why it is impossible to completely formalise requirements: it is because they cannot be fully separated from their social context. More specifically, the qualities of situatedness explain why the lifecycle phases cannot be fully formalised. Indeed, the activities that are necessary for a successful system development project cannot always be expected to fit in a natural way into any system of pre-given categories, and practising software engineers often report (informally) that they have to spend much of their time circumventing 'the system'. Nevertheless, it is the very essence of requirements engineering to use and construct such dry structures, because they are necessary for constructing actual computer-based systems. What is unnecessary is a slavish adherence to narrowly prescriptive plans and categories. Note that in general, abstractions (immutable mobiles) have only a practical utility, and must be interpreted concretely in order for that utility to be made manifest.

These considerations have consequences for tools to support requirements engineering. Perhaps the most important consequence is that requirements tools must provide very strong support for retrospective revision; in particular, they must be very flexible, to accommodate the frequent changes in requirements and their links with other objects (such as specs and code). Another requirement is that varying degrees of formalisation should be accommodated, ranging from raw data to mathematical formulae. Moreover, information that is heavily situated should come with pointers into its context (e.g. background ethnographic information, such as audio and video clips of work and interviews, questionnaires and their results, and sample documents from the work environment), in order to make it understandable by workers who have not had direct contact with the client organisation. This suggests that multimedia documents may have great potential for the support of requirements engineering.

The area that we have called the social theory of information offers some hope of furthering requirements engineering, by clarifying the situated nature of the information involved, and indeed, of the requirements process and the whole lifecycle. This should help us to effect an ongoing, practical reconciliation between formal technical issues and socially situated issues in the actual *practise* of requirements engineering, as is needed for building systems that work successfully in their social context.

APPENDIX: FORMAL SPECIFICATION FOR THE HENLEY REGATTA

This appendix gives a formal specification of an abstract data for the structure of the Henley Regatta, using the executable part of the programming and specification language OBJ3. It is not feasible to give a complete tutorial on OBJ3 here; the interested reader should look elsewhere for details (Goguen *et al.*, 1993). However, a few remarks may help the untutored reader to obtain a rough overview of the specification given below. There are four modules, each of which begins with the keyword 'obj' and end with the keyword 'endo'. Immediately after 'obj' comes the name of the module. Sorts, operations, subsorts, variables, and equations are declared after fairly obvious keywords; also, 'cq' indicates a conditional equation, while 'pr' and 'dfn' indicate module importations, the latter with a renaming of the principle sort (in this case, from List to Index).

The first module, named '12', merely introduces two constants, '1' and '2'; these are used for indicating one or the other of the two boats in a heat. Note that this is an abstract data type, in the sense that we could have chosen different representations for the two boats, such as 'A' and 'B', or 'L' and 'R'; any such choice will yield an isomorphic (two element) initial algebra. The second module, named 'LIST', is a *parameterised module* for forming lists of anything; the list constructor has concatenation syntax '_ _' for placing a new element at the head of a list; nil is the empty list. Inside the third module, we form and import the module LIST[12], renaming its principal sort List to be Index; these lists are used for picking out particular instances of a boat racing in a regatta; a typical term of sort Index is '1 1 2 nil'. This module also introduces the constructor heat for regattas, the method swin for setting winners of heats, and the selector winner. The final module SREG adds a method sreg for restructing regattas. The line vars-of HENLEY' just imports the variable declarations from the previous module HENLEY.

```
obj 12 is sort 12 .
  ops 1 2 : -> 12 .
endo

obj LIST[X :: TRIV] is sort List .
  op nil : -> List .
  op _ _ : Elt List -> List .
endo

obj HENLEY is sorts Boat Reg Boat? Reg? .
  pr QID .
  subsorts Id < Boat < Reg Boat? < Reg? .
  dfn Index is LIST[12] .

  op ? : -> Boat? .
  op heat : Reg? Reg? Boat? -> Reg? .
  op heat : Reg  Reg  Boat  -> Reg .

  var B B' : Boat? .  vars R R' R'' : Reg? . var I : Index.

  op winner : Reg? Index -> Boat? .
  eq winner(heat(R,R',B), nil) = B .
  eq winner(heat(R,R',B), 1 I) = winner(R,I) .
  eq winner(heat(R,R',B), 2 I) = winner(R',I) .
  eq winner(B,nil) = B .
  cq winner(B,I)   = ? if I =/= nil .

  op swin : Reg? Index -> Reg? .
  eq swin(heat(R,R',B), nil)    = heat(R,R',B).
  eq swin(heat(R,R',B), 1 nil)  = heat(R,R',winner(R,nil)).
  eq swin(heat(R,R',B), 2 nil)  = heat(R,R',winner(R',nil)).
  eq swin(heat(R,R',B), 1 I)    = heat(swin(R,I),R',B) if I =/= nil.
  eq swin(heat(R,R',B), 2 I)    = heat(R,swin(R',I),B) if I =/= nil.
  eq swin(B,I) = ? .
endo

obj SREG is
  pre HENLEY
  op sreg : Reg? Reg? Index -> Reg? .

  vars-of HENLEY .
  eq sreg(heat(R,R',B), R'', 1 nil) = heat(R'',R',B).
  eq sreg(heat(R,R',B), R'', 2 nil) = heat(R, R'',B).
  eq sreg(heat(R,R',B), R'', 1 I)   = heat(sreg(R,R'',I),R',B).
  eq sreg(heat(R,R',B), R'', 2 I)   = heat(R,sreg(R',R'',I),B).
  eq sreg(heat(R,R',B), R'', nil)   = ? .
endo
```

Note that all of this code has actually been run in OBJ3.

ACKNOWLEDGEMENTS

I thank the members of the Centre for Requirements and Foundations for many stimulating conversations on the topics discussed here, particularly Marina Jirotka and Matthew Bickerton. I also wish to thank Dr Susan Leigh Star for several interesting and helpful conversations, and my wife Kathleen for carefully reading several drafts of this chapter and offering many helpful comments. Thanks to André Stern for some interesting remarks about time and requirements. Thanks to Frances Page for preparing the figures. Finally, special thanks to Dr Charlotte Linde for our long collaboration, during which I learned much of what I know about discourse analysis.

REFERENCES

Abbott, R. (1983). Program design by informal English descriptions, *Communications of the ACM*, **26**(11) 882–894.

Barwise, J. and Perry, J. (1983). *Situations and Attitudes*, Bradford Books.

Becker, A. L. (1979). Text-building, epistemology, and aesthetics in Javanese shadow theatre, in A. L. Becker and A. Yengoyan (Eds), *The Imagination of Reality: Essays on Southeast Asian Symbolic Systems*, Ablex.

Bickerton, M. and Siddiqi, J. (1993). The classification of requirements engineering methods, in S. Fickas and A. Finkelstein (Eds), *Requirements Engineering '93*, pp 182–186, IEEE Press. (Also, Technical Report, Centre for Requirements and Foundations, Oxford University Computing Lab, 1992.)

Boehm, B. (1981). *Software Engineering Economics*, Prentice-Hall.

Boehm, B. (1986). A sprial model of program development and enhancement, *Software Engineering Notes*, **11**(4) 14–24.

Boland, R. (1991). *In search of management accounting: Explorations of self and organization*, Technical report, Case Western University.

Conklin, J. and Bergman, M. (1988). gIBIS: A hypertext tool for exploratory policy discussion, *ACM Transactions on Office Information Systems*, **6** 303–331.

Davis, A. M. (1990). *Software Requirements: Analysis & Specification*, Prentice-Hall.

Finkelstein, A., Kramer, J. and Goedicke, M. (1990). Viewpoint oriented software development. *Proceedings Third International Workshop on Software Engineering and its Applications*, pp 337–351, Springer-Verlag.

Garfinkel, H. (1967). *Studies in Ethnomethodology*, Prentice-Hall.

Goguen, J. (1991). Types as theories, in G. M. Reed, A. W. Roscoe and R. F. Wachter (Eds), *Topology and Category Theory in Computer Science*, pp 357–390, Oxford. (Proceedings of a Conference held at Oxford, June 1989.)

Goguen, J. (1992a). The denial of error, in C. Floyd, H. Züllighoven, R. Budde and R. Keil-Slawik (Eds), *Software Development and Reality Construction*, pp 193–202. Springer, 1992. (Also in *Four Pieces on Error, Truth and Reality*, Programmming Research Group Technical Monograph PRG–89, October 1990, Oxford.)

Goguen, J. (1992b). The dry and the wet, in E. Falkenberg, C. Rolland and El-Sayed Nasr-El-Dein El-Sayed (Eds), *Information Systems Concepts*, pp 1–17. Elsevier North-Holland. (Proceedings, IFIP Working Group 8.1 Conference (Alexandria, Egypt); also, Programming Research Group, Technical Monograph PRG-100, March 1992, Oxford.)

Goguen, J. (to appear). *Theorem Proving and Algebra*. MIT.

Goguen, J. and Linde, C. (1978). *Cost-benefit analysis of a proposed computer system*, Technical report, Structural Semantics.

Goguen, J. and Linde, C. (1981). *Structural semantic analysis of the information structure of organizations*, Technical report, Structural Semantics.

Goguen, J. and Linde, C. (1983). *Linguistic methodology for the analysis of aviation accidents*, Technical report, Structural Semantics, December. NASA Contractor Report 3741, Ames Research Center.

Goguen, J. and Linde, C. (1993). Techniques for requirements elicitation, in S. Fickas and A. Finkelstein (Eds), *Requirements Engineering '93*, pp 152–164. IEEE Press. (Also Technical Report, Centre for Requirements and Foundations, Oxford University Computing Lab, 1992.)

Goguen, J., Linde, C. and Murphy, M. (1984). Crew communication as a factor in aviation accidents, in E. J. Hartzell and S. Hart (Eds), *Papers from the 20th Annual Conference on Manual Control*. NASA Ames Research Center.

Goguen, J., Thatcher, J. and Wagner, E. (1976). *An initial algebra approach to the specification, correctness and implementation of abstract data types*. Technical Report RC 6487, IBM T.J. Watson Research Center, October. (In *Current Trends in Programming Methodology, IV*, R. Yeh (Ed.), Prentice-Hall, 1978, pp 80–149.)

Goguen, J., Weiner, J. and Linde, C. (1983). Reasoning and natural explanation, *International Journal of Man-Machine Studies*, **19** 521–559.

Goguen, J., Winkler, T., Meseguer, J., Futatsugi, K. and Jouannaud, J.-P. (1993). Introducing OBJ, in J. Goguen (Ed.), *Applications of Algebraic Specification using OBJ*. Cambridge, to appear. (Also to appear as Technical Report from SRI International.)

Goodwin, C. and Heritage, J. (1990). Conversation analysis, *Annual Review of Anthropology*, **19** 283–307.

Jirotka, M. (1991). *Ethnomethodology and requirements engineering*. Technical Report PRG-TR-92-27, Centre for Requirements and Foundations, Oxford University Computing Lab.

Kawakita, J. (1975). *KJ Method: a Scientific Approach to Problem Solving*, Kawakita Research Institute.

Kendon, A. (1990). Conducting interaction: patterns of behavior in focused encounters. Cambridge University. *Studies in Interactional Sociolinguistics*, no. 7.

Labov, W. (1972). The transformation of experience in narrative syntax, *Language in the Inner City*, pp 354–396. University of Pennsylvania.

Latour, B. (1987). *Science in Action*, Open University.

Leigh Star, S. (1988). The structure of ill-structured solutions: heterogeneous problem-solving, boundary objects and distributed artificial intelligence, in M. Huhns and L. Gasser (Eds), *Distributed Artificial Intelligence* Vol 3, pp 37–54. Morgan Kaufmann.

Lévi-Strauss, C. (1964). *The Raw and the Cooked*, Penguin. (Translation by John and Doreen Weightman, 1986.)

Levinson, S. (1983). *Pragmatics*, Cambridge University.

Linde, C. and Goguen, J. (1978). Structure of planning discourse, *Journal of Social and Biological Structures*, **1** 219–251.

Livingston, E. (1987). *The Ethnomethodology of Mathematics*, Routledge & Kegan Paul.

Lyotard, J.-F. (1984). The postmodern condition: a report on knowledge, Manchester University. *Theory and History of Literature*, Vol. 10.

Marco, T. De (1978). *Structured Analysis and System Specification*, Yourdon.

Opie, I. and Opie, P. (1951). *The Oxford Dictionary of Nursery Rhymes*, Oxford.

Penrose, R. (1989). *The Emperor's New Mind*, Oxford. (Vintage paperback edition, 1990.)

Polanyi, M. (1967). *The Tacit Dimension*, Routledge & Kegan Paul.

Sacks, H. (1974). An analysis of the course of a joke's telling in conversation, in R. Baumann and J. Scherzer (Eds) *Explorations in the Ethnography of Speaking*, pp 337–353. Cambridge University.

Sacks, H. (1992). *Lectures on Conversation*, G. Jefferson (Ed.), Blackwell.

Sacks, H., Schegloff, E. and Jefferson, G. (1974). A simplest systematics of the organization of turn-taking in conversation, *Language*, **504** 696–735.

Saeki, M., Horai, H., Toyama, K., Uematsu, N. and Enomoto, H. (1987). Specification framework based on natural language. *Proceedings of the Fourth International Workshop on Software Specification and Design*, pp 87–94, IEEE Press.

Shannon, C. and Weaver, W. (1964). *The Mathematical Theory of Communication*, University of Illinois.

Sharrock, W. and Anderson, B. (1991). Epistemology: Professional scepticism, in G. Button (Ed.), *Ethnomethodology and the Human Sciences*, pp 51–76, Cambridge University Press.

Sharrock, W. and Button, G. (1991). The social actor: social action in real time, in G. Button (Ed.), *Ethnomethodology and the Human Sciences*, pp 137–175, Cambridge University Press.

Suchman, L. (1987). *Plans and Situated Actions: The Problem of Human-machine Communication*, Cambridge University Press.

Toulmin, S. (1958). *The Uses of Argument*, Cambridge University Press.

U.S. Government Accounting Office (1979). Contracting for computer software development – serious problems require management attention to avoid wasting additional millions. Technical Report FFGMSD-80-4, U.S. Government Accounting Office, November.

Whitehead, A. N. (1898). *A Treatise on Universal Algebra, with Applications, I*, Cambridge University Press. Reprinted 1960.

Yourdon, E. (1989). *Modern Structured Analysis*, Prentice-Hall.

Eight

Rethinking requirements analysis: Some implications of recent research into producer–consumer relationships in IT development[1]

Steve Woolgar
*Centre for Research into Innovation, Culture and Technology (CRICT),
Brunel University, Uxbridge, Middlesex, UK*

1 INTRODUCTION

In recent years, a number of social scientists have carried out ethnographic studies of development in various aspects of information technology (IT). A central rationale for this work is to provide a picture of the actual processes of development, by contrast with the partial and idealised depictions which often appear in textbooks or in participants' retrospective reconstructions. The strategic importance of the 'ethnographic' perspective is explained below. Thus far, this line of work has looked in particular at case studies in hardware development, software system development and information system implementation.

This chapter describes some aspects of these ethnographic studies of IT development, drawing in particular on a case study of the development of microcomputers (Woolgar, 1991). The main aim is to demonstrate some important implications of ethnographic research for requirements analysis. To do this, however, we first need to consider the general nature of problems encountered in requirements analysis. In

---

[1] A previous version of this chapter, under the title 'Producer–consumer relations in IT development: some possible implications of recent research for requirements analysis', was presented to the conference on Requirements Capture and Analysis, Hertford College, Oxford, 19–20 December 1991 and to Hewlett Packard Research Laboratories, Bristol, 23 June 1992. Thanks to participants for comments and to Matthew Bickerton and Marina Jirotka. Much of the discussion and specific examples in this chapter are taken from Woolgar (1991).

Requirements Engineering
ISBN 0–1238–5335–4

particular, we first need to look carefully at typical responses to the recurrent problems of requirements analysis. Why do the same kind of problems seem to turn up again and again? The chapter then outlines two key concepts which can assist our rethinking of problems in requirements analysis: the idea of system as text, and the notion of configuring the user. These concepts are then illustrated with reference to experiences deriving from a recent ethnography of computers.

One caveat is necessary. The application of results from existing ethnographic studies of IT development to requirements analysis is necessarily speculative. There are as yet few sustained ethnographic studies of the requirements process itself – we urgently need more. Consequently, although some of my suggestions may seem relatively unsophisticated to those more versed in the requirements business, there is a *prima facie* case that requirements analysis and sociological (and ethnographic) methodology share some key problems. The aim here is to explore the foundations of these problems as the basis for new and different ways forward.

2   THE FAMILIAR PROBLEMS OF REQUIREMENTS ANALYSIS

The problems of requirements capture and analysis are well known. The familar problems include the following:

- The user doesn't know his/her requirements.
- The user knows his/her requirements but can't articulate them.
- The user changes his/her mind.
- Individual users say different things to different people.
- Users disagree as to what their joint requirements are.
- Individual users are not representative of (all) relevant users.
- The user turns out to be a customer rather than (just) a user.

Those experienced in the day-to-day business of dealing with users/customers will find it easy to add to this list; it is vastly extendable. Here are the 1001 reasons which make it so difficult to capture requirements. It is worth noting, however, that these problems have direct analogues in the classic problems of sociological method, especially sociologists' use of interviews and questionnaires. In the above list, we need only substitute the terms 'subject' or 'interviewee' for 'user' or 'customer' to come close to an articulation of traditional sociological difficulties of method.

3   THE PROBLEMS OF REQUIREMENTS ANALYSIS CONSTRUED AS DIFFICULTIES OF METHOD

Of course, we are all aware of these difficulties. The point of spelling them out is not just to remind everyone how bad the situation is. Instead, I want to suggest that we need critically to consider how we construe these as difficulties in the first place. My argument is that, by construing them as mere difficulties of method, we unwittingly prevent ourselves from moving beyond the current situation. To put it another way, my argument is that we need to become much more aware of the nature of, and our reaction to, these difficulties.

When I refer to the tendency to construe these problems as difficulties of method, I mean 'method' in the sense that denotes the enduring assumption that actual requirements pre-exist our efforts to 'capture' them. It is the very use of the metaphor 'capture' which supports and reaffirms this realist preconception. This preconception, I suggest is at the heart of our current flounderings in requirements analysis.

A first response to these problems as difficulties of method proposes that the fault lies in inadequate methods. The remedy, it is suggested, is to devise 'more sophisticated' ways of triangulating in upon the 'actual' requirements. The problem, it might be said, is that we need to be more rigorous and scientific in order to discover 'what is actually going on'. However, it is fairly easy to see that if the initial construal of the problem is erroneous, this first response is merely going to exacerbate rather than ameliorate the situation; it is a response which reaffirms rather than questions the realist preconception.

A second response which views requirements analysis problems as problems of method builds on the recognition that the capture (interview/questionnaire) process is a social process. Since the exchange involves communication between members of different social organisations, social (human, cognitive, etc.) factors (interests, motives, etc.) are said to be involved. This is unobjectionable, except that in this response, such 'social factors' are viewed as a source of distortion. They are seen as the intervening variables which detract from the detection of the actual requirements held by individuals. Once again we see how the response reaffirms the realist preconception. This response often leads to efforts to 'factor out' the social dimensions of requirements capture, so as to reveal (actual) requirements in their pure form. Thus, for all its apparent recognition of the relevance of 'the social', this response still subscribes to a view of problems in requirements analysis as 'technical', because it preserves the ideal of pre-existing requirements awaiting their detection (and capture) through careful screening out of the social[2].

A third, more sophisticated response takes the view that 'requirements' do not simply pre-exist the occasion of their 'capture'. The view here is that what turns out to count as 'requirements' is what emerges in the course of negotiation between 'capturers' and users; requirements are the upshot of a process of (often protracted) social interaction and communication across organisational boundaries. This last kind of response provides support for the nexus of efforts around participative, collaborative and user centred design. Thus, for example, attention is directed to

---

[2] Of course, this argument applies equally to all reactions to problems which cite the relevance of 'circumstances', sociological or otherwise. The point is not just that sociological variables are being given the wrong emphasis, but that the very conception of 'circumstantial' variables as distinguishable from the core essence of requirements is misconceived.

replacing traditional linear communication structures with a 'method of cooperative requirements capture' which 'pays attention' to the social process by which consensus is reached (chapter 3). Suffice to say that important questions still remain about what counts as adequate negotiation, co-operativeness and user centred-ness, and who decides[3]. More significantly, this form of response adopts some of the base assumptions about the notion of 'the user' and tends not to adopt a very critical attitude towards ideas about the capacity of the evolving system.

4   THE PROBLEMS OF REQUIREMENTS ANALYSIS AS CONCEPTUAL PROBLEMS

An alternative is to view the many problems of requirements capture and analysis as stemming from conceptual problems arising from deeply entrenched assumptions about requirements analysis. Let us take a look at some of these assumptions.

From a sociologist's point of view, the requirements process will always involve the creation and maintenance of (often new) social relationships across social organisational (and sometimes institutional) boundaries. This in turn suggests that requirements will always involve processes of negotiation and translation between producers and consumers, or between the representatives of each. Since this is an omnipresent feature of communication, it is neither possible nor desirable to 'factor out' or 'take account of' social factors. Such social 'factors' are constitutive of the communication involved, so should not be viewed merely as 'distorting variables' which can be disengaged from a separate 'core reality' (for example, what individuals really want). This then is a rather stronger claim for the constitutive character of the social than saying, for example, that 'the dry' and 'the wet' aspects of information 'need to be reconciled' (chapter 7). Instead, the constitutive view is that, in line with the demonstration in much recent research (in the sociology of science and technology) of the impossibility of separating the technical from the social, it is inappropriate to treat 'the social' as a residual ('nontechnical') category. As chapter 1 points out, one adverse consequence of presupposing this kind of distinction is to provide a 'stable core' of objectives which severely delimit orthodox approaches to requirements engineering. Hence, such categorical divides must be understood as the upshot of contingent social process. Precisely in those situations where a particular sub-set of issues appear technical (when, for example, they appear to be 'context insensitive' – Goguen, 1993), social forces are most powerfully at play (Latour, 1987; see also Low and

---

[3] A common supposition of 'user-centred' approaches is that the more participation the better. However, some of the examples from the case study described below suggest there are occasions when it is to the advantage of everyone concerned that the user is not involved in design decisions (Woolgar, 1991)!

Woolgar, 1993). It is in this constitutive sense that what counts as a 'requirement' is a social matter.

These considerations suggest that, rather than tackling the difficulties of requirements analysis as problems of method, to be solved by better or more careful techniques, or by using social science methods as an adjunct to existing procedures, we need to find a fresh conceptual frame. In particular, such a frame needs to take issue with the core, but as yet unexplicated assumptions which guide requirements analysis. We might, for example, begin to consider that 'the user' is perhaps not the most appropriate unit of analysis in all this. In particular, the problems of requirements analysis are perhaps much less to do with individual cognitive propensities and capacities, for example, and more to do with the wider organisational frame in which 'being a user' comes to have currency and makes sense. At the same time, this suggests that we should understand users' much celebrated inability to say exactly what they want of a system, not as the result of their failings, but in the context of the very many different ways in which IT and systems' capacities are represented to and by different social constituencies. More generally, we need to be more sceptical about any definitive claims for what different systems can and can not do.

I suggest two key concepts which can help build a fresh theoretical frame: the system as text and configuring the user.

5   THE SYSTEM AS TEXT

The metaphor of system as text is a vivid way of stressing the 'interpretatively flexible' nature and capacity of a machine or system. In this view, machines (systems) do not have inherent capacities; rather their capacity and capability is the upshot of users' interaction with the system. In the post-modernist adage, it is the reader who writes the text. Relatedly, the notion of machine/system as text encourages us to view processes of design, construction and use of systems as analogous to processes of producers writing and consumers reading a text. Thus, as far as requirements are concerned, the capacity of the system is likely to vary, before, during and after any specific 'requirements phase'.

Construing the system as a text encourages us to see that the nature of a system is in its reading. But this does not mean that any reading is possible. So how do we account for the fact that in practice only a limited set of readings are possible? Our question is how to account for this delimitation. Following Smith (1978), we can suggest it is the organisation of the text which makes one or other reading differentially possible[4]. For Smith, the important point is that the organisation of the text is isomorphic with the concept we use to make sense of it. In her example, a text

---

[4]   In Smith (1978) and other textual analysts influenced by ethnomethodology, the deterministic status of the text is present although muted. The usual formulation is that the organisation of the text provides for a particular reading. It thus delimits the interpretative options, rather than determining them.

'about' mental illness is organised in such a way as to make this reading possible. By direct analogy, I suggest, the system text is organised in such a way that 'its purpose' is available as a reading to the user. In her analysis, Smith notes how certain organisational features of texts provide 'instructions' which enable readers to make sense of content in terms of conclusions stated at the outset. To adapt Smith's terminology to our concern, the user is encouraged to find in her dealings with the system an adequate puzzle for the solution which the system offers.

A small extension of this analytic stance on texts suggests that the organisation of the text hinges not so much on mundane features like the length of sentences, the amount of space devoted to different topics and so on, but rather on associations made available within the text and between text and reader. Textual organisation refers critically, as far as the sense to be made of it is concerned, to the relationships made possible between the entities within and beyond the text. Certain characters become central to the story and others peripheral; groups of actants join forces while others disperse; the activities and achievements of some are highlighted, while others are relegated to the background, silenced and unnoticed. The reader (who is, I am afraid, the writer) of the text is invited to join with certain groups and disassociate herself from others.

6   CONFIGURING THE USER

In the system text metaphor, the user of a system is the reader of the text. As writers like Friedman (1989) have pointed out, the 1980s have seen considerable attention devoted to 'the problem of the user' amongst the designers and builders of computer systems. In the examples discussed below, I pursue the idea that the emergence of a new range of microcomputers crucially entails the definition, delineation and emergence of The User. We could say that this process amounts to the (social) construction of the user. However, it is not just the identity of the user which is constructed. For along with negotiations over who the user might be, comes a set of design (and other) activities which attempt to define, delimit and enable the users' possible actions. Consequently, it is better to say that by setting parameters for the user's actions, the evolving system effectively attempts to configure the user.

In configuring the user, the architects of a new system, its hardware engineers, product engineers, project managers, salespersons, technical support, purchasing, finance and control, legal personnel and the rest are all contributing to a definition of the reader of their text and establishing parameters for readers' actions[5]. Indeed,

---

[5] 'Configuring the user' involves much more than just marketing. It refers to underlying (and overriding) intangible conceptions of outsiders to the organisation which may not be possible to take into account in the process of market research and marketing more generally. For example, the organisation's beliefs and culture may result in specific decisions about which aspects of the market and which methods to deploy in carrying out market research.

the whole history of a system project can be construed as a struggle to configure (that is, to define, enable and constrain) the user. These different groups and individuals at different times hold different views and offer varying accounts of 'what the user is like'. Knowledge and expertise about the user is likely to be distributed within the company (producing organisation) in a loosely structured manner, with certain groups claiming more expertise than others in knowing what users are like. It is particularly important to note that this distribution of knowledge about users both precedes and survives any particular attempt explicitly to articulate what users require.

7   AN ETHNOGRAPHY OF COMPUTERS

Ethnography entails sustained participant observation in a setting being studied. The idea is that the participant observer joins the tribe and works for a prolonged period as one of the 'natives'. There are a number of different variants of ethnography currently being practised (see chapter 10). Arguably, however, the interpretation of ethnography most suited to the study of technical settings stresses two features. Firstly, the importance of accumulating empirical materials and observations *in situ*. The observer has to learn to be (like) a native, to develop a somewhat sophisticated appreciation of the specific technical problems which face participants. More than that, the observer must have access to design and other decisions as and when they happen, rather than having to reconstruct them retrospectively, when the benefits of hindsight have tended to blur the original rationale (if any!). Secondly, the importance of maintaining a level of analytic scepticism. Whereas traditional anthropologists have the task of merely describing the strange happenings which occur before them, ethnographers of technical settings also have to work at making features of their situation seem strange. This applies especially to what participants tell you about users! More generally, this kind of analytic scepticism is important in the context of natives' claims about the definitive qualities of the system, which aspects are amenable to renegotiation and so on (cf Low and Woolgar, 1993).

I carried out an 18-month participant observation study in a medium sized company which manufactures microcomputers and allied products, primarily for education. My research design was to follow a major project in detail from inception through to launch, first shipment and after-sales feedback. I joined the company as a project manager assistant on a project to produce a new range of microcomputers built around the new 286 chip. (For some details of the company and this development project see Appendix A). In the remainder of this chapter, I discuss selected aspects of the materials arising from this case study, using the twin notions of system as text and configuring the user.

8   KNOWLEDGE ABOUT USERS IS SOCIALLY STRUCTURED

8.1   Difficulties of knowing the user from within the company

My first vivid introduction to the socially structured character of knowledge about users occurred during an early meeting of a group of technical writers in the User Products section. The discussion centred on plans for carrying out usability trials. Who should be invited to act as subjects for these trials? The problem was that constraints of confidentiality made it difficult to select subjects who would know nothing about the new system. Getting in 'the man on the street' as they put it, was not a realistic option. At this point, parties to the discussion started to consider the possibility of finding 'true novices' amongst the workforce in the company.

In a fit of helpfulness, I offered my services. If they were really stuck, I said, I would be very happy to act as a subject since I would have no problem in acting as a naive user. I was very surprised when SallyP turned on me vehemently. Didn't I realise how differently users approached this? Didn't I realise how extraordinarily difficult it was for anyone in the company to appreciate the way users looked at things? People in the company couldn't possibly appreciate the user's point of view. Indeed, this was a major problem which pervaded the company: a failure to understand what it was really like to be a user.

I realised I had inadvertently stepped out of role. As a relative newcomer to the company, I had expressly volunteered my naivety in the Company Perspective. But SallyP was apparently unaware of my 'real' identity as participant observer. She assumed I was part of the project management team, and it was in that guise that she was addressing me. I had unwittingly reaffirmed her worst fears about insensitive 'techies' and their inability to see beyond a company mind-set. So I was admonished for presuming to be able to act like an outsider.

8.2   Alleged deficiencies in company knowledge about users

As this anecdote suggests, certain individuals could claim the right to speak authoritatively on behalf of users. At the same time, it was said that some of the individuals and groups you would expect to know about users were manifestly deficient in just this kind of knowledge. For example, one of the technical writers spoke of her amazement in discovering that the Marketing section apparently had no well defined target market lists. I was told by a long-serving member of Technical Support that 'typically, the engineers don't have a clue about users'. She told the tale of an early attempt by 'engineering' to encourage users initially to configure their new systems by input-ing a long line of characters which would have been 'meaningless to your average teacher'. She poured scorn on what she saw as the engineers' presumption that users would be happy to have to do this.

8.3   Stories about users

Members of the User Products section felt that their conception of users was affected by a wide range of influences, ranging from their own first time of using computers through to 'hearing tales about what happens outside'. Knowledge about users thus involved the circulation of stories and tales about the experiences of users. Frequently, stories about 'what happens outside' seem to have originated in the Technical Support and Service sections of the company[6]. These sections were generally reckoned to represent 'the sharp end' of dealings with customers. The view was that whereas, for example, the engineering and design sections worked in some isolation from users, those in Technical Support had much more experience of users since they dealt with user complaints and queries at first hand. Some of those in Tech Support had themselves 'moved out' from working in the engineering sections and seemed keen to emphasise their new-found responsibilities in dealing with users.

Significantly, these stories about users were nearly always couched in terms of insider-outsider contrasts: what was happening (or had happened) 'on the outside' was a recurrent motif. The boundaries of the company thus played an important part in the telling of these tales. For example, one respondent recalled the experience of one particular 'outside' visit leading to the realisation that in schools someone, perhaps a teacher, had had to devise extremely plain instructions for use alongside the computer. The same respondent related a story passed on to her by a colleague in Technical Support:

> Another tale I remember hearing is that a school who had a machine up to like four months. They wouldn't unpack it or anything, they were too scared. There was no one around they thought was able to do much with it ... Yes. I mean GOOD GRIEF!

8.4   User singular and users multiple

Whereas participants often referred to 'the user' in the singular, it is not clear they thought users of the Stratus 286 would all exhibit identical, monolithic sets of attributes. They could presumably imagine a wide variety of purposes and uses; they would have been aware that Marketing stressed the versatility of the systems when promoting the company's products. All this makes curious the continued singular reference to 'the user' in the company, until this is understood as a generalised formulation produced for purposes of establishing contrasts between insiders and outsiders. The generalised user provides a more successfully stark contrast with us/the company/members of the company, than would a heterogeneous rag-bag of

---

[6] The notion that the Technical Support section is the fount of the various 'atrocity stories' circulating in the company is developed in an analysis of hot-line calls to the company (Woolgar, 1993).

customers with varying attributes. The contrast is rhetorically important for example, as we have seen, in stressing the difficulties of knowing what precisely it is that users want. Given the extent of the (claimed) difference between the way 'we' look at the world, and the way 'the user' looks at the world, it becomes necessary to rely upon especially skilled spokespersons – those few with knowledge of these very different entities. When someone in User Products says that Engineering have no notion what the user expects, the achieved distinction between the monolithic entity – the user – and the monolithic entity – the engineer – makes a political point about the inadequacies of all members of Engineering. More pervasively, this generalised formulation reaffirms divisions between us and them. Company boundaries, differences between insiders and outsiders, are more greatly emphasised through deployment of 'the user' than by admitting that some users are more familiar with our systems than others. This rhetorical rendering of the generalised user also afforded some interesting variations on the more familiar examples of prejudiced rhetoric: He was a user but he seemed to know what he was talking about.

8.5   Users don't necessarily know best

References to the user emerging from the Engineering sections of the company included the view that, although it was important to have an idea of who 'the user' was and what they wanted in the system, users' views should not be unproblematically adopted in design. The suggestion was that designers should respond instead to ideas about 'where the market was going' or 'where things were going', a more generalised conception of the future requirements of computing. Significantly, such conceptions were frequently referred to as 'visions' of the future, which seemed to stress technical progression and which were couched in terms which transcended individual users' desires for particular technical features. A variant of this line of argument was the more familiar view that there was no point in asking users what they wanted because they themselves didn't know. According to this view, such ignorance arose primarily because users were unaware of likely future developments. This provided an effective rationale for not placing too much emphasis on users' views. According to this perspective, configuring the user involves the determination of likely future requirements and actions of users. Since the company tends to have better access to the future than users, it is the company's view which defines users' future requirements.

9   CONSTRAINING AND ENABLING USER ACCESS: THE IMPORTANCE OF THE CASE

The start of the usability trials for the new system text was delayed several times. The User Products section was caught, as it was on several other occasions, between the need to ensure usability testing as early as possible in the development of the product, and the late availability of a 'finished' product. It was reasoned that the most fruitful assessments of usability could only be carried out with the product in a form as near as possible to that which would be experienced by the user. One of the main reasons for the delay in the project as a whole centred on the availability of the case. Members of User Products took the view that usability trials could only properly take place when a cased version of the system was available. Some negotiation ensued when the first prototype case appeared, but Product Engineering argued that it was too risky to loan the sole case for purposes of usability testing.

It is significant that User Products felt the necessity for a physically bounded entity for use in usability testing. The system would not be a real system unless it was in its case. 'Real' in this usage specifically denotes 'the kind of system a user would expect'. This contrasts markedly with what counts as a real system within the company. Particularly within the engineering sections (notably Hardware Design and Engineering Quality), systems were mostly left open on desktops and workbenches, their innards displayed, precisely so that the engineers had quick access to the inside of the system. In these sections, it was unusual to find a system inside its case.

The following contrast between the treatment of computers 'outside' and 'inside' the company was provided by one of my students employed by the company for a summer work placement:

> When I joined the company I was a 'soft' user (Turkle, 1984). Although I did not believe the computer was 'magical', I could not recognise the internal parts of a computer and had never taken the casing off a computer. In fact I had always been deterred from doing so. However in the EQ [Engineering Quality] section, no such squeamishness was expected. Machines were perched on 'breadboards' – metal frames or boards, or they were missing their top covers. ... At school I had been told that the ideal place for computers was a dust free atmosphere kept at a controlled atmosphere. In the company, there was no such reverence for the computer. They were regularly taken apart. In fact, when a machine which was in its case did not work, the top was removed immediately and the boards were jiggled around just to check that the connections were all right. (Dobbins, 1990)

The surprise of finding the innards of computers regularly on display around the desks and benches in the company is part of the experience of moving from the outside to within the organisation. The system's boundary symbolises that of the company, so that access to the inner workings of the system is access to the inner workings of the company.

Many similar examples[7] underscore the symbolic importance of the system's (text's) boundary. The video record of the usability trials shows putative users working out how to relate to (and in one instance, literally, how to connect to) a technol-

---

[7] These include the induction programme – a series of meetings for those newly starting with the company; attempts to purchase the system; meetings and discussions to decide the name of the new system; debates about whether or not to include a new user interface; various exercises in compatibility testing; internal launches to the sales force; and so on.

ogy which has already been black-boxed. The task for subjects of the usability trials is to work out how to access the interior of the black box, in order to extract what they need from the system/company. The system's task is to make sure these putative users access the company in the prescribed fashion: by way of preferred (hardware) connections or through a predetermined sequence of keyboard operations. The user will find other routes barred and warnings posted on the case itself. Labels bear warnings of the dire consequences of unauthorised boundary trangression: electrocution, invalidation of the warranty and worse. These labels often also redirect users to company sources – for example, to 'user documentation' or to the company technical support hotline – where they can be told the 'correct' pattern of user action, in line with the approved configuration of the user's relationship with the company[8].

10   CONCLUSION

I began by suggesting an essential similarity between the (increasingly) familiar difficulties of requirements analysis, and the classic difficulties experienced by social scientists in eliciting information from their subjects. Just as with other sets of relationships between producer/professional and customer/client – doctors, lawyers, and so on – these difficulties centre on problems of negotiation and translation, as the producer/professional attempts to force the experience, beliefs, discourse of the customer/client into the conceptual and technical categories which make sense to the sphere of the professional/producer. In particular, this negotiation and translation invariably seems to entail communication across social organisational boundaries.

The general and enduring character of these difficulties suggests that they be regarded, not as difficulties which can be eased by the use of more sophisticated (or just more) scientific methodology, but as conceptual problems which will be encountered on every occasion that existing assumptions are reduplicated in the relationship between producer and consumer. Rethinking requirements analysis means we have to build an alternative theoretical model of the producer–consumer relationship.

One way to do this is to construe the technical artefact (machine. software system) as a text, the interpretatively flexible upshot of a variety of writing practices, which invites readings (uses, interpretations, actions) from a more or less well defined community of users. The nature of the relationship of readers to the achieved text can in part be understood by construing the production/writing as a process of configuring the user: the identification, definition and construction of putative readers. Configuring the user is a process of establishing legitimate and illegitimate ways in which readers may relate to the text; it both enables and constrains users' relationships to the producing company and defines the set of 'permissible' actions in rela-

---

[8]   For a further example of the symbolic value of the system boundary, played against the metaphor of transgressing organisational boundaries, see the analysis of computer virus stories in Woolgar and Russell (1989).

tion to (uses and interpretations of) the technical artefact. The process of configuration involves the juxtaposition of a wide variety of assumptions, preconceptions and beliefs about 'users' within the producing company, itself characterised by socially structured knowledge and expertises about users.

Notably, user configuration involves boundary work. The user's character and capacity, her possible future actions are structured and defined in relation to the system. As is dramatically illustrated in the case of usability trials (Woolgar, 1991), when there is still considerable ambiguity both about the capacity of the system and about the character of the user, the system becomes its relationship to the user, and vice versa. In this, the system is a metaphor for the company so that, in particular, the boundaries of the system are the boundaries of the company. The system's case symbolises the user's relationship to the company. Insiders know the system, whereas users have a configured relationship to it, such that only certain forms of access/use are encouraged. This never guarantees that some users will not find unexpected and uninvited uses for the system. But such behaviour will be categorised as bizarre, foreign, perhaps typical of mere users. More generally, of course, the more significant this boundary, the more likely will be the prevalence of this kind of racist talk[9].

The notion of 'capturing' requirements, like its counterpart in some versions of social science research, 'gathering' data, does not make much sense in these examples. It certainly does scant justice to the complexity of the relationships between producers and consumers in the case I studied. It is clear, for example, that the 'requirements' of these users were defined, constructed, nurtured and redefined as part of a long complex process of development which extended beyond the formal parameters of a particular system project. The requirements that the company saw itself addressing did not pre-exist the company's choice of design alternatives. Instead, user requirements emerged from a complex process of discussion, contention and political manoeuvring, only one small fraction of which approximated the formal project phase designated 'requirements analysis'.

This can sound like cynical manipulation of what was a relatively captive customer base. But it is important to note that much more than simple manipulation of users is at stake. For example, it is clear that many of the company's preconceptions about users were ingrained in company culture. To generalise, we should subscribe to the view that requirements don't just happen: they are in an important sense a producer's fiction. Certainly they are actively constructed. But this will also involve implicit (and perhaps company or organisation specific) preconceptions about users and their requirements.

---

[9] It is in this light that we might best understand the occurrence of 'atrocity stories' – tales about the nasty things that users have done to our systems (see footnote 6). Such tales portray nastiness in terms of users' disregard for instructions (violation of the configured relationship users are encouraged to enter into) and their disregard for the case (violation of the system's boundary). Whereas many of the company members engage in the exchange of such atrocity stories, it is also possible to identify liberals who are willing to speak up for the user. Users can't help the way they behave; they just need to be educated to understand what we are trying to achieve here. Readers can't help the way they interpret the text; they just need to be educated. . . .

Clearly, the case study described here is hardly typical of all situations where requirements specification is invited. Microcomputer development is a largely technology driven market; the company studied was trying to cater for a wide range of potential users; the case study involved (predominantly) hardware development rather than software products; arguably, the particular users under study were relatively unsophisticated; and so on. Nonetheless, the preceding discussion suggests there is merit in thinking further about the ways in which the requirements analysis process inadvertently (and perhaps inevitably) constitutes the phenomenon it sets out to 'capture'. As a result of the process of configuring the user, analysts of requirements are likely to reproduce a version of user requirements which meet preconceptions about users.

In sum, the central implication of the ethnographic research described in this chapter is that we need to understand requirements analysis in the broader context of organisational and company culture. The pursuit of requirements should not centre around the application of disembodied formal rules – premised on the mistaken belief that actual requirements exist independently of local organisational preconceptions about users; it should instead be the occasion for taking a close look at the taken for granted assumptions which permeate the producing organisation. There is, I suggest, much value in having the scepticism of an ethnographer to hand when embarking upon the requirements process.

Finally, it is worth noting that the extent to which the requirements process differs in different situations raises some interesting further questions for the notions of system as text and configuring the user. How does the development of products for a mass market (involving a substantial heterogeneous community of users) differ from the development of a bespoke software system for a single client? More interestingly, perhaps, what are the constraints of configuration upon innovation? The case study discussed above concerns user configuration in the context of relatively minor changes to an existing PC standard. In such a situation it may be a relatively straightforward matter to configure users who are used to the general form of the product. By contrast, how does one generate and deal with user requirements in an innovative situation, where the objective is to devise an entirely new type of software or technical artefact? Or, relatedly, we might expect quite different sets of readings and preconceptions about users according to whether our efforts are aimed at merely automating existing features of a work situation, or whether we want to suggest a radically different organisation of work practices. In every case, we will need to be alert to the particular forms of social relationship between producer and consumer[10].

---

[10] This discussion has steered clear of the thorny issue of evaluating how successfully requirements have in fact been identified and captured. The evidence from the case study again suggests many diverse criteria of adequacy. For example, users' (which ones?) 'satisfaction' with a product may be a gratifying outcome for producers, but it is not clear that this is the same as having satisfied their 'requirements'. The artefact at the centre of the case study was said to have been successful in the particular sense that the new range of computers were said to have 'sold well'. Perhaps this is a measure, not of the accurate capture of users' requirements, but of the success of a social relationship which tutored users about what it was they could want.

APPENDIX A

Since certain members of the company are still uncertain about the benefits of publicity arising from the kind of analysis undertaken in this chapter, I currently refer to the company anonymously. They are a very successful company, having been founded some 14 years prior to my study, having grown in size by an average of approximately 20% per year over the previous five years, and having increased its turnover by an average of about 35% per year in the same period. By the time of my study they had achieved a position such that both they and their main competitors were claiming in excess of 50% of the market share!

After some negotiation, it was agreed that I should join the company as part of the newly expanded project management team. We felt this would be a strategic position from which to carry out the study since, as a project manager assistant with responsibility for liaison and coordination between different sections within the company, I would be able to enjoy relatively free access across disparate parts of the company. The project I joined – DNS – entailed following the lead established by IBM in the production of their IBM PS/2 standard.

The DNS range was the third in a recent series of microcomputer product ranges which brought the company more into line with IBM compatibility standards. The first of these – the 'Stratus PC' – had been built around the 186 chip to 'provide an educational computer which was appropriate for schools'. I was told that the Marketing section had received the acclaim of the press for the Stratus PC with some glee, especially when one review went so far as to praise the system by speaking of the IBM PC as a good Stratus clone. In fact, the Stratus PC was not designed as IBM compatible, and although IBM was not at that point seen as the main competitor, a further range – the 'K series' – was developed to compete with the IBM XT at the high end of the market. Subsequently, DNS (later marketed under the name Stratus 286) was developed to fill a position between the two previous ranges, combining the educational virtues of the Stratus PC (186) with the IBM compatibility of the K series (286).

REFERENCES

Dobbins, J. (1990). Good for business, death for the joy of work: an ethnography of quality in a microcomputer company. Unpublished BSc Dissertation, Department of Human Sciences, Brunel University, June.

Friedman, A. L. (with D. S. Cornford) (1989). *Computer Systems Development: history, organisation and implementation*, John Wiley.

Garfinkel, H. (1967). *Studies in Ethnomethodology*, Prentice-Hall.

Latour, B. (1987). *Science in Action*, Open University Press.

Latour, B. (1988). The prince for machines as well as for machinations, in B. Elliott (Ed.), *Technology and Social Process*, pp 44–69, Edinburgh University Press.

Low, J. and Woolgar, S. (1993). Managing the social-technical divide: some aspects of the discursive structure of information systems development, in P. Quintas (Ed.), *Social Dimensions of Systems Engineering*, pp. 34–59, Ellis Horwood.

Smith, D. (1978). K is mentally ill: the anatomy of a factual account, *Sociology* **12**, 23–53.

Turkle, S. (1984). *The Second Self*, Simon & Schuster.

Woolgar, S. (1989). Stabilisation rituals: steps in the socialisation of a new machine, *PICT National Conference*, Brunel University, May.

Woolgar, S. (1991). Configuring the user: the case of usability trials, in J. Law (Ed.), *A Sociology of Monsters*, pp. 58–100, Routledge.

Woolgar, S. (1993). The user talks back, pp 58–100, *CRICT Discussion Paper Series*, no. 40, Brunel University.

Woolgar, S. and Russell, G. (1989). The social basis of troubles with software: the case of computer virus stories, *PICT Workshop on Social Perspectives on Software*, Manchester. (Also to appear in F. Murray and S. Woolgar (Eds), *Social Perspectives on Software*.)

Nine

Occasioned practices in the work of software engineers

Graham Button,
Rank Xerox EuroPARC, Cambridge, UK
Wes Sharrock,
University of Manchester, UK

1 INTRODUCTION

This chapter is, in part, concerned with the *practical use and implementation* of a methodology which has been designed to ensure a disciplined approach to requirements analysis and a structured approach to the development process in general[1]. It examines the work of a group of software engineers who are developing the embedded software for a new photocopier, and it is concerned with how part of their work consists of *making the method work* by fitting it to the contingent circumstances of their project. The object is not, however, to criticise the methodology for its failure to meet the demands placed upon it by the software engineers, nor to criticise the engineers for failing to strictly follow the methodology. Rather, the object is to develop an understanding of *what it is* to follow a methodology that has been designed to systematically approach the problem of requirement analysis by examining how it is applied in the working circumstances of an actual development project.

The relevance of the chapter to requirements analysis in general resides in the attempt to understand the *relationship between methods and systems development*. Appreciating the particulars of that relationship may suggest that understanding the social organisation of the work of systems development is as important as formulat-

---

[1] The methodology is *The Yourdon Development Methodology* (Yourdon and Constantine, 1979). In addition to considering the use of Yourdon methodology, we also examine the situated use of a development environment, CASE technology, and the programming language C. Like Yourdon methodology we regard these as formally organised, thus our remarks on formalisation and methodology are also directed towards the use of development technologies and programming languages.

Requirements Engineering
ISBN 0–1238–5335–4

ing a set of methods for developers to follow. This is because part of that work consists of making the method organisationally[2] accountable in the practices of making it work. In this respect, the difficulties that were encountered in the development which we will describe were not just technical difficulties, and we share the reservation expressed by Mullery (1991) that the causes of project difficulties should invariably be ascribed to "technical difficulties in the approach to their development". The case study we report here details the extent to which the project's problems arose from the organisation's own difficulties in, for example, recruiting staff with appropriate technical skills. We further emphasise the extent to which the development methodology which was adopted was used for purposes other than its strictly technical one. As a result the technical requirements were frequently subordinated to other, *organisational*, demands[3].

This chapter thus treats requirements analysis as *itself* a topic for analysis or investigation as it is encountered as part of the work of systems development, and its object is to explicate facets of that work in the situated circumstances of development. As sociologists we are concerned with understanding the details of the social practices through which that work is ordered and produced[4]. We hope that having drawn out these details and having shown that there is a more complex relationship between a method for requirements analysis and the situated and local processes of development than merely following the method, that computer scientists and software engineers may then be able to reflect upon ways of enriching their supportive practices in the light of that complexity[5].

2   SOCIAL SCIENCE METHODOLOGY AND REQUIREMENTS ANALYSIS

Before we begin to address the case study upon which this chapter is based we need to make a number of introductory remarks about the type of sociological concerns

---

[2]   We should note that here as on other occasions in this chapter we are not reifying organisations, only using the word as a shorthand for individuals, groups, etc.

[3]   We have no reason to believe from our own observations, nor were we given reason to believe from the people involved that this project was any different *in kind* to other development projects that members of the development team had been previously involved in.

[4]   More accurately, this interest originates in the type of sociology we pursue, *ethnomethodology*. See Button (1993) for a collection of other ethnomethodologicaly influenced studies of technology.

[5]   Experience has taught us, however, that some computer scientists often want snappy solutions and answers from sociologists to what we consider to be complex matters, as if their own discipline was capable of fulfilling such a tall order. Bearing in mind these experiences we will conclude this chapter by formulating a number of development maxims based upon our study. We hope, however, that it is the explication of the relationship between methods and development as that is organised in the contingent and situated work of development which will hold the attention of most readers and will be the occasion of reflection about how to understand ways of analysing or capturing requirements.

involved in our understanding of the way in which requirements analysis and development are undertaken. Our principal interest here is in how, through the use of particular development tools, computer scientists and software engineers produce and use *formalisations*, as part of their development work. We do not expect that computer scientists and software engineers should take a passionate or deep interest in the internecine disputes of sociology, but, given that some at least are showing an interest in sociological methods[6] they should at least be aware that the discipline of sociology is far from unified or harmonious. In that context, they should also be informed that the sociological approach which has gained much of their attention, ethnomethodology[7], is by no means the prevailing one but is very much a minority and dissenting tradition within the broader discipline, and that part of that dissent revolves around the sociological production and use of formalisations.

The predominant drive in sociology has been to formalise the discipline's intellectual apparatus. However, from the point of view of other sociologists, ethnomethodologists included, these attempts have proven highly problematical and this has motivated an interest in examining the problems of developing and implementing formal schemes. Appreciating that the development and implementation of formal schemes is by no means confined within sociology; it has been found illuminating to investigate other settings of social life where the following out of formal prescriptions is involved, and it is not surprising, then, that such constructions as the formal methodologies contrived for the organisation of software development (and other aspects of the development of new technology) have come to the attention of sociologists like ourselves.

Ethnomethodology's interest in what is involved in following a formal prescription as part of the accomplishment of the work of those concerned originates in a small, illustrative study conducted by Garfinkel (1967), into the work of 'coders' on a sociological project. Coders are routinely required to work to a set of rules which instruct them in how to classify the respondent answers that are recorded on the interview schedules which they are engaged in coding.

The aim in the case reported by Garfinkel was to make the coding rules as exhaustive and explicit as possible, so as to eradicate any discretion on the coders' part. The finding of his study was, though, that this could not be done, that however full and detailed the rules in the coders' handbook were made, there was nonetheless a need for decision and discretion in the coders' work. The coders would resort

---

[6] See, Bently *et al.* (1992), Hughes, Randall and Shapiro (1992), Somerville *et al.* (1991), Robinson (1990), Norman and Thomas (1990), Finkelstein and Fuks (1990), and Cawsey (1990).

[7] Suchman's (1987) book *Plans and Situated Action* was the first to consider aspects of AI and computer science in terms of ethnomethodological interests. Garfinkel's (1987) *Studies in Ethnomethodology* is the foundational text in ethnomethodology. Useful introductions to ethnomethodology are Benson and Hughes (1983), Heritage (1984), and Sharrock and Anderson (1986). Also see Button (1991) for a development of ethnomethodological interests for foundational issues in the human sciences, and Button (1993) for a range of ethnomethodologically influenced studies of technology.

to a variety of practices, which were *ad hoc* relative to the coding manual's purportedly systematic character, to decide what the coding rules actually required of them and whether what they were doing was actually (or virtually) in correspondence with those rules.

The prime thrust of Garfinkel's argument is against some sociological conceptions of the nature of social action (particularly those which seek to conceive it as generated algorithmically), demonstrating that the capacity to follow out a line of conduct would requite understandings on the part of those executing that line, which would necessarily exceed what could be specified 'in so many words'. Its meaning for concerns of the sort which are addressed in this volume, however, has to do with the extent to which the implementation of 'formal schemes' depends upon the *ad hoc* practices of those subject to them, upon their resort, in actual situations, in the face of real circumstances, to their own 'good sense' of what is needed and what can be done in order to decide what the rules, procedures or instructions require of them. In the case study which follows, it will be seen that the software engineers had on occasion to decide whether to stick with the step-by-step requirements of their development method, or to (temporarily) abandon these so that schedule deadlines be met and/or the demands of fellow workers be accommodated.

The point of Garfinkel's study of coders was not to suggest the futility of creating 'methodologies' or to imply that these have inbuilt shortcomings but was, instead, to emphasise the extent to which the implementation of such methodologies requires that they be 'made to work' in application. The coders were not engaged in circumventing the coding prescriptions, nor did they even act in disregard of them, for they were assiduous in consulting the handbook and in discussing what a correct decision would be in a particular case. Their *ad hoc* practices were, rather, directed at determining what the manual was telling them to do and in relating that, as closely as they could, to what was practically possible with respect to any given coding decision. The coders routinely invoked their reciprocally recognised 'good sense' understanding of how things generally worked, of the objectives of the project and of the purposes of the coding manual itself to assure (as best they could) a correspondence between what they were doing and what they were supposed to do. In summary, the coders were 'making the method work'. Similarly, the software engineers described below were engaged in determining how to relate what they were *supposed* to do to what they could actually do. They were not, however, dissatisfied with their software development methodology even though they patently could not faithfully follow its prescriptions; for them, it was just a fact of the contingencies of development with which they had to grapple.

They were aware that they were intended to follow the methodology for a number of good reasons which had to do with the development of good software design, but they were also aware that the application of this methodology required the phasing of activities in ways that they could not necessarily control and that adherence to its step-by-step organisation would take such time as to mean they would be 'holding up the rest of the project'.

Mullery's (1991) point about coordination is applicable here. The Yourdon development methodology which was adopted for the project called for the coordination of hardware and software work. However, the hardware work had been done in advance of the software development, thus the hardware engineers applied pressure for early (premature, from the software engineers' point of view) software releases. Recognising that meeting deadlines – and enabling others to meet theirs' – so that the project would not be 'held up' was the dominant *practical priority*, and the engineers would suspend the operation of the methodology to ensure that software could be provided. They had not given up on the objective of producing good software, but, for the moment, the working out of the software design according to the method had to be postponed in recognition of overriding organisational realities.

We do not comment on the wisdom or realism of such decisions (for the hopes that software engineers had that they would be able to get back to working out the software in accord with the method and without further disruption and distraction must have been fragile) but merely point out that the deviation from Yourdon was something about which, *under those circumstances*, the developers thought they had no choice. Their conviction that they had 'no choice' in such a matter must, of course, depend upon their estimation of the chances that, were they to insist in adhering to the methodology regardless of its consequences for the project's scheduling – leaving hardware engineers with 'nothing to do' for some time, for example – they would be supported by their superiors.

The fact that the implementation of software development methodologies instantiates ethnomethodological themes pertaining to the implementation of formal schemes in actual settings in a rich and varied way accounts for our interest in the topic. The fact that ethnomethodology emphasises the argument that it is an unavoidable feature of the use of methods that they will have to be 'ad hoced' and improvised on the occasions of their use explains some of the interest that computer scientists and system developers have found in ethnomethodology. However, although there are mutual interests here, studies such as Garfinkel's pose epistemological problems for sociology that may not be relevant for computer scientists. We hope, though, that a mutual interest can be maintained, for we argue that such studies may point computer scientists who are thinking about the use of sociological methods in requirements analysis in a particular direction. If methodologies are thought of as procedural recipes to follow in the design of a system, then the work of the actual implementation of the methodology may, considering ethnomethodological understandings of the situated work involved in applying methods, go unrecognised. This would mean that what is a crucial feature of development, actually applying and making the methods work in the circumstances of their application, may not have been explicitly noticed and recognised. However, realising that methodologies cannot be divorced from their practical use, then knowing about that use and how methodologies are implemented on actual occasions may allow developers to better understand the actual process of development itself. In turn, a better understanding of the development process may enable them to reflect upon better ways of supporting the actual work of development.

3   AN INTRODUCTION TO THE SOFTWARE ENGINEERING TEAM

Project 'Archer' is being undertaken by the European subsidiary of an international company that is primarily known for its production of photocopiers and computer systems. It is re-engineering a copier that is in commercial production in Japan where it was built by the company's Japanese subsidiary. The project involves making the copier fit multi-national requirements. The embedded software is being developed at a site in England and the hardware at a site in Holland. At the time that this study took place, the hardware had already been built and the software development was twelve months into its development cycle and was suffering from time-slippage.

'Archer' is part of the company's overall production strategy of re-engineering Japanese designs to multi-national requirements. It fitted that strategy for a number of reasons, primarily that in Japan the original machine was selling very well and that it had a number of features that marked it out from its closest rival. In particular, it was a very fast machine. Project 'Archer' was embarked upon because, as it was argued, the machine was already in commercial production and 'all' that the English company would have to do was to 'customise' it for the multi-national market; the company could thus introduce into a new market a proven and popular machine that had a strong technical pedigree and with a short-time to market horizon. Further, the Japanese company had an international reputation in its own right before becoming part of the parent company which was eager to benefit from the Japanese knowledge and expertise that was involved in engineering such a fast machine. Consequently, project 'Archer' also fitted into the overall corporate strategy of attempting to export this knowledge and expertise to other parts of the company.

Initially, the 'customisation' of the machine for the European market appeared to be straightforward[8]. The engineers would have the Japanese machine to work with and would be able to consult with members of the original Japanese development team should the need arise. Thus developing the requirements for the machine seemed quite straightforward, although new ones were to be added at the behest of the marketing department who felt that the ability for the machine to produce covers and inserts was seen to be a particularly strong sales point.

The development team was to be a relatively small one of seventeen-and-a-half heads. It was thought that because the project was a re-engineering one that the development of the software would be relatively straightforward. If problems arose then the English team would, as we noted, have access to their Japanese counterparts who could advise them on the basis of the original development. Indeed, the managers of the Japanese project had visited the English site and together with the

---

[8]   It was necessary to make the machine meet European safety standards and to re-design aspects of the control panel interface.

project manager and task leader had put in place a machinery for contacting the original Japanese engineers via phone and e-mail.

A number of technical and organisational factors, however, thwarted the original intentions of the project managers. First, when the documentation for the original design was delivered it was found to be in Japanese. The manager and task leader had, however, begun to assemble a development team, one of whom spoke and read Japanese. Nevertheless, although he could provide improvised and impromptu translations, it was also found that the documentation was so incomplete and partial that it made little sense to someone who had not been part of the original development team. This meant that the embryonic team that was forming had to contact their Japanese colleagues, the intention being to interrogate them about their design. It then transpired, however, that although the Japanese managers they had originally met could speak English, the actual Japanese engineers they needed to talk to could not, and thus the easy resolution to their dilemmas and difficulties was not just a phone call or e-mail away; for all practical purposes the phone was redundant, and the e-mail took some days of response time whilst a translation of their queries and a translation of the response was put together. Even then the responses were not full and the English managers began to speculate that the Japanese were being intentionally uncooperative and put this down to yet another example of the difficulties of working with the Japanese part of the company which, it was felt, was generally resisting the dissemination of its expertise throughout the worldwide organisation as a whole.

These problems arose in the early days of planning the re-engineering of the software, and before more than a couple of the final head-count had been appointed. The manager and the task-leader for the project explained that as they encountered the contingencies recounted above they began to realise that the project was not as straightforward as it had at first seemed. Far from being a 'customisation' and 're-engineering' project, the software was going to require a major redesign, which would make the project a very technical one requiring a high degree of experience and competence, especially in the area of photocopier design. They were faced with the task of having to redesign what, due to the speed requirement, was technically difficult software with the added complications of including new requirements such as "covers" and "inserts" which in themselves were not considered to be simple engineering matters.

To support the software development, the project manager and the task leader argued for the introduction of development support tools. This argument revolved around the technical complexity of the development. Because the development would make exacting technical demands they argued that the engineers needed to be supported in their development work to a higher degree than was normal for a development project within the company. They thus proposed what for the company would be new moves. First, so that a proper definition of requirements could be produced, it was argued that the engineering should be done strictly under the procedures of Yourdon methodology. Second, to ensure that the engineers would write to requirements and produce full documentation it was proposed that a considerable monetary investment be made in CASE technology[9]. Third, that the normal programming language used at the site[10] be abandoned in favour of C.

With this sketch of the project in hand we want to now turn to examining the use of the methodology, the environment and the language in the actual work of engineering the software. It will be suggested that this work turns on the orientation to, and invocation of, two rationales for their use: a technical rationale and a social/organisational rationale. In the *technical deployment* of the methodology, the development environment and the language it is possible to see an *organisational accountability*.

4 TWO RATIONALES AT WORK IN THE PROJECT

Two rationales were embedded within the argument for the use of the method, the environment and the language. Whilst one rationale was oriented to the *engineering of the software* the other was oriented to the *engineering of the development team*. That is, within the arguments that were given for the organisation of the development around Yourdon principles, within a CASE environment and programming in C, all three were being offered as both and at the same time technical and organisational artefacts. As technical artefacts they would be used in the engineering of the software and as organisational artefacts they would be used in the engineering of the development team.

4.1   The technical character of the development

The argument in favour of using Yourdon methodology, CASE and C was articulated in terms of proprietary and textbook rationales. This consisted of fitting the abstract rationales for each of them to the project-in-hand. It also involved setting aside the social and organisational character of the development.

It was argued that the complex technical character of the development necessitated a proper and methodical approach to requirement analysis which could be achieved by using Yourdon methodology. As noted, the original machine was very fast and this was also a requirement for the multi-national version. To work to this requirement a proper understanding of what it consisted of was necessary, and the engineers would have to engage in a full and proper analysis of this and other requirements for the machine. Further, the project would be structured so as not to compromise requirements by, for example, making premature design decisions.

---

[9] The particular computer-aided software engineering (CASE) package they purchased was *Teamwork* by Cadre.

[10] This was *Sequel*, an in-house language developed for the production of the embedded software for photocopiers.

Inasmuch as Yourdon provides a very tight structured approach to development, it was argued that it would fit the bill.

The use of CASE technology for this project was made by invoking the fact that the engineers in project 'Archer' were working in a multi-engineering environment. This meant that they required a proper definition of interfaces and a proper documentation of the software, because within such environments there are problems of writing the software to requirements. If CASE technology was used it would make the engineers follow Yourdon methodology and thus write to requirements.

Also, the problems caused by the lack of proper documentation accompanying the original design were highlighted, and it was argued that the use of CASE tools would provide for proper and adequate documentation, and thus the company would be well served in the long run. Having just experienced the difficulties that are associated with lack of proper documentation, the use of CASE technology was championed by the argument that inasmuch as they would allow this development to be properly documented then future maintenance of the software would be easier and more cost effective. A contrast was drawn between 'how things were' and with 'how they were to be'. How things had been, the lack of proper documentation had in part caused the problem that was now faced, thus ensuring that there would be proper documentation accompanying the development would help mitigate the possibility of a similar outcome in the future. The long-term view was contrasted with the short-term view. The short-term view was to restrict the documentation process to gain the advantage of a shorter development time. The long-term view was that proper documentation would provide for a more efficient project at the end of the day, a design that could be easily worked on in the future. This was for the good of the company because, in the long run, it would be easier to maintain and hence cheaper and more cost effective.

Regarding the change of the programming language, it was argued that Sequel did not support micro-processing needs of modern hardware requirements. C, however, it was reasoned, supports up-to-date hardware and although they could have used Ada or PLA they decided that C had a technical advantage in flexibility, structured analysis and real-time programming.

4.2   The organisational character of the development

To elaborate upon the organisational character of Yourdon methodology, CASE and C, it can be emphasised that the project was considered by the management to be a very technical one which would give the engineers a high degree of responsibility and freedom, but would also require that they work together as part of a team. Different members of the team, or sub-groups within the team had responsibility for different sections of the development. However, it was necessary for those sections to non-problematically interface with one another. Thus the managers not only required engineers with enough experience to be able to shoulder the responsibility of individual development, but also with enough experience to organise that development so as to ensure that it would eventually interface with the other developments with minimal difficulties. The engineers would thus have to organise their own work and organise its compatibility with each others' work.

However, experienced photocopier software engineers are few and far between, even within a company known for the production of photocopiers, and the managers of the project were afraid that they would not be able to recruit sufficiently experienced engineers onto the project. This problem was compounded by the fact that although the project was a technically complicated development, nevertheless the fact that it was also originally planned as 'merely' a re-engineering project *stigmatised* it within the company. The project was perceived as, in the words of one of the engineers who subsequently signed up for it, 'mickey mouse'.

The development manager and the task leader thus faced a problem. On the one hand it was a highly technical project requiring highly experienced engineers whilst on the other hand because it had been stigmatised it was unlikely to attract the calibre of engineer required.

The fact that Yourdon methodology was to be properly followed, that the development would involve CASE technology and that C was to be the programming language were used as *lures* for the engineers. Given that no development project on the site has used CASE technology nor C and that there was only a partial and patchy history of the use of Yourdon then even highly experienced engineers were being offered an incentive, for they would be able to include on their CVs that they had experience of CASE, were expert in C, and had properly used Yourdon methodology[11].

The eventual composition of the development team testified to what, in the main, was the successful deployment of the lures. Thus only a couple of the development team had programmed in C before and the engineers were often observed to consult *C The Complete Reference* (Schildt, 1990), and although under the pressure of time and working twelve hour days to meet the development schedule, they were sent on an outside one week training course, after which they could be found doing textbook exercises at odd moments. An expert in the proprietary CASE tools they were using was hired in to help them and also give them 'on the job training'. In addition, each of the engineers had new copies of the Yourdon course on their bookshelves, and an inspection of these would reveal that the engineers were doing the exercises that followed each of the course sections and awarding themselves marks on their attainments.

Thus, although there was a technical rationale for the use of Yourdon methodology, CASE and C there was also an organisational rationale, for whilst the techni-

---

[11] Even then it was difficult to recruit a full complement of engineers from amongst the employees based at the site where the development was taking place, and it was necessary to bring in one person from one of the company's European sites. He was prepared to live in hotel accommodation during the week, returning to Holland for the weekend to gain the experience of working with Yourdon, CASE and C. In addition, two consultants were hired to consolidate the team and in order to make up the head-count.

cal rationale portrayed their use as a feature of good development, the organisational rationale ensured that there were engineers of sufficient experience and standing to engage in the development. Both the engineers and the management oriented to these rationales.

5   A DEVELOPMENT PROBLEM

The project was a year into its development cycle and was beginning to experience slippage. The company's internal audit team had already rescheduled the project when it was realised that the development was more complicated than was first expected. However, 'Archer' was now falling behind its new target and audit dates. Part of the reason for this was the very management decision to use CASE, Yourdon methodology and C, and the decision to do a 'full and proper' analysis of requirements and write to requirements with full documentation.

The method, the development environment and the programming language had contributed in different ways to the slippage. Thus, the CASE technology was causing problems quite simply because none of the engineers had used it before and therefore were not using it effectively. Management had recognised that this might be a problem and had hired an independent consultant whose job it was to troubleshoot for the team and to provide them with some sort of 'on-the job' training. However, in the actual course of the development the consultant came to recognise that his continued employment was dependent upon his continued utility to the group and that it was, thus, in his vested interests that the other engineers continued to require and rely upon his expertise. Consequently, he would take on engineering tasks himself rather than educating others to do those tasks using CASE technology and ever burdened engineers would let him, pleased to be relieved of 'yet another job'. The consultant ventured the opinion that the CASE technology was only being used to about 10% of its capacity, and rather than being used in the way in which it had been designed to support the engineers in the development process, it was merely being used as a 'drawing instrument'.

The programming language they were using also resulted in problems that exacerbated the time slippage problem. The problem was not so much one of having to learn a new language[12], rather it was a problem of using C within a multi-engineering environment. C does not lend itself easily to tight specification and to a tight structure. In its low level mode, C allows the programmer a tight control over the movement of data, the manipulation of information and the storage of a result, but this means that the structure of a program is likely to be more esoteric than for other languages. This may not be a problem for individuals who are writing code for their own purposes, but it can become a problem when programming in teams and where the ready availability of the structure of the code and the mutual intelli-

---

[12] The engineers prided themselves on their professional ability to pick up new languages.

gibility of code is of paramount importance. As each engineer or group of engineers had responsibility for particular areas of development, it was found that there was a problem of interfacing the code written within the different areas of responsibility, and it became time consuming to change code and work out ways of interfacing. Although CASE technology could have helped with this interfacing problem, the fact that the engineers were not really using it for many of the purposes it was designed for meant that, in practice, it did not simplify the solution to this interfacing problem.

Building software to Yourdon principles involves working to a sequential development pattern, one step proceeding another, so that the whole development cycle unfolds in a structured manner. However, as we have noted, the hardware had already been built and was waiting for the software to be developed before it could be tested. Whilst test software could have been developed and run, the hardware group argued that they required a release of the software for the machine, not test software. However, if Yourdon principles were strictly followed, the software would not be ready for the required time. Thus, from the point of view of the hardware division, the software division's decision to use Yourdon methodology was producing an unacceptable time delay, and the hardware division was consequently putting pressure upon the software division and questioning their processes.

Thus, for various reasons, the decision to use CASE, C and Yourdon methodology, to organise and order the software so as to engage in a full and proper analysis of requirements, with a structured approach to the development and with engineers writing to requirements and producing full documentation, was resulting in the exacerbation of time slippage for the project. Time slippage is taken very seriously within the company, and most of the engineers had previously worked on projects that had been cancelled because of this problem, thus the possibility that the development could fall even further behind was a source of concern for them inasmuch as it was felt that this could result in the cancellation of the project.

6   THE SITUATED USE OF THE METHOD, THE ENVIRONMENT AND THE LANGUAGE

It was possible to observe that in the situated and circumstantial use of the CASE tools, Yourdon methodology and C, the engineers worked out ways of overcoming the time-slippage problem, but in such a way that they did not undermine the rationales for using them even though they were exacerbating the time-slippage. That is, they worked out ways of making Yourdon, the CASE technology and C work in the circumstances and thus made their technical work of engineering organisationally accountable. The engineers built into their technical work the organisational character of the methodology, the technology and the language and their use of them testified to their entwined technical and organisational character.

In engineering the development team the organisational character of Yourdon,

CASE and C was revealed. They had acted as constituting mechanisms for the group. Their deployment was the lure that was used to recruit good engineers onto the project: engineers with sufficient photocopier experience. Yet, it was the utilisation of Yourdon methodology, C and the CASE tools for the development that was in part causing the time-slippage. However, in the face of these circumstances the engineers developed strategies and employed situated and local *ad hoc* practices for the implementation of Yourdon, C, and CASE to make them fit the circumstances of their use[13]. That is, the methodology, tools and the language were contingently deployed in ways not covered by the formal documentation for their use to solve the problematic circumstances that their formally documented deployment had resulted in. In so doing, the engineers tailored them for the circumstances of their use, utilising practices not covered by the formal practices for using them. This use oriented to the social/organisational character of the three devices for the engineers' artful use of them testified to the actual decision to use them for the development in the first place. To illustrate this we will describe a number of the *ad hoc* practices and strategies that the engineers devised.

6.1   Yourdon methodology in use

Part of the reason they were experiencing time problems was that following Yourdon principles for the development was preventing them satisfying the demands that were being placed upon them by the hardware division. Yourdon methodology requires that development takes place in a number of sequential steps, thus an analysis of requirements should precede design decisions. It is a method that has been developed in order to ensure the disciplined analysis of requirements in a structured way. Yet it was, in part, through following that method that slippage was developing and which was also resulting in friction with the hardware division.

To provide hardware with the software it demanded but which would be unavailable if the software development continued on its originally planned course and if software was developed through the disciplined analysis of requirements, the software engineers worked out a strategy for using Yourdon. This strategy was developed in preference to other options, one of which was to abandon the methodology. The strategy was therefore developed to *preserve* the use of Yourdon, and it was thus aimed at organising the use of Yourdon within the working circumstances of its deployment. This strategy was to distinguish between *following Yourdon* and

---

[13] We do not mean that they would not have developed practices of this order had they not been faced with a problem of time-slippage or pressure from hardware. As we mentioned in the introduction, for us it is just a feature of applying formal schemes whether they are methodologies or programming languages or instructions for using software packages that their application will involve local practices of implementation that are not covered by the formal schemes. However, it is possible to see that the particular practices they developed are sensitive to the particular circumstances of this development.

saying that they were following Yourdon. By following Yourdon they would not have been able to satisfy the demands made by hardware, simply, hardware would not have software to test its machine. By following Yourdon they would therefore compromise the rationales for its use and therefore compromise the very organisation of the team. However, by *saying* that they were following Yourdon they were able to provide hardware with its software and at the same time testify to the rationales in the decisions for its use. For in *saying* they were using Yourdon they would be able to deliver software which from the point of view of those who would be consuming it had been produced *as if* they were following Yourdon. Thus to say they were following Yourdon was to publicly testify to the rationale for its use.

The strategy of 'saying they were following Yourdon' was used in conjunction with and also involved devising a number of version release dates within the original time frame for the development cycle. These versions could not have been produced had Yourdon procedure been followed as laid down in Yourdon documentation. Thus rather than working to a sequentially planned development cycle that results in the delivery of debugged, tested and operational software, the engineers were prepared to deliver a release of the software to hardware knowing that it would not operate properly, knowing that it was badly designed and knowing that it was full of bugs, and knowing that they would have to return to it[14]. In fact the strategy was devised *so* that they could return to it, for once the version had been delivered they could return to it and begin to work on the problems they knew were inherent within its design, free, for the moment, of the pressure from hardware. They could thus work towards the next release date by which time they would have caught up on some of the problems they fully recognised they were delivering.

In developing the software in this fashion they fully recognised that they were compromising Yourdon principles. Yet in compromising Yourdon principles they were able to organise its use within the circumstances of the development. But *saying* they were using Yourdon was to ground the development in the method and testify to the technical rationale for its use. In so doing they were, in the activities of using it within the strategy they had devised, making the use of the method organisationally accountable. Thus, actually using Yourdon was to knowingly compromise its principles so as to justify the rationale for its use in the first place which was to organise a proper structured development.

6.2   C in use

One of the problems the engineers were experiencing with C was that they could not, for some processes, program the processing chip in real-time even though one

---

[14] This is not to say that this is bad engineering nor is it to say that the engineers were not competent. The point is that they knew what the problems of the software were and they knew what they were doing when they delivered such software. Their concern was to get it right *in the end*, and to give themselves space within the confines of this development to do so.

of the reasons for choosing C was that it could be used to do real-time programming. Their solution to this was to drop C for the moment and use assembler programming language instead[15]. Their 'abandonment' of C – even temporarily – was undertaken with the utmost reluctance. They rated C very highly among the programming languages, and some of the engineers had even signed onto the project to learn the language. Further, it was one which would have specific advantages for the work they were doing, especially with its capacity to facilitate the documentation of the code. However, a management decision had been made to use a particular – and relatively cheap – processing chip in the machine and the fact was that this chip could not handle the numerous lines of code that writing in C would involve. The engineers were of the opinion that this was a false economy, but the fact that they could not persuade their managers to review it meant that they had no realistic choice but to shift to writing assembler code. As we have explained, the nature of assembler code involved the writing of fewer lines of code than C would, but made documentation (an important consideration) vastly more problematic. The decision to use C had been the right one, and the use of assembler in many ways confirmed this, for what made assembler useful here was one of the features that it shared with C, that it conserved memory and allowed fast processing. The purpose for which C had been introduced was a valuable one, and a better overall job would have resulted from its use but that was being frustrated by the inappropriately 'economising' attitude to the price of chips. Again, as with the manager's decision to use Yourdon, the technical wisdom of their decision to introduce C was also acknowledged by the engineers: the technical rationale for C was convincing, but they saw the problem as being the failure of managers to follow through the implications of their technical decision. Thus *abandoning C was done in the name of using C.*

The engineers also had to devise a strategy for making C *workable* within the circumstances of the development. Part of the technical rationale for the use of C made reference to the fact that the engineers were working within a multi-engineering environment. This environment occasioned the possibility of an interfacing problem and it had been argued by the manager and the team-leader that writing code in C would give a structure to the code that would alleviate this problem. However, C has always been considered to be 'a programmers language' because it allows programmers to use their knowledge of the architecture of a machine. This means that it is less structured than some programming languages. For example, modern ALGOL-derivative languages have compilers that provide error messages that alert programmers to the fact that they have made a mistake before they actually run the program. C, however, does not make use of these devices to the same extent and not only may the intelligibility of error messages be in question, but also finding the causes of any errors may be difficult. It was the exacerbation of these problems in a multi-engineering environment that was, as noted above, causing some of the time-related difficulties the project was experiencing.

---

[15] Assembler programming language is closer to machine code than 'high level languages' such as C, and therefore requires less processing to turn its procedures into machine code.

To address this problem, the engineers devised a strategy, not part of the programming language itself, to use the language within their collaborative circumstances. The strategy was to produce an internal set of guidelines to standardise work practices, and to ensure that the engineers produced similar documents and used similar ways of describing their work. The guidelines were oriented to providing for the mutual intelligibility of their code. They could not ensure that in and of itself any one person's or one groups' code would be intelligible to others in the development team. Thus knowledge of the language did not ensure an understanding of the code written in it; the meaning of their code was not stable and given to it by the language it was written in. In use, the engineers had to devise ways of writing code in C to ensure it was intelligible to other members of project 'Archer'. Consequently, the engineers made a distinction between C *as presented in the textbooks* and C *as a working tool*: textbook C and working C. Textbook C would not yield them workable code within their collaborative circumstances, yet working C would.

The engineers, then, engaged in transformation processes as a situational feature of their work. The way in which textbook C was transformed into working C was through their production of the set of guidelines. The guidelines became an instrument through which they could use the language within their community. Yet it was not a guideline for other communities. It was assembled from out of the circumstances of their work and being contingent upon their work was applicable to just their work. A contextual assemblage, it ensured the workability of the language for their practical purposes and was a method for remedying the inevitable susceptibility of the formal language to the situational vagaries of ambiguity and esotericism. The compilation of the guidelines made their technical work organisationally accountable. Its use ensured the usability of C within the context of their development and in so doing testified to the technical judgement to use it in the first place.

6.3 CASE in use

The core of CASE technologies are structured methodologies such as Yourdon. The technical reasons for using CASE tools on project 'Archer' recognised this, for it was argued that using CASE technology would make the engineers follow Yourdon methodology and thus engage in a proper analysis of requirements and a proper development of design specifications based upon that analysis.

There are a number of aspects to the relationship between CASE and structured methodologies. Structured analysis can be conceived as a set of tools for the production of a structured specification. These tools are: (1) data flow diagrams, (2) data dictionaries, and (3) process specifications. CASE technology has been designed to work with these tools. For example, with respect to data flow diagrams, CASE tools make tasks such as their creation, editing and sharing relatively quick and straightforward. Also, the construction of aspects of a data flow diagram are constrained by physical limitations such as the space on a page. Thus the data flow diagram under a particular process node will be limited to ten or twelve subordinated process nodes, because once this number is exceeded there is too much detail to represent at that level than will fit onto a page or a screen, and it is therefore necessary for further subordination. With CASE this can be easily accomplished because it is possible to open a diagram under the indicated node where the subordinate data flow diagram can be drawn.

Data dictionaries, the second structured analysis tool mentioned above, form the underpinnings of data flow diagrams and CASE tools automatically maintain a data dictionary. Lastly, with respect to the third structured analysis tool, process specification, CASE tools usually have facilities for performing data dictionary consistency checking and also check for undefined entries, circular definitions aliases, self-defining terms and syntactically correct definitions. The fact that project 'Archer' was a multi-engineering environment meant that interface problems could arise, but the tools provided by CASE technology, integrated into the structured approach of Yourdon would, it was argued, minimise development problems in this regard.

In addition to furnishing engineers with useful development tools, supporters of CASE environments also point to the fact that it can draw out the analytic and design skills of the software engineer: "The goal is to provide freedom for the lone designer, or the most skilled team member, allowing this person to concentrate fully on developing the requirements and design specifications" (Fisher, 1991; p 33). However, within the context of project 'Archer', it was, in part, this feature of CASE that was contributing to the time slippage that the project was experiencing, for there had been no time to train the members of the project in CASE technology and the consultant that was hired in was not necessarily 'the most skilled team member' for developing requirements and specifications. As a multi-engineering project, 'Archer' very much depended upon the proper coordination and collaboration of the different engineering groups within the project, and the CASE technology was not effectively promoting this sort of collaboration.

However, despite the fact that the CASE environment was contributing to the slippage, it was possible to observe that, similar to the ways in which the engineers used Yourdon and C, the way in which the engineers also used CASE *in practice*, testified to the organisational decision to use CASE. Their strategy for using CASE in these circumstances was to use CASE technology to package the development for presentation rather than using the technology to order the development. That is, in the practices of their work, the engineers distinguished between *the processes of development and the presentation of the development processes*. The engineers eventually came to only use the CASE environment for particular tasks, and, as we noted above, the outside consultant reckoned that this only utilised about 10% of the capacity of the technology. The capacity of the technology that they continued to use was, as the consultant put it 'its drawing capabilities'. These 'drawings' were the documentation of the development, thus, in practice, CASE was used to document the development processes rather than being used as part of the development process.

However, for 'readers' of the document it could appear that CASE was being used to partly order the development process. This was because the documents provided a tangible demonstration of the effectiveness of CASE inasmuch as they constituted concrete artefacts of the development and were thus available to be 'read' for the role played by CASE in that process. They thus occasioned the possibility that readers of the documents could infer that CASE was being used to order the development. That is, with the documents of the development in hand, it could be inferred that the development was being ordered and organised using CASE technology; the documents could be, and were, used as artefacts that testified to the use of the technology. These artefacts were used as *documentary evidence* that CASE technology was successfully ordering the development, for the project manager used them in the presentations that he made to those above him in the company. In his hands, they documented the sound decision to use CASE technology because their display was evidence that the technology was making the engineers document the development. However, inasmuch as they were not the product of that technology (that is, they did not document a development process that had been ordered and organised in their use) their use in this way constituted them as *organisational artefacts*.

7   THE RELATIONSHIP BETWEEN DEVELOPMENT METHODOLOGIES AND DEVELOPMENT TOOLS AND THE SITUATED WORK OF DEVELOPMENT

It would be wrong to think that the software development described in this chapter is an example of a badly managed and organised project[16]. This examination is not meant to be a criticism of either the way the company organises its software development, or the organisational prowess of the managers, or the competence of the engineers. In fact, nothing emerged from the study to suggest that there was anything unusual about either the management of the project, or the quality of the engineering work. Software development, even a relatively small project such as project 'Archer', is very complex, and it is inconceivable that a project will not encounter organisational problems, and ones that may result in time-slippage. Indeed, software development projects are embarked upon knowing that there will be problems, but without always knowing just what they will be, and thus are embarked upon without knowing what a solution to them will look like, though also knowing that practical solutions will have to be found if the project is to continue, and it is the experience of many engineers that solutions are found and that projects do arrive at their launch date.

It would also be wrong to think that this chapter is meant to be an attack upon

---

[16]   Indeed, since this study was conducted the development has beeen completed and the product successfuly launched.

Yourdon methodology, CASE and the use of C for complex and commercial software development. There *are* debates about all three, thus Yourdon has its champions and its detractors, CASE is being improved because current examples do not support certain activities, and C is a source of argument amongst programmers. However, the descriptions that have been presented in this study of their deployment and use in project 'Archer' is not meant to contribute to any of these issues: it is not meant to give succour to any in the arguments over Yourdon, it is not meant to reinforce the need for new CASE environments, nor to lend support to one side in the programmer's 'cultural wars'.

Rather, this chapter invites some reflection on what is being asked of software development methods and tools, and raises the possibility that they are often effectively expected to provide, through technical means, solutions to problems which are, in fact, those created by the organisational environment within which the methods and tools are to find their use. In the case we have reviewed, the engineers were satisfied that were they able to make proper use of the tools they were provided with, they could have delivered improved results of the sort that the tools were meant to engender, but the opportunity to master and apply the procedures involved in using the tools was repeatedly pre-empted by other, more immediate and urgent priorities. The fact that software development methods and tools have much and varied functionality means that their efficient use will require learning, and that the learning will often have to be done in and through actual practice. But in circumstances where schedules are tight and milestones taken seriously and where delay in the software's progress can seriously impact other parts of the project, taking the time to investigate, work out and experiment with the resources provided by a methodology or tool is going to be the last thing that engineers feel they can do.

In thinking about the introduction of methodologies and tools into organisations, it is worth bearing in mind that even with respect to individual projects the organisation does not necessarily have clear, coherent or clearly and consistently prioritised objectives, and that design work will often involve the expeditious reconciliation of competing demands, and in such situations the requirements of methodologies and tools will compete with other, and no less legitimate, calls on their work. Grudin (forthcoming) makes a suggestion which our work can reinforce, which (to put the point crudely) is that the design and introduction of methodologies and tools needs to be considered relative to the interests of those who are to use them. These methodologies and tools are not necessarily designed to facilitate the work of the particular individuals who will use them, but are, rather, often intended to serve the purposes of others. It is certainly not *necessary* that individuals should follow the ways of the methodology or use the tool as its designers intended to get their work done. As we have clearly indicated, the software engineers were able to get their software up and running only by setting aside the methodology, the potential of the CASE tool and the coding language C.

The methodologies and tools are often designed to address the problem of achieving *orderly* software development, and the concerns which are serviced by such devices are often those of other parties than the ones implementing the steps in the methodology or putatively using the tool. Many aspects of methodologies have to do with the organisational accountability of the work, with producing a record of the work done, with organising the work itself in such a way that other people can make sense of that work and can 'pick it up' or 'build on it' at some later stage in the process. Clearly, for example, the fact that someone will later have to maintain code and that (unless that code has been written and documented in 'orderly' ways) they will have trouble understanding that code is something that gives rise to concerns about the way in which the code is put together and documented in the first place. In the actual work situation, subject to the demands of workload and schedule, and in the face of the roster of problems that they face in getting their part of the work done at all, the requirements of methodologies and tools may be perceived to embody the needs of others, ones which – though undoubtedly real and legitimate – are currently remote from the developer's immediate problems, and, if they do not contribute directly to the fulfilment of the task in hand (may even require additional effort or the taking of a long way round) then these requirements may be treated as dispensable. Making sure that the order is preserved, that the methodology's requirements are complied with and that the tool's procedures are used in the intended, and intendedly standard, ways may be perceived as worthy objectives in themselves but ones which are, after all, ultimately in someone else's interest.

This discussion has been pervaded by an assumption about the general nature of methods, rules and procedures, which is that their proper understanding is inseparable from their examination *in use*, for it is there that the irreducible 'gap' between the necessarily general prescriptions of the method, rule or procedure, and the specifics of the instance or case to which it must be applied will be bridged by the practical judgement of those who are seeking to implement the method, follow the rule, or respect the procedure. Matters which are not, which *cannot* be, mentioned in the manuals and textbooks (for they have to do with the local conditions under which the methodology will find its actual use) are decisive in determining the extent to which and the ways in which the formal prescriptions will be followed through.

This, chapter has addressed a feature of what is a generic problem in software engineering that methods such as Yourdon and development environments such as CASE are oriented to, as indeed is the situated and local work of planning and organising a software development project, and as is the contingent work of development. This problem is one of *orderly software development*, and this chapter has been concerned with the situated work of that ordering. Thus, whilst examinations of Yourdon and CASE may debate their utility for ordering software development, typically that debate is done independently of a consideration of their actual deployment, in the hands of engineers engaged in using them for development purposes. That is, typically, discussion of methodologies and development environments is done without reference to the actual circumstances of the situated work of their implementation. Part of the context of that use and part of the circumstances of their implementation is the social/organisational character of the development work.

This chapter has directed attention to the locally organised practices of the *use* of development methods such as Yourdon, development environments such as CASE and programming languages such as C. It highlights that part of the work of development resides in making such artefacts work for the occasions of their use, and that making them work is an integral feature of their use. It is to suggest that understanding how they are made to work is important in the consideration of their role in software development, and that understanding this cannot be removed from the actual practices of and settings in which they are made to work. Thus making them work is contingent upon the circumstances of their use. In this respect we have to appreciate that any discussion about and understanding of the technical robustness or prowess of a methodology or an environment has to take into account that part of its technical character is organised in the way in which its use makes it organisationally accountable. That is, we should not consider methodologies, environments or languages divorced from praxis, since part of their technical character is organised in praxis.

This has a consequence for the way in which we think about the relationship between methods and development. It has a consequence for thinking about developing what might be considered to be more pertinent methodologies for analysing requirements, and, to return to the points made in the introduction, for thinking about the role of social science methodologies in analysing user requirements. If we think that methods are procedural recipes to follow we might think that all we have to do is to develop or alight upon the best method for our purposes and our problems will be solved by cranking the methodological handle. If we do this, however, we miss the point that methods are *worked at* phenomena, that they are made to work in the circumstances of their deployment and that the details of that work are part and parcel of the development process. If instead of thinking of methods as procedural recipes to be used in the course of development, we think of them as tools in the organisation of development, then the artful and contingent *use* of those tools is as important as the character of the tools themselves. This chapter has attempted to show that there is indeed an artful use of development methodologies, development environments and programming languages, and that part of this use testifies to the social/organisational circumstance. Thus, we argue, understanding the social organisational work of the development is as important as constructing a development method and environment.

8   CONCLUSION: SOME MAXIMS FOR REQUIREMENTS ANALYSIS

In our attempts to familiarise ourselves with the work of software developers we have become aware of how difficult, and often intractable, are the problems with which they contend. It would, therefore, be presumptuous of us to use this study to offer advice to those developers in other than the most tentative fashion. How the procedure of requirements capture might develop in the long run is not, either, something that we are equipped to anticipate, but it does seem to us that, in the short-term, there is often a tension between the methodologists' ambition to impose clarity, coherence and closure upon the design (which leads them to treat requirements capture as something that can be done definitively, early in the project and in a once and for all way), and the significantly indeterminate character of many of the matters with which they deal. This tension encourages them to think of the requirements capture procedures which they contrive as ways of (more-or-less adequately) elucidating the requirements inherent in the situation they seek to design for, but from our point of view, these requirements capture devices often resemble, rather, forcing devices, which *impose* standards of definiteness, clarity and completions upon situations which do not inherently feature these. The situation with requirements capture, then, is one which is, in practice, a matter, currently at least, of an accommodation between the resources and skills available to the developer and the complexities of the problems with which they must contend. Thus, it seems to us important that the appraisal of requirements capture devices should not employ too exacting (and unrealistic) a standard, and that the use of such devices should proceed on the basis of an awareness that in practice they will not, alone, be enough, and that their most effective use will not be where designers 'use the formula' instead of 'using their heads', but when designers use their heads when using the formula. In the light and spirit of these remarks, we offer the following maxims for requirements analysis.

First, *requirements are enmeshed in organisational processes*. Everything we know about organisations tells us that they involve conflicts, some of which are essential to the life of the organisation, and it should not therefore be expected that the business of requirements capture can ever provide a way of reconciling the assorted demands and expectations that may legitimately be made of a system.

Second, *requirements are not objective; they come from a point of view*. Design is an *intervention* in the organisation's life, and the designer cannot be a neutral figure within that context. Alignments will, in practice, be made, and these can be more or less unwittingly made, and consequently more or less systematically thought through.

Third, *ending the specification of requirements for any development is a practical matter*. The mind set which looks for definitive solutions to the problem of requirements capture will seek for principled ways of defining those requirements and terminating the process, but the search for requirements may, in reality, be one which is never ending, and which may even create the requirements that it 'finds'. The termination of the requirements process will always be, in practice, a practical matter.

Fourth, *any methodology is always a trade-off*. One of the much criticised features of methodologies is the way in which they falsely segment the design process and thus distort understanding of its practice. Too single-minded a focus on 'requirements capture' as a problem may obscure the fact that it is only one problem, and that it competes with other issues and tasks for time and resources, and that, therefore, the decisions in the design process might often be measured in terms of 'opportunity cost'.

Fifth, *no method is genuinely foolproof*. There is a limit to the extent to which you can seek to design procedures for doing a job without having to depend upon the good sense of those who are to follow them.

Sixth, *'a requirement' is a gloss for a swarm of changing contingencies*. Projects of the greatest philosophers and logicians have foundered on the assumption that the structure of ordinary language is formally determined and structured, but the system developer is often practically compelled to seek a precise matching between the formal devices used in his/her work and the communicative processes involved in transactions between designers and users. This compounds the risk of misunderstanding, of the developer attributing to the expressions of users a clarity and definiteness of a sort those expressions do not possess. The idea that one can surely, conclusively and without revision say, in so many words, just what someone wants is perhaps, and certainly in many contexts, a will o' the wisp. The definiteness of the requirements may serve more to protect the legal position of the developer than to pin down the requirements of the user.

Seventh, *capturing a requirement is like capturing a butterfly, once it's pinned down it's no longer what you chased, it's dead*. User requirements are contextually organised matters, and their intelligibility resides in understanding their relationship to a whole range of other work and organisational matters. They gain a life and an animation within this context. Requirements analysis rips them from out of this life-giving context and in the process they lose their very substance as known to users. Thus, a decontextualised definition of a requirement cannot be a literal description, it can only be for the practical purposes of defining, and the resulting defined requirement will not be the phenomenon it is to users.

ACKNOWLEDGEMENTS

We would like to thank Marina Jirotka, Matthew Bickerton, Joseph Goguen, William Newman, Paul Luff, Bob Anderson and Hervé Gallaire for their comments on earlier drafts of this chapter, and Hervé Gallaire for a very detailed description of the problems and difficulties involved in the organisation of software engineering.

REFERENCES

Benson, D. and Hughes, J. (1983). *The Perspective of Ethnomethodology*, Longmans.

Bently, R., Rodden, T., Sawyer, P., Sommerville, I., Hughes, J., Randall, D. and Shapiro, D. (1992). Ethnographically-informed systems design for air traffic control, *Proceedings of CSCW '92: Sharing Perspectives*, pp. 123–129.

Button, G. (Ed.). (1991). *Ethnomethodology and the Human Sciences*, Cambridge University Press.

Button, G. (Ed.). (1993). *Technology In Working Order: Studies of Work, Interaction and Technology*, Routledge.

Cawsey, A. (1990). A computational model of explanatory discourse: Local interactions in a plan-based explanation, in P. Luff, N. Gilbert and D. Frohlich (Eds), *Computers and Conversation*, Academic Press, pp. 221–234.

Finkelstein, A. and Fuks, H. (1990). Conversation analysis and specification, in P. Luff, N. Gilbert and D. Frohlich (Eds), *Computers and Conversation*, Academic Press, pp. 173–186.

Fisher, A. S. (1991). *CASE Using Software Development Tools*, John Wiley.

Garfinkel, H. (1987). *Studies in Ethnomethodology*, Prentice-Hall.

Grudin, J. (forthcoming). Evaluating opportunities for design capture, in T. Moran and J. Carroll (Eds), *Design Rationale*, Lawrence Erlbaum Associates.

Heritage, J. C. (1984). *Garfinkel and Ethnomethodology*, Polity Press.

Hughes, J., Randall, D. and Shapiro, D. (1992). Faltering from ethnography to design, *Proceedings of CSCW '92: Sharing Perspectives*, pp. 115–122.

Mullery, G. (1991). Methods Engineering. Paper presented at the *Oxford Workshop on Requirements*.

Norman, M. and Thomas, P. (1990). The very idea: Informing HCI design from conversation analysis, in P. Luff, N. Gilbert and D. Frohlich (Eds), *Computers and Conversation*, Academic Press, pp. 51–66.

Robinson, H. (1990). Towards a sociology of human-computer interaction: A software engineer's perspective, in P. Luff, N. Gilbert and D. Frohlich (Eds), *Computers and Conversation*, Academic Press, pp. 39–50.

Schildt, H. (1990). *C The Complete Reference* (2nd Edn), McGraw-Hill.

Sharrock, W. W. and Anderson, R. J. (1986). *The Ethnomethodologists*, Ellis Norwood.

Somerville, I., Rodden, T., Sawyer, P. and Bentley R. (1992) Sociologists can be suprisingly useful in interactive systems design, *Proceedings of HCI, '92*, York.

Suchman, L. (1987). *Plans and Situated Actions: The Problem of Human Machine Communication*, Cambridge University Press.

Yourdon, E. and Constantine, L. C. (1979). *Structured Design: Fundamentals of a Discipline of Computer Program and System Design*, Prentice-Hall.

Ten

Steps toward a partnership: Ethnography and system design

Dave Randall, John Hughes and Dan Shapiro
Department of Sociology and the Centre for Research into CSCW, Lancaster University, UK

1 INTRODUCTION

The recognition that many systems for use in cooperative environments are failing to meet the needs of those who use them has in, recent years, prompted a considerable interest in the insights to be gained from the development of Computer-Supported Cooperative Working (CSCW) as a collection of disciplines designed – if this is not too strong a word for what is a serendipitous amalgam – to meet the challenges posed by the relocation of the computer interface 'deeper and further into the user and the work environment' (Grudin, 1990, p 261: see also Bannon, 1985). This shift has provoked the need to devise methods of requirements elicitation which acknowledge the socially organised character of work and its environments. There are, of course, no shortage of candidate methods to meet this particular need, including task analysis and job design, the socio-technical approach pioneered prior to the widespread use of computing, the 'soft systems' approach, user participative design and, most recently and our especial concern, ethnography. Of the ones mentioned, ethnography is the most recent and the most untried and, perhaps, the one that most resists the formalities of logical tightness demanded by requirements capture. Its home resides in the research traditions of sociology and anthropology rather than technical systems design. Its disciplinary focus has seldom been directed towards the regimen of a 'service' role in quite the way that the CSCW community might anticipate (Randall *et al.*, 1991). Nevertheless, as with any method or tool it is important to try to spell out what it can and cannot achieve, what needs it can serve and what it cannot. Matters in this regard are made less straightforward given that the term 'ethnography' is a gloss for very wide-ranging concerns, interests and theoretical presumptions. As Hammersley and Atkinson (1983) put it in a standard text on the method,

"... across the numerous fields in which ethnography, or something very like it, has come to be proposed, one finds considerable diversity in prescription and

Requirements Engineering
ISBN 0–1238–5335–4

practice. There is disagreement as to whether ethnography's distinctive feature is
the elicitation of cultural knowledge ..., the detailed investigation of patterns of
social interaction ..., or holistic analysis of societies ...."

Ethnography is, even within its home territories, something of a contested enterprise. Nevertheless, the appropriation of ethnography as method of investigation in
CSCW has not so far been accompanied by the necessary attention that needs to be
given to issues such as *what kind* of ethnographic practice might be suitable for the
task of gearing into the procedures of eliciting requirements, or how its analyses
and descriptions can be related effectively to systems design. Matters are complicated by the ever present risks of serious confusion between practitioners working
in an interdisciplinary field when coming to terms with methods that, for them, are
unfamiliar. In the absence of clear statements of practice that risk is multiplied.
This chapter represents an initial effort to evaluate the contribution of ethnography
to system design on the basis of one research project in which the method has been
explicitly used to describe, and in detail, the work activities of air traffic controllers
with a view to assessing how and in what ways these could be effectively supported
by automated systems. In other words, it represents an attempt to bring an ethnographic study of work to bear on system design.

There are, as with any method, considerable risks in making strong claims as to
the virtue of ethnographic investigation, not least in the raising of expectations
which cannot be fulfilled. Thus, in what follows we are trying to begin some *evaluation* of the method, looking to both its virtues and its vices to begin to see what
role it can play in system design. The experiences of collaboration with software
engineers that we recount should not be read as a programmatic statement of ethnographic practice to be applied indiscriminately to all examples of collaborative
endeavour. Quite the reverse. The research on which we draw is academic, and it
remains, for instance, to be seen whether the approach can be adequately managed
in commercial contexts where time/cost constraints are more rigidly applied than in
an academic environment. Further, in ethnography a great deal of responsibility for
the description and analysis rests on the experiences of the ethnographer rather than
in the ability to produce publicly available, though sometimes intellectually dubious, 'hard data'[1]. In which case there are, potentially, problems of generalising
across settings and domains[2]. A final preliminary point is that while we recognise
that ethnography is distinct from other methods, it may well be that it has a complementary role to them once their interrelationships are unravelled.

The project on which we draw involves an ethnographic study of air traffic controllers directed toward the design of a user interface to the flight progress database

---

[1] This posture clearly draws on a whole host of arguments, which are beyond the purview of this
chapter, to do with the epistemological and related issues concerning the nature of social science
measurement. But see, for example, Cicourel (1964), Hughes (1988) and Benson and Hughes (1991).

[2] Against this it can be argued, as we would so argue, that one of the important stances of CSCW is the
need to resist the easy urge to generalise prematurely about the nature of work.

(Bentley *et al.*, 1992a; 1992b; 1992c; Hughes *et al.*, 1988)[3]. In the current UK air traffic control system, aircraft descriptors are printed from the database onto paper strips. Controllers use these strips, in conjunction with a real-time radar display and communication with aircraft, for in-flight controlling. The ATC system is non-trivially cooperative in at least two respects. First, work around the control suite involves a group of persons who have to cooperate in providing assistance of various kinds to the active controller. Second, each suite has to coordinate its work with that of others, a feature which is oriented to in the work on individual suites. The need for effective computer support is largely prompted by the pressure of traffic loadings which has meant that flow control restrictions have been in operation at busy periods since the mid-1980s[4]. Hitherto, the constraint on traffic loads, the 'reverse salient' to use Hughes's (1987) phrase, has been taken to be the work capacity of the controller, hence the impetus to enhance this through appropriate computer support. Thus, it is a working environment in which there is considerable pressure for innovation and change.

ATC is an evolved, highly skilled occupation in which the methods of working have remained substantially unchanged since the 1960s. It has an occupational culture which has demonstrated its reluctance to embrace technological solutions which fail to improve the work and maintain standards of safety as controllers interpret these (see Harper *et al.*, 1991). Given that ATC is a safety critical system, there is a strong *prima facie* case for arguing that it exemplifies the need for viewing effective systems as being those which resonate with existing working practices (Hirschheim and Newman, 1988; Schmidt, 1991). Thus, and to put it simply, the justification for using ethnographic methods is to describe what the working practices are with a view to better understanding how they may be appropriately supported.

Our research in the Air Traffic Control domain had the advantage of a prior study (Hughes *et al.*, 1988; Harper *et al.*, 1989; 1991). The new study was different, however, in that it was intended to focus on the work of Air Traffic Controllers (ATCOs) in using the paper 'Flight Progress Strip', a piece of card with dimensions of about 20 × 3 cm containing printed information about a particular flight, with the objective of contributing to the design of an electronic equivalent. The site of the research therefore was the 'suite' which provides the technical facilities for communications with aircraft and with other suites, and the radars and flight

---

[3]   The research is funded by an HCI Initiative Grant, 'Social Analysis of Control Systems for HCI Design', ref: G8931590. Our computer science collaborators are Professor I. Sommerville, Dr T. Rodden, Dr P. Sawyer and Mr R. Bentley. This chapter has benefitted immensely by their critical, but friendly, scrutiny.
[4]   Flow control is a system whereby a fixed number of slots are stipulated for incoming traffic. Among air traffic controllers this measure, though recognised as necessary, was felt to be a disgrace since they had for a long time prided themselves on being able to take 'anything as it comes along'. It should also be pointed out that flow control is not a particularly efficient way of coping with traffic demands, since the UK has little control over how its slots are allocated by, for example, French ATC, German ATC, or whatever. It is largely flow control restrictions which are responsible for the delays increasingly experienced by package holiday flights.

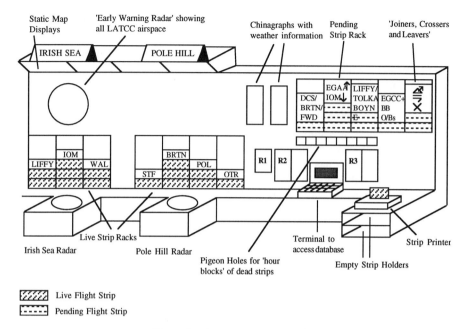

Live Flight Strip

Pending Flight Strip

Figure 1   An *en-route* sector suite.

progress strips for displaying the position and various characteristics of the aircraft currently in, and expected within, the control responsibility of the sector. Each suite conventionally is divided into two sectors[5].

The radar provides a 'real-time' representation of airspace in which each aircraft is indicated by a 'blip' accompanied by a data block showing its call sign and height[6]. The radar cannot, however, give a full picture of the traffic situation, since the situation encompasses not only what is happening now but also what is likely to happen in the near future. The evolving conjunction of aircraft is immensely relevant to the controller in that he or she will be making decisions and acting on the basis of an anticipation of likely problems. For this reason, the flight strip, which incorporates information relevant to that decision making, is, along with the radar picture, vital to the controlling process.

Briefly, the flight strip stands proxy for the passage of an aircraft through controlled airspace. It is produced from a database consisting of flight plans filed by airlines prior to the departure of the aircraft through the Flight Data Processing

---

[5] The airspace in England and Wales is typically divided into 16 sectors and 8 suites at the London Air Traffic Control Centre (LATCC), although according to traffic density these sectors can be reconfigured either by 'splitting' or 'bandboxing'.

[6] The radar can display other information such as sector boundaries, coastlines, major and minor airports, etc.

(FDP) application, and can be updated in a limited fashion through links with Radar Data Processing (RDP), or through inputs from either the controller or the 'wings'. The information for each flight, including call sign, flight level, requested flight level, destination and route, eta at next navigation point, radio 'squawk' code, etc., is printed on a strip up to 40 minutes before the aircraft reaches navigation points in the relevant sector. Since the updating of the database is not a continuous process, the real situation of the aircraft is represented by written annotations and symbols.

Replacing a paper based information display of this kind with an electronic equivalent has some evident purposes which have to do both with current and additional functionalities (see Shapiro *et al.*, 1991 for further details). However, any new technology would need to pay due attention to the need for incremental change in the domain, given not only the cost of retraining but also the possible consequences for safe working inherent in any change. The use of the strips is an evolved and trustable part of a complex system of working, wherein the consequences of changing one aspect of the system for other aspects cannot easily be determined. In effect this means that electronic re-representation would need, at least, to capture *all* current functionalities (or provide alternatives) in order not to impoverish or problematise the accomplishment of controlling.

2   PROBLEMS OF ETHNOGRAPHIC FOCUS UNDER INTERDISCIPLINARY AUSPICES

Ethnography, in all of its many forms and within a sociological/anthropological context, at a minimum is concerned with the description of social life and its activities in their natural setting or context. The emphasis is on the portrayal of the setting as it is seen and understood by its inhabitants. Such a naturalistic stance requires that it begins with what people *do*. And what people do is discovered through the ethnographer's active involvement in the setting under investigation.

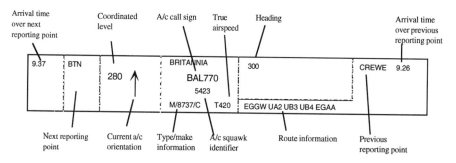

Figure 2   An *en route* flight progress strip.

The ethnographic fieldworker's task is to become enculturated in the understandings and activities which constitute the setting. Of course, beyond such a minimal specification are the procedures and practical details about the conduct of the fieldworker within the relevant setting, the inferential principles of drawing conclusions from the data gathered, judgements about typicality of the scenes encountered, and many more including those to do with relating the material gathered to the objectives of the research.

In the context of CSCW, however, by far the most serious additional difficulty is the process of relating the ethnography to designers' concerns. In our experience there are two aspects to this worth noting. The first has to do with the 'innocence' of the ethnographer with respect to the designer's concerns. The fieldworker can either function explicitly from the beginning in a 'service' role for the system designer or lay these on one side for the time being and concentrate on describing and analysing the work and its activities. While these are not necessarily incompatible objectives, our view was that it was more important to take the latter route in order to avoid focussing too early on any constraints there might be arising from problems of design. By suspending these concerns at the beginning, the fieldworker could concentrate on furnishing a sociological description of the work, its activities, its contexts and its culture as constituted by parties to the work[7]. In this way we hoped to be in a better position to evaluate the feasibility and consequences of design decisions.

A second problem, and closely related to the first, is the ethnographic record itself and its relationship to requirements analysis. More particularly, it involves recognising that the ethnographic record does not constitute an adequate framework for requirements analysis. In essence, the problem is one of translating the rich, textured, and highly detailed description of sociality that is associated with ethnographic enquiry into a form usable by system designers. In part, this is a problem of translating the highly qualitative natural language descriptions that constitute the ethnographic record into a more formal set of specifications for system designers. Moving from the natural language description of requirements analysis in its early stages toward the abstraction or formalisation necessary to the software design process is an activity which, from an ethnographic point of view, inevitably loses much of the texture of the 'real world' of working life; a texture which, from a sociological point of view, is hardly irrelevant. Within software engineering the design process is conceived as a progression from a natural language or quasi-formal denotation of the requirements of a system, when the functionalities of the system are outlined against the needs of the user, toward a level of formality suitable for the technical problems of design specification. Typically, therefore, the work of the

---

[7] This is in keeping with the ethnographic injunction to entertain as few presumptions as possible about the social character of the setting to be studied. One assumption that is not relaxed, however, is that the setting is socially organised. The task of the ethnographer is to show how it is socially organised. By contrast, in Wise *et al.* (1992), one searches without success for an analysis of teamwork as consequential for technological intervention in the domain.

designer starts with what Sommerville (1992) refers to as 'requirements definition', namely, "that process of establishing what services the system should provide and the constraints under which it must operate...". This constitutes the first stage of the 'software lifecycle'. Sommerville goes on to specify the format of an adequate requirements definition which consists, principally, of a distinction between it and a software specification. The latter is intended for the systems designer and is, thus, an abstract definition of software components. By contrast, the requirements specification should be expressed in terms which are understandable to the user. The substantial part of that definition is constituted in 'those system services which are expected by the user of the system' and is otherwise termed the functional requirements definition. As Jones (1990) points out, functional definitions are that part of the design analysis which may describe "what the product does, but they do not specify how it is done." Requirements definition is an analytic framework from which formal requirements specification will evolve. However, accepting the necessity of such changes of emphasis is one thing, realising it as an effective programme for requirements specification is quite another. For one, although sociologists have rarely been reluctant to move into domains where even angels might fear to tread, the invitation to play a part in systems design and become what is in effect an applied discipline, an adjunct to computer science, is a difficult one not least in the very different ways in which problems are posed within the respective disciplines. In the light of this, the following points are important to note.

Firstly, the materials produced by ethnography usually consist of no more than the fieldworker's notes and records, usually taken at the time of the observation. These, particularly in the early stages, may look little more than random jottings of remarks, sketches of activity, recordings of discrete sequences, descriptions of the physical environment, quotes, and so on. As pointed out above, ethnography is informed by the principle that it should in the beginning contain a minimum of assumptions as to the detailed character of the activities, understandings, etc that are to be found within a particular setting. It was Becker (1958), in an early formulation of the principles of ethnography, who first identified the 'sequential' analytic process characteristic of the method. Becker argued that much of the data collection phase and its analysis is carried out while the fieldwork is in progress and, as such, forms an integral part of that phase of the research. In other words, ethnography is a developing affair, in which sociological interpretations of what is seen inform the direction of subsequent investigations.

The second and related point is that though, typically, ethnography entertains a minimum of presumptions about the character of the setting to be investigated, it is not devoid of analytic or theoretical purpose. Nevertheless, there is a world of difference between framing the research problem as a sociological one and framing it as an interdisciplinary one. Sociologically, the method involves, again at a minimum, the presumption that the work site is socially organised, the task being *to uncover how and in what ways* that is worked out in the relevant context. The ethnographer's task is to gain access to and knowledge of the social practices, knowledge, beliefs, attitudes and activities, as they are exhibited by participants, and to present these as a socially organised way of life. However, in the context of CSCW this picture does have to be related to issues of design and, particularly, the requirements the system will need to meet. Currently, there are no formal methods of relating ethnographic materials to orthodox requirements definition. In this respect, the rich and textured conclusions associated with ethnographic enquiry would seem to contribute little to resolving the designers' problem on their own. Such a problem, and the brief excursus above should make it clear that it is really a collection of problems, are not objections in principle to the use of ethnography (Sommerville *et al.*, 1992). They are rather a statement about the importance of trying to identify, as adequately as can currently be done, the lineaments of the problems and the role that ethnography can play in resolving them.

3   SOME EXPERIENCES – DESIGNING AN ELECTRONIC FLIGHT STRIP

As indicated earlier, the story we tell involves procedures that, while not *ad hoc*, are, nevertheless, to be viewed as practical responses to problems encountered in an evolving collaboration between sociologists and system designers. In the absence of a universally acceptable method of subsuming descriptions of cooperative work into the requirements analysis process, it could hardly be otherwise. In a nutshell, we believe that rehearsing the history of our collaboration may prove to be of value to others for the pragmatic purpose of establishing the boundaries of ethnographic enquiry. As mentioned earlier, it is our contention that at this stage no practical purpose is served by making claims for the universal applicability of the method. While ethnography may prove to be a valuable resource for systems design, there are important questions which need to be addressed if this potential is to be realised. In the following exposition, we outline what our experience suggests those questions to be. Of course, others' experiences may be different and such differences are important for the identification of commonalities and specificities of the method as well as the contexts in which it may be appropriately used to inform system design.

The first task of the fieldwork was to furnish a detailed, adequate and accurate rendering of the activity of controlling. This required a lengthy and sustained observation on the part of the ethnographer. In essence, the ethnographer was required to learn something of the art of controlling by watching, asking questions, and generally talking to, controllers on a suite at London Air Traffic Control Centre. At the same time, the broad design principles of an electronic alternative to the strip were being established. The interests of the computer scientists were to do with the visualisation of database information in interactive command and control systems, with ATC as the exemplar. The kind of issue that was of interest to them were problems such as, for example, information overload at the user interface, and the feasibility of tailoring displays. In addition, the environment needed to allow for the construction of a multi-user, multi-screen system where the same database entities could be simultaneously displayed and manipulated by different users (see Bentley *et al.*, 1992a, b, for further details). It was intended that the ethnographic research would inform the rapid prototyping of the tool.

As pointed out earlier, we made the methodological decision not to take on board the concerns of the system designers. We felt, rightly or wrongly, that it was important not to prejudge what might be discovered by treating the designers' concerns as an initial focus for sociological enquiry. This is not to say we felt they were unimportant, but that we did not wish to 'buy into' any particular concerns at such an early stage in case what might turn out to be important features of working practices were missed by an initial over attention to designer's problems. Rather, at the beginning we were concerned to explicate the work as it is understood, experienced and organised by those who do the work, thus meeting Garfinkel's (1967) measure of the sociological enterprise by treating the activities in question as the 'outcomes' or 'accomplishments' of the practical common-sense reasoning on the part of members. Only by describing the controller's activities in that way could we begin to capture their identity as activities within the setting as, in this case, *controlling activities*. We were thus concerned specifically to avoid the reductive and behaviouralised descriptions redolent of cognitive and task approaches to work activity, but instead to undertake a protracted study of the system 'from within' as a real world and socially organised working environment.

During the first period of fieldwork, which lasted about three months, there were lengthy debriefing sessions at least once a month, based both on the fieldnotes and on the reported experiences of the ethnographer. The structure of the collaboration is set out in Figure 3.

Over the period, and after the initial 'innocent' ethnography, the designer's questions gradually shaped the fieldwork toward the focus of the research, namely, the flight strips. But, and importantly, the initial phase of the ethnography had succeeded in portraying the wider context of work activities in which the strips played their part. Although it was rare during the debriefing sessions to identify an explicit software requirement, the designers did gain an intuitive impression of the kind of facilities required by the controllers and the team to perform their work.

We cannot reproduce all of the details of these debriefing sessions, but at an early stage a number of important aspects of controlling work were evident. Firstly, it was apparent that controlling is a teamwork activity. Not simply in the sense that there were formally defined positions around the suite, but also in the vital sense that controlling requires an orientation to the active coordination of tasks on the part of all the personnel around the suite in ways that fundamentally go beyond the formal specification of roles. A typical radar suite is staffed by two radar controllers, a Chief Sector Controller ('chief'), and a number of assistants, or 'wings'[8]. Each of these are formally responsible for particular tasks, although in practice

---

[8]   In addition, there may be London Joint Operations officers from the RAF, with responsibility for liaison with civilian controllers when military aircraft are traversing controlled airspace.

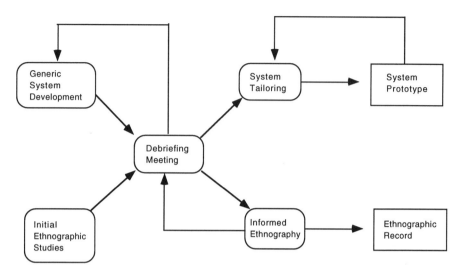

Figure 3   Ethnographically informed systems development.

some of these tasks may be shared. The 'wings', for example, while they are primarily required to do much of the routine work, such as removing paper strips from the printer and placing them in the relevant racks in front of the controller, also act as a first level 'check' on the accuracy of information. Errors in printed information are not uncommon, and the ability of the 'wings' to notice and point out inconsistencies is sometimes invaluable to the controller. The 'wings' also prepare substitute strips when, for example, a controller has to deal with an aircraft before printed strips are available. The 'wings' also do much of the inputting work, as and when important new information needs to be entered into the database. The chief is responsible for monitoring traffic and making strategic decisions including the allocation of flight levels, and pointing out possible conflictions, and coordinating traffic between sectors. The work of the radar controller issues instructions to aircraft, and verifies that instructions have been carried out. They also spend time coordinating activities with other sectors and with other members on the suite. But what is important about this teamwork is that the various tasks which members undertake are woven into a 'working division of labour' (Anderson *et al.*, 1989). The individuals, whatever they may be doing at a given moment, are individuals-in-a-team and orient to their work as such. The work consists in the ability to organise the distribution of individual tasks into an ongoing assemblage of activities which constitute the working division of labour. There was no single activity that could be said to manifest that teamwork since it saturated all features of the work.

The above, of course, is, necessarily, a brief description of the work of controlling. It should be stressed that the process of debriefing was important because it furnished a much richer account than could have been obtained from the fieldnotes alone. Further, the debriefing sessions were intended not merely to provide a systematic account of the controlling process but, additionally, to ensure that the account was a very detailed one. In particular, and unsurprisingly given the stated objective of the research, much of the questioning concerned the role of the flight strips in the teamwork. Importantly, the strips are the site of all the activities we have talked about. They serve as a historical record of decisions taken and as a resource for decisions to be taken. They can be written on by any and all members of the team, can be reconfigured and reordered, and manipulated in various ways. In this respect, the strips are a 'shared resource' used by all members of the team to inform not only their own particular tasks but to see 'at a glance' how these tasks are related to others and to the evolving state of the sector[9]. The strips are the key to 'good' controlling for those who work with them. They constitute a documentary record of an aircraft's passage through the airspace, from the initial printed information on them, through the accumulation of information about decisions taken and effected as they are written on. Information added is largely according to agreed protocols, but also sometimes incorporating a whole variety of 'attention getting' devices, including circles, arrows, and so on, conveying information about unusual destinations, 'joiners, crossers, and leavers' and so on[10]. They may also include a record of coordination activities, changes in eta or route, changes in call sign, etc. The strip thus represents a notepad on which is written information about what has been, is being, and is about to be, done to particular aircraft, and more importantly it enables that information to be related to what is known about other aircraft also in the sector. It is thus a fundamental means of comparison. Since any member of the team may write on the strips using different coloured pens, thus providing a record of who has made decisions in addition to what decisions have been made, the strip thus also provides a record of accountability. The strip is a public document, available 'at a glance', to all around the suite.

The strips have significance not only for what is on the strip, but also in their position relative to each other. The fundamental problem for the controller is creating order out of the stream of traffic that is entering his/her sector, threading each aircraft into the flow as and when they arrive. The active organisation of the strips is one of the ways in which this scheduling can be achieved. The 'live' strips[11] in front of the controller are actively organised in ways that enable controllers to assess overall traffic flow and the problems to be contended with 'at a glance'. To the experienced and knowledgeable eye, arrays of indicated arrival times at beacons, heights, aircraft speed, and headings give information about the general situation in the sector, and more importantly, about those situations such as clashing

---

[9] The importance of such 'shared resources' in control systems has been noted and recorded by other researchers. See, for example, Heath and Luff (1991).

[10] Some aircraft follow routes which are not wholly within controlled airspace. Such aircraft, perforce, must 'join, cross, or leave' the airspace at various points, and sometimes require more attention.

[11] Other strips are to be found on the 'wings', including 'pending' strips which are printed for the first sector of UK airspace the aircraft will enter, and 'transfer' strips, which enable coordination with other centres such as Scottish.

arrival times and heights, and 'climbing through' or 'catching up' problems, which might cause conflictions. The activity of moving the strips so as to reflect the controller's concerns at that moment serves to generate patterns that both contribute to, and reflect, the sequence of activities that the controller must undertake so as to expedite the smooth flow of traffic in airspace itself.

4   TOWARDS INFORMING SYSTEM REQUIREMENTS

Our account of the use of strips, and this has been only indicative, in ATC is obviously informed by our own sociological interests in work as a socially organised phenomenon. Our colleagues in computer science, however, and quite understandably, were less interested in this notion. Their concerns were more explicitly to do with the specific ways in which the strips are worked with, exactly what the strip markings mean, what relationship there is between information on the strips and on the radar, etc. Sociological interests in the character of social interaction are of course not inconsistent with those of designers but they are indicative of different relevances, namely, our interest in the social organisation of work, and for computer scientists more explicitly in the requirements the electronic display tool would have to serve. The process of directing sociological attention towards systems design issues, and, by contrast, of ensuring that the designers' understanding of the work is adequate, is in principle difficult to formulate. For us, these matters were worked out through the debriefing sessions. Initially, this took the form of questioning the fieldworker, typically with 'what if ?', 'how ? . . .', and 'what consequences?' kinds of question as ways of explicating what happens, under what conditions, how often, what else is happening while this goes on, and so on. Scenarios were evolved in which the 'routine' and the 'exceptional' were distinguished, the absence of particular information on the strips was discussed; the constraints on the system imposed by coordination addressed, as was the workload and the skills of the controller. These early sessions were anything but systematically organised. Nevertheless, they served important purposes; not least, a means of reaching design decisions about the scope of the system. In the nature of some of the issues raised it quickly became apparent that the form that the working practices took prompted some initial conclusions about what the system should encompass and what its limits should be. In the first place, there was the recognition that tailorability of the interface would be deeply problematic given its public availability and use by different controllers. Equally, the amount of coordination work that went on while an evident constraint on the current system seemed also to be a resource for safe operation. The designers quickly reached the conclusion that the electronic distribution of information could not unproblematically replace the current coordination work. In particular, it was decided that the system should not organise electronic versions of the strips to some default order, but that this should remain the responsibility of the controller. These early discussions also sensitised our computer colleagues generally to salient issues, constraints, and resources in the work which, in turn, enabled them to ask the kind of questions that gave direction to subsequent field-work. While the ethnography generated rather more problems than solutions, these were problems germane to the reviewing of design possibilities and options, and vital. Subsequently, the computer scientists posed four 'guiding questions' which were intended to provide a framework for directing the ethnographic research toward issues of system design. The questions were:

- What aspects of the work which are currently manual are not important or consequential to system purposes, and need not be supported in a computerised system?
- What are the important manual activities which are characteristic of the system because it is manual? In other words, what activities need not be supported in an electronic system because the system will replace them?
- What aspects of the manual system must be replicated without change in a computerised system?
- What aspects of the work needs to be supported but need not be, or cannot be, replicated in the same way in an electronic version?

These questions, though firmly posed and suggesting definite patterns of analysis, still raised practical difficulties that stemmed directly from interdisciplinary collaboration. For us, the questions simply could not be answered in an unequivocal fashion without, seemingly, compromising the subtlety and complexity of the work as portrayed by the ethnography. The questions seemed to require us to make generic distinctions about elements of an organisation of social action which, again to us, seemed better described as a 'motile configuration' of activities (Anderson *et al.*, 1989). The questions also appeared to reduce the social organisation of work to sets of discrete tasks and ignoring the specifically social properties of the interaction around the suite: properties which were not incidental to the work but integral to it. For brief example, although many of the current manual activities could, in principle, be automated, including manipulation of the strips themselves, writing on them, and coordination between suites, the significance of these activities for 'gearing' team members in the ongoing work means that automation could have radically unknown consequences. One of the consequences of automating activities might be to reduce operators to a more passive role within the system, which might have important consequences for safety critical activities such as controlling (Hopkin, 1984). The tasks of controlling are activities within a socially organised working division of labour which accords them significance and meaning within the work itself as 'activities organising the flow of traffic'.

In important respects, the questions and our response to them brought to the surface problems of interdisciplinary working of this kind. It was not a problem of terminology but one of viewpoint and the different interests that disciplines take in the world and how these are instantiated in practice and procedures. For computer engineers, designing systems requires that relevant elements of real world systems are decomposed into discrete objects whose properties, and the relations between them, can be clearly and unequivocally specified and defined. On the other hand, however, reducing an ethnography to a series of apparently individualistic activities in this way does no sociological justice to the activities. The insistence on the social character of the work is particularly significant if the proposed system has the consequence of reconfiguring the working system, rather than removing some tasks from the manual realm. If decision making in ATC is best viewed as a cooperative activity based on the mutual understandings in the team, it is because its apparent seamlessness, its smooth and safe operation, cannot be guaranteed by interventions designed to replace some of the activities that make it so since it is a product of the skills and socially oriented activities of the team itself. As already said, these difficulties, for all of us involved in the project, are at the 'cusp' of interdisciplinary working and in this case crucial to understanding the role ethnography can play in system design.

Nonetheless, these were, and are, undoubtedly important questions to address in any form of system design even though it took the sociologists on the research team some time to appreciate their importance. For their part, the system designers began to recognise the difficulties of providing answers to them. However, there were a number of 'conventional assumptions' of system design that we felt able to challenge in respect of cooperative systems. First, that computer systems should automate tedious manual tasks and, second, that user interfaces should provide facilities for end-users to tailor them to suit their personal ways of working (Bentley *et al.*, 1992c). Our observations strongly suggest that the manual manipulations of the strips were significant activities in keeping the controller 'geared into' the work and, accordingly, should not be positioned according to some default order when added to the display. Further, and relatedly, some manual activities are related to checking the feasibility of the information on the strip and, accordingly, also retained. As far as tailorability of the interface is concerned, our argument is that in cooperative systems where the representation is a 'shared resource', and available 'at a glance', such tailorability should be limited. Finally, exploring the questions effectively is a justification for the rapid prototyping of the system in which various possibilities can be explored.

5 CONCLUSION

Our review of our own collaboration is, it is important to remember, conditioned by our own research objectives. Our 'product' is small in scale, and we were under no commercial pressure. The research is the work of a small number of people and not conducted in the institutional constraints of large-scale commercial design, where the coordination of teams of designers, programmers, etc. is of paramount importance. But by rapid prototyping the system design has been able to go hand in hand with our ethnographic conclusions. Even so, and notwithstanding the possibility that larger systems might pose different problems, we feel that some features of the research are worth highlighting.

Ethnography, with its focus on the practical realities of working life is an important tool for drawing attention away from the abstracted versions of work which have tended to predominate in system design. Although within sociology there are different perspectives on work, it remains an obdurate fact that work is social. The problem for sociology in the context of system design is providing adequate accounts of this 'real world' character of work, and it is in this respect that ethnography comes into its own. Ethnographic portraits of activities as part of a socially organised setting avoids some of the pitfalls in treating tasks as discrete, isolated chunks of behaviour as if they were representations of how the work is actually done. For brief example, it is not any particular task that guarantees the 'trustability' of radar and strip information for the controlling team. If it is true, as members of the controlling team constantly claim, that printed information is unreliable, then how reliability is accomplished becomes an important practical issue for them. It is, in fact, woven into all of the activities on the suite, including those which appear routine, even redundant. A considerable amount of mutual checking goes on not merely to do with the printed strips, but including the various activities of members of the team. The 'at a glance' availability of the organisation of the strips for all members of the team enables them to monitor, not as discrete fixed activities, 'what is going on now' as and when they like. 'Trusting the system' is not any *one* thing but infuses the whole of the work. A similar argument can be adduced for the problem of coordination between the suites. The need for coordinating work is a time consuming constraint on the expedition of traffic, but is based in the current system on the requirement for maintaining safe separation. That work involves not only the passing of specific information, but in reality is the occasion for a substantial amount of explanation, justification, questioning, joking, etc. It is part of the process whereby attentiveness is ensured and maximised through activity. Such conclusions have considerable consequence for design decisions about, for instance, the feasibility of automatically passing information from sector to sector in that if it leads to an attenuation of the teamwork character of controlling, it may also reduce attentiveness and therefore safety levels. This identification of skills and the subtle, pervasive, and interdependent ways in which they can be deployed according to the demands of the situation, is an important consideration for the design of systems which blend with and support working practices.

A second but related point has to do with ethnography's potential for uncovering the tacit knowledge and understanding embedded in activity. It is sometimes argued, and with some justification, that the articulation of this knowledge is difficult for practitioners by virtue of its very familiarity. Bound up in this may also be a sense of their interests and satisfactions which may otherwise limit a willingness to make admissions, recognise alternatives, and explore options. The ethnographer by virtue of his/her tyro status in the culture can ask the naive questions that would not be permissible for experts, and on establishing the kind of relationships that are possible from the practised ethnographer, the kind of questions that require critical self examination from the domain expert. The ethnographer, however, cannot be expected to acquire knowledge of the domain in the way that domain experts know it, and indeed should not, since it might mean losing the analytical and theoretical distance that is an important quality of the method. User participative approaches have the advantage that they can encompass even the most abstruse and technical of methods, but they rely on presumptions of who the users are, their particular versions, regardless of the interests that may be in play. Thus, and to stress again, it is possible that, to some extent, user participative design and ethnography have complementary roles to play. The ethnographer can act as a bridge between domain and system experts, recognising the partiality of some accounts, translating the technicalities of the domain, and generally effecting another dialogue between users and designers. Thus, although the ethnographer is a surrogate for the domain, it is a distanced and critical substitute. It is the ethnographer who is able to locate and contextualise the knowledge that domain experts have in the context of design concerns. It is not that users cannot talk about what they know, or how things are done, but they may not be familiar with the problem of organising their explanations in the context of design problems. However, although these are important activities for achieving better *informed* design, in our own case we cannot claim that there is a literal traceability between the ethnography and the specification of the system components. We can claim that many of the features the system will offer to a user have depended on ethnographic insights.

A third, and perhaps least well articulated, view of the ethnographer's role stems from the neutrality of the ethnographer *vis-à-vis* the wider organisational context. Even accepting the importance of involving users in the design process, it is by no means clear how the determination of the 'user' is to be made. In the context of ATC, it is apparent that automating flight strips may have a wide ranging set of implications which may be quite distinct for different categories of person working at LATCC. It may threaten the jobs of some people, most notably those of the 'wings', and progressively perhaps those of chiefs. For controllers, it may routinise their work, and make it less active, less satisfying, less skilful. A new computer system may impact on employment patterns and on levels of work satisfaction experienced, but be significant for the provision of enhancements to system functionality which expedite work and remove some of the routine frustrations endemic in current practices. It may evoke complex managerial decisions implicating the pace of innovation, training requirements, cost/benefit appraisal and technical expertise. In short, 'real world' organisations are full of divergent interests, conflicts, efficiencies and otherwise, which interact in difficult to predict ways. The success or failure of a new system in a given context will depend not only on its presumed functionalities but on several strands of organisational practice and their interweaving. Important considerations in ATC will, without doubt, include training requirements, configuration of the airways and other procedural changes, as well as decisions about personnel requirements. The ethnographer, of course, cannot help but become aware of these organisational factors, and perhaps acquire a view. Whilst this in many ways is part of the potential strength of the ethnographic method, it may be a source of its limitations as well. The sheer width and depth of perception that should evolve from extensive ethnography opens up a space for a sophisticated understanding of real organisational life and its interrelationship with technical artefacts. One of the main ways in which this could prove significant is in understanding the rhythms of work, how it may vary from one time to another, and one period to another. Ethnography can, in principle, provide more than a mere 'snapshot' of the work and the organisation by uncovering some of the fluctuations in workload and intensity, and the differences between normal and some exceptional conditions.

Conversely, its very openness creates a number of problems. There are important questions to be asked about how research selectivity and relevance for system purposes can be guaranteed. It is not clear how the boundaries of ethnographic enquiry can be established, nor under what conditions it can be presumed to be complete. We know in our own case that there are certain conditions we have not investigated, including for instance air crashes and 'hijacks'. Ultimately, a system such as ATC must be able to cope with any circumstance, no matter how exceptional, and we have no first hand knowledge of how the ATC system reacts in a number of circumstances. Neither can our own research be said to be demonstrably applicable for research on larger scale systems, for organisational work on systems, and in commercial contexts. It may be that time, cost and other market disciplines prove to be major constraints on the use of a research style, which one of our colleagues in computing described as 'leisurely'. We do not know how these wider issues will impact on decisions about the suitability of ethnography for system design and building, nor even whether the same issues have arisen in other contexts where attempts have been made to relate ethnographic practice to these purposes. And, not unconnected to the above issues, is the fact that ethnography deals with patterns of interaction as they are currently organised not with how they might be changed as a consequence of system intervention. It is a matter of walking a tightrope between informed systems which resonate better with existing working practices, but knowing that any system is likely to alter these practices, and in ways that it is not easy to anticipate. However, this is a limitation faced by many other methods and a balancing act that remains to be worked out. It is hoped that recounting our own experiences will prompt some suggestions.

REFERENCES

Anderson, R. J., Hughes, J. A. and Sharrock, W. W. (1989). *Working for Profit: The Social Organisation of Calculability in an Entrepreneurial Firm,* Avebury.

Bannon, L. J. (1985). *Extending the Design Boundaries of Human-Computer Interaction,* ICS Report, 8505, University of California, San Diego.

Becker, H. (1958). Problems of inference and proof in participant observation, *American Sociological Review,* **23**, 682–90.

Benson, D. and Hughes, J. A. (1991). Evidence and inference, in Button, G. (Ed.), *Ethnomethodology and the Human Sciences,* Cambridge University Press.

Bentley, R., Hughes, J. A., Randall, D., Rodden, T., Sawyer, T., Shapiro, D. and Sommerville, I. (1992a). Ethnographically-informed systems design for air traffic control, *Proceedings of CSCW'92*, Toronto, ACM Press.

Bentley, R., Rodden, T., Sawyer, P. and Sommerville, I. (1992b). A prototyping environment for dynamic data visualisation, *Proceedings of the 5th IFIP Working Conference on User Interfaces*, Ellivuiri, Finland, Elsevier.

Bentley, R., Rodden, T., Sawyer, P. and Sommerville, I. (1992c). An architecture for tailoring multi-user displays, *Proceedings of CSCW'92*, Toronto, ACM Press.

Cicourel, A. V. (1964). *Method and Measurement in Sociology,* The Free Press.

Garfinkel, H. (1967). *Studies in Ethnomethodology*, Prentice-Hall.

Grudin, J. (1990). *The Computer Reaches Out: The Historical Continuity of Interface Design*, ACM Press.

Hammersley, M. and Atkinson, P. (1983). *Ethnography: Principles in Practice,* Routledge.

Harper, R. R., Hughes, J. A. and Shapiro, D. Z. (1989) *The Functionalities of Flight Data Strips,* Report for CAA, Department of Sociology, Lancaster University.

Harper, R. R., Hughes, J. A. and Shapiro, D. Z. (1991). Working in harmony: An examination of computer technology in air traffic control, in J. Bowers and S. D. Benford (Eds), *Studies in Computer Supported Cooperative Work: Theory, Practice and Design,* North-Holland.

Heath, C. C. and Luff, P. (1991). Collaborative activity and technological design: Task coordination in London underground control rooms, *Proceedings of ECSCW*, 1991, Amsterdam.

Hirschheim, R. and Newman, M. (1988). Information systems and user resistance: Theory and practice, *The Computer Journal,* **31**(5).

Hopkin, V. D. (1984). Some human factors implications of expert systems, *Behaviour and Information Technology,* Vol. 3.9.

Hughes, J. A., Shapiro, D. Z., Sharrock, W. W., Anderson, R. J., Harper, R. R. and Gibbens, S. (1988). *The Automation of Air Traffic Control,* Final Report, SERC/ESRC Grant No. GR/D/86157, Department of Sociology, Lancaster University.

Hughes, T. P. (1987). The evolution of large technological systems, in W. E. Bijker, T. P. Hughes and T. T. Pinch (Eds), *The Social Construction of Technology,* MIT Press.

Jones, G. W. (1990). *Software Engineering*, John Wiley.

Randall, D., Hughes, J. A. and Shapiro, D. (1991). Systems development – The fourth dimension: Perspectives on the social organisation of work, *SPRU/CICT Workshop*, Brighton, 18–19 July.

Rasson, M. B., Maas, B. and Kellog, W. A. (1988). The designer as user: Building requirements for design tools from design practice, *ACM Communications,* **31**(11).

Schmidt, K. (1991). Riding a tiger, or computer supported cooperative work, *Proceedings from the 2nd European Conference on CSCW,* Kluwer.

Shapiro, D. Z., Hughes, J. A., Randall, D. and Harper, R. R. (1991). Visual re-representation of database information: The flight strip in air traffic control, *Proceedings, 10th Interdisciplinary Workshop on Informatics and Psychology: Cognitive Aspects of Visual Language and Visual Interfaces,* Scharding.

Sommerville, I. (1992). *Software Engineering,* 4th Edn. Addison-Wesley.

Sommerville, I., Rodden, T., Sawyer, P. and Bentley, R. (1992). 'Sociologists can be surprisingly useful in interactive systems design', *Proceedings of HCI '92*, York.

Wise, J. A., Hopkin, V. D. and Smith, M. L. (1992). *Automation and Systems Issues in Air Traffic Control*, Springer-Verlag.

Eleven

Work, interaction and technology: The naturalistic analysis of human conduct and requirements analysis

Paul Luff, Christian Heath and David Greatbatch
University of Surrey and University of Nottingham,
Rank Xerox, EuroPARC, Cambridge, UK

So Taurus was to be the perfect, all-electronic, paperless system that would not just replace the British settlements system but would connect into other settlement systems around the world for international securities. Of course, as with so many other grand British technical visions, they could not get it to work. Not only was it too complicated: it required legal changes and regulatory changes. And importantly, many of the personal customers for whom it was supposed to be a great advance did not want it: they rather liked the idea of having share certificates to show what they had bought.

Hamish McRae; *Independent* 12/3/93

The full introduction of the computer system effectively did away with the radio and telephone calls to stations, with the computer dispatching crews to answer calls. But within hours, during the morning rush, it became obvious to crews and control room staff that calls were going missing in the system; ambulances were arriving late or doubling up on calls. Distraught emergency callers were also held in a queuing system which failed to put them through for up to 30 minutes.

Ian MacKinnon and Stephen Goodwin; *Independent* 29/10/92

Management were misguided or naive in believing that computer systems in themselves could bring about [such] changes in human practices. Experience in many different environments proves that computer systems cannot influence change in this way. They can only assist in the process and any attempt to force change through the introduction of a system with the characteristics of an operational "straight jacket" would be potentially doomed to failure.

London Ambulance Service Inquiry Report (Page *et al.*, 1993, p. 40)

Requirements Engineering
ISBN 0–1238–5335–4

1 INTRODUCTION

A series of highly publicised failures and disasters have highlighted the difficulties of developing computer systems to support complex organisational activities. The collapse of the Taurus system for the London Stock Exchange and the introduction of a Computer Aided Dispatch (CAD) system into the London Ambulance Service are just two of the more serious cases which have led to questions concerning the viability of computing systems and the ways in which advanced technologies are designed to support routine working practices. Hence, industrial designers, software engineers and researchers are becoming increasingly concerned with conventional methods for system design. In particular, they are beginning to look for distinct and innovative approaches to requirements analysis and the earliest phases of the design process.

Whilst there remains some ambiguity as to the meaning of many of the terms which permeate requirements analysis, including the term 'requirements' itself (cf. McDermid, Chapter 1 in this volume), we have begun to witness the emergence of a burgeoning body of methods and techniques for the earlier stages of system development. Being particularly concerned with the organisational context into which technology is introduced, many of these methods reveal a growing commitment to the 'social'. This concern, however, raises new problems and difficulties for requirements analysis. For example, it has been noted that participants in the design process may have differing views of the scope and functionality of the system; they may even question the necessity of introducing a computer system altogether. Moreover, it is recognised that the requirements for a system can change while it is being designed and built. Despite the emergence of more flexible approaches, such as 'participatory design' and 'prototyping', to address these issues, there are still difficulties concerning how material gathered in such exercises can be utilised and analysed.

In this chapter, we wish to explore the ways in which developments in social science, namely ethnomethodology and conversation analysis, may provide a distinctive approach to requirements analysis and design. We wish to suggest that despite recent innovations and advances, many of the methods and techniques used within requirements analysis rely upon a relatively individualistic conception of tasks and activities that severely delimits the domain of the 'social'. Taking three very different organisational settings, we begin to sketch the ways in which the detailed, naturalistic analysis of video-recordings of (real world) work and interaction may generate requirements for technological support and innovation and lead to a thoroughgoing reconsideration of our traditional conceptions of task and cooperation. In particular, by directing analytic attention to the moment-by-moment production of (technologically mediated) organisational conduct, we can begin to explore the tacit, socio-interactional foundations of *in situ* human conduct in the workplace, and delineate requirements for technological innovation.

This chapter discusses three different organisational settings to show how the analysis of *in situ* human conduct can contribute to different stages of the requirements process. We begin with a study of general medical consultations that makes use of video-recordings and field observation to assess current information systems. The second study involves a technology that is being prototyped: the introduction, evaluation and successive modification of a media space in a research laboratory. Finally, we consider London Underground Line Control Rooms to show how the analysis of work and interaction can delineate the requirements for innovative technologies to support a particular form of collaborative work. Drawing on these various studies, the chapter then discusses more generic considerations for the design of technologies and suggests ways in which we can begin to develop a distinctive approach to requirements analysis which places the socio-interactional foundations of organisational activities at the heart of the analytic domain.

2   ASSESSING THE USE OF COMPUTER SYSTEMS: NEW TECHNOLOGIES IN GENERAL PRACTICE

the inability of the system to cope easily with certain established working practices (e.g., the taking of a vehicle different to the one allocated by the system) – this causes exception messages to be raised for manual exception rectification – in itself a somewhat laborious process;

(Page *et al.*, 1993, p.32)

With the increasing number of "awaiting attention" and exception messages it became increasingly easy to fail to attend to messages that had scrolled off the top of the screen. Failing to attend to these messages arguably would have been less likely in a "paper-based" environment.

(Page *et al.*, 1993, p. 53)

Observations of the use of computer systems in work settings, such as those in the London Ambulance Service, frequently suggest deficiencies in their design. Although some of these difficulties can be accounted for in terms of poor interface design and insufficient functionality, it has become increasingly recognised that systems need to be assessed in relation to the requirements of the particular context for which they were intended. Although considerable effort has been expended into exploring computer use in experimental settings, particularly in the field of Human-Computer Interaction (HCI), there have still been few studies of technology use in real-world domains.

In the light of these concerns, we are examining the introduction of computer systems into an inner-city medical practice, focussing primarily on the ways in which they impact on the consultations between doctors and patients. The data comprise video-recordings of medical consultations conducted before and after the introduction of the computer, augmented by field observation and discussions with the doctors concerned. The software used in the practice is called IGP VAMP, which is currently installed in a third of general practices throughout the UK.

VAMP is accessed through terminals, consisting of a standard keyboard and monitor, located in the reception area and in each consulting room. It provides two features that are used in the consultation: a computerised record system for the documentation and retrieval of medical biographical information and a facility for issuing prescriptions. Since the introduction of the system in 1990, the practice has made use of both of these functions[1]. However, within the consultation, computer use is concentrated largely in the prescription phase. Thus, for medico-legal reasons, the doctors continue to update their paper records and, despite the availability of the computerised records, still rely heavily on them as an aid to diagnosis and prognosis. One of the reasons for this is the absence of pre-1990 information in the screen-based records. Another is that, because the system restricts the doctors to 19 characters of free-comment, the paper records generally contain more detail about major illness and psycho-social problems.

Analysis of the audio-visual recordings has begun to reveal how the use of the computer system displays sensitivity to and is shaped by socio-interactional considerations. Thus, the apparently individual activities of documenting and retrieving information are frequently coordinated with the real-time contributions of patients. For example, doctors may delay the initiation or completion of sequences of keystrokes until either a patient has finished speaking or the thrust of their talk has become apparent.

However, the coordination between a doctor's activities and a patient's contributions is less apparent when conversations centre on issues not directly related to the

Figure 1   Computer use in the medical consultation.

[1] Computerised record facilities such as VAMP are seen as offering important advantages over manual systems in that they provide comprehensive, cross-indexed data bases of textual information that can be rapidly searched and manipulated for a variety of purposes (e.g. Bradeley, 1989).

computational task at hand. For instance, psycho-social issues, other medical complaints, problems in the family, as well as everyday topics such as holiday plans or the weather, are often discussed as prescriptions are being issued. During such discussions it is noticeable that the use of the computer is often more prominent than the use of a prescription pad and pen. In particular, the doctors often display a preoccupation with the task at hand by, for example, restricting their participation in the interaction to minimal, largely undifferentiated responses as they type and/or look at the screen; failing to respond even though a patient has produced talk inviting reactions such as expressions of sympathy or surprise; and delaying utterances until they have completed a sequence of keystrokes.

The prominence of the computer system appears to derive, in large part, from the ways in which it places demands on the doctor that did not apply when they wrote prescriptions by hand. For example, the provision of a standard keyboard and monitor means that, in entering prescription details and viewing the resultant text, the doctors have to attend to artefacts that are located in different parts of the local environment. Moreover, because the system is reactive, they will often need to monitor closely its operation to ensure that appropriate responses have been elicited, as well as to enable them to coordinate their actions with the movement of the cursor along the prompt line (and other changes on the screen). They may also be required to attend to output messages, such as requests for clarification or corrections of input and/or warning beeps. In addition, once they have started along the prompt line, they have little control over the order in which information is entered.

On occasions, these constraints appear to undermine the doctors' ability to participate simultaneously in discussions with patients concerning topics that are not directly related to the production of prescriptions. Nonetheless contrast cases do occur. As one would expect, these are largely located in the recordings made after the doctors had several months experience of using the system and were becoming increasingly familiar with its use, operation and potential. Here, the doctors conduct themselves in ways which minimise their displayed involvement in the use of the computer. They regularly cease typing and/or reading in order to gaze at the patient, and when continuing to use the system minimise their displayed involvement by, for example, slowing the tempo of their typing, striking the keys very softly, and asking the patient questions.

However, with one exception, the doctors' increasing familiarity with the system has not as yet led to a marked reduction in the extent to which its use adversely affect social interaction. There are at least three reasons for this. First, some prescriptions are less routine than others. As such, whereas with routine cases, the doctors may be confident about entering the correct information and thereby eliciting appropriate responses, with others the need to monitor input and responses closely may persist. Moreover, even with routinely prescribed items, there may be considerable variations in the forms, strengths, dosages and quantities that are issued to particular patients, with an attendant need to pay close attention to the system.

Second, as the doctors have become more familiar with the system, an additional phenomenon has emerged. On occasion, when producing what appear to be routine prescriptions, they have begun to enter information in larger packages, anticipating the system's responses and often typing through changes on the screen. This is not only disruptive to ongoing interaction (undermining the ability of the doctors to participate simultaneously in discussions with their patients), but also may inhibit patients speaking in the first place.

A third factor concerns the ecological mobility of the prescription pad and pen as opposed to the system. The former can be placed between doctor and patient on the desk so that only a minor shift in orientation is required to shift gaze from one to another. With the computer, however, if the screen is placed away from the patient to the centre or far end of the desk, shifts in orientation are necessarily more marked. (Similar issues also apply in the case of the medical record cards, which can be held in the hand while standing, placed over the knee while sitting facing the patient, propped on the corner of the desk while conducting an examination or held in front of the patient in order to facilitate a shared reading.)

The impact on the use of the computer system on doctor–patient interaction does not only turn on the conduct of the doctors. Patients may also contribute to this by attempting to coordinate their conduct with the use and operation of the system. Thus, for example, when producing utterances that have not been solicited by the doctors, patients frequently attempt to coordinate their talk with potential junctures in the doctor's use of the keyboard; thereby seeking to avoid interrupting an activity-in-progress. In doing this they rely upon visible and audible aspects of system operation and use, locating likely junctures on the basis of the movement of the doctors' hands and fingers, the relative intensity of keystrokes, shifts in the doctors' gaze from the keyboard to the monitor, and the character of the system's responses (Greatbatch *et al.*, 1991, 1993).

The prominence of the use of the system does not, then, derive solely from the conduct of the doctors. It is also due, in part, to patients attempting to synchronise their conduct with the visible and audible aspects of system operation and use. However, the extent to which patients do this appears to depend largely on the conduct of the doctors. For the most part, patients coordinate their actions with the use and operation of the system in contexts in which the doctors' exhibit an ongoing preoccupation with the computational task at hand. In general, the more a doctor succeeds in backgrounding the use of the computer as he interacts with a patient, the less likely it is that the patient will attend to his use of the computer as constraining his actions.

The use of the system has also had other consequences, including the development of new forms of patient involvement in the consultation. Although comprising an individual workstation, the system can be used to support collaborative readings. Thus, those doctors who have placed the monitor next to the patient (and angled the screen towards them) often invite patients to read items in their screen based records and to look through, and possibly choose from, lists of drugs. In addition, patients sometimes refer to the screen-based text on their own volition; for example, identifying drugs that they do or do not wish prescribed as doctors scroll through the drug dictionary, or asking questions concerning entries in their medical records.

Although the study is in its early stages, it has already demonstrated that the analysis of video recordings can reveal aspects of situated computer use that were

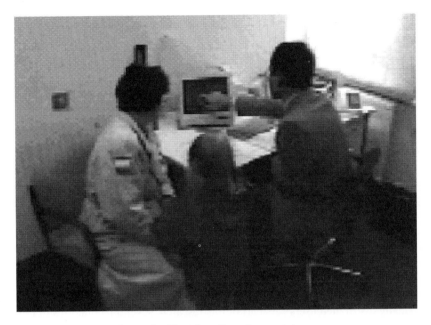

Figure 2 Shared reading of a computer screen.

hitherto unavailable for repeated observation. Without these recordings it would not be possible to describe systematically how doctors coordinate their use of the system with the actions of patients, how patients shape their contributions with respect to the doctor's use of the technology, or how doctors' contributions are shaped by reference to their use of the system (and *vice versa*).

The study has revealed that the design of VAMP overlooks various constraints and contingencies that surround its situated use. This deficiency appears to derive from the earliest stages of the system's design. For the initial requirements of VAMP failed to take account of the ways in which tasks for which the system is used are inextricably enmeshed with the interaction between doctor and patient. This failure has had a considerable impact on the system's integration into the medical consultation, both in terms of its adverse affect on doctor–patient interaction and perhaps, on its under-utilisation within the consultation as a whole.

3 PROTOTYPING: THE CASE OF AN AUDIO-VISUAL INFRASTRUCTURE

"The main lesson to be learnt from Taurus is that the approach to change must be through a series of manageable phases rather than a large complex, project".

Barclays Bank, in *Independent* 12/3/93

the early decision to achieve full implementation in one phase was misguided. In an implementation as far reaching as CAD it would have been preferable to implement in a stepwise approach, proving each phase totally before moving onto the next;

(Page *et al.*, 1993, p. 5)

In recent years, prototyping has been seen as a more flexible and reliable way of establishing requirements and building systems. It allows the technology to be respecified following a particular 'iteration', and provides a series of opportunities for reflecting on and reconsidering the design. In this section we wish to show how the naturalistic analysis of video-recordings of system use can be used in prototyping. The technology in question is an audio-visual infrastructure or 'media space' which was introduced into a research laboratory in order to encourage informal sociability and collaboration amongst both scientists and administrative personnel. At the outset, the requirements were largely unknown, and it was thought it would be useful to carry out successive assessments and modifications to the system.

The development of audio-visual networks (or 'media spaces') is related to the growing interest in developing systems to support collaborative work between physically distributed users[2]. As part of this research, several laboratories in Europe and the United States have experimented with media spaces primarily designed to support informal communication between personnel located within different physical locations within a particular organisation. Personnel are provided with microphones, speakers, cameras and monitors and are able to communicate, in real time, with colleagues in other locations (see, for examples, Fish *et al.*, 1990; Condon, 1993). The media space at EuroPARC (the Rank Xerox Research Laboratory in Cambridge) is not untypical of these systems. It consists of an audio-visual infrastructure which allows scientists and administrative staff, located in offices spread over three floors, to establish audio and visual contact with each other or to view one of the several common areas within the Laboratory (Gaver *et al.*, 1992). Several other facilities were progressively introduced into the media space, including a computer application which allows personnel to 'browse' through the building, to see for example, who is in their offices and whether they are available.

As in other cases where prototyping is adopted, we reconfigured the system in the light of reactions to and comments on the use of the system. An important concern was the threat that the technology posed to privacy, and in line with conventional prototyping a range of facilities were added to alleviate these worries. These included the introduction of different types of connections, allowing users easily to glance at each other or to set up longer term 'office shares'. A mechanism was also added to allow personnel to specify who was allowed to connect to their offices. However, general observations of the use of the infrastructure revealed that despite its common availability and the range of functions it provided, the system was relatively under-used and rarely provided a medium for collaborative work. Indeed,

---

[2]   The collection by Baecker (1993) contains a range of papers relating to recent research in this area.

Figure 3   An office within EuroPARC: the camera is above the monitor to the left of the workstation. The microphone is multi-directional, consisting of a small, flat metal plate on the wall, operated by a foot switch.

although much effort had been taken to enable connections to be made quickly and efficiently, the most common connections were either to a permanent display of the 'commons area' or a long-term 'office share' between two individuals.

The data, which consist of audio-visual recordings of personnel using the system, begin to reveal some curious features of interpersonal communication mediated through audio-visual technology; features that contrast with the organisation of social interaction in more conventional environments where participants are co-present. In particular, whilst the technology provides both audible and visual access to individuals distributed at different physical locations, the non-vocal actions of the participants appear at times to be ineffectual. In face-to-face interaction, gestures and other forms of bodily activity can serve not only to provide certain information about the talk that it accompanies, but also to shape, even during the delivery of a single utterance, the way in which a recipient participates in the activity at hand. For example, gestures are used to elicit the gaze of a recipient, and speakers coordinate the production of the utterance, and gesture, with the visual alignment of the person to whom they are speaking (cf. Heath, 1986). In video mediated communication we find that whilst individuals presuppose the effectiveness of their visual conduct, and rely upon gesture, gaze and other forms of bodily movement to engender and shape the activities of their co-participants during the delivery of talk, many non-vocal actions lose their local performative impact, their interactional significance when mediated through video.

The relative weakening or insignificance of visual conduct when communicated through video, in contrast to face-to-face interaction, is also consequential to the articulation of talk. A speaker's failure to secure an appropriate form of co-participation in the delivery of talk may be accompanied by various forms of perturbation, including pauses, restarts and self repairs; themselves devices which may be used by speakers to secure the appropriate form of attention or involvement from the recipient(s) (cf. Goodwin, 1981; Heath, 1986; Heath and Luff, 1992a). The relative weakening of visual conduct and, in particular, gaze, undermines the free flowing exchange of talk and engenders practical difficulties in the accomplishment of collaborative tasks and the maintenance of an appropriate 'co-present' environment. For example, it is interesting to note that actions such as glances, of which we can be 'peripherally aware' when co-present, pass unnoticed within a video-mediated environment. A person's inability to notice another looking at him in the media space allows the other, however inadvertently, to retain their gaze on their colleague, to stare, whilst the 'recipient' remains ignorant of the attentions that he is receiving from the other. By undermining the performative impact of a range of apparently trivial or minor actions, the infrastructure introduced the systematic possibility of individuals' privacy being invaded.

More generally, we find that the media space introduces communicative asymmetries that are not found, as far as we are aware, in other conversational environments. On the one hand, participants have visual access to each other; they can monitor each other's conduct and remain sensitive to the ways in which a recipient is 'attending' during the delivery of talk. On the other, the resources speakers ordinarily use, both gestural and spoken, in organising the relevant forms of co-participation from the person(s) to whom they are speaking, are undermined by the technology. The technology appears to interfere with the local, sequential significance of a range of visual actions, revealing a continually shifting imbalance between the participants. As they shift between the role of speaker and hearer they generate an environment which is similar to switching, during the course of a single conversation, continually between the telephone and face-to-face.

These asymmetries appear to arise in the light of two, interrelated issues. Firstly, 'recipients' have limited and distorted access to the visual conduct of the other. The other's conduct is available on a monitor which not only distorts the shape of a movement, transforming its temporal and spatial organisation, but also presents the image of the other *in toto*, and undermines the relative weighting of different aspects of an individual's conduct. More importantly perhaps, the presentation of the other on the monitor undermines the possibility of peripherally monitoring the different aspects of the co-participant's conduct. Secondly, an individual's limited and distorted access to the other and their local environment, undermines their ability to design and redesign movements such as gestures in order to secure their performative impact. These problems become more severe when one recognises that in contrast to physical co-presence a person undertaking an action, such as speaking, cannot change their own bodily orientation in order to adjust their perception of the recipient and the local environment. The speaker is unable to see how his or her actions appear to the other, and in consequence has relatively few resources to enable him or her to modify conduct to achieve a performative impact. It is not surprising, therefore, that in reviewing the data corpus one finds numerous instances of upgraded and exaggerated gestures and body movements, as speakers attempt to achieve some impact on the way that others are participating in the activity, literally, at hand.

The technology, therefore, at least as it is currently designed and configured, provides physically distributed individuals with incongruent environments for interaction. Despite this incongruity, individuals presuppose the effectiveness of their conduct and assume that their frame of reference is 'parallel' with the frame of reference of their co-participant. This presupposition of a common frame of reference, a reciprocity of perspectives is a foundation of socially organised conduct.

Now it is a basic axiom of any interpretation of the common world and its objects that these various co-existing systems of coordinates can be transformed one into the other; I take it for granted, and I assume my fellow-man does the same, that I and my fellow-man would have typically the same experiences of the common world if we changed places, thus transforming my Here into his, and his – now to me a There – into mine.

(Schutz, 1962, pp. 315–316)

In video mediated presence, however, camera and monitor inevitably transform the environments of conduct, so that the bodily activity that one participant produces is rather different from the object received by the co-participant. The presupposition that one environment is commensurate with the other undermines the production and receipt of visual conduct and provides some explanation as to why gesture and other forms of bodily activity can be ineffectual when mediated through video rather than undertaken within a face-to-face, co-present social environment.

In the light of the analysis developed from scrutiny of the details of audio-visual recordings, it was possible to explore ways of addressing the more severe difficulties which emerged in relation to the media space. In the first instance we investigated how we might simulate the range of actions through which individuals in co-presence can become aware of others, and make themselves known to their colleagues. Various sounds were introduced into the system which were designed to simulate particular actions and activities, so that, for example, when one colleague glanced at another through the media space, the recipient will hear the sound of a door gently opening. Whilst, in part, such sounds serve to alleviate individual concerns about privacy, allowing people to know when they are being glanced at (and by whom), it is very difficult to simulate the broad range of actions through which individuals, often through bodily comportment and gaze, can have another know that, either delicately or more forcefully, they are receiving the attentions of another.

The analysis also led to innovations in the ways in which images were presented to users. In particular, we explored whether larger monitors, placed vertically rather than horizontally on the individual's desk and close to the user's workstation might provide a stronger sense of co-presence and facilitate the design and presentation of visual conduct. The idea was to simulate a situation in which one individual was sitting to one side of another. The data (audio-visual recordings of the connections) revealed that users became far more sensitive to the visual conduct of the other, and that they seemed more able to monitor peripherally each other's conduct. However, increased awareness also has its disadvantages, in particular individuals found it difficult to become accustomed to the intense proximity of another, and felt that, when not communicating through the system, the other was overly obtrusive within their working environment. In the light of these findings we have recently begun a series of experiments aimed at radically transforming the types of connection provided by the media space, particularly by providing users with variable access to each other and their respective working domains (Gaver *et al.*, 1993).

The original aim of introducing an audio-visual infrastructure into EuroPARC was to encourage and support informal interaction and sociability between members of the laboratory. Its initial development was through a series of rapid iterations in which small changes and additions were made to the system in response to users' comments and ideas. More detailed analysis of individuals using the system to work with colleagues uncovered some interesting properties of video-mediated communication; properties which perhaps account, in part, for the relative inability of the system to facilitate communication and collaboration amongst members of the laboratory. In particular, by using video-recordings of actual use of the technology to examine aspects of the organisation of interaction between users, it was possible to discover phenomena that would have been unavailable for detailed analysis otherwise. These phenomena appear to be crucial aspects of video-mediated communication, and are perhaps relevant both to our understanding of the relative success or failure of current systems of this sort, and the ways in which we might begin to develop more innovative, and delicate, technologies to support physically distributed work and collaboration.

Prototyping, by allowing for an iterative approach to design, has often been seen as a way of coping with vague and changing requirements. It had been hoped that potential users experimenting with the prototype may reveal new requirements or alter the current design, particularly if those experiments took place in a setting similar to the one in which the system was intended. However, the prototyping process still relies on some initial formulation of the scope and functionality of the final system, no matter how preliminary this is. In the case of the media space at EuroPARC this initial formulation, in terms of supporting informal interaction and collaborative work shaped the subsequent iterations in the design. It appears that from the analysis of this experimental technology, even these vague requirements were misconceived. It may be that alternative requirements for systems to support cooperative work may be informed by examining the details of collaborative work and interaction in real-world settings.

4   IDENTIFYING REQUIREMENTS: CRISIS MANAGEMENT AND COMMUNICATION IN LONDON UNDERGROUND CONTROL ROOMS

The physical changes to the layout of the control room on 26 October 1992 meant that CAC staff were working in unfamiliar positions, without paper back-up, and were less able to work with colleagues with whom they had jointly solved problems before.

(Page *et al.*, 1993, p.3)

It is increasingly recognised that requirements analysis will need to focus on informing the design of technologies to support real-time cooperative and collaborative work. As yet, however, despite the commitment to the social and the organisational, many requirements methods preserve a conception of the collaborative which is little more than a summation of an individual's skills and contributions. Even more radical developments in cognitive science, such as the growing commitment to distributed cognition (Hutchins, 1985; Olson, 1990), tends to retain an individualistic and psychologistic conception of organisational activities and artefacts. In many settings however, if not all, individual skills and abilities, the ways in which tasks are produced and recognised, are inseparable from a body of tacit and indigenous practices and reasoning in and through which organisational members systematically accomplish their own actions and participate in activities of their colleagues. In undertaking a requirements analysis and building technologies, it would seem critical to examine the tacit, the 'seen but unnoticed' organisational practices and procedures through which work is systematically accomplished. Such practices are not available to unguided intuition and it is unlikely that participants would be able to describe the organisation through which they organise their ordinary conduct. Indeed, it is a systematic feature of such practices, that members conceal from view, mask, the ways in which they produce and render intelligible their ordinary conduct.

Taking the tacit and, in particular, the socio-interactional foundations of *in situ* organisational conduct seriously, may not only support the evaluation of technologies and rapid prototyping, but also allow us to identify systems to further support indigenous practices and reasoning. Thus far, we can perhaps envisage for example, how the detailed analysis of talk and work in the medical consultation could provide a background from which to consider innovative technological support for general practice, but it might be helpful to consider a rather different setting. A setting in which the work is essentially collaborative, though even here, some earlier reports commissioned by management, have tended largely to ignore the collaborative organisation of the work. The setting is the London Underground Line Control Room.

Whilst drawing on materials from a number of Line Control Rooms on London Underground, we focus particularly on the Bakerloo Line. The Line Control Room has recently undergone extensive modernisation. Traditional manual signalling has been replaced by a complex computerised system which is operated centrally by signal assistants who are based in the Line Control Room. The Bakerloo Line Control Room now houses the Line Controller, who coordinates the day-to-day running of the railway, the Divisional Information Assistant (DIA) whose responsibilities include providing information to passengers through a public address (PA) system and communicating with station managers, and two signal assistants who oversee the operation of the signalling system from Queens Park to the Elephant and Castle, the busiest section of the line. It is not unusual also to find a trainee DIA or Controller in the Control Room or a relief Controller when problems and crises emerge. Figure 4 shows the general layout of the Control Room.

The Underground service is coordinated through a paper timetable which specifies: the number, running time and route of trains; crew allocation and shift arrangements; information concerning staff travel facilities, stock transfers, vehicle storage and maintenance, etc. Each underground line has a particular timetable, though in some cases the timing of trains will be closely tied to the service on a related line. The timetable is not simply an abstract description of the operation of the service, but is used by various personnel including the Controllers, DIAs, Signalmen and Duty Crew Managers (DCMs), to coordinate traffic flow and passenger movement. Both Controller and DIA use the timetable, in conjunction with their understanding of the current operation of the service, to determine the adequacy of the service and, if necessary, to initiate remedial action. Indeed, a significant part of the responsibility of the Controller is to serve as a 'guardian of the timetable', and even if he is unable to shape the service according to its specific details, he should, as far as possible, attempt to achieve its underlying principle; a regular service of trains with relatively brief intervening gaps.

The timetable is not only a resource for identifying difficulties within the operation of the service but also for their management. For example, the Controller will make small adjustments to the running times of various trains to cure gaps which are emerging between a number of trains during the operation of the service. More severe problems such as absentees, vehicle breakdowns or the discovery of 'suspect

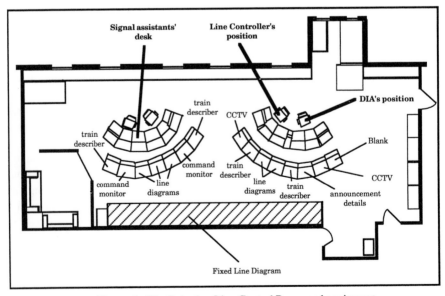

Figure 4   The Bakerloo Line Control Room and equipment.

packages' on trains or platforms, which can lead to severe disruption of the service, are often successfully managed by reforming the service. These adjustments are marked in felt pen on the relevant cellophane coated pages of the timetable both by the Controller and the DIA, and communicated to Operators, Signalmen, DCMs and others when necessary. It is critical that the DIA and others receive information concerning changes to the timetable, otherwise they may not only misconstrue the current operation of the service, but also take the wrong courses of action.

Despite important differences in the formal specification of the responsibilities of the Controller and DIA, the various tasks they undertake rely upon extremely close collaboration. Indeed, Control Room personnel have developed a subtle and complex body of practices for monitoring each other's conduct and for coordinating a varied collection of tasks and activities. These practices appear to stand independently of particular personnel, and it is not unusual to witness individuals who have no previous experience working together systematically, coordinating their conduct. One element of this interweaving of sequential and simultaneous responsibilities is an emergent and flexible division of labour which allows the personnel to lend support to the accomplishment of each others' tasks and activities and thereby manage difficulties and crises.

It is relatively unusual for Control Room personnel to tell each other what tasks they are undertaking or explicitly to provide information concerning, for example, the changes they have made to the service, the instructions they have provided to other personnel, or the announcements they have made to passengers. Indeed, given the demands on the Controller(s), DIA and Signal Assistants, especially when dealing with emergencies or difficulties, it is impossible to abandon the tasks in which they are engaged to provide explicit information to each other as to what they were doing and why. Yet, it is essential that personnel remain sensitive to each other's conduct, not only to allow them to coordinate specific tasks and activities, but also so that they gather the appropriate information to grasp the details of the current operation of the service.

Control Room personnel distribute information, monitor each other's conduct and coordinate their actions and activities with each other through a set of indigenous and taken-for-granted practices, procedures and reasoning. These practices remain largely unexplicated; they are not formalised in handbooks or training manuals and yet they form the foundation to line control, signalling and passenger information. They are robust and reliable, allowing personnel to work, unproblematically, with different colleagues, in different Line Control Rooms, using very different technologies. The practices inform the ways in which participants produce their 'distinct' activities and coordinate those activities in real time with the contributions of colleagues. These practices provide for the sense, or the intelligibility, of their own actions and the activities of colleagues, and allow the participants to maintain a mutually compatible (though not necessarily 'shared') understanding of the current state of affairs. The production, intelligibility and coordination of 'specialised' tasks with the Control Room, is inseparable from the socio-interactional organisation which participants use, orientate to, and take for granted.

For example, Controllers will often deal with problems in the service by rescheduling trains and crews. The activity involves rewriting the timetable, a process known as reformation. It is critical that others, both within the Line Control Room and outside are aware of the changes undertaken by the Controller, otherwise they will not only misinterpret the various information displays, but produce inappropriate actions. The problem for the Controller, however, is that during crises and emergencies he may have little opportunity to suspend the activity in which he is engaged to inform explicitly his colleagues of the changes he is making. In consequence, we find that Controllers have developed various procedures for rendering their potentially 'private' activities, 'publicly visible' within the local milieu. For instance, as they are undertaking a complex reformation they will talk through, out-loud, the task in which they are engaged, so that the DIA, Signal Assistants, and others can retrieve details of the changes which are being made. Moreover, Controllers will not only render visible the actual changes, but talk through the various options, so that the reasoning involved in the decision and its background is made available. It is observable that even as they talk through the activity Controllers are coordinating the production of the task with the ways that colleagues simultaneously participate in the activity in which the Controllers are engaged. The production of the task therefore, and its character, is inseparable from the concurrent conduct of others within the local milieu; the task, however 'individual' is interactionally accomplished[3].

Our original study was concerned with the ways in which personnel within the Line

Figure 5   DIA and Controller, CCTV and timetable.

[3] Further details of these and other work and interactional practices in the London Underground Control Rooms are given in Heath and Luff (1992b and forthcoming).

Control Room adapt to the introduction of new, multimedia technology, and with the addition of staff responsible for signalling. It has been found that the indigenous practices through which Control Room personnel gather and distribute information and coordinate their actions with each other, have become increasingly fragile following these changes. For example, in crisis situations, where the Controller has to undertake multiple reformations, we are finding that certain personnel who may not be directly involved in managing the difficulties, the relief Controller, the second Signal Assistant or the duty operations manager, may fail to gather the relevant information, and may inappropriately intervene in the management of the problem. Moreover, we have also found that, as the situation becomes more complex, particularly when opportunities arise to undertake rescheduling of the service, that Controllers may lack 'intelligence' concerning the 'knock on' consequences of particular decisions. Finally, it was also observed that Control Room personnel were having to spend time and effort coordinating information for and delivering information to specific colleagues based in other locales within the Underground service. These staff, who include Station Managers, Crew Managers, and staff located at depots, also have to be informed of real-time changes to the service.

In the light of these observations, we have begun to identify the requirements for a system which would support the ways in which Controllers, Signal Assistants and DIAs work with the paper timetable and use it as a resource in collaboration and coordination. The system would be designed to preserve the textual flexibility of the paper timetable and the ways in which it is rewritten, corrected and recorrected, whilst providing the communications and functionality afforded by electronic media and computational technology.

Perhaps the simplest design for such a system would be a network of real time, screen-based timetables each with a touch-sensitive screen and stylus marking device which preserve the orientation and size of the existing timetable. The displays would present individual pages of the timetable with running times alongside the scheduled times. Changing the timetable would be done in a similar fashion to marking the acetate sheets of the current document, enabling the Controller to sketch in corrections and recorrections to the running order and times of particular trains. These changes would be communicated directly to the electronic timetables of the Signal Assistants and DIA and would appear precisely in the ways in which those staff currently mark changes on their own timetables. This would not exclude these staff also 'marking up' their timetables, though this information would overlay the indications provided by the Controller. Rather than the current procedure of communicating these changes through a command monitor, Signal Assistants could effect changes to signalling directly through the screen based timetable. In this way, the system would support not only how the timetable is currently used as a reasoning device by Controllers, but also the ways in which information is currently exchanged within the Line Control Room.

The system could also support communications between the Line Control Room and other domains within London Underground and reduce some of the time spent by Controllers, Signal Assistants and DIAs in keeping others updated on problems with, and changes to, the service. A screen-based version of the timetable with the marked up changes could be displayed in Station Control Rooms and the offices of the DCMs at Queens Park and Elephant and Castle, so that both Station Inspectors and DCMs could be warned of any changes, as soon as they occur, and see at a glance the current state of the service and its future modifications. The system could also provide relevant information to other staff such as Duty Operation Managers, and other Managers who have an interest in the successful operation of the day-to-day running of the service (and who are called to account on a daily basis for any problems or difficulties which have occurred).

The system would also provide the opportunity for assembling a data base of actual changes to the service and the possibility of providing 'intelligence' or expertise. At its most basic, such intelligence could forewarn Controllers of the consequences of candidate decisions, say to crewing arrangements and stock, prior to the selection of a particular course of action. In the longer term, however, we envisage that it will be possible to have the system offer potential courses of action to the Controller given the circumstances in which a decision is having to be made.

As well as identifying requirements for computer systems we have also been able to contribute to discussions concerning proposed designs for new technologies for the Control Rooms. For example, one suggestion has been to replace the large, fixed line diagram with personal displays through which each individual could focus on a relevant segment of the line. However, such a proposal overlooks some of the practices through which personnel currently communicate and coordinate tasks within the Control Room; the very size and orientation of the fixed line diagram appearing to assist individuals to make sense of the activities of others in respect to particular problems on the line. Indeed, preliminary observations of Control Rooms where individual screen displays have been adopted suggest a localisation of activities between Controllers and Information Assistants, individuals appearing to be relatively insensitive to the details of their colleagues' activities in relation to the particular problems that they are facing on the line (Luff and Heath, 1991).

From the scrutiny of video-recordings of the Bakerloo Line Control Room, coupled with fieldwork undertaken in the setting, we have begun to delineate the practices through which tasks and interaction are accomplished in a real-world setting. Such an analysis appears to provide valuable resources for the identification of requirements for systems to support the accomplishment of communication and cooperative work. It may also suggest directions for the design of new technologies that could fulfil those requirements.

5   INNOVATIVE TOOLS AND GENERIC REQUIREMENTS

It could be possible to utilise existing technologies, such as touch screen displays, reactive databases and local area networks, to implement a system to support collaborative work in Line Control Rooms of London Underground. However, in the case of the London Underground, as in the other settings discussed above, it is possible to envisage more innovative forms of computer support.

For example, even after the introduction of comprehensive computer systems, in both the medical consultation and London Underground Control Rooms, participants continue to rely upon paper documents. This is despite the introduction of computer systems designed to support activities usually carried out on paper (Luff et al.,1992). In the light of this observation, and the analyses outlined above, it may be possible to draw out some general requirements for computer systems. It may be that recent developments in computational technology and novel experiments with 'augmented' computer systems suggest ways by which these generic requirements might be met.

First, paper allows participants to customise or tailor their documents in order to differentiate and highlight particular items. For example, staff in the Line Control Rooms mark temporary changes on their timetables with a felt-tip pen and doctors use a range of annotations on the patients' medical record cards. Annotations of this kind consist of a wide variety of marks making use of different pens and colours. In more general applications, such as the use of calendars and diaries, it also appears that the ability to annotate a document contributes to the preferred use of paper over recent electronic alternatives (Payne, 1991). Customisation allows for contributions to the document to be differentiated, providing other personnel with a rich body of resources with which to draw various inferences concerning the specific contributions of colleagues. Annotating a document should not only to be considered as an individual activity, since it also supports various forms of collaborative work. Given that there are similar documentary practices in architecture practices, City Dealing Rooms and other settings, the ability to differentiate and highlight contributions to a document may be a more general requirement for computer systems. Some support for this requirement may be provided for electronic documents by recent developments in pen-based systems and 'gestural interfaces'. Although they do not offer the wide variety offered by the paper medium, they do provide some flexibility for marking documents.

One of the reasons why paper documents are still used during a medical consultation appears to be their mobility within the local environment, facilitating being read on the knee by the doctor while talking with the patient or held in front of the patient for joint readings. The screen-based system can be placed in a variety of fixed positions: away from the patient, in front of the doctor or between doctor and patient. If it is centrally-placed, with the screen tilted towards the patient, the system can facilitate shared readings. However, in this position the reactiveness of the screen seems further to undermine the doctor's ability to read and enter information 'in the background'. The system's lack of mobility means that the computer does not provide for the seamless movement between private and public activities afforded by the paper document. Even in settings like London Underground Control Rooms and architecture practices where there are severe limitations on the participants' abilities to pass paper documents to each other, practices have emerged for making potentially private activities, publicly visible. Such practices appear to suggest a general requirement for collaborative systems to allow for the seamless movement between public and private activities.

Pen-based systems with gestural interfaces may thus not only provide for flexible annotation of electronic documents, but also, if small enough, may offer the mobility around the local environment that would facilitate transitions from seemingly private activities to public ones. Careful design of these systems may also ensure that they are minimally reactive[4]. Where such mobile technologies are inappropriate there may be other possibilities for fulfilling the requirement of allowing transitions between private and public activities. One possibility may be to allow for the continued use of paper documents integrated, in some way, with the use of computer systems. This would provide for computational capabilities whilst supporting practices that surround the use of paper. This is the motivation behind recent work involving 'direct interaction'. One development being currently explored is to integrate various technologies, including cameras, digital tablets, video projectors and electronic displays in order to provide users with the means to manipulate both screen-based objects and paper documents on their desks and work-surfaces (e.g. 'DigitalDesk' by Wellner, 1991)[5]. The manipulation of objects on such a large surface may allow aspects of an individual's activities to become available to others within the local environment.

A third and related requirement for technologies, implied by the studies of interactional organisation of work, is the need to support the ways in which individuals orient to, monitor and 'collaborate' in the activities of others within a particular setting. The relative failure of the media space to facilitate interaction derived, in part, from the limited conception of collaborative activity for which it was designed to support. The infrastructure had been primarily intended for face-to-face communication, and yet it became increasingly apparent that in task-based interactions it was necessary to support object-focussed collaboration. Indeed, our studies of co-present collaboration reveal the ways in which individuals are continually engaged in shaping their mutual alignment with respect both to each other and the local environment of objects, and artefacts, including paper- and screen-based documents. Moreover, these studies demonstrate how visual conduct and visual alignment is a critical resource in the accomplishment of mutual frames of reference. Hence, media spaces and their unanticipated consequences for visual conduct, renders task-focussed collaboration, particularly problematic. The general focus on 'face-to-face' interaction of audio-visual infrastructures has tended to neglect possibilities for making the activities of individuals, rather than simply the individuals, available to others.

---

[4] These systems, becoming known as Personal Digital Assistants (or PDAs), may also alleviate problems, found in medical consultations and other service encounters, associated with individuals shifting visual attention between three domains: the client, monitor and keyboard. However, the ways in which hand-writing recognition is carried out by these systems may conflict with the requirement for minimal reactivity.

[5] See also the related innovations by Tang and Minneman (1991) and Ishii *et al.* (1992).

Technological innovations such as the DigitalDesk, appear to offer support for task-focussed activities when users are co-present. We have recently begun a series of experiments in which we investigate the possibility of providing users with variable forms of access to each other when they working in physically dispersed domains (Gaver *et al.*, 1993). These experiments have entailed interconnecting two offices with multiple cameras, monitors and a switch. In this way a user can select particular views of his or her colleague and their local working environment, including high resolution access to documents on the desk. Following preliminary analysis of the audio-visual recordings, it is interesting to note that subjects predominantly select object-centred or working domain views rather than face-to-face ones for accomplishing various tasks. Also, it appears that even with the support of a 'vanity' or feedback monitor, there are difficulties in preserving mutually compatible perspectives. In particular, whilst benefiting from their ability to adopt various views of the other and their working domain, subjects continually find that their own perspective is incongruent with the perspective of their interlocutor. These problems in preserving an interchangeability of standpoints or a 'reciprocity of perspectives', form the foundation to our current research into supporting variable accessibility between participants in media space.

Observations from the studies of three settings have begun to suggest some more general requirements for technologies to support both co-present and physically distributed collaborative work. By taking into account the continued use of paper documents in settings where computer systems have been introduced, it appears necessary to facilitate a range of documentary practices of participants, particularly in regard to the ways by which individuals can distinguish contributions made to a document. It also appears to be important to move easily from seemingly 'private' activities to public ones or, even, to allow for apparently individual activities to be shaped with respect to the ongoing tasks and interaction with others. These requirements point to the adoption of recent technological innovations, the development of novel forms of 'human-computer interaction' and experimentation with radical ways of supporting both co-present and distributed collaborative task and activities.

6   RECONCEIVING 'TASK'

It has long been argued that problems with computer systems derive from the failure to identify the appropriate functions that a system should perform. However, it has been noted that there may be a range of viewpoints concerning the tasks a system should carry out, and therefore requirements analysts should seek to establish a consensus from these differing viewpoints (see Easterbrook and Macaulay, Chapters 2 and 3, respectively, in this volume). Within many conventional approaches to requirements analysis there is a phase where views concerning the potential scope and functionality of a system are gathered. There is little consistency over terminology, this phase being variously termed problem definition (Roman,

1985), requirements definition (Berzins and Gray, 1985) and context analysis (Ross, 1977). It is in this phase where analysis concerning the context into which the proposed computer system is to be introduced is undertaken, and where the problems the system must address are defined. Hence, systems designers are encouraged to collect data about the appropriate setting by carrying out interviews and questionnaires, and sometimes, by observing the workplace. In order to define the eventual functionality of the computer system, it is usual for some form of analysis of current tasks to take place from these materials.

The nature of such an analysis is not uncontroversial. It has been claimed that the methods by which requirements engineers analyse activities are unsystematic (e.g. Diaper and Addison, 1992). An alternative approach would be to draw from relevant work on Task Analysis in HCI (e.g. Diaper, 1989), and for requirements analysis, at least in its preliminary phase, to be more 'user-centred'. However, the ways in which tasks are conceived and defined in HCI have also been called into question. Despite various task analysis techniques adopting widely different definitions of 'task', these definitions still conceive of tasks too narrowly, either by neglecting particular tasks from analysis, or by failing to abstract from the particular (Draper, 1993; Benyon, 1992)[6]. Although various requirements methods provide ways of organising and abstracting from the representations of activities produced by an analysis, the means by which the gathered material is assembled into representations is generally assumed to be unproblematic. For example, the identification of objects in Object Oriented Analysis is generally assumed to be straightforward, not requiring advice on how this analysis should be performed (Davis, 1990)[7]. However, the emphasis on objects and entities appears to encourage an association of tasks and activities with individuals. When such approaches do take account of the 'social' or the collaborative, these are either conceived in terms of a conjunct of individual activities or in terms of 'a context' in which individual tasks take place. The conception of task in both requirements engineering and HCI is problematic. In the one its definition is left open, the identification of activities for analysis being assumed to be straightforward. In the other, the conception appears to be too narrow and too restrictive for subsequent system specification and design.

Analysis of video-recordings of activities in real world environments reveal the ways in which the accomplishment of specific tasks and activities are thoroughly embedded in the individual's interaction with others, whether they are colleagues or clients, co-present or physically distributed. Even in cases where the activity would appear to be thoroughly localised and individual, such as entering a professional diagnosis into a medical record card, we find the activity to be systematically produced with respect to the co-participation of the patient. The production of a task,

---

[6] The extent to which the conception of task in HCI takes account of multiple views and perspectives of participants is also debated (Benyon, 1992; Diaper and Addison, 1992).

[7] As an exception, Coad and Yourdan (1989) do give some guidance on how to identify 'objects' from observations of real-world entities and organisations.

even during the course of its articulation, is sensitive to, and inseparable from, the conduct of others. Tasks are interactionally produced and rely upon a body of 'seen but unnoticed' practices through which particular actions and activities are accomplished.

If we reconsider the concept of 'task' and begin to explore the ways in which its accomplishment is embedded in the interaction of colleagues and clients, then it also leads us to question other conventional ideas in system design. In particular, the concept of 'the user' and its complex variations, informs a substantial body of literature concerned with the research and development of computer systems. For example, it has been recently proposed that system design should be 'user-centred' (Norman and Draper, 1986), and that developers should take seriously the attitudes of individuals who employ particular systems to accomplish some set of tasks. This focus, perhaps, draws too sharp a distinction between a person handling the system and those within the 'local' environment whose actions, however trivial, have a bearing upon the accomplishment of particular tasks and activities. So, for example, whilst a signalman in the Line Control Rooms may be scrolling through a line diagram, apparently insensitive to the conduct of those within the work domain, his colleagues will undoubtedly monitor the activity, and even retrieve relevant information from the screen as the successive images pass by. Noticing his colleagues noticing his own activity, the signalman may well begin subtly to coordinate his viewing of the diagram with respect to the peripheral participation of his colleagues. Similar issues arise in the medical consultation and in the use of the media space at Cambridge EuroPARC. Indeed, it could be argued that direct use of many systems and the information they provide, form a relatively small part of the ways in which a system is utilised. Technology, even individual computer systems such as VAMP, engender and facilitate a rich and complex web of social actions and activities, only some of which will be undertaken by an individual user in direct 'interaction' with the system. In one sense, all of the various ways in which individuals may, if only minimally, participate in the system's use, should lead us to question the usefulness of designing for a single user who theoretically has a relatively circumscribed set of tasks to perform.

Whilst there has been a growing interest in developing Computer systems to Support Cooperative Work (CSCW), it is not necessarily the case that such work will lead to a radical reconceptualisation of activities for system design. The current emphasis on cooperation or collaboration is primarily concerned with developing systems to interrelate individual contributions to a particular task or activity, or to support the real-time cooperative activity of groups. Studies of work in real world, organisational settings, however, reveal the ways in which ordinary tasks and activities are shaped with respect to real-time contributions of others, and that the forms of cooperation and collaboration in which individuals are engaged are continually emerging and in flux. Indeed, even during the course of a single activity such as entering a diagnosis into a computer system, the task may necessitate very different forms of participation and collaboration at different stages of the task. In the medical consultation, as in the other settings, we find participants continually moving from the individual to the collaborative, from the private to the public, and from direct to system-mediated interaction[8]. It would be unfortunate if the growing interest in CSCW allowed designers of more conventional systems to ignore the interactional and collaborative organisation of many of the tasks they are attempting to support, just as it is important that CSCW does not allow the emphasis on the cooperative to ignore the more delicate and minimal ways in which individuals participate in the activities of colleagues in organisational environments.

The studies of technology use and communication in three settings has begun to specify the range of ways in which tasks are embedded within interaction between individuals within the workplace. Indeed, tasks are accomplished step-by-step with the participation of others and coordinated moment-to-moment with the ongoing and emerging interaction. In this sense, the accomplishment of tasks in real-world settings is thoroughly collaborative. However, this interactional organisation of tasks is overlooked by those methods for requirements analysis and HCI which adopt an individualistic or cognitive conception of activities, and by designers of systems aimed at supporting cooperative work. The analysis of how activities are systematically accomplished in workplaces, suggests a more general reconsideration of task is necessary for computer system design; a reconsideration that takes into account the *in situ* production of tasks-in-interaction and attends to the details of that accomplishment. Rethinking the concept of task not only has implications for task analysis and the early phases of requirements analysis, but also questions a range of related concepts commonly used in system design; for example the 'user', the 'interface', 'consistency', 'communication', 'cooperation' and 'collaboration'[9]. A reconsideration of these concepts may in turn lead to a review of the various methods which utilise them. Indeed, it may point to a rather different approach to the analysis of Human–Computer Interaction as well as an alternative approach to user-centred system design.

7   METHODOLOGICAL IMPLICATIONS

It has been recognised that user-centred system design tends to focus too narrowly on the screen-based activities of individual 'users' and to conceive of these activities as 'goal-based' (e.g. Suchman, 1987; Winograd and Flores, 1986). Consequently, several researchers have attempted to broaden the analysis of systems' use in terms of 'distributed cognition' (Hutchins, 1985; Olson, 1990) and begun to develop technologies to support collaborative work. In requirements analysis there

---

[8] Heath *et al.* (1993), in a study of City Dealing Rooms, delineate a range of interactional and work practices that could be glossed over as 'collaborative'.

[9] A range of other problems associated with the term 'user' and 'interface' are raised by Grudin (1990). Greatbatch *et al.* (1993) briefly considers the current conception of 'consistency' in HCI system design.

have been corresponding attempts to incorporate, and sometimes model, the social and organisational aspects of the domain in which a new technology is to be introduced (Goguen, Chapter 7 in this volume). However, it is, as yet, unclear how such an analysis should be attempted. Thus, several approaches can be seen to have emerged that aim to take account of the 'context' into which technologies are to be introduced. These include: adopting a pre-specified framework for structuring a requirements analysis; introducing the system in discrete stages; and involving customers, stakeholders and users in the design process.

In wishing to avoid general prescriptive recommendations to take account of the 'social, political and organisational aspects' of the domain, several researchers have proposed the utilisation of frameworks within which to structure a particular requirements analysis. Hence, the suggestions that such diverse frameworks as cybernetics (Espejo, 1980), socio-technical systems (Mumford, 1983), critical social theory (Flood and Jackson, 1991) and social norms (Stamper, Chapter 5 in this volume) be employed by requirements engineers. These frameworks offer a correspondingly broad range of categories on which to base an analysis, including rôles, authority, transformations of information, job satisfaction and responsibility. Although guidance for collecting data for such analyses is mostly left vague, it is often assumed that stakeholders be interviewed, sometimes observed and occasionally asked to participate in discussion groups.

The studies of medical consultations, the media space and control rooms reveal socio-interactional practices that are tacit and unavailable through interviewing and participation in group meetings. Furthermore, it may be problematic to assign the tasks and activities revealed by an analysis to pre-specified structures and categories. For example, in Information Systems Methodology (Wilson, 1990) each activity in a 'task set' is treated as an information transformation process, defined in terms of inputs and outputs to the transformation. Although such descriptions can be straightforward to construct and may facilitate the subsequent specification of a design, they gloss over the range of interactional and work practices through which tasks are accomplished. For example, it is possible to characterise diverse interactional activities in London Underground Control Rooms as 'transformations of information'. Glancing at a DIA's screen, overhearing a Controller's telephone call and speaking aloud train numbers to oneself could all be conceived in terms of transfers and transformations of information between DIAs and Controllers. However, as outlined above, the ways in which these activities are accomplished, moment-to-moment, can be relevant to design. Imposing, beforehand, the categories into which activities should be classified, even if these are as general as inputs, outputs and transformations, constrains the analysis of requirements. A restricted analysis of the domain may lead to oversights in the final design, and could be a reason why systems are sometimes considered inappropriate to the setting into which they are introduced.

The lack of flexibility in the design process has been one of the principal motivations behind rapid prototyping. Indeed, developing a system in a series of short iterations is often viewed as a way of avoiding premature commitment to a particular design. However, even in innovative forms of prototyping, where requirements activities are intended to be carried out throughout the process, the early conceptions of the activities, tasks or functions, utilised when eliciting requirements, are likely to shape subsequent analysis and design. In the case of the media space at EuroPARC, trials of prototypes pointed to problems with the existing design, and yet a more radical reconsideration of the requirements for the system appeared to be necessary. It may be that even a vaguely expressed requirement, such as the need to support informal interaction, can still be too restrictive and constrain possibilities for technological innovation.

One way of developing systems that, in part, aims to avoid premature imposition of a particular technology on a setting and the pre-specification of the set of tasks a system should perform, is by enlisting users to participate in the design process. Such 'participative' approaches (Ehn, 1988) are also seen as a way of coping with the possibility of conflicting and ambiguous definitions of the 'non-functional requirements' of users, customers and various other stakeholders. In these methods considerable attention has been focused on the process by which views are elicited and ensuing conflicts resolved (e.g. Mumford, 1983; Checkland, 1981; Easterbrook, Chapter 2 in this volume). Although involving the user and other stakeholders in the design process appears to have some worth, analysis and assessment of the products of the various meetings and interviews is necessary. When analytic frameworks are suggested for participative design they seem to be based on similar *a priori* classifications and categorisations of human behaviour to those incorporated in the methods mentioned above. Despite proposing a radical alternative for system analysis, participative methods either give little guidance for analysts or continue to constrain the possibilities for analysis.

Given the provisos offered by Button and Sharrock (Chapter 9 in this volume), any guidance for the analysis of requirements would itself have to reflect the organisational contingencies facing requirement engineers in their work. Perhaps, instead of guidelines for analysis and representation, it may be worth considering a methodology more akin to those adopted in the social sciences. Whatever form such a requirement analysis method would take it appears, from the studies above, that it should move away from individual and cognitively infused conceptions which underpin current methods. An alternative analytic orientation towards examining (technologically supported) work and communication in real world organisational environments should involve uncovering the tacit competencies and practices, the knowledge-in-use (cf. Ryle, 1963), through which participants produce their own activities and recognise the actions of others. This provides an opportunity to delineate the ways in which the production and intelligibility of organisational conduct, ranging from seemingly individual use of computer systems through to collaborative activity, is thoroughly dependent, and inseparable from, talk and interaction within the workplace. By revealing the socio-interactional foundations of task-based activities, this orientation should direct the attention of requirements analysts to a hitherto unexplicated domain of technologically supported tasks and activities.

8   SUMMARY

[The mobilisation of the optimum resource to any incident] was perceived to overcome many of the working practices seen by management to be outmoded and not in the best interests of providing the best service to London. Such practices included the previous abilities of the crews themselves or the stations to decide which resource to mobilise to an incident. CAD would eliminate this practice, or so management thought. Unfortunately, such practices could not so easily be eliminated and the CAD system could only accommodate them only with difficulty and with a reduced level of efficiency.

(Page *et al.*, 1993, p. 40)

It is important to understand that in any system implementation the people factor is important, and is arguably more important, than the technical infrastructure.

(Page *et al.*, 1993, p. 39)

Several of the chapters in this volume suggest that requirement methods should take account of the social and political aspects of the organisations for which a new technology is intended. Similarly, recent reports of dramatic failures of computer systems have emphasised that systems should be sensitive to the practices of personnel in their work settings. By considering three different studies of real-world work and interaction, this chapter has suggested some issues that have to be resolved if these admonitions are to be followed. By fine-grained analyses of video-recordings of systems-in-use, it is possible to suggest certain deficiencies in the original definition of a system's requirements. Analyses of the details of tasks and interaction can also lead to the reconsideration of the requirements for a technology and, by being utilised within a prototyping paradigm, can inform the design's evolution. These studies may also have more general relevance for the design of new technologies in other settings. This chapter has pointed to the ways in which workplace studies, driven by a common analytic orientation, can begin to generate a body of substantive findings concerning the socio-interactional organisation of task-based activities in complex technological environments. From these findings it has been possible to delineate more general requirements for computer systems to support both co-present and distributed collaborative work. These findings also suggest a reconsideration of concepts, such as 'task', 'user' and 'collaboration', that are fundamental to HCI, CSCW and to requirements engineering. Re-specifications of this kind are informing a growing body of work concerning task-based, technologically-mediated, actions and activities, which appears to form the foundation to a novel approach for the elicitation of requirements. Furthermore, by also being relevant to other stages in the development process, this work suggests a distinctive approach to 'user-centred' system design.

ACKNOWLEDGEMENTS

Part of the work reported in this chapter has been carried out on the MITS (Metaphors for Integrated Telecommunications Systems) Project funded by the EC RACE Programme. The authors would like to thank Marina Jirotka, Joseph Goguen and Matthew Bickerton for their valuable comments on previous drafts of this chapter and are grateful for earlier discussions with colleagues at Rank Xerox Cambridge EuroPARC and the Universities of Lancaster, Paris and Oxford.

REFERENCES

Baecker, R. M. (Ed.) (1993). *Readings in Groupware and Computer-Supported Cooperative Work*, Lawrence Erlbaum.

Benyon, D. (1992). The role of task analysis in systems design, *Interacting with Computers*, **4**(1) 102–123.

Berzins, V. and Gray, M. (1985). Analysis and design in MSG 84: Formalizing functional specifications, *IEEE Transactions on Software Engineering*, **11**(8) 657–670.

Bradeley, P. (1989). *Information Technology in General Practice: Some Guidelines for Introducing Computers into General Practice*, Department of General Practice, University of Liverpool.

Checkland, P. B. (1981). *Systems Thinking, Systems Practice*. John Wiley.

Coad, P. and Yourdan, E. (1989). *Object-Oriented Analysis*. Prentice-Hall.

Condon, C. C. (1993). The Computer won't let me – cooperation, conflict and the ownership of information. In D. Diaper and C. Sanger (Eds), *CSCW: Cooperation of Conflict?*, 171–185, Springer-Verlag.

Davis, A. M. (1990). *Software Requirements: Analysis and specification*, Prentice-Hall.

Diaper, D. (Ed.) (1989). *Task Analysis for Human-computer Interaction*, Ellis Horwood.

Diaper, D. and Addison, M. (1992). Task analysis in systems analysis for software development, *Interacting with Computers*, **4**(1) 124–139.

Draper, S. W. (1993). The notion of task in HCI, *Proceedings of INTERCHI '93 (Short Paper)*, pp. 207–208.

Ehn, P. (1988). *Work Oriented Design of Computer Artifacts*, Arbetslivscentrum.

Espejo, R. (1980). Information and management: the cybernetics of a small company, in H. Lucas *et al.* (Eds), *The Information Systems Environment*, North-Holland.

Fish, R. S., Kraut, R. E. and Chalfonte B. L. (1990). The videowindow system in informal communication, *Proceedings of the Conference on Computer Supported Collaborative Work.* pp. 1–11, Los Angeles, CA.

Flood, R. L. and Jackson, M. C. (1991). *Creative Problem Solving: Total systems intervention*, Wiley.

Gaver, W. W., Moran, T., MacLean, A., Lovstrand, L., Dourish, P., Carter, K. A. and Buxton, W. (1992). Realizing a video environment: EuroPARC's RAVE system, *Proceedings of CHI 92.* Monterey, CA, May 3–7, 1992: 27–35, ACM Press.

Gaver, W. W., Sellen, A., Heath, C. C. and Luff, P. (1993). One is not enough: Multiple views in a media space, *Proceedings of INTERCHI '93*, Amsterdam, April 24–29. pp. 335–341.

Goodwin, C. (1981). *Conversational Organisation: Interaction between a Speaker and Hearer*, Academic Press.

Greatbatch, D., Heath, C. C., Luff, P. and Campion, P. (1991). *Utterance Initiation and Computer Keyboard Use in Medical Consultations: Preliminary Observations*. Rank Xerox Cambridge EuroPARC, Working Paper.

Greatbatch, D., Luff, P., Heath, C. C. and Campion, P. (1993). Interpersonal communication and human-computer interaction: An examination of the use of computers in medical consultations, *Interacting with Computers*, 5(2) 193–216.

Grudin, J. (1990). Interface, *Proceedings of CSCW '90*, October, Los Angeles, 269–278.

Heath, C. C. (1986). *Body movement and speech in medical interaction*. Cambridge University Press.

Heath, C. C., Jirotka, M., Luff, P. and Hindmarsh, J. (1993). Unpacking collaboration: The interactional organisation of trading in a city dealing room, *Proceedings of ECSCW 1993*, Milan, September 13–17, pp. 155–170.

Heath, C. C. and Luff, P. (1992a). Media space and communicative asymmetries: Preliminary observations of video mediated interaction, *Human-Computer Interaction*, 7(3) 315–346.

Heath, C. C. and Luff, P (1992b). Collaboration and control: Crisis management and multimedia technology in London underground line control rooms, *CSCW Journal*, 1(1)–(2) 69–94.

Heath, C. C. and Luff, P. (forthcoming). Converging activities: Line control and passenger information on London underground. In D. Middleton and Y. Engestrom (Eds), *Distributed Cognition*, Sage.

Hutchins, E. (1985). *The Social Organisation of Distributed Cognition*. Unpublished Manuscript. University of California, San Diego.

Ishii, H., Kobayashi, M. and Grudin, J. (1992). Integration of inter-personal space and shared workspace: Clearboard design and experiments, *Proceedings of CSCW 92*. Toronto, Oct. 31–Nov. 4, 33–42, ACM Press.

Jirotka, M., Luff, P. and Heath, C. (1993). *Requirements for Technology in Complex Environments: Tasks and Interaction in a City Dealing Room*. Do users get what they want? Industrial Seminar, CRICT, Brunel University, April.

Luff, P. and Heath, C. C. (1991). *Preliminary Observations of the Docklands Line Control Room*, WIT Report, University of Surrey.

Luff, P., Heath, C. C. and Greatbatch, D. (1992). Tasks-in-interaction: Paper and screen based documentation in collaborative activity, *Proceedings of CSCW '92.*, Oct. 31–Nov. 4, pp. 163–170.

Mumford, E. (1983). *Designing Human Systems for New Technology: The ETHICS Method*. Manchester Business School, Manchester.

Norman, D. and Draper, S. (Eds) (1986). *User Centered System Design*, Lawrence Erlbaum Associates.

Olson, G. M. (1990). *Collaborative Work as Distributed Cognition*. Unpublished Manuscript. University of Michigan.

Page, D., Williams, P. and Boyd, D. (1993). *Report of the Inquiry into the London Ambulance Service*, South West Thames Regional Health Authority, February.

Payne, S. (1991). Shared calendar use, *Human-Computer Interaction*, 6.

Roman, G-C. (1985). A taxonomy of current issues in requirements engineering, *IEEE Computer*, 18(4) 14–23.

Ross, D. T. (1977). Structured analysis: A language for communicating ideas, *IEEE Transactions on Software Engineering*, 3(1) 2–5.

Ryle, G. (1963). *The Concept of Mind*, Penguin.

Schutz, A. (1962). *The Problem of Social Reality: Collected Papers 1*, M. Natanson, (Ed.), Martinus Nijhoff.

Suchman, L. A. (1987). *Plans and Situated Actions,* Cambridge University Press.

Tang, J. C. and Minneman, S. L. (1991). VideoDraw: A video interface for collaborative drawing, *ACM Transactions on Information Systems*, **9**(2) 170–184.

Wellner, P. (1991). The DigitalDesk calculator: Tactile manipulation on a desk top display, *Proceedings of the ACM Symposium on User Interface Software and Technology (UIST '91)*, November.

Wilson, B. (1990). *Systems: Concepts, methodologies and applications*, John Wiley.

Winograd, T. and Flores, F. (1986). *Understanding Computers and Cognition: A New Foundation for Design,* Addison-Wesley.

Index